South Carolina Women

South Carolina Women

THEIR LIVES AND TIMES

Volume 1

EDITED BY

Marjorie Julian Spruill, Valinda W. Littlefield,
and Joan Marie Johnson

The University of Georgia Press   *Athens and London*

Library of Congress Cataloging-in-Publication Data

South Carolina women : their lives and times /
edited by Marjorie Julian Spruill,
Valinda W. Littlefield,
and Joan Marie Johnson.
p.   cm.
Includes bibliographical references and index.
ISBN-13: 978-0-8203-2935-2 (hardcover : alk. paper)
ISBN-10: 0-8203-2935-5 (hardcover : alk. paper)
ISBN-13: 978-0-8203-2936-9 (pbk. : alk. paper)
ISBN-10: 0-8203-2936-3 (pbk. : alk. paper)
1. Women—South Carolina—Biography.
2. South Carolina—Biography.
I. Spruill, Marjorie Julian, 1951–
II. Littlefield, Valinda W., 1953–
III. Johnson, Joan Marie.
CT3262.S65S68   2009
975.7'043082—dc22
[B]   2008050102

British Library Cataloging-in-Publication Data available

To our mothers:
Edna Whitley Spruill
Bessie M. Pearley
Dorothy Ann Infosino

Contents

Preface

The three volumes of *South Carolina Women: Their Lives and Times* highlight
the long and fascinating history of the women of the Palmetto State, women
whose stories have often been told as well as women whose lives warrant far
more attention than they have received. The collection of essays is designed
to enrich our understanding of the history of South Carolina and the nation
as we examine the lives and times of the dozens of women whose stories appear within. The essays are intended to be of interest to a wide audience as well
as useful to scholars at every level. For that reason we have chosen a "life and
times" approach, through which the lives of individual women are explored
within the context of time and place.

As editors we have not attempted to be inclusive: there are countless notable
women in the history of the Palmetto State. Readers seeking information on
these women should refer to *The South Carolina Encyclopedia*, edited by Walter B. Edgar.[1]

We do seek, however, to be representative, to include in these pages accounts
of women from the Carolina Lowcountry, the Midlands, and from Upstate;
from all social classes; and from the many racial, ethnic, and religious groups
that have made the history of South Carolina so full and rich. The women featured in the three volumes range from the well known to the largely forgotten
and were involved in many different occupations. They include, among others,
a Native American queen, a Catholic mother superior, an entrepreneurial farmwife, a NASCAR driver, and a Supreme Court justice. There are enslaved women
and slave mistresses, free black women and poor white women, black and white
civil rights activists. Some of these women are quite famous, having earned
distinction in a wide variety of areas. Many were path breakers for their sex.
Others led quiet, even ordinary lives, serving their families and society in ways
that were fairly typical and that rendered their stories quite obscure though no
less meaningful. Most lived in an era when prevailing customs dictated that
women were not to play public roles or to engage significantly in activities beyond home and family, a time when a respectable woman's name appeared in

the papers only in the announcement of her engagement or in her obituary. A proper woman, it was said, did not seek the limelight.

Thus we have the saying "well-behaved women seldom make history," which is true all too often—although not always—in South Carolina.[2] Most of these women were "well behaved" and well respected even in their times, though some created considerable controversy—a few to the point that they felt they needed to leave the state. For the most part, however, even those who were social critics and sought to reform their society seemed to navigate South Carolina and southern culture—with all its restrictions on the lives of women—in such a way that they lived comfortably or at least quietly among fellow South Carolinians—even as they fostered change through their ideas and actions. For some, the ability to so navigate was the key to their success. This was of course easiest to do if a woman was from the white elite, protected by racial and class privilege and influential relations. The South Carolina women who were reformers and African American had the most to protest and the least protection but still won great admiration in many circles and, at least in the late twentieth century, managed to prevail.

As we began the task of collecting essays for this project, we anticipated publishing only one volume. As we learned, however, of more and more women whose stories we wanted to tell and found more and more talented scholars interested in writing about them, the project soon grew to three volumes. And still, there are so many wonderful stories left untold. Therefore we hope that these three volumes will not only inform and inspire but also encourage further research and writing on South Carolina women.

The history of women in South Carolina has grown along with the field of women's history. Early books on southern women, including Julia Cherry Spruill's *Women's Life and Work in the Southern Colonies* (1938), did not focus on South Carolina women in particular but included them.[3] This was also true of the work of pioneering historian Mary Elizabeth Massey, who spent much of her distinguished career at South Carolina's Winthrop College, and whose work, especially *Bonnet Brigades: American Women and the Civil War* (1966), was an enormous contribution.[4] South Carolina women also appeared prominently in Anne Firor Scott's *The Southern Lady: From Pedestal to Politics, 1830–1930* (1970) which established southern women's history as a field.[5] This book was particularly important given the fact that the outpouring of scholarship on American women that accompanied the success of the modern women's movement focused principally on women in the Northeast with its highly influential regional culture, the area where the women's movement originated and was most successful and where many of the scholars in the emerging field of women's history lived and worked.

Just as much of the early work in women's history focused on elite white women, so too did the work on South Carolina women. Women of the planter class received considerable attention as did the middle- and upper-class white women who were most prevalent in the campaign for women's rights. The publication of Gerda Lerner's award-winning biography, *The Grimké Sisters from South Carolina: Rebels against Authority* (1967), about two extraordinary women who were born to an elite white slaveholding family but were among the earliest leaders of both the antislavery movement and the women's movement in America, directed attention to the South and especially to the Palmetto State.[6] C. Vann Woodward's edition of the Civil War diary of South Carolinian Mary Chesnut (1981), for which he won the Pulitzer Prize, Elisabeth Showalter Muhlenfeld's biography of Chesnut (1981), and later, Thavolia Glymph's award-winning essay "African-American Women in the Literary Imagination of Mary Boykin Chesnut" (2000) also brought South Carolina women into the public eye.[7] South Carolina women who participated in the campaign for woman suffrage also attracted early attention, beginning with A. Elizabeth Taylor's articles on the movement in the state published in the 1970s, and continuing with important work by Barbara Bellows, Sidney Bland, and others.[8]

From these important beginnings, women's history, including the history of women in South Carolina, has broadened as it has flourished. The last fifteen years has produced an impressive array of scholarship on a diversity of women and subjects. We now know more about South Carolina plantation mistresses and even poor white women. Cara Anzilotti, Barbara Bellows, and Jane H. Pease and William H. Pease have examined the lives of slaveholding women, while Stephanie McCurry's important work has provided valuable insights regarding gender and the state's yeoman class.[9]

We also know much more about the African American women whose labors supported the plantation mistresses and who were largely excluded from the suffrage movement. The outpouring of new scholarship on black women in South Carolina is as welcome as it is overdue; after all South Carolina long had a black majority and continues to have one of the highest concentrations of African Americans in the United States. Marli Weiner, Cynthia Kennedy, Emily West, and Julie Saville unearthed important details of slave women's lives, labors, and loves. Leslie Schwalm traced how African American women transformed their lives after the Civil War, defining freedom for themselves in work and family life during Reconstruction.[10] Joan Marie Johnson helped us to understand how middle-class African American clubwomen fought segregation and established social services for their community at the beginning of the twentieth century, while Voloria Kibibi Mack examined the relations between clubwomen and working women in her book on class relations among African

American women in Orangeburg.[11] Significant work has also been produced about outstanding professional women, including, for example, the work of Darlene Clark Hine on Dr. Mathilda Evans.[12]

Racial identification was essential in both the slave South and the segregated South and played a crucial role in the lives of all South Carolina women. In a state where proslavery defenders dominated antebellum political life, where an African American majority was violently disfranchised and subjected to Jim Crow and economic deprivation, and where whites were so determined to avoid school integration that they voted to remove responsibility for public education from the state constitution as a potential means of avoiding it, choices for black women were quite limited. Yet the large urban population in Charleston, which included a substantial number of both slaves and free African Americans, made it possible for some black women to create financial independence for themselves. Neither the imposition of segregation nor the violence of lynching stopped South Carolina's black clubwomen and professionals from seeking to improve African American living conditions and challenging the state to provide more substantial resources in education and health.

White women, too, were constrained by the system, and slaveholding mistresses rarely opposed slavery even if they complained privately about its injustice or inconveniences to them. The extraordinary Grimké sisters, who left Charleston and became abolitionists, lived out their lives in exile in the North. Even those women who were sometimes considered outsiders because of their religion, like the Quaker Mary Fisher or the Catholic mother superior Ellen Lynch, did not renounce slavery. White suffragists, including Eulalie Salley and Emma Dunovant, fought for their own enfranchisement while accepting the disfranchisement of African Americans: like most white suffrage leaders in the region, either they favored disfranchisement or knew their cause would be doomed if they allied it with the cause of black suffrage.

Yet by the 1930s and 1940s, conditions in the state had changed to the point that several white women were willing and able to challenge racial oppression in several different ways. Two such women were Hilla Sheriff, a white public health professional who sought to empower and educate black midwives, and Wil Lou Gray, who extended her adult education program to reach African Americans. These women were often inspired by African American women, some of whom had been toiling quietly to raise money and improve conditions, and included Modjeska Simkins and Septima Clark, who were already active in the early phase of the modern civil rights movement. Certainly, the citizenship schools Clark developed and the schoolteacher equalization salary movement underlie recent scholarship that emphasizes that the movement was a "long civil rights movement." One of the earliest white women of South Carolina to work along with African American leaders to end segregation was Alice Buck Norwood Spearman Wright, executive director of the biracial South Carolina Council on Human Relations from 1954 to 1967, a woman deeply committed to advancing civil rights for African Americans.

This collection also emphasizes that many women, even in this most conservative of states with its strong emphasis on traditional gender roles, took on very public roles. From the Lady of Cofitachequi, a Native American woman of considerable political power in the 1500s, to Jean Toal, the current state supreme court chief justice, women in South Carolina have a long tradition of influencing local and national affairs. During times of war, women, including Rebecca Motte of Revolutionary War fame, Lucy Pickens and Mary Chesnut of the Civil War era, and the Delk sisters, Julia and Alice, who worked in the Charleston Navy Yard during World War II, demonstrated the ability of women on the home front not only to follow political developments but also to affect them through their willingness to work and sacrifice for a cause.

When social reformers in the late nineteenth and early twentieth century began to make public speeches, lobby legislatures, and advocate woman suffrage, they were careful to disarm critics with their manners and charm. African American reformers in particular had to maintain a reputation of virtue and refinement owing to the negative stereotypes of African American women's character. Given the importance South Carolinians attached to family, women like the Poppenheims, the Pollitzers, Susan Frost, and Marion Birnie Wilkinson legitimized some of their activism simply by the power of who they were. This attention to character, deportment, and family name continued to serve white women who broke with convention and advocated for African Americans in the 1940s and 1950s. Women without wealth or prominence, however, also broke barriers, including Polly Woodham, a leader among farmers, and Louise Smith, who pioneered in the unlikely field of NASCAR racing.

Women in politics, especially those who wished to run for office, faced particular challenges in South Carolina, where many equated leadership with maleness, saw the aggressiveness and confidence politics called for and a willingness to be in the limelight as unladylike, and expected women to remain in a supporting role. Mary Gordon Ellis, the first female state senator, received little recognition during her lifetime. Since the 1970s, women who broke barriers have received a bit more support and appreciation, though throughout the twentieth century not enough to encourage large numbers to seek political leadership in the state. South Carolina continues to trail the other fifty states in the numbers of women who win statewide elective office. Yet there are distinct signs that this pattern is about to change. And the appointment of Jean Toal as the chief justice of the South Carolina Supreme Court is for women of the state a point of considerable pride.

The essays in this three-volume collection help us to understand the ways that South Carolina women have been similar to and different from other women in the South, and indeed, the nation. They allow us to understand the complex roles that gender played in the lives of women from many different backgrounds and ethnicities as well as the varying contributions and experiences of women in the history of the Palmetto State.

Marjorie Julian Spruill
Valinda W. Littlefield
Joan Marie Johnson

NOTES

1. Walter B. Edgar, ed. *The South Carolina Encyclopedia* (Columbia: University of South Carolina Press, 2006).

2. This phrase was coined by historian Laurel Thatcher Ulrich in a scholarly essay and then began to appear on countless T-shirts, bumper stickers, mugs, and so forth. As a result Ulrich decided to write a book about the phrase and its meaning (*Well-Behaved Women Seldom Make History* [New York: Knopf, 2007]).

3. Julia Cherry Spruill, *Women's Life and Work in the Southern Colonies* (Chapel Hill: University of North Carolina Press, 1938; New York: W. W. Norton, 1998).

4. Mary Elizabeth Massey, *The Bonnet Brigade: American Women and the Civil War* (New York: Knopf, 1966).

5. Anne Firor Scott, *The Southern Lady: From Pedestal to Politics, 1830–1930* (1970; repr., Charlottesville: University Press of Virginia, 1995).

6. Gerda Lerner, *The Grimké Sisters from South Carolina: Rebels Against Slavery* (1967; repr., Chapel Hill: University of North Carolina Press, 2004).

7. *Mary Chesnut's Civil War*, ed. C. Vann Woodward (New Haven, Conn.: Yale University Press, 1981); Elisabeth Muhlenfeld, *Mary Boykin Chesnut: A Biography* (Baton Rouge: Louisiana State University Press, 1981). See also Mary Boykin Chesnut, *The Private Mary Chesnut: The Unpublished Civil War Diaries*, ed. C. Vann Woodward and Elisabeth Muhlenfeld (New York: Oxford University Press, 1984), and Thavolia Glymph, "African American Women in the Literary Imagination of Mary Boykin Chesnut," in *Slavery, Secession, and Southern History*, ed. Louis Ferleger and Robert Paquette (Charlottesville: University Press of Virginia, 2000).

8. A. Elizabeth Taylor, "South Carolina and the Enfranchisement of Women: The Early Years," *South Carolina Historical Society Magazine* 77, no. 2 (1976): 115–26; A. Elizabeth Taylor, "South Carolina and the Enfranchisement of Women: The Later Years," *South Carolina Historical Magazine* 80, no. 4 (1979): 298–309; Barbara (Ulmer) Bellows, "Virginia Durant Young: New South Suffragist" (MA thesis, University of South Carolina, 1979); Sidney R. Bland, "Fighting the Odds: Militant Suffragists in South Carolina," *South Carolina Historical Magazine* 82, no. 1 (1981): 32–43; Sidney R.

Bland, *Preserving Charleston's Past, Shaping its Future: The Life and Times of Susan Pringle Frost* (Columbia: University of South Carolina Press, 1999).

9. Cara Anzilotti, *In the Affairs of the World: Women, Patriarchy and Power in Colonial South Carolina* (Westport, Conn.: Greenwood Press, 2002); Barbara Bellows, *Benevolence among Slaveholders: Assisting the Poor in Charleston* (Baton Rouge: Louisiana State University Press, 1993); Jane H. Pease and William H. Pease, *Ladies, Women, and Wenches: Choice and Constraint in Antebellum Charleston and Boston* (Chapel Hill: University of North Carolina, 1990); Stephanie McCurry, *Masters of Small Worlds: Yeoman Households, Gender Relations, and the Political Culture of the Antebellum South Carolina Low Country* (New York: Oxford University Press, 1995).

10. Marli F. Weiner, *Mistresses and Slaves: Plantation Women in South Carolina, 1830–1880* (Urbana: University of Illinois Press, 1998); Cynthia M. Kennedy, *Braided Relations, Entwined Lives: The Women of Charleston's Urban Slave Society* (Bloomington: Indiana University Press, 2005); Emily West, *Chains of Love: Slave Couples in Antebellum South Carolina* (Urbana: University of Illinois Press, 2004); Julie Saville, *The Work of Reconstruction: From Slave to Wage Laborer in South Carolina 1860–1870* (New York: Cambridge University Press, 1996); Leslie A. Schwalm, *A Hard Fight For We: Women's Transition from Slavery to Freedom in South Carolina* (Urbana: University of Illinois Press, 1997).

11. Joan Marie Johnson, "'How Would I Live without Loulie?': Mary and Louisa Poppenheim, Activist Sisters in Turn-of-the-Century South Carolina," *Journal of Family History* 28, no. 4 (2003): 561–77; Joan Marie Johnson, *Southern Ladies, New Women: Race, Region and Clubwomen in South Carolina, 1890–1930* (Gainesville: University Press of Florida, 2004); Voloria Kibibi Mack, *Parlor Ladies and Ebony Drudges: African American Women, Class, and Work in a South Carolina Community* (Knoxville: University of Tennessee Press, 1999).

12. Darlene Clark Hine, "The Corporeal and Ocular Veil: Dr. Matilda A. Evans (1872–1935) and the Complexity of Southern History," *Journal of Southern History* 70, no. 1 (2004): 3–34.

Acknowledgments

No book, but especially a three-volume anthology like this, is possible without a great deal of support. We would like to thank several people who were particularly helpful in selecting the subjects and essayists, including Walter Edgar, director of the Institute for Southern Studies at the University of South Carolina and editor of the *South Carolina Encyclopedia*, and Amy Thompson McCandless, dean of the Graduate School and associate provost for research at the College of Charleston and an associate editor for the section on women in the *Encyclopedia of South Carolina*. Robin Copp, Henry Fulmer, and Allen Stokes of the South Caroliniana Library also provided valuable suggestions, as did Beth Bilderback, who helped us locate illustrations.

We would like to thank several administrators at the University of South Carolina who have been generous with support at crucial junctures: Lacy Ford, chair of the History Department; Mary Anne Fitzpatrick, dean of the College of Arts and Sciences; and Harris Pastides, president.

It has been a pleasure working with the University of Georgia Press. We are especially grateful to Nancy Grayson, associate director and editor-in-chief, whose support for this anthology and the series of which it is a part has made this project possible. We are also thankful for the help provided by others at the press: Nicole Mitchell, Courtney Denney, Regan Huff, Derek Krissoff, John McLeod, David E. Des Jardines, Pat Allen, and Samantha Knoll. Finally, we thank Larry Lepianka for his editing, MJ Devaney for her meticulous copyediting, and Robert Ellis for his skillful indexing.

The authors of the essays have been a pleasure to work with and we appreciate their talents, diligence, and patience as this anthology has become a reality.

Marjorie Julian Spruill
Valinda W. Littlefield
Joan Marie Johnson

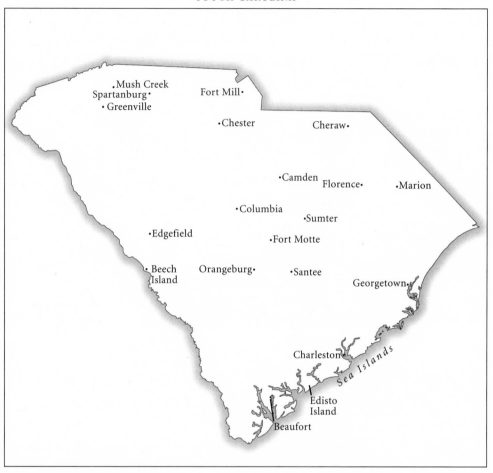

Locations that figure prominently in volume 1.

Introduction

MARJORIE JULIAN SPRUILL, VALINDA W. LITTLEFIELD,

AND JOAN MARIE JOHNSON

❀ ❀ ❀

The most striking aspect of the essays in volume 1 of *South Carolina Women: Their Lives and Times* is the diversity of the subjects. From the Native American queen featured in the first essay to the governor's wife whose image appeared on Confederate currency and whose story concludes the volume, they are remarkably different in their religion, economic status, racial and ethnic identity as well as in their experiences and achievements. The range of women discussed in this volume compels us to confront the complexity of southern women's history, to remember that antebellum southern history encompasses much more than the stories of mistresses and slaves, and to examine southern identity in its many manifestations.

Such extraordinary diversity will push the readers of this volume to reconsider their notions about the slave South. In particular, the significance of women to the state's economy can be more fully appreciated when the lives of overseers' wives, free African American women in antebellum Charleston, and the non-slaveholding white farm women of Mush Creek are studied. The unusual history of religious toleration in South Carolina as well as the religious diversity of the state are better understood through the essays examining the experiences of Quaker, Catholic, and Protestant women; these essays also explore the roles that religion played in their lives and the price religious minorities sometimes paid for social acceptance. Moreover, women in South Carolina carved out far richer public lives than historians have often attributed to antebellum southern women—they published, taught, preached, and one even managed a convent. Women of color, despite the enormous oppression they suffered, seized what opportunities were available to negotiate forms of economic and social opportunity for themselves and their families.

Owing to the importance of slavery to the southern economy and the plethora of source materials left by wealthy, literate planters, the first historians to study women in the antebellum South focused more often on slaveholding mistresses and even slave women (using many of those same sources) than on other women in the antebellum South. But the women in this volume were not all elite women living on plantations. Even Judith Giton Manigault, whose descendants were members of Charleston's wealthiest and most elite planter families, arrived in the colony with no money. A Huguenot who left France to escape political persecution, Giton had to indenture herself in order to earn her passage to South Carolina. Almost two hundred years later, the Civil War letters of the farm women of Mush Creek reveal how the Civil War affected yeoman farm women and slaveholding women quite differently. Essays on slave women and free women of color in antebellum South Carolina also demonstrate that the degree of freedom possible for African American women varied greatly, depending on whether they were enslaved or free and on the nature of their particular connections with whites.

Furthermore, the women in this volume represent the notable religious and ethnic diversity that distinguished colonial and antebellum South Carolina. The first colony to adopt a policy of religious tolerance, South Carolina had significant Jewish, Catholic, and Quaker populations in addition to its Protestant majority. The lives of Mary Fisher, Sophia Hume, and Mother Baptista show how women from very different faiths practiced their religion and understood their identity in a slaveholding society. In addition, the essays reflect the fact that immigrants to South Carolina were not all English. Many early South Carolinians were Scots Irish, French, or German and came to Carolina from the West Indies and colonies belonging to European countries other than England. They were from all economic groups: for instance, descendants of Irish immigrants included the well-educated and privileged mother superior, Baptista, who looked askance at some of her fellow Irish men and women because of their lower social standing.

As the theme of the subordinate role that women were expected to play in the colonial and antebellum South is so pervasive in this volume, it is ironic that the book opens with the story of a Native American woman, the Lady of Cofitachequi, the head of a hierarchical chiefdom in the region who led her people during famous encounters with Spanish explorers in the sixteenth century. Historian Christina Snyder explains that although female chiefs were not common, their power was possible because the position was inherited. The Lady of Cofitachequi demonstrated her power not by threatening warfare (a tactic common to men in her culture) but instead by using diplomacy and giving gifts.

This strategy was effective—she was one of the most powerful chiefs Spanish explorer Hernando de Soto encountered in the Southeast. Once she realized the extent of de Soto's entourage and of his avarice, the Lady abruptly disappeared, hoping, Snyder speculates, that he would turn to another chiefdom for supplies and riches. He did, but not before capturing her and requiring her to accompany his expedition to provide food and other goods. In so doing de Soto implicitly recognized her power over her people. Undaunted, she escaped de Soto—and disappeared from the historical record. The Cofitachequi chiefdom lasted over one hundred years before succumbing to disease and economic distress. The Lady's use of charm and diplomacy, which Snyder contends was clearly linked to her position as a woman, presaged tactics many women in South Carolina would use for the next several centuries as they attempted to win support for their activism.

Unlike the Lady of Cofitachequi, who was carried about in a litter so that her feet did not touch the ground, Judith Giton Manigault, though from a noble family in France, was neither honored nor privileged when she arrived in Charleston early in the history of the colony. According to historian Bertrand Van Ruymbeke, Giton and her family, who were Huguenots (French Calvinists), escaped legal, financial, and violent persecution in Catholic France by traveling across France and Germany to London, where they boarded a ship that took them to Bermuda. When the ship was seized she had to indenture herself to pay for her passage from Bermuda to South Carolina. Giton complained that when she arrived, she went hungry and worked "like a slave," but then she married into what ultimately would become one of the state's most prosperous families. Giton's experience dramatically illustrates historian Peter Woods's contention that in the late seventeenth century, the social and economic chasm that later divided blacks and whites in South Carolina had not fully developed and that therefore few could escape the hard work that defined the lives of most residents of the colony.

Like Judith Giton, Mary Fisher suffered because of her religion before coming to South Carolina. In England, Fisher was one of the original sixty converts to George Fox's Quakerism. She became an itinerant Quaker preacher, traveling as far as the Ottoman Empire to deliver her message. Across England and in Massachusetts (Fisher and a companion were the first Quakers in Massachusetts) Fisher was jailed and beaten for her teachings. South Carolina, with religious tolerance guaranteed in its Fundamental Constitutions and proprietors welcoming Quakers, provided a haven for Fisher when she arrived in 1680 with her second husband. The persecution that Judith Giton and Mary Fisher suffered did not lead them to oppose slavery. Rather, in South Carolina, Mary

Fisher Crosse's family owned slaves, as did the Manigaults. The descendants of both women remained in Charleston, where they amassed fortunes, married outside their faith, and otherwise became integrated into the larger society. Mary Fisher Crosse's granddaughter Sophia Hume, however, ultimately returned to her Quaker faith after her husband suffered from a financial scandal and died soon afterward. After a brief time in London, Sophia returned to Charleston to preach, probably then including an antislavery message. According to historian Randy Sparks, the Quaker faith dramatically transformed the lives of these women. Mary Fisher went from being a servant in London to an international itinerant preacher and challenged South Carolina's traditions with respect to women's roles in the church and society. Her granddaughter extended the family's activism by opposing slavery and questioning the luxurious lifestyle and frivolity of the gentry. Fisher and Hume remind us that South Carolina, and Charleston in particular, allowed for a surprising level of religious diversity and even challenges to gender conventions in the seventeenth and eighteenth centuries in comparison to other colonies.

Like Judith Giton, Mary-Anne Schad and Mrs. Brown (first name unknown), two overseers' wives in colonial South Carolina, were compelled to work very hard owing to difficult economic circumstances. They experienced some degree of upward mobility, though they never reached the elite status that Giton eventually achieved. Historian Laura Sandy contends that women like Mary-Anne Schad provided valuable housekeeping, farming, nursing, midwifery, slave management and other services. Their ability to produce food and clothing enabled plantations to become self-sufficient. They also received payment for their services, which, although it did not make them wealthy, may have provided the additional funds needed to move their family from overseeing to land ownership. Sandy argues that the desire of many planters to hire overseers with wives indicates their appreciation of the economic contributions of these resourceful and hard-working women.

While the experiences of the Lady of Cofitachequi, Judith Giton, Mary Fisher, and Mary-Anne Schad and Mrs. Brown highlight the diversity of class and religion in colonial South Carolina, the experiences of plantation mistresses, Eliza Pinckney, her daughter Harriott Horry, and Rebecca Motte, emphasize the growing wealth and refinement of life in South Carolina, the interconnectedness among elite South Carolina families, and the importance of slavery to the colony by the Revolutionary era. Eliza Pinckney is best known for her skill in plantation management, an occupation she was cast into after the deaths of her father and later, her husband. She is also known for agricultural experimentation, particularly the successful cultivation of indigo, which made it one of South Carolina's most important crops in the eighteenth century. Historian Constance Schulz reminds us that Eliza Pinckney was also celebrated in her lifetime for her role in establishment of one of South Carolina's most powerful political families: she reared a talented daughter as well as two illustrious sons, Charles Cotesworth Pinckney and Thomas Pinckney, and maintained a close, mutually supportive kinship network to the family's benefit. Schulz argues that the labels historians have used to type women's work in the colonial and early republican eras did not always fit women's lived experiences. Eliza Pinckney is often presented as the prototypical "republican mother"; Schulz, however, maintains that although she raised her sons with the values extolled in the new republic, she did so for the sake of her family rather than the nation. During the Revolution, her daughter Harriott offered sanctuary to General Francis Marion, South Carolina's celebrated Swamp Fox, doing her part to aid the rebellion despite the fact that her husband abandoned the cause of American independence in an effort to protect his property. The family gradually recovered from its economic losses during the war owing in part Harriott's agricultural and industrial initiatives.

Like Eliza Lucas Pinckney, Rebecca Brewton Motte was from one of the colony's wealthiest families and blessed with both social and business skills that worked to the advantage of her family. The two women were related by marriage: Rebecca's daughter Elizabeth married Eliza's son Thomas Pinckney. Rebecca inherited much of her brother Miles Brewton's fortune, including his magnificent home that still stands in Charleston, which the British commandeered during the war. The British also occupied her country plantation to which Motte had retreated, and when American forces approached, she found herself and her home in the midst of the Revolutionary conflict. When American commanders found it advantageous to burn her home, literally in the center of the British forces, she not only assented but proved her patriotic mettle by offering a flaming arrow to start the conflagration. British troops surrendered, patriots began to control the state, and Motte became a heroine. Though this situation was unique, historian Alexia Helsley argues that Motte's wartime experiences mirrored those of many elite women in South Carolina as they attempted to keep households running and families united during the extraordinary circumstances of war. Not only were men absent, but with combatants nearby, the departure of many slaves, and food and other necessities in short supply, life on the home front was difficult and often frightening.

The lives of elite women, including these plantation mistresses, are often well documented in letters and papers; their slaves, and the thousands of slave women across the state, left few documents. Much of what we know about them and their experiences, in fact, comes from the documents left by their owners. Despite these limitations, Emily West has been able to use a variety of sources to examine the patterns of slave marriage across a variety of settings (urban, large plantation, and small farm) in South Carolina. She concludes that, because enslaved people did not gain economic or legal benefits through marriage, slave women had more freedom than some elite white women when it came to selecting marriage partners. They were, West claims, "pioneering in the concept of marriages based on romantic love," often marrying slaves from other plantations, unions that would not lead to tangible benefits such as better housing or rations. At the same time, like other recent historians of enslaved women, West documents the difficulties slaves encountered in marriages due to their bondage, especially those in "abroad" marriages who could only visit their spouses on other plantations once a week.[1] Rare sources of information about slaves (letters written by enslaved women and a set of WPA interviews of the same woman conducted by an African American and by a white woman) provide insight into the physical abuse, sale of family members, relationships with mistresses, and interracial sexual contact that slave women endured across the state and the region.

Sources for studying the lives of free African American women in antebellum South Carolina are also in short supply. South Carolina had a relatively large free population in Charleston, and slaves and free blacks in that city had a unique experience due to the urban setting. Historians have found that their participation in the city's economy—as peddlers, washerwomen, seamstresses, cooks, prostitutes, and in other occupations—was significant, and slaves who were hired out to work for wages helped drive Charleston's growth. A few free women were able to catapult themselves into great economic wealth, though historian Amrita Myers cautions that their position as free African American women in a slave society was precarious. Their freedom depended in part on their relationships with whites. Margaret Bettingall lived with Adam Tunno, a wealthy white man, for forty years. Though not legally married, they were considered married by those who knew them. Margaret and her daughters Barbara and Hagar amassed considerable wealth, but always aware of the contingent nature of their freedom, they did what they could to ensure it through various strategies, including carefully crafted instructions regarding inheritance through which each successive generation of women looked out for the next generation of daughters. Although their story is different from that of the many free black women with husbands or children who were enslaved, the Bettingall/Tunno experience reflects the difficulties faced by free black women across the South as they tried to secure family unity.[2] Taken together, these two essays on enslaved and free African American women demonstrate the possibilities for freedom and agency as well as the extent of oppression experienced by women of color in antebellum South Carolina.

The emphasis on keeping white women in their prescribed role within a highly stratified society discouraged virtually all of them from speaking out against slavery, even those deeply troubled by it. South Carolina, however, produced the two most notable exceptions to this rule, Sarah and Angelina Grimké. There was nothing to predict that Sarah and Angelina, members of a prominent slaveholding family, would leave South Carolina and make their home in Pennsylvania—and reject slavery. Yet, in 1835, violence against abolitionists, including incidents that took place in Charleston, moved Angelina to take a public stand against slavery. A year later, she wrote one of her most important essays, "An Appeal to the Christian Women of the South." Unlike most scholars, who have tended to write about the Grimké sisters together and focus on their primacy in the antislavery and women's rights movement in the North, literary scholar Charles Wilbanks focuses on Angelina's determination to "redeem" southern slaveholders, not just to reform them. He insists that, though exiled from her family and the South, Angelina continued to care about her South Carolina relatives, indeed that "she could not have feared more for the ultimate salvation of her family." Her emotional ties to southern slaveholders and her religious fervor led Angelina to make a unique contribution to the antislavery effort. She shifted the debate from an argument over the welfare of the slave to that of the slave owner, thereby making a crucial contribution to the antislavery effort that justifies a separate focus on her and her antislavery rhetoric.

Most white southern families of the planter class, however, supported and relied heavily on the institution of slavery. The Allston family, for example, was one of the region's largest slaveholding families. Elizabeth Allston and her mother, Adele, tried to manage their family's rice plantations when Bessie's father Robert Allston left home to join Confederate forces during the Civil War and then after his death in 1864. When the war ended, the two women, like many other former slaveholders across the South, struggled with former slaves as they asserted their independence and with the loss of wealth that accompanied emancipation. Bessie married but was widowed and childless before she turned thirty. From then until the end of her long life she managed Chicora Wood, her father's largest plantation, and White House, the plantation of her former husband. Rice cultivation left Bessie struggling financially, and so, like many other white southern women at the time who were searching for respectable employment, she took up her pen. In 1912 she began to write letters from the rice plantation for publication. They were first published in the *New York*

Sun and later in book form as *A Woman Rice Planter*. Charles Joyner discusses how Bessie layered autobiography and fiction in this memoir and how she emulated the patriarchal world in which she grew up. Despite overstepping the bounds of gender roles in her own life as a planter, she never sought to make larger claims for her gender.

The survival of a significant number of letters also allows us to learn about one of Bessie's contemporaries, a Catholic nun of Irish descent, Mother Mary Baptista Aloysius (née Ellen Lynch), who lived a very different kind of life. Her letters, never intended for publication, were written to her brother, Bishop Patrick Lynch, third bishop of the Diocese of Charleston. Despite South Carolina's history of religious toleration, there had been hostility to Catholics, including Irish Catholics, in the state long before the potato famine of the 1840s brought thousands more to the United States and stimulated a wave of vicious anti-Irish and anti-Catholic hostility. Historian Nancy Stockton, writing about Mother Baptista, argues that, despite this hostility, Baptista felt quite comfortable in South Carolina society owing to her family's prosperity and support for slavery and the Confederacy. Baptista also felt that Catholicism, with its emphasis on hierarchy and patriarchy, was quite congenial to southern society. Stockton argues that Baptista, who as an Ursuline nun ran a school for girls, defended traditional roles for women even as she, pursuing an option available to Catholic women, chose to eschew marriage and children. Baptista's letters indicate that she relished the independence and power she retained as the mother superior. Mother Baptista provides an illuminating comparison to the "masterless mistresses" at the Ursuline convent in New Orleans, who, according to recent scholarship by historian Emily Clark, were more explicit in their rejection of gender conventions.[3] That Baptista, a woman from an elite background in South Carolina society, felt comfortable with many southern conventions, mitigated, but did not entirely erase, her ambition.

We learn much also from the writing of Mary Boykin Chesnut, another member of South Carolina's planter class, whose diary became one of the best and most widely read Civil War diaries ever published. Drawing from the diary and other sources, Elisabeth Muhlenfeld, her biographer, describes Chesnut, the wife of a U.S. senator, as an astute political observer and writer about African American life and other aspects of South Carolina society. Chesnut's intelligence and wit won her many admirers, especially among her husband's male associates, and she had keen insight into the political process. She took seriously her role as a political wife and hostess, offering a space for conversation, a refuge from the war, and solace to soldiers. After the war she gave equal attention to her role as author, carefully revising conversations and details in her diary to provide an exacting story that centered on the disruption of families caused by the war.

Historian Sara Eye's discovery of Civil War letters from the women of a white, nonslaveholding family in the Upstate region of South Carolina makes it possible for us to learn about another understudied but fascinating group of women, a group that was often illiterate and left few written records. Eye argues that the Neves family, who lived along Mush Creek, experienced less change and deprivation during the war than wealthier white women of the planter class in parts of the state where slavery was prevalent. In the antebellum period, the wealthiest plantation mistresses did less physical labor themselves (instead they supervised that of the slaves) than poorer white women such as Frances Neves, her mother, and her sister, who were accustomed before the war to performing a variety of farm chores, including raising animals, spinning wool, dying fabric, and making clothes. When the young men in the family left for war, the women in the family, aided by Frances's father, who remained home, continued to produce enough food and supplies for their own consumption. This contrasts with the experience of another yeoman farmwife of the South Carolina Upcountry, Emily Harris, who, according to her husband's journal, found it difficult to adapt in his absence.[4] Furthermore, Eye argues that because the Neves were isolated by the fighting, they experienced relatively less deprivation than other slaveholding or yeoman women. Their community as a whole suffered less drastic economic and societal changes as a result of the war. Perhaps because of this, the Neves women expressed more loyalty to the Confederacy than other historians have ascribed to white women of their class.[5] The letters the Neves women, particularly Frances, wrote to their menfolk during the war provide a window into the experiences of poor, white farming women—the majority of white women in the South—and demonstrate how their relative economic weakness turned out to be a relative strength and source of stability.

As for the women of the planter class, the Civil War brought considerable change, and privilege did not typically keep it at bay. But for Lucy Holcombe Pickens, one of the most prominent of this class, elevated status insulated her from the suffering many women endured. Pickens, the wife of Francis Pickens, former U.S. ambassador to Russia and the Civil War–era governor of South Carolina, spent the first years of the war caught up in politics. As first lady of the state, she was an unofficial diplomatic aide to her husband, smoothing over tensions with his political enemies as she entertained. As secretary and advisor to her husband, she used her marriage to a politically influential and wealthy man to create a meaningful and powerful role for herself. Like Elizabeth Allston Pringle and Mary Chesnut, Lucy Pickens wrote a great deal, finding that

˙writing allowed her to express ideas that, as a woman, she could not easily express more directly. From her first book on "the Cuban affair," written before the Civil War, she displayed remarkable interest in and understanding of foreign affairs. Like many other elite white women around the South, she remained loyal to the Confederacy despite frustrations during the war, and afterward she was involved in memorial work. Georganne and Vernon Burton argue that Pickens, like the other women of her generation whose lives and times are described in this volume, did not show empathy to slaves or overtly challenge women's roles. However she subtly crafted wider possibilities for women. More overt challenges to the racial and gender hierarchies in South Carolina would be the province of the next generation of women, born during or after the Civil War.

NOTES

1. Brenda E. Stevenson, *Life in Black and White: Family and Community in the Slave South* (New York: Oxford University Press, 1996).

2. Loren Schweninger, "The Fragile Nature of Freedom: Free Women of Color in the U.S. South," in *Beyond Bondage: Free Women of Color in the Americas*, ed. David Barry Gaspar and Darlene Clark Hine (Urbana: University of Illinois Press, 2004), 106–24.

3. Emily Clark, *Masterless Mistresses: The New Orleans Ursulines and the Development of a New World Society, 1727–1834* (Chapel Hill: University of North Carolina Press for the Omohundro Institute of Early American History and Culture, Williamsburg, Virginia, 2007), 5–6.

4. Philip N. Racine, ed., *Piedmont Farmer: The Journals of David Golightly Harris, 1855–1870* (Knoxville: University of Tennessee Press, 1990), 3, 4, and 309.

5. Laura Edwards, *Scarlett Doesn't Live Here Anymore: Southern Women in the Civil War Era* (Urbana: University of Illinois Press, 2000), 69, 85.

The Lady of Cofitachequi

Gender and Political Power among Native Southerners

CHRISTINA SNYDER

On May 1, 1540, Hernando de Soto and his army approached the first major town of Cofitachequi, one of the South's wealthiest and most storied Native chiefdoms. The Spaniards had conceived of this journey many months earlier when Native Floridians told them of a chiefdom rich in silver and gold and ruled by a powerful woman. Such riches were the expedition's raison d'etre; conquistador Hernando de Soto, veteran of Pizarro's ruthless campaign against the Incas, was willing to go to any length to secure even greater wealth and fame. Marching northeast from peninsular Florida, the expedition had endured arduous travel, intense hunger, and bellicose Native warriors. After traversing an uninhabited area that stretched from the Oconee River in modern central Georgia to the Congaree River in South Carolina, the expedition reached Hymahi, the first village subject to Cofitachequi. Perhaps seeking to protect their chief, the people of Hymahi refused to tell the Spaniards the way to Cofitachequi, so de Soto's men captured several of them. De Soto ordered his soldiers to burn the captives alive one by one until someone disclosed Cofitachequi's location. Finally, a villager relented, and others informed the Spaniards that the chief was aware of their presence and awaited their arrival.[1]

The conquistador and his army went to the principal town of Cofitachequi—the Mulberry site—which lay at the confluence of Pine Tree Creek and the Wateree River, near present-day Camden, South Carolina.[2] From across the river, some of Cofitachequi's principal citizens, including a female relative of the chief, spotted the Spaniards and rowed out in dugout canoes to greet them. Through an interpreter, the Cofitachequis questioned the Spaniards' intentions and then

LADY OF COFITACHEQUI

There are no extant illustrations of the Lady of Cofitachequi, but this engraving of an elite Timucuan woman provides an image of a similarly privileged woman who was a contemporary of the Lady. Theodor de Bry engraving after an original drawing by Jacques LeMoyne de Morgues, *Brevis narratio eorum quae in Florida Americae provi[n]cia Gallis acciderunt* (Frankfurt, Germany, 1591), vol. 2, plate 37. Courtesy of the North Carolina Collection, Manuscripts Collection, Wilson Library, University of North Carolina, Chapel Hill.

reported that their ruler would soon greet the newcomers. Within moments, the Cofitachequis carried their chief, known to history as the Lady of Cofitachequi, from the town to the water's edge on a litter draped in white cloth.[3] Never did her feet touch the ground. The Lady's subjects then placed her in a fine canoe that had an awning to shade her from the sun and ample cushions to make her comfortable. When the Lady approached the Spaniards, they noticed she wore a finely woven white shawl. They described her as beautiful, graceful, and self-assured.

This flourish of chiefly power deeply impressed the Spaniards, just as the Cofitachequis had intended. The Cofitachequis were participants in what archaeologists have dubbed "Mississippian culture," a tradition that thrived from roughly A.D. 1000 to 1600. Although Mississippian culture was less pronounced in certain areas (including portions of what is now South Carolina), the tradition dominated much of the Southeast, changing the lifestyle of nearly all its inhabitants. Before the Mississippian era, Native southerners lived in smaller tribal societies and relied on a wide variety of gathered and cultivated plants as well as deer, fish, and small game for their subsistence. With the dawn of the Mississippian era came a new sort of political and social organization—chiefdoms. These regional, hierarchically structured polities emerged at the same time that southern Indians began to rely on a single crop, corn, for up to 70 percent of their caloric needs, on a large scale. Clearly, the trends toward political centralization and agricultural production were linked, and lineages likely rose to power through securing access to surplus foodstuffs.[4]

Atop Mississippians' social and political order were chiefs, who reigned by virtue of their birth into the highest-ranking lineage. These lineages were closely associated with the sacred, which gave their members a sort of divine right to rule. Evidence from throughout the region suggests that Mississippians believed their chiefs to be descendants of the Sun, a deity of great importance to these agricultural people. A French chronicler described the following ritual linking chiefs to celestial power.

> The Sun is the principal object of veneration to these people; as they cannot conceive of anything which can be above this heavenly body, nothing else appears to them more worthy of their homage. It is for the same reason that the great Chief of this Nation, who knows nothing on earth more dignified than himself, takes the title of brother of the Sun. . . . To enable them better to converse together, they raise a mound of artificial soil, on which they build his cabin, which is of the same construction as the Temple. The door fronts the East, and every morning the great Chief honors by his presence the rising of his elder brother [the Sun], and

salutes him with many howlings as soon as he appears above the horizon. Then he gives orders that they shall light his calumet; he makes him an offering of the first three puffs which he draws; afterward raising his hand above his head, and turning from the East to the West, he shows him the direction which he must take in his course.[5]

As this account reveals, Mississippian chiefs used monumental architecture, including large earthen mounds, as well as esoteric rituals to confirm their relationship to the sacred. Additionally, by controlling external trade, chiefs secured access to rare and beautiful things—finely crafted jewelry, ornamental weapons, and valuable raw materials. Chiefs either displayed these goods or gave them away to allies and supporters to further their own social and political capital. Sumptuary rules also set Mississippian chiefs apart from nonelites; when the Cofitachequis carried their chief on a litter, they literally elevated her above all others.[6]

Early historical records indicate that Mississippian chiefs were usually men, and, as already mentioned, Mississippian chiefs were born rather than made. Significantly, Native southerners traced their ancestry exclusively through their mothers' bloodlines. In contrast to Europeans, who emphasized paternity rather than maternity, southern Indians did not count their fathers as blood relatives. Their matrilineal kinship system made women rather than men central figures in reckoning descent. Native southern women traditionally controlled agricultural production, farming family plots with other female relatives. Matrilineal descent and agricultural production empowered southern Indian women, who dominated the household and provided most of its sustenance. Still, although Native southern women may have used their power as creators and sustainers of life to influence the political decisions of their male relatives, they rarely enjoyed direct rule. Usually, the office of chief passed from uncle to maternal nephew.[7]

The Lady of Cofitachequi's rule demonstrates, however, that manhood was not requisite for Mississippian chiefs. She commanded great power across the Carolinas and dominated subordinate chiefdoms controlled by men. Neither historical nor archaeological data offer any explanation of how she rose to power. It may be that the Lady was the only legitimate heir in her generation. In fact, the de Soto chroniclers documented a recent pestilence in the province that had carried off a great many souls; perhaps male heirs were among the dead. Other evidence suggests that women chiefs were more prevalent among chiefdoms in the Carolinas than elsewhere in the Southeast. Juan Pardo, a Spaniard who explored the area from 1566 to 1568, met with a number of women chiefs. From a town near modern Salisbury, North Carolina, a woman ruled Guatari, maintaining control over thirty-nine lesser chiefs. At Guatari, Pardo also encountered a woman *orata*—ruler of a village. Not far away, at Joara, just north of modern Morganton, North Carolina, Pardo dealt with not only a male ruler but also an older woman whom he also called a *cacica*, meaning "woman chief."[8]

When the Lady of Cofitachequi met de Soto, she greeted him through an interpreter, saying she hoped he had come in goodwill. The Lady's warm greeting suggests that she thought of de Soto as an important visiting dignitary. As de Soto traveled throughout the American South, Mississippian chiefs adopted a number of strategies for dealing with the unexpected arrival of six hundred armed Spaniards: some fled their towns; others tried to use threats or force to keep the soldiers away; still others, including the Lady, attempted to use their considerable political power and material resources to seal a friendly alliance with de Soto. Native southerners in general did not believe that the Spaniards possessed godlike power, and the Lady was no exception. But she clearly saw that they were militarily strong, and she had probably already heard that de Soto was quite willing to use force to secure his demands. Thus, she no doubt concluded that peace was the wisest course.

After greeting de Soto, the Lady placed a string of pearls around his neck and gave hides, blankets, meat, corn, and salt to his men. Among Native southerners, gift giving was far more than an economic transaction—it was a sign of peaceful intentions. When the Lady of Cofitachequi gave de Soto precious pearls, skins, and large stores of food, she sought to coax him into a peaceful alliance by creating bonds of obligation. Although de Soto and his men must have seemed quite foreign, the Lady attempted to incorporate them into her own world, drawing on long-standing diplomatic traditions.[9]

After this initial meeting, the regal Lady left the Spaniards feeling, as one chronicler recalled, "very gratified and charmed, both with her discretion and with her great beauty, which she had in extreme perfection."[10] As a woman, the Lady of Cofitachequi may have been a more effective cultural mediator than male chiefs. Among Native southerners, masculinity was intimately linked to warfare. Virtually all male children began to train for war at an early age; those who did not commonly took on women's roles and occupied a special place in society as a third gender.[11] Dualism was (and is) pervasive in southern Indian cultures, especially with respect to gender roles. As such, masculinity was associated with war and femininity with peace. Although women warriors are not unknown in the annals of southern Indian history, they were rare.[12] More typically, Native women served as nonviolent mediators. In the eighteenth century, when Native diplomats made alliances with other nations, they typically brought along several women as a sign of their peaceful intentions.[13] Europeans also thought of Native women as less violent and threatening than their male counterparts and eagerly accepted them as translators, guides, and sexual partners. Women such as La Malinche in Mexico, Pocahontas in Virginia, Mary Musgrove in Georgia, and Molly Brant in New York acted as crucial mediators in colonial Euro-Indian relations. Indeed, the Lady of Cofitachequi's femininity disarmed the Spaniards. Several chroniclers mentioned her beauty, while another commented on her wit and intelligence, writing that the Spaniards were amazed "to hear such sensible and well-chosen words," especially from an Indian woman.[14]

In addition to her own province on the Wateree, the Lady, as a paramount chief, controlled other chiefdoms from the area near the middle of the Pee Dee River through the Carolina piedmont and into the mountains, perhaps even southward to the Atlantic coast.[15] Of the dozens of rulers the Spaniards met during their four-year entrada across the Southeast, the Lady of Cofitachequi was among the most powerful. Through military conquest or strong-arm diplomacy, the Lady of Cofitachequi had gained control of weaker polities, which, as a result, owed her tribute in the form of food, animal skins, and perhaps even laborers. The Lady's subjects, strewn across the modern Carolinas, numbered in the thousands. Although most Native southerners, including inhabitants of Cofitachequi, broadly shared Mississippian culture, local traditions persisted. The paramount chiefdom of Cofitachequi itself was a multiethnic, multilingual polity. While the Lady's tongue was in the Muskogean language family (the most widespread among Native southerners), her subjects included speakers of Catawban and Cherokee languages.[16]

The Spaniards thought the Lady's land beautiful and bounteous. Although de Soto would never find the precious metals he so desperately wanted, Cofitachequi was otherwise an exquisitely rich land, abounding in walnuts, mulberries, deer, and—to the delight of the Spaniards—freshwater pearls. Eyeing the rich bottomlands of the Wateree, de Soto's men also speculated that Cofitachequi was quite an arable land, and some wished to remain behind and found a settlement there.[17] Owing to rich environs and goods received from tributary chiefdoms, the people of Cofitachequi also seemed extraordinarily salubrious and gracious. Rodrigo Rangel, de Soto's personal secretary and one of four chroniclers of the expedition, remembered the Cofitachequis as the most beautiful people in the Southeast. He recalled, "All the Indians walked covered down to the feet with very excellent hides, very well tanned, and blankets of the land, and blankets of sable, and blankets of mountain lions[.] . . . [T]he people are very clean and very polite and naturally well developed."[18] Another chronicler, known simply as the Gentleman from Elvas, wrote, "The people were dark, well set up and proportioned, and more civilized than any who had been seen in the land . . . and all were shod and clothed."[19] By "civilized," the Gentleman from Elvas meant that the Cofitachequis' lifestyle most closely resembled that of his own people; they lived in permanent villages, engaged in agriculture, possessed a centralized government, and respected an entrenched social hierarchy. Although neither Christian nor European, the Cofitachequis and their culture seemed intelligible, perhaps even respectable, to the Spaniards.

The Lady explained to the Spaniards that she did not reside at this town at the Mulberry site but was merely on a visit to discipline her subjects. Apparently, some elite men of the town had refused to pay her tribute, and the Lady had come to chastise them.[20] Like other Mississippian chiefs, the Lady's strategy for retaining her authority was to keep subjects in awe of her seemingly sacred power and, if necessary, use threats or force. She demanded her subjects provide her with the first of their harvests, which she then stored in a granary. The Lady could then distribute stores to visiting dignitaries, as she did with de Soto, or dole them out to her subjects during times of famine.

Understanding that the Spaniards sought precious things, the Lady took them to the temple of this principal town. During the Mississippian era, major towns throughout the Southeast included temples, usually built atop raised earthen mounds. These temples contained the remains of former chiefs and other members of ruling families as well as precious ceremonial objects. As the temples were the most sacred places in the towns, access to them was restricted to chiefs, religious officials, and guards. And yet the Lady allowed de Soto and other high-ranking Spanish officials to enter. Although the Lady's motives are unclear, she was probably attempting to impress the Spaniards with her wealth and simultaneously placate them with treasures. Significantly, this was not the Lady's own temple, which was at Talimeco, but rather that of her unruly subjects. Thus, the bones that rested at the Mulberry site's temple were not those of her own ancestors.

As the Lady expected, the temple's treasures greatly impressed de Soto and his men. Strewn across the bodies of the dead, the Spaniards saw many thousands of pearls. Greedily, the men began to seize pearls by the handful; in all, they collected roughly two hundred pounds of them.[21] Unfazed, the Lady told them that these pearls were few in number compared to the riches of Talimeco.[22] Additionally, the Spaniards found glass beads, rosaries, and Spanish axes, which they correctly concluded had come from the failed colony of a fellow Spaniard, Lucas Vázquez de Ayllón. In 1526, Ayllón attempted to found a settlement, San Miguel de Gualdape, probably at Sapelo Sound, along the coast of what is now

Georgia.[23] Like many other early colonial ventures on mainland North America, San Miguel de Gualdape was a great disaster. Sapelo Sound offered only sterile soil, and settlers had little or no knowledge of agricultural practices suited for the landscape and climate of the American South. Starvation and disease quickly ensued, killing 450 out of the original 600 settlers. The survivors managed to sail back to Hispanola. The Cofitachequis may have obtained the Ayllón artifacts themselves through direct trade with the Spaniards. It is more likely, however, that Indian groups residing closer to Sapelo Sound obtained the axes, beads, and rosaries and then offered them as gifts or tribute to Cofitachequi. Regardless of how the artifacts came to rest in the Lady's temple, the chief and her people considered these foreign objects to be rare, exotic, and perhaps even powerful.

Beads and steel axes were not the only evidence of contact with Ayllón's failed colony; epidemic disease had also recently visited Cofitachequi. Many settlers at San Miguel de Gualdape had died of a disease or diseases not specified in historical documents. Whether smallpox, measles, influenza, typhus, malaria, or some other Old World disease, the pestilence was probably a new one to Native southerners. To make matters worse, waves of several diseases may have hit simultaneously. Europeans and Africans gained a measure of immunity to such diseases through their mothers' antibodies or their own exposure in childhood, but American Indians had no such acquired immunity to these "virgin soil epidemics." Scholars estimate that such epidemics killed up to 90 percent of all American Indians within the first 150 years of exposure.[24]

The people of Cofitachequi told members of the de Soto expedition that pestilence had recently visited them. According to the Gentleman from Elvas, "Within the compass of a league and a half league were large uninhabited towns, choked with vegetation, which looked as though no people had inhabited them for some time."[25] Another chronicler, citing eyewitness Alonso Priego de Carmona, asserted that plague had depopulated Talimeco and that the Spaniards found four charnel houses full of bodies there.[26] As debilitating as this pestilence had been, it did not destroy the Cofitachequis, perhaps because they adopted a quarantine strategy, abandoning plague-ravaged towns.[27]

After a few days of hosting the hungry, demanding Spaniards, the Lady abruptly disappeared. Although initially she had given generously of her food stores, the Lady apparently realized that the Spanish army—over six hundred strong—threatened to rob the chiefdom of all its supplies. Abandoning her former strategy of allying with de Soto, the Lady now attempted to cut ties with him. She correctly surmised that de Soto could only supply his army through securing massive stores of resources, and he could only gain access to such resources through her. Thus, the Lady probably reasoned that without her aid, the Spaniards' hunger would drive them to seek out another chiefdom.

Indeed, after the Lady's departure, de Soto's army was forced to procure food in other ways; officer Baltasar de Gallegos rode to a tributary town and stole its stores of dried corn.[28] As he pillaged his way across the Southeast, de Soto also made a practice of pressuring chiefs to give him guides, burden bearers, and sex slaves. The Gentleman from Elvas believed that the Lady ran away to avoid "giving guides or *tamemes* [burden bearers] for carrying because of offenses committed against the Indians by the Christians."[29] In any case, the Lady was clearly disgusted with the Spaniards' behavior and wished to rid her chiefdom of them as quickly as possible.

In the Lady's absence, de Soto and his army ranged across her land, looking for food and precious metals. As they did so, according to chronicler Garcilasso de la Vega, the Spaniards found "many Indians native to other provinces who were held in slavery."[30] The Cofitachequis lived in a strictly ranked society, at the bottom of which were enslaved Indians from other chiefdoms. During the Mississippian era, in addition to exchanging material goods when making or confirming alliances, chiefs sometimes also made gifts of captives, so subordinate chiefs may have given some of the slaves to the Lady.[31] Most of the enslaved Indians, however, were probably enemies taken during wartime.

Mississippian chiefs directed warfare, which they used not to conquer territory but to control the material resources and labor of other chiefdoms. Warfare came in two forms: small surprise attacks and large-scale battles. Either way, chiefs sought to inflict great damage in a short amount of time on their enemies, who would then agree to submit to their authority. Archaeological and historical records indicate that the Cofitachequis had fought the Ocutes for at least several generations prior to de Soto's arrival. The chiefdom of Ocute lay in the Oconee River Valley roughly two hundred miles west of Cofitachequi. Since about A.D. 1450, the land between the chiefdoms—including the Savannah, Saluda, and Broad river valleys—had been completely depopulated. War rendered this otherwise quite habitable country a no-man's-land. When de Soto passed through Ocute in the spring of 1540, he demanded that guides show him the way to Cofitachequi, but, as chronicler Luys Hernandez de Biedma recorded,

[t]hey told us that there was no road by which to go, since they had no dealings with one another because they were at war; sometimes when they came to make war on one another, they passed though hidden and secret places where they would not be detected, and they spent twenty or twenty-two days on the road and ate only herbs and some toasted corn that they brought.[32]

Doubtless, among the enslaved Indians at Cofitachequi were captured warriors of Ocute who dared to venture too close to the lands of their powerful enemy.

Like other spoils of war, captives fell under the purview of chiefs. These captives endured a variety of fates: torture, adoption, hard labor. One de Soto chronicler reported that enslaved Indians worked the agricultural fields at Cofitachequi: "As a safeguard against their running away, they disabled them in one foot, cutting the nerves above the instep where the foot joins the leg, or just above the heel. They held them in this perpetual and inhuman bondage in the interior of the country away from the frontiers, making use of them to cultivate the soil and in other servile employments." Maiming captives to prevent escape seems to have been fairly widespread among Mississippians, and the practice endured among Native Carolinians until the eighteenth century.[33]

In the sixteenth century, shipwrecked Spaniards were among those enslaved by Mississippian elites, and those who lived to tell their tales reported that labor was at times extremely arduous. Juan Ortiz, who had been a member of Panfilo de Narvaéz's failed 1528 expedition, lived for a decade as a captive of two Floridian chiefs, Ozita and Mocozo. Under Ozita, Juan Ortiz fetched wood and water for the townspeople during the day and guarded a charnel house full of decaying bodies at night.[34] Fortunately for him and for the de Soto expedition, Ortiz found them soon after their 1539 landing near modern Tampa Bay and thereafter acted as a translator, having mastered two Native languages during his captivity. Chiefs also retained slaves as domestic servants. The Lady of Cofitachequi commanded a retinue of female slaves, who always accompanied her and tended to her personal needs.[35] When Mississippian chiefs died, a retinue of dependents, including slaves, typically accompanied them into the afterlife.[36]

While the Lady was in hiding, the Spaniards entered her temple at Talimeco, a Muskogean place-name meaning "chief's town."[37] Rodrigo Rangel thought Talimeco beautifully situated: "This town has very good savannahs and a fine river, and forests of walnuts and oak, pines, evergreen oaks and groves of sweetgum, and many cedars."[38] Located about four miles upstream from the Mulberry site, Talimeco was clearly a planned town with a central ceremonial center and carefully arranged houses.[39] It was, however, depopulated at the time, probably due to the recent wave of epidemic disease.

A number of tall, flat-topped earthen mounds dominated the landscape at Talimeco. Atop the largest mound at Talimeco, the Spaniards saw the great house of the Lady. Her temple crowned the top of another impressive mound. Captain Gonzalo Silvestre, a veteran soldier later stationed in Peru, told an interviewer that this temple "was among the grandest and most wonderful of all the things that he had seen in the New World." The roof was constructed of cane woven so tightly that it was waterproof; skeins of marine shells and festooned pearls decorated the exterior. Inside, as Silvestre recalled, "it was large being more than a hundred paces long and forty wide; the walls were high in keeping with the size of the room." Six finely carved warrior effigies guarded each side of the temple door. In addition to more shells and pearls, the Spaniards found plumes of colorful feathers, dressed skins and mantles of albino deer, and finely crafted shields made from buffalo hide—rare and beautiful things designed to enhance the prestige of the ruling lineage. The temple also contained the corporal remains of the Lady's ancestors, which rested in chests along the wall. Each chest was accompanied by a wooden statue depicting the individual in life.[40] When the Spaniards later asked the people of Cofitachequi about the "ostentation and pomp" of the temple they replied, according to Garcilasso de la Vega, that "the lords of that kingdom, especially those of that province and of others that they would see beyond, regarded the ornateness and magnificence of their burial places as the greatest [sign of] their dignity, and thus they endeavored to embellish them with all the arms and wealth they could, as they had seen in that temple."[41]

After roughly ten days, de Soto and his men had exhausted the chiefdom's food stores, and they determined to go into the Appalachians, which were rumored to contain gold.[42] Predictably, de Soto had no intentions of leaving peacefully. He ordered his men to find and capture the Lady of Cofitachequi, which they did. Because de Soto knew that the Lady was a paramount chief who controlled many others, he forced her to join the expedition so that she could order tributaries to provide the Spaniards with food. Against her will, the Lady went along. She did, however, manage to bring a number of enslaved women to serve her as she traveled.

The expedition marched from Cofitachequi's seat on the Wateree due northwest toward the headwaters of the Catawba River. De Soto's strategy worked; as one chronicler noted, "We traversed her lands for a hundred leagues, in which, as we saw, she was very well obeyed, for all the Indians did with great efficiency and diligence what she ordered of them."[43]

As the expedition left the foothill town of Joara, the Lady hatched a plot to escape. Located on the upper Catawba, just north of modern Morganton, North Carolina, Joara marked the northernmost reaches of the Lady's dominion.[44] She knew she had to break away from the Spaniards before she reached lands controlled by other chiefs, who might well have been her enemies. A few days into the mountains, near the town of Guasili, the Lady told the Spaniards she needed "to attend to her necessities." She went into the woods, and three enslaved women followed with her baggage. Together, the women managed to escape back to Joara, where the Lady's subjects gave her succor.[45] Interestingly, several members of the expedition also deserted around this time. The deserters included several enslaved men of West Indian and African descent, who probably offered to aid the Lady in return for her protection. One who later rejoined the expedition told the others that the Lady had taken one former slave as her lover, and that the two planned to return to her capital.[46]

The Lady's escape from the Spaniards at Guasili marks her final appearance in the historical record. She probably returned to Talimeco and continued to rule her chiefdom. Assuming that the Lady retained power, she would have faced difficult times. The Spaniards had drained much of Cofitachequi's food stores, and a severe drought plagued the area from 1565 to 1575. In 1566, the Spaniards established Santa Elena, the first capital of La Florida, at Port Royal Sound. Goods, people, and germs from throughout the Atlantic World circulated in Santa Elena, which doubtlessly facilitated further spread of Old World diseases among the South's Native peoples.

Yet, the chiefdom of Cofitachequi endured. In 1670, the year English colonists founded Charleston (originally called Charles Towne or Charlestown), diplomat Henry Woodward visited Cofitachequi on behalf of the Carolinians. At that time, Cofitachequi still maintained control over a considerable portion of South Carolina's piedmont and coastal plain. A male chief, called "Emperor" by Woodward, had succeeded to Cofitachequi's highest office. Within the next thirty years, however, the chiefdom disintegrated. Like other Mississippian chiefdoms, Cofitachequi could not withstand the disease and dislocation wrought by European colonialism. Fewer inhabitants and decreased agricultural production led to the downfall of the chiefdoms, which were replaced by the more egalitarian Native confederacies of the eighteenth century—the Catawba, Cherokee, Choctaw, Chickasaw, Creek, and Seminole.[47]

The Lady of Cofitachequi made only a brief appearance in historical records, but her story illustrates the nature of gender relations and political power among Native southerners. Because political power in chiefdoms ultimately flowed from rank, not gender, women could and did succeed to the highest offices of their lands. Though her gender made the Lady of Cofitachequi rather extraordinary among Mississippian chiefs, she clearly wielded political power effectively, for she maintained control of a sprawling paramount chiefdom. However, as chiefdoms crumbled in the seventeenth century and Native societies instead began organizing themselves as confederacies, women no longer joined the ranks of political leaders. Southern Indian women retained their traditional authority within the home and in clan affairs, but they did not hold government offices. In large part, American Indians formed these confederacies to protect their people from ambitious colonial powers and later the fiercely expansionistic United States. Native confederacies, most notably the Cherokees, self-consciously styled aspects of their governing bodies after Euro-Americans, who maintained an intensely patriarchal social and political culture. The twentieth century, however, saw the return of women chiefs among Native southerners. In 1967, the Seminoles of Florida elected Betty Mae Jumper head of their tribal council. The Cherokee Nation of Oklahoma (whose ancestors had been forcibly removed from the South in the 1830s) voted Wilma Mankiller principal chief in 1985. Ten years later, the Eastern Band of Cherokees chose Joyce Dugan as their chief. Although twentieth-century liberalism accounts for part of these women's rise to leadership, women chiefs are nothing new among Native southerners. Despite centuries of disease, war, and cultural imperialism, the descendants of Mississippian chiefdoms and their distinctive gender relations endure to the present.

NOTES

1. Rodrigo Rangel, "Account of the Northern Conquest and Discovery of Hernando de Soto by Rodrigo Rangel," trans. John E. Worth, in *The De Soto Chronicles: The Expedition of Hernando de Soto to North America in 1539–1543*, ed. Lawrence A. Clayton, Vernon James Knight Jr., Edward C. Moore, 2 vols. (Tuscaloosa: University of Alabama Press, 1993), 1:275; Charles M. Hudson, *Knights of Spain, Warriors of the Sun: Hernando de Soto and the South's Ancient Chiefdoms* (Athens: University of Georgia Press, 1997), 177–78; Gentleman from Elvas, "The Account by a Gentleman from Elvas," trans. James Alexander Robertson, in *De Soto Chronicles*, 1:82–83; Garcilasso de la Vega, "La Florida by the Inca, Garcilasso de la Vega," trans. Charmion Shelby, in *De Soto Chronicles*, 2:249.

2. Hudson, *Knights of Spain*, 173–74.

3. The four chroniclers of the de Soto expedition disagree on whether the Lady of Cofitachequi was actually the ruler of the chiefdom. Perico, a Native Floridian boy, told them that the Lady's aunt was actually the chiefdom's ruler. However, the Portuguese Gentleman from Elvas and Rodrigo Rangel, de Soto's secretary and the most reliable source for the expedition, assert that the Lady was in fact the chief (Rangel, "Account of the Northern Conquest," 278; Gentleman from Elvas, "The Account by a Gentleman from Elvas," 82; Luys Hernandez de Biedma, "Relation of the Island of Florida," trans. John E. Worth, in *De Soto Chronicles*, 1:231; Hudson, *Knights of Spain*, 175).

4. A comprehensive discussion of research on the Mississippian era is beyond the scope of this essay, but for more information, see Charles M. Hudson, *The Southeastern Indians* (Knoxville: University of Tennessee Press, 1976), 77–96, 122–68, and John F. Scarry, "The Late Prehistoric Southeast," in *The Forgotten Centuries: Indians and Europeans in the American South*, ed. Charles M. Hudson and Carmen Chaves Tesser (Athens: University of Georgia Press, 1994), 17–35.

5. Mathurin le Petit to Père d'Avaugour, July 12, 1730, *The Jesuit Relations and Allied Documents: Travels and Explorations of the Jesuit Missionaries in New France, 1610–1791*, vol. 68, ed. Reuben Thwaites Gold (Cleveland: Burrows Brothers, 1900), 127.

6. F. Kent Reilly III, "People of Earth, People of Sky: Visualizing the Sacred in Native American Art of the Mississippian Period," in *Hero, Hawk, and Open Hand: American Indian Art of the Ancient Midwest and South*, ed. Richard Townsend and Robert Sharp (New Haven, Conn.: Yale University Press, 2004), 125–37; Susan C. Power, *Early Art of the Southeastern Indians: Feathered Serpents and Winged Beings* (Athens: University of Georgia Press, 2004), 140; Lewis H. Larson Jr., "The Etowah Site," in *The Southeastern Ceremonial Complex, Artifacts and Analysis: The Cottonlandia Conference*, ed. Patricia Galloway (Lincoln: University of Nebraska Press, 1989), 139–41; David H. Dye, "Art, Ritual, and Chiefly Warfare in the Mississippian World," in *Hero, Hawk, and Open Hand*, 196–98; Hudson, *Knights of Spain*, 17.

7. Hudson, *The Southeastern Indians*, 185–88; Hudson, *Knights of Spain*, 14–17.

8. Juan de la Bandera, "The 'Long' Juan de la Bandera Relation," April 1, 1569, in *The Juan Pardo Expeditions: Exploration of the Carolinas and Tennessee, 1566–1568*, trans. Paul E. Hoffman, ed. Charles M. Hudson (Tuscaloosa: University of Alabama Press, 2005), 62, 262–63.

9. David J. Hally and Marvin T. Smith, "Chiefly Behavior: Evidence from Sixteenth Century Spanish Accounts," in *Lords of the Southeast: Social Inequality and the Native Elites of Southeastern North America*, ed. Alex W. Barker and Timothy R. Pauketat (Washington, D.C.: American Anthropological Association, 1992), 99–109; David H. Dye, "Feasting with the Enemy: Mississippian Warfare and Prestige-Good Circulation," in *Native American Interactions: Multiscalar Analyses and Interpretations in the Eastern Woodlands*, ed. Michael S. Nassaney and Kenneth E. Sassaman (Knoxville: University of Tennessee Press, 1995), 289–316.

10. Rangel, "Account of the Northern Conquest," 278; Hudson, *Knights of Spain*, 177–78; Gentleman from Elvas, "The Account by a Gentleman from Elvas," 82–83; Garcilasso, "La Florida by the Inca," 288.

11. Early French explorers called these people berdache. Native American societies commonly included a third gender or transgender individuals. See, for example, Rene Goulaine de Laudonnière, *Three Voyages*, trans. Charles E. Bennett (Tuscaloosa: University of Alabama Press, 2001), 13.

12. Perhaps the most famous in the Southeast was Nancy Ward, war woman of the Cherokees (Theda Perdue, "Nancy Ward," in *Portraits of American Women*, ed. Catherine Clinton and Ben Barker Benfield [New York: St. Martin's Press, 1991], 83–100).

13. Greg O'Brien, "The Conquerer Meets the Unconquered: Negotiating Cultural Boundaries on the Post-Revolutionary Southern Frontier," *Journal of Southern History* 67, no. 1 (2001): 39–72.

14. Quotation from Garcilasso, "La Florida by the Inca," 287; Clara Sue Kidwell, "Indian Women as Cultural Mediators," *Ethnohistory* 39, no. 2 (1992): 97–107.

15. Hudson, *Knights of Spain*, 182–84.

16. Karen M. Booker, Charles M. Hudson, and Robert L. Rankin, "Place Name Identification and Multilingualism in the Sixteenth-Century Southeast," *Ethnohistory* 39, no. 4 (1992): 399–451.

17. Gentleman from Elvas, "The Account by a Gentleman from Elvas," 83.

18. Rangel, "Account of the Northern Conquest," 278–79.

19. Gentleman from Elvas, "The Account by a Gentleman from Elvas," 83.

20. Ibid., 86.

21. Chroniclers' estimates vary, ranging from 6.5 to 9 arrobas (between 160 and 250 pounds) (Biedma, "Relation of the Island of Florida," 231; Rangel, "Account of the Northern Conquest," 279).

22. Rangel, "Account of the Northern Conquest," 280.

23. Ibid., 279–80. For a discussion of San Miguel de Gualdape's location, see Paul E. Hoffman, "Lucas Vázquez de Ayllón's Discovery and Colony," in *The Forgotten Centuries*, 43–46.

24. Alfred W. Crosby, "Virgin Soil Epidemics as a Factor in the Aboriginal Depopulation in America," *William and Mary Quarterly* 33, no. 2 (1976): 289–99; Henry F. Dobyns, *Their Number Become Thinned: Native American Population Dynamics in Eastern North America* (Knoxville: University of Tennessee Press, 1983).

25. Gentleman from Elvas, "The Account by a Gentleman from Elvas," 83.

26. Garcilasso, "La Florida by the Inca," 306.

27. Paul Kelton, "Avoiding the Smallpox Spirits: Colonial Epidemics and Southeastern Indian Survival," *Ethnohistory* 51, no. 1 (2004): 45–71.

28. Rangel, "Account of the Northern Conquest," 280.

29. Gentleman from Elvas, "The Account by a Gentleman from Elvas," 85.

30. Garcilasso, "La Florida by the Inca," 312.

31. Dye, "Feasting with the Enemy."

32. Biedma, "Relation of the Island of Florida," 229. See also Hudson, *Knights of Spain*, 182–83.

33. Spaniards also saw such captives in the Mississippi River Valley. Garcilasso, "La Florida by the Inca," 312, 400. For the eighteenth-century Carolina captives, see John Lawson, *A New Voyage to Carolina*, ed. Hugh Talmage Lefler (Chapel Hill: University of North Carolina Press, 1967), 59, 208.

34. Hudson provides a more detailed account of Ortiz's captivity in *Knights of Spain*, 78–85.

35. Gentleman from Elvas, "The Account by a Gentleman from Elvas," 87.

36. John R. Swanton, *Indian Tribes of the Lower Mississippi Valley and Adjacent Coast of the Gulf of Mexico* (Washington, D.C.: U.S. Government Printing Office, 1911), 100–105; George R. Milner, *The Cahokia Chiefdom: The Archaeology of a Mississippian Society* (Washington, D.C.: Smithsonian Institution Press, 1998), 83–84, 136, 160–61; Thomas E. Emerson, *Cahokia and the Archaeology of Power* (Tuscaloosa: University of Alabama Press, 1997), 228; Melvin L. Fowler, Jerome Rose, Barbara Vander Leest, and Steven R. Ahler, *The Mound 72 Area: Dedicated and Sacred Space in Early Cahokia* (Springfield: Illinois State Museum Society, 1999).

37. Booker, Hudson, and Rankin, "Place Name Identification," 418–19; Biedma, "Relation of the Island of Florida," 230–31.

38. Rangel, "Account of the Northern Conquest," 280.

39. Hudson, *Knights of Spain*, 178; Garcilasso, "La Florida by the Inca," 297.

40. Garcilasso, "La Florida by the Inca," 298–306; Rangel, "Account of the Northern Conquest," 280.

41. Garcilasso, "La Florida by the Inca," 306.

42. Biedma, "Relation of the Island of Florida," 231.

43. Gentleman from Elvas, "The Account by a Gentleman from Elvas," 86.

44. Hudson, *Knights of Spain*, 191–92.

45. Gentleman from Elvas, "The Account by a Gentleman from Elvas," 87; *The Juan Pardo Expeditions*, 90.

46. Gentleman from Elvas, "The Account by a Gentleman from Elvas," 87; Rangel, "Account of the Northern Conquest," 282; Hudson, *Knights of Spain*, 191–92.

47. Chester B. DePratter, "The Chiefdom of Cofitachequi," in *The Forgotten Centuries*, 197–226; Hudson, *Knights of Spain*, 417–40.

Judith Giton

From Southern France to the Carolina Lowcountry

BERTRAND VAN RUYMBEKE

Sometime in 1690 a disillusioned and yet hopeful French woman named Judith Giton Manigault wrote a letter to one of her brothers back in Europe. Judith was a Huguenot who escaped from France in 1684 and settled the following year in the South Carolina Lowcountry. In her letter she detailed her flight and journey across the Atlantic and the various hardships she suffered both along the way and after arrival in the Lowcountry. After the death of her first husband, the artisan Noé Royer, she married into the Manigault family, which had become one of the most prestigious Carolina dynasties by the time of the Revolution. What we know of her eventful life is essentially based on this document and bits and pieces gathered from probate records.

Seventeenth-century France counted about 730,000 Huguenots (French Calvinists), or less than 4 percent of a total population estimated at 20 million. This Calvinist population was concentrated in a series of contiguous provinces that formed a southern crescent extending from La Rochelle, on the Atlantic coast, to Dauphiny in the Alps. Initially protected by the Edict of Nantes of 1598, a document that guaranteed this Protestant minority religious, civil and judicial rights, they came under a policy of legal and financial harassment adopted in the 1660s that was meant to marginalize and impoverish them. The monarchy eventually resorted to violence against them in the years preceding the 1685 Revocation of the Edict of Nantes.[1] The use of violence led many Huguenots to flee the kingdom to a neighboring Protestant city or country. This exodus, known in French historiography as *le Refuge*, extended through the early decades of the eighteenth century, reaching a peak in the years immediately preceding and following the revocation, from 1684 to 1687.

Estimates concerning the number of refugees have varied greatly over time, but historians now agree that slightly less than 200,000 (perhaps only 180,000) Huguenots left France. Many were reluctant to leave given their hope that Louis XIV would reverse his religious policy under the diplomatic and military pressure of Protestant nations at war with France and that they would consequently have their rights restored. Most of the refugees relocated in the Netherlands, the British Isles, the Swiss cantons, and the German states. It is not surprising, considering the distance and the overall reluctance of seventeenth-century Europeans to move overseas, that only a tiny fraction of them, perhaps twenty-five hundred, crossed the Atlantic.[2] These Huguenots settled primarily in New York and South Carolina, unexpectedly few of them going to Calvinist New England and hardly any to Quaker Pennsylvania.[3]

Huguenot letters from America are few. There are assuredly more of them than historians know about but they are disseminated in archival repositories in France, the British Isles, the Netherlands, Germany, and Switzerland and are usually found by chance.[4] In a sort of epistolary web, refugees wrote to their families—parents, brothers, sisters, or cousins—from across the Atlantic, but these documents usually contain little personal information. Authors, almost exclusively men, were typically merchants who discussed shipments, prices, and other types of business matters, pastors who reported to vestries, or lonely refugees who extolled the benefits of a town or a colony in an effort to draw relatives and friends to wherever they settled. Judith Giton's letter, written in the early 1690s, is different; indeed in many respects it is unique. Written by a woman, it tells how the Giton family—Judith, her mother, Madeleine Cottin, and two of her brothers, Pierre and Louis—escaped from France and about the hardships they had to overcome on their journey and after their arrival in the Carolina Lowcountry. Additionally it reveals, although discreetly, personal information and, in contrast to the archetypical letter, does not portray South Carolina as an Eden.

This well-known and oft-cited South Carolina document has its own history.[5] Acquired by the South Carolina Historical Society, it was filed among the Manigault papers (because Judith Giton married Pierre Manigault, the founder of the Carolina branch of the Manigault family) and placed next to a contemporaneous note recording the family's transatlantic passage. The descendants of Judith and Pierre Manigault later used this receipt to prove that she was a free migrant, not an indentured servant. For the same reason, the passage in the

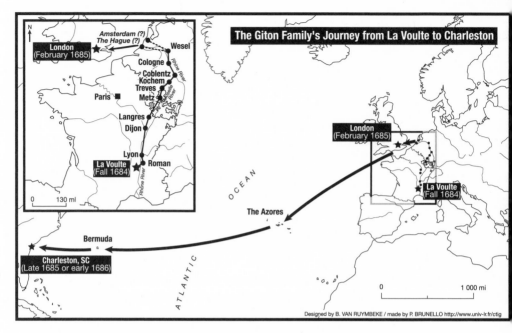

The Giton Family's Journey from La Voulte to Charleston

Amsterdam (?)
The Hague (?)
London
(February 1685)
Wesel
Cologne
Coblentz
Kochem
Treves
Metz
Paris
Langres
Dijon
Lyon
La Voulte
(Fall 1684)
Roman

Rhine River
Moselle River
Rhône River

0   130 ml

London
(February 1685)
La Voulte
(Fall 1684)

OCEAN

The Azores

Bermuda

Charleston, SC
(Late 1685 or early 1686)

ATLANTIC

0   1 000 mi

Designed by B. VAN RUYMBEKE / made by P. BRUNELLO http://www.univ-lr.fr/ctig

MAP OF JUDITH GITON'S JOURNEY

The map was designed by Bertrand Van Ruymbeke, Université de Paris
VIII, and created by Pascal Brunello, Université de La Rochelle.

original letter in which Judith explained that she and her brother Louis had to indenture themselves in Bermuda in order to gather funds to pay for the rest of the voyage was omitted in the early nineteenth-century transcription, the only copy available to historians since the original is no longer extant. Although indenturing oneself was not necessarily disgraceful, even in the eyes of descendants eager to boast an impeccable pedigree, in a letter dated 1808, Gabriel Manigault II confessed to David Ramsay that he crossed this part off. The family was adamant that others believe Judith had migrated freely to the Lowcountry.[6] In fact, with her tales of dragooned homes and nightly escapes, Judith offered the Manigault descendants a Pilgrim-like custom account of persecution and flight, which is absent from the Manigault side of the family (Pierre and his brother Gabriel having converted to Catholicism before leaving France). This probably explains why the letter, even if amended, was a family treasure before becoming an historical document.

The Manigaults became a wealthy and prestigious South Carolina family while the Gitons disappeared from the colony's records. Pierre Giton died of a fever soon after settling in the colony, and Louis Giton passed away in 1696, both without descendants. Yet, although Judith arrived in Charleston penniless, she belonged to a family of the provincial nobility and held a higher status than her husband's family. In the Carolina Lowcountry, Pierre Manigault cultivated economic fortune through his business endeavors but acquired additional social status by marrying Judith.

Although her experiences were somewhat unusual, Judith's letter still reveals much about the conditions of the Protestants in late seventeenth-century France. She opened her letter with the words "I want to give you an account of our leaving France and reaching Carolina since you wish to have it."[7] She was writing to a brother (first name unknown) whose regiment was stationed in Lüneburg, possibly the Lüneburg in Lower Saxony, present-day Germany.[8] Her noting that her brother wanted information about their arrival in Carolina implies that her brother had written her there. The purpose is clearly stated. Judith was satisfying his curiosity not so much about the Lowcountry but about how the family managed to escape from France and cross the Atlantic. This brother was serving in the elector of Hanover's army. Many members of the Huguenot nobility joined the military as their occupational options were gradually limited by an increasingly restrictive legislation that kept them from administrative and judicial careers. Judith's brother first served in one of Louis XIV's regiments but most likely left the kingdom when the same military was instructed to obtain conversions forcibly among his fellow Calvinists. Once abroad he was eager to have information about his family's escape from France, knowing that the familial home was occupied by the soldiery.[9]

A chronological reconstruction of the family itinerary allows us to date their escape and their arrival in Charleston roughly. Judith mentioned that they were in England "in eighty-four or eighty-five[,] . . . the year King Charles of England died." This was in February 1685. The Gitons probably left their home in late 1684, perhaps December, or in January 1685. Judith explained that they suffered the presence of soldiers at home for eight months, which would have been from May or June 1684. Troops had actually occupied provinces of southern France since July 1683. These were the infamous dragoons used by the crown to pressure Huguenots into converting to Catholicism. Instances of violence occurred, but what made the *dragonnades*, as these domestic military campaigns were called, particularly difficult to bear for the Huguenot population was the soldiers' rough behavior and constant demands. Boarding perhaps four or five soldiers at home for so long was a real financial burden and a psychological ordeal. Although she does not give any details, Judith unsurprisingly mentions suffering "the contributions and billeting of soldiers, for the sake of religion, with much evil."

The Gitons lived in La Voulte-sur-Rhône, a small town located on the western bank of the Rhone River south of Lyon between Valence and Montélimar in Vivarais, a Protestant region in eastern Languedoc. Judith was then nineteen. Her father was deceased. Her sister was married and lived in Pont-en-Royan, a market town in nearby alpine Dauphiny, and, as we have seen, one of her brothers was away in the military. The family in La Voulte therefore consisted of Judith, Pierre (the oldest brother), Louis, and the mother.[10]

The Gitons escaped at night "leaving the soldiers in the bed and the house all furnished." Leaving literally in the dark and without notice was imperative. Everything had to be abandoned. Huguenot merchants shipped their goods abroad to an agent who would then sell them and hold the money for them, thereby enabling them to transfer part of their capital out of France. Those whose wealth was principally in real estate, however, could not sell anything without arousing suspicion from Catholic neighbors and local authorities and could only take cash and jewelry with them. In some cases, a son volunteered or was designated by the father to convert and stay behind so that the property would remain in the family. Huguenots who opted to leave the kingdom nonetheless believed that the Edict of Nantes would some day be reinstated. They thought that their migration abroad would be temporary and that they would return someday and recover their estates. The Gitons, however, all decided to leave, thereby forfeiting their property. Local authorities later recorded that the "demoiselle Giton" left an estate worth 2,000 livres or 154 pounds sterling.[11]

In accordance with the legislation regarding refugees' properties, the Gitons' estate was to be confiscated by the state, temporarily joined to the king's domain, and administered by the *intendant*, the representative of the monarchy in the province. The personal property was to be auctioned off to cover the administrative and judicial costs of the confiscation procedure.[12] The Gitons' furniture was sold to pay the troops that had occupied their home. Choosing to relocate across the Atlantic inevitably made the Gitons' migration more definitive. Moving to South Carolina was literally starting a new life. As might be expected, going away permanently caused a profound sadness in Judith that was reflected in her letter when she mentions the "deep grief" she felt when Pierre did not let them go to visit their brother in the military. Judith therefore lost "such a perfect opportunity to see [him], at least one more time."

The Gitons immediately headed north and crossed the Rhone River to Romans-sur-Isère where they "hid for ten days while they [the troops] were searching the area looking for them." Apparently it was a narrow escape since the dragoons literally followed in their steps. They were saved by their "secretive hostess who said nothing when the soldiers asked her if she had seen them." She was a trustworthy and courageous acquaintance who risked a heavy fine and the anger of local Catholic authorities for assisting Huguenot fugitives. The Gitons resumed their northern route and proceeded to Lyon, then Dijon (in Burgundy), and then Langres. It was when they were in Langres that Pierre wrote a letter to their brother in Germany informing him of their decision to leave France. They stopped at "Madame de Choiseule's," most likely a family friend, but were not welcomed as expected since she had passed away and her son-in-law, who was "the master of every thing [maître en tout]," warned them that if they asked him anything he would turn them in. Needless to say the Gitons did not linger there and continued on their route. Their objective was to reach Metz, in Lorraine, then an independent duchy. Once in Metz they were safely out of France.[13]

Their escape itinerary was unusual. Huguenots from southeastern France typically traversed the Alps to cross the kingdom's borders as quickly as possible, stopping in Geneva on their way to the Netherlands. The Gitons, however, did not take the shortest and safest route but went north and remained in France at least two weeks, putting their lives at risk. They neither left with other fugitives nor did they hire a guide. They traveled on their own, perhaps thinking that they could more easily go unnoticed that way. Still, however unusual the route, the escape was obviously carefully planned, the fugitive family having arranged in advance stops along the way where it could expect support.

From Metz, the Gitons followed a river route, descending the Moselle and Rhine through Treves, Kochem, Coblentz, and Cologne, in southwestern Germany. In Cologne they took a coach to Wesel where, apparently to Judith's relief, they found "a host who could speak some French." There Judith learned that Lüneburg, where their brother's regiment was currently wintering, was only "thirty leagues away." Judith and her mother pleaded with Pierre to let them all go to Lüneburg or to go by himself. This was in the "dead of winter." Pierre refused, arguing that this detour would delay them and perhaps jeopardize their plans. Judith added that he "had only Carolina on his mind [n'ayant que la Caroline en son esprit]." She strongly protested and later reproached him for his lack of compassion, but, she added, "He was our master [il était notre maître], we had to do as he said." Along with illustrating the patriarchal characteristic of the early modern French family, her stating they had to do his bidding seems to imply that Judith did not initially want to settle in South Carolina nor, perhaps, even leave France. It was apparently Pierre's arbitrary decision, and the others followed. Pierre's Carolina obsession possibly came from reading promotional pamphlets published in French in Geneva that illegally circulated through the Alps and down to the Rhone valley.[14]

From Wesel, the Gitons continued on to the Netherlands and then to England. Judith did not specify whether they crossed the English Channel from Amsterdam or The Hague but the former, where the largest concentration of Huguenot refugees lived, is more likely. The family reached London in February 1685. The English capital, which like Geneva and Amsterdam had a large population of French refugees (at least twenty thousand), was the place where Huguenots interested in migrating to South Carolina obtained information about the colony and made arrangements for their departure. The Gitons remained there only "three months waiting for a Carolina-bound ship." A receipt dating April 11, 1685, records their departure from England.[15]

The ocean voyage was long and eventful. First, scarlet fever broke out on board killing many passengers. Judith's mother, "being elderly," was among the dead. The ship went by way of "a Portuguese island" [the Azores] and Bermuda, where they had to stop to repair the ship following a storm. The captain, who had "committed some rascality," was placed under arrest and imprisoned, and the ship was seized. The Gitons found themselves stranded and penniless in Bermuda. Judith and Louis indentured themselves (Pierre, being the eldest, does not seem to have bothered to help) to raise the necessary funds to pay for a passage to Charleston for the three. They probably reached the Lowcountry in January 1686, a full year after they left their hometown.

Once in South Carolina they met more hardship. Judith wrote that "she worked the land like a slave" and that she was six months without eating bread (it would be, she added, "three or four years" before she could have "it when she wanted"). Finally, eighteen months later—in June 1687—Pierre, who had been so intent on starting a new life in the Lowcountry, weakened by hard physical work he was not accustomed to doing, died of a fever, possibly malaria. Judith ended her letter by thanking God for helping her to withstand so much adversity and to change "her lot to a happier one."

About five hundred Huguenots settled in the Carolina Lowcountry between 1680 and 1710. Yet these French settlers, although they were but a small fraction of the overall Huguenot exodus, represented about 15 percent of the colony's population in the 1690s. The first ship arrived in 1680, the year Charleston was transferred down the Ashley River to its present-day peninsular site. This early migration enabled the French to receive one-sixth of the over three hundred town lots granted between 1680 and 1698. Nearly half of the total Carolina Huguenot population lived in Charleston, and this community remained the largest and the wealthiest of all the Huguenot enclaves in South Carolina throughout the proprietary period (1680–1719). In fact, the Charleston Huguenot Church was the only one in the Lowcountry important enough to resist anglicanization and remain independent and active throughout the eighteenth century. Most Huguenots acquired contiguous lots along present-day Broad and Meeting Streets near the original, pre-1695 location of the French church; a few others lived on present-day Church Street.[16]

With no accounts or further letters, Judith's life in South Carolina is sketchy at best and must be pieced together from scattered probate records. As we have seen, she lost her mother on the ocean voyage and her brother Pierre a year and a half after their arrival in Carolina. She remained with her brother Louis, who died in 1696.[17] Judith's first years in South Carolina were painful and difficult. Not only did she lose beloved relatives but, as she put it in her letter, she met only with "maladies, famine, poverty, and hard work." Yet she survived and eventually prospered.

Probably soon after her arrival she married Noé Royer (1663–98). Two years older than she, Noé was a weaver from Tours, a midsized town in the Loire Valley, southeast of Paris, who arrived in the colony on board the *Margaret* in spring 1685.[18] This marriage represented both a geographic and social adaptation for Judith. Her husband was from northern France and therefore from a culturally—and to some extent linguistically—different region. As an artisan, he did not share her social status. This marital union, derogatorily called *mésalliance* (social mismatch), could not have occurred in France; it was only the dislocations engendered by the dispersion and a tight French matrimonial market in South Carolina that made it possible there. First-generation Low-country Huguenots wanted to marry within the group or, in the case of a few male refugees, avoid remaining single, even if they had to cross ancien régime French social barriers to do so. The Royers (Noé, Judith, and their three sons, Noé, Jean [John], and Pierre) lived in Charleston, on Church Street, where Noé had been granted lot number 43 in December 1686. A town lot was potentially a great source of income since with time, as Charleston grew from a peripheral village to a port town, it acquired value and could be sold in quarters or even in eighths. This is what the Royers did. Records show that Noé Royer Sr. and Noé Royer Jr. sold and purchased parts of town lots over the years. Although only an artisan, Judith's first husband must have enjoyed a certain visibility within the Charleston French community since in 1696, along with Jonas Bonhost and Peter Poinset, he led a group to petition the colonial assembly for naturalization.[19]

In November 1698, Noé Royer died, aged 35.[20] Exactly a year later Judith signed a bond of 240 pounds over to Pierre Manigault in return for which she was "to pay to Noa Royer, son of Noa Royer, late of Charles Towne and Judith his wife, the sum of £60 [Carolina money, or roughly 10 pounds sterling] within one month next after said Noa (Royer) is 21 years and also deliver to John Royer, son of same, £60 when 21 years and educate and clothe said Noa and John during their minority." Another deed sheds useful light on this transaction:

> I, Judith Royer of Charles Towne, widow, for maternal affection I bear to my children, Noa and John Royer, and particularly for my late husband, who by his last will gave me all his estate leaving it to my discretion to provide for said children as I should think fit, do give to son Noa sum of £60 c.m. of province and also John £60 to be paid when either becomes 21 years. . . . [M]y children shall pay Lewitt Lebott for a lot my late husband sold by virtue of said Lebott's Power of attorney when said Lebott shall demand same for better security of the payment of said sum to my said sons, have entered into Obligation bearing same date with Pierre Manigault in sum £240.[21]

Thus Noé Royer, who had been empowered to sell a town lot for this Lewitt Lebott but had never paid him (perhaps he had never been asked to) and who bequeathed his entire estate to Judith, left her with a potential debt. Probably because she did not want to sell part of the family estate to pay off this debt,

Judith asked Pierre Manigault, who was then a fellow artisan (cooper) and had not reached the wealth and status of his later years, for help. A year later, Judith married her benefactor. Pierre Manigault was a neighbor and obviously a close family friend of the Royers. Judith was a widow with an estate, and she was French. Although it was far from essential, she might even have been good looking. Regardless, to Pierre Manigault, who was still single at thirty-four, a highly unusual situation for a successful male in the early modern period, Judith was an excellent match.

The Manigaults were an old family from La Rochelle who joined the Huguenot church as early as 1559, the year the first national synod secretly met in Paris. In 1685, however, Gabriel, the father, converted to Catholicism, presumably to keep the estate within the family while his two sons, Gabriel (?–1704) and Pierre (1664–1729), escaped to London. In early 1686 a Manigault (first name not recorded) appeared before the consistory (board of elders) of the Huguenot Threadneedle Street Church to make his *reconnaissance*.[22] The church was the largest London Huguenot congregation that had not conformed to the Church of England. Refugees who left France after the revocation (October 1685) were presumed to be new converts and were therefore required to publicly recant their Catholicism and make a public testimony of their Calvinist faith (called "reconnaissance" from the phrase "reconnaître son erreur") in front of the elders before being readmitted into the Huguenot communion. Refugees who intended to relocate across the Atlantic were given priority since it was not guaranteed that they would find a Huguenot church wherever they planned to settle.[23]

The date of the arrival of the Manigault brothers and the conditions under which they arrived in Charleston are conjectural. A warrant dated July 1695 records that Gabriel arrived with "one negro man by [the] name Sambo."[24] The presence of the slave implies that at least Gabriel (but most likely the two brothers) came to Carolina by way of the Caribbean, where he would have acquired the slave.[25] The Manigaults first settled in Santee, a predominantly Huguenot settlement located north of Charleston and founded in the late 1680s. Running a farm in a subtropical climate, however, was a challenge for two artisans from La Rochelle. The brothers unsurprisingly did not remain long in Santee and by 1699 had moved to Charleston.

The following year, Pierre married Judith. In 1701 they had a daughter, Judith, and in 1704, the year Pierre's brother died falling off a roof, they had a son whom they named Gabriel in remembrance of his late uncle. Judith and Gabriel were both baptized at the Huguenot Church by Paul L'Escot.[26] The French Calvinist congregation in Charleston was founded as early as 1681, but the first building was not constructed until 1687. The French church was originally located on present-day King Street. In 1695 the Huguenots abandoned this site and built another church on Church Street (its current location) within the walls of the city and closer to the docks of the Cooper River. The first building on this site, a wooden church, was leveled by a hurricane in the summer of 1700. It was replaced by a brick structure in 1701 or 1702. Paul L'Escot, its pastor from 1700 to 1719, was born in Nevers, a town located southeast of Paris, but left France for Geneva with his parents, at age eighteen. L'Escot studied theology at the Geneva academy and, after serving various wealthy noble patrons, obtained his first ecclesiastical position in Charleston through the London Threadneedle Street Church. L'Escot was a Calvinist serving a nonconformist church, but he looked up to the Anglican hierarchy. He befriended Gideon Johnston, the bishop of London's representative in South Carolina, and corresponded with members of the Anglican Society for the Propagation of the Gospel.[27] Like many Charleston Huguenots, Pierre Manigault, who had converted to Catholicism and then returned to the Calvinist faith, straddled two religions. He had his children baptized in the French Calvinist church by an Anglican-leaning pastor but purchased a pew in St. Philip's, an Anglican (Episcopal) church; he was interred in the French churchyard, but he bequeathed an equal sum of 10 pounds to both the Huguenot and Anglican congregations.

Like the vast majority of settlers, Pierre started small. He first raised cattle in Santee, registering his cattle mark in 1696, and by 1699 had become a cooper in Charleston.[28] Pierre and Judith had a house on Church Street, where she had lived during her first marriage. They took in boarders to be financially more comfortable.[29] Pierre then opened distilleries and by 1710 had made a fortune. Judith died in 1711, at age forty-six. Following Judith's death, Pierre married Ann Reason, with whom he had no children. Ann died in 1727 and Pierre, who had by then become a Charleston merchant, passed away in 1729.[30] In his will Pierre gave his daughter Judith a portion of his town lot, with a house, slaves (two women and a child), half of his household goods, and 1000 pounds, which Gabriel was to invest and pay Judith 10 percent interest on annually. To his son he gave three slaves (a woman, a girl, and a child), the remainder of the lot with its dwelling house and stores, the other half of the household goods, and the other half of the personal property after deductions for gifts. Pierre also bequeathed his granddaughters (Judith's daughters), Judith and Mary, each a slave girl but nothing to his grandson. Pierre was most likely preoccupied with leaving his granddaughters with dowries.[31]

Judith Giton had five children: Noé, John, Peter, Judith, and Gabriel. In 1717 Noé Royer lived in Santee, and he briefly appears in the records of the commissioners of the Indian trade as a tanner buying raw skins from an unlicensed trader.[32] In 1717 John Royer, identified as a mariner, lived in Charleston and had a note (an epilogue to the 1699 agreement between his mother and his stepfather) recorded acknowledging "to have received of Peter Manigault the sum of £105 c.m. which is in full for that due me or any other legacies left me by my mother."[33] In his will, dated 1722, John named Peter Manigault his executor and mentioned his half brother Gabriel and his half sister Judith as well as his wife, Hannah, and their three children (John, Samuel, and John).[34] Peter Royer died sometime between November 1698 and November 1699. In 1717 Judith married James Banbury, a sea captain from Bedford, England, and had six children (Judith, Mary, William, Peter, Gabriel, and James). James died in 1732 and Judith married Thomas Witter, a planter from James Island. She died in 1778, at age seventy-four.[35]

Judith Giton lived no ordinary life. At age nineteen, with her home occupied by royal troops, she left France to travel across the Atlantic to settle in a remote English colony where she overcame adversity, married twice, had five children, and died not long after building herself a comfortable existence. Whereas she married two Frenchmen and had her children christened in the Huguenot Church, her daughter twice married outside the group. The contrast between the two generations reflects the integration of the Huguenots into South Carolina society. Judith's daughter, however, named three of her children after her French relatives (Pierre, named for her father, Judith, named for her mother, and Gabriel, named for her uncle). Her Huguenot cultural heritage was thus transmitted within a family matrix.

NOTES

1. Philip Benedict, *The Huguenot Population of France, 1600–1685: The Demographic Fate and Customs of a Religious Minority* (Philadelphia: American Philosophical Society, 1991); Elisabeth Labrousse, *La révocation de l'Edit de Nantes: Une foi, une loi, un roi?* (Paris: Payot, 1990).

2. Jon Butler, *The Huguenots in America: A Refugee People in New World Society* (Cambridge, Mass.: Harvard University Press, 1992); Warren Scoville, *The Persecution of Huguenots and French Economic Development, 1680–1720* (Berkeley: University of California Press, 1960), 118–21.

3. Butler, *The Huguenots in America*, and Paula W. Carlo, *Huguenot Refugees in Colonial New York: Becoming American in the Hudson Valley* (Brighton, U.K.: Sussex Academic Press, 2005).

4. See for example the letters recently published: Harriott Cheves Leland and Dianne W. Ressinger, eds., "'Ce Païs Tant Désiré.' This Much Longed-for Country," *Transactions of the Huguenot Society of South Carolina* 110 (2006): 1–41, and Molly McClain and Alessa Ellefson, eds., "A Letter from Carolina, 1688: French Huguenots in the New World," *William and Mary Quarterly*, 3rd ser., 64, no. 2 (2007): 377–94.

5. The letter is mentioned in the earliest history of the Huguenot exodus, N. Charles Weiss,

Histoire des réfugiés protestants de France depuis la révocation de l'Edit de Nantes jusqu'à nos jours (Paris: Charpentier, 1853), translated and published in the United States the following year, and appears in extenso in Charles W. Baird, *History of the Huguenot Emigration to America*, 2 vols. (New York: Dodd and Mead, 1885), 2:396–97.

6. Maurice A. Crouse, "The Manigault Family of South Carolina, 1685–1783," (PhD diss., Northwestern University, 1964), 7, n. 13.

7. All Judith's quotations are taken from an undated letter of hers, Manigault Family Papers, 11/275/3, 1 fol., South Carolina Historical Society, Charleston (hereinafter cited as SCHS).

8. On the back of the letter, Pierre Manigault wrote "lettre de ma femme écrite à son frère [letter from my wife to her brother]" (undated letter, Manigault Family Papers, 11/275/3, SCHS).

9. Slann Legare Clement Simmons, ed., "Early Manigault Records," *Transactions of the Huguenot Society of South Carolina* 59 (1954): introduction. Refusing to convert to Catholicism was not the factor that led this brother out of France since until the revocation Huguenots could serve the military and remain Calvinist. His leaving France to join a German regiment before the revocation is therefore atypical since Huguenot regiments under foreign monarchs and princes were formed only after October 1685.

10. Because the receipt of the Gitons' transatlantic voyage is registered under Pierre's name, it can be assumed that he was the oldest son, at least among the children present (receipt for transatlantic passage, Manigault Family Papers, 11/275/5, SCHS).

11. "A déserté la demoiselle Giton, et s'est retirée en Picardie, d'où elle est sortie. Ses meubles furent vendus pour la subsistance des gens de guerre. A l'égard de ses bien-fonds, elle avait une métairie de valeur de 2000 livres," quoted in Samuel Mours, *Le protestantisme en Vivarais et en Vélay: Des origines à nos jours* (Valence, France: Imprimeries réunies, 1949), 282, n. 26.

12. Emmanuel Jahan, *La confiscation des biens des religionnaires fugitifs de la révocation de l'Edit de Nantes à la Révolution* (Paris: R. Pichon and R. Durand-Auzias, 1959).

13. Lorraine was acquired by France in 1766. Officials knew that the Gitons had taken the northern route but thought that they left the kingdom by way of Picardy, a region located northwest of Paris.

14. See, for example, *Description de la Carolline* (Geneva: Jacques de Tournes, 1684) and *Suite de la Description de la Carolline* (Geneva: Jacques de Tournes, 1685). On this promotion that targeted Huguenot refugees, see Bertrand Van Ruymbeke, *From New Babylon to Eden: The Huguenots and their Migration to Colonial South Carolina* (Columbia: University of South Carolina Press, 2006), 40–49.

15. Receipt for transatlantic passage, Manigault Family Papers, 11/275/5, SCHS.

16. Van Ruymbeke, *From New Babylon to Eden*, 203.

17. Louis Giton appears only once in the records when he witnessed the sale of a town lot in February 1693 (Miscellaneous Records [Proprietary Series], 1675–95:295, South Carolina Department of Archives and History, Columbia [hereinafter cited as SCDAH]).

18. Noé Royer appears in the South Carolina records on March 15, 1687, when he served as a witness for the will of fellow refugee Alexandre Pépin (Caroline T. Moore and Agatha Aimar Simmons, comps. and eds., *Abstracts of the Wills of the State of South Carolina, 1670–1740* [Charlotte, N.C.: The *Observer* Printing House, 1960], 11).

19. "The Humble Petition of Noah Royer, Jr., Jonas Bonhost, [and] Peter Poinsett . . . ," Miscellaneous Records (Proprietary Series), 1694–1705:83, SCDAH. Here Noah Royer Jr. refers to Judith's husband and not her son because Noah emigrated with his father, who had the same first name and who was still alive.

20. Noé Royer's will is no longer extant but on November 11, 1698, Judith Royer, John Francis Gignilliat, and Jonas Bonhost made his inventory (no longer extant either) (Caroline T. Moore, comp. and ed., *Records of the Secretary of the Province of South Carolina, 1692–1721* [Columbia, S.C.: R. L. Bryan Company, 1978], 108).

21. Pierre, Judith's third son, is not mentioned in the deed because he died between November 1698 and November 1699 (Moore, comp. and ed., *Records of the Secretary of the Province,* 175–76).

22. Livres des Actes du Consistoire, 1679–1692, ms. 7, January 14 and February 17 and 24, Archives of the French Protestant Church of London.

23. In February 1686, while already in London, the Manigaults would have received letters from a Catholic priest to introduce them to any French priests they might find in Carolina. It was unlikely that they would have found French Catholic clergymen in proprietary South Carolina, but it is entirely possible, given that we know they converted to Catholicism, that the Manigault brothers moved within Catholic circles before leaving France. The letter was burned by their descendants in 1854 as a sign of wavering faith, but in no way does it mean that they were more than nominal Catholics (Crouse, "The Manigault Family," 3 and n. 5).

24. Alexander S. Salley and R. Nicholas Olsberg, eds., *Warrants for Lands in South Carolina, 1672–1711* (Columbia: University of South Carolina Press, 1973), 506. Crouse wrote that the Manigaults remained ten years in England to accrue capital, which is highly doubtful, and Thomas Gaillard conjectured that they arrived in Charleston in 1686. Actually the Manigaults arrived in the early 1690s by way of the Caribbean, where they most likely had stayed a few years (Crouse, "The Manigault Family," 10 and n. 3).

25. Pierre possibly arrived in Charleston slightly ahead of his brother.

26. Crouse, "The Manigault Family," 12.

27. Van Ruymbeke, *From New Babylon to Eden,* 146–49.

28. "A Book for [the] Recordeing of the Cattle Markes and Others . . . ," Miscellaneous Records [Proprietary Series], 1709–25:n.p., SCDAH.

29. Crouse, "The Manigault Family," 10.

30. Ibid., 13.

31. Moore and Simmons, comps. and eds., *Abstracts of the Wills,* 18 and 19. No inventory has remained, so Pierre's exact wealth cannot be determined.

32. W. L. McDowell Jr., ed., *Journals of the Commissioners of the Indian Trade (20 September 1710–29 August 1718)* (Columbia: South Carolina Department of Archives and History, 1955), 170.

33. Moore, comp. and ed., *Records of the Secretary of the Province,* 278.

34. Moore and Simmons, comps. and eds., *Abstracts of the Wills,* 74.

35. Crouse, "The Manigault Family," 12 and n. 23.

Mary Fisher, Sophia Hume, and the Quakers of Colonial Charleston

"Women Professing Godliness"

RANDY J. SPARKS

The opening of the Atlantic World, coupled with the rise of new religious movements in the wake of the English Revolution, transformed the lives of thousands of English men and women whose inward spiritual journeys led them to undertake equally dramatic physical journeys as well. Of the new religious movements that sprang up during the seventeenth century, none was more successful than the Society of Friends, which proposed a radical new vision of religion and society. Many members of the Society of Friends, better known as Quakers, came to the English colonies, including Mary Fisher. She and her granddaughter Sophia Hume were Quaker preachers who lived in Charleston, South Carolina, in the seventeenth and eighteenth centuries.

The proprietors who founded the South Carolina colony, especially Anthony Ashley Cooper and his personal secretary John Locke, envisioned an enlightened colony, and religious toleration was written into the Fundamental Constitutions.[1] That same document, however, formalized a colony based on inequality, servitude, and slavery. The guarantee of religious liberty brought a remarkable variety of religious-minded colonists into Carolina and created one of the most religiously diverse colonies in America. But as Carolina grew and prospered on the basis of slave labor, many of those religious colonists found much to criticize. Though their numbers were never large, the Quakers were an important presence in early Charleston; they provided an alternate vision of society to many men and women, and the religion proffered the power to transform radically the lives of those who followed the inner light.

Quakerism began with the religious revelations of George Fox (1624–91), a shoemaker's apprentice who became convinced that the Holy Spirit, the inner light, resided within every individual and that therefore all people had within them the capacity for divine revelation. Established churches, he believed, had drifted away from this fundamental truth. The Reformation had attempted to restore the religion as practiced among early Christians, but that effort too had failed. Fox insisted that anyone, regardless of sex or station, could be called to preach, and he rejected the idea of a paid or "hireling" ministry. Quakers sat in silence until someone felt guided by the inner light to speak.

No aspect of Fox's preaching was more radical than his views on women's equal role within his movement. The status of women in the early Christian church was more egalitarian, but as the church took institutional form, women's roles were sharply constrained. Church fathers claimed that as daughters of Eve, all women had a share in the Fall, and they turned particularly to the writings of the apostle Paul who insisted that women should be silent in church and that only men should teach and govern. Fox, however, believed that both women and men were created in God's image and that women's subjection to men was a result of the Fall. For him, gender inequalities were one of Satan's tools, intended to separate humankind from God, when, in reality, both sexes were completely dependent on God. Fox taught that when Christ was resurrected, original sin was erased and the equal relationship that existed before the Fall was reestablished. He argued that the scriptures provided many examples of female prophetesses, that Jesus reached out to women, and that it was women who first announced the joyous news of Jesus's resurrection. Fox's movement began to take shape during a 1652 trip to the northwest of England; he preached out of doors to emotional crowds, many of whom became convinced that his words were genuine revelations of the divine spirit.[2]

As converts gathered around Fox, some of them felt the call to preach, and women were among them. Revered by Quakers, these first converts were known as the "Valiant Sixty," the early and courageous missionaries who suffered severe persecution and hardship to spread the faith.

Mary Fisher was one of this number and among the most famous female Quaker preachers of the first generation. Born in 1623 in a village near York, Fisher labored as a servant in the home of Richard and Elizabeth Tomlinson in Selby, Yorkshire. When the first Quaker preachers came to her area in 1652, the thirty-year-old woman converted along with the Tomlinsons, and Mary immediately felt herself called to prophesy. A short time later, she addressed a congregation in Selby at the close of a worship service, and for that offense she spent sixteen months imprisoned in York Castle. There she met and befriended several other Quaker preachers, and from her cell, she wrote to a local judge protesting the death sentences he imposed on three horse thieves. She warned

QUAKER MEETING IN THE GRACE CHURCH
STREET LONDON MEETINGHOUSE, 1788
Sophia Hume appears in the balcony, third from left. Courtesy of the
Library of the Religious Society of Friends in Britain, London, U.K.

the magistrate, "Examine thy heart and see what thou hast done . . . and let the oppressed go free." She signed her letter "one who desires the good of all people . . . who cryeth for justice and true judgment." Moved by her warnings, the judge rescued two of the convicts as they stood on the gallows, but it was too late to save the third.[3]

Imprisonment did nothing to dissuade Quakers like Fisher; if anything, it deepened their faith and strengthened their resolve. Upon her release from York Castle, Fisher and another female Quaker preacher, Elizabeth Williams, headed south, where they caused an uproar at Cambridge University by standing outside Sidney Sussex College and calling it a "cage of unclean birds." Outraged students stoned the women, and the mayor of Cambridge had them arrested for disorderly conduct and taken to the market area, where they became the first Quaker preachers to be stripped to the waist and publicly whipped until the blood ran down their backs. Had she not converted to Quakerism, a servant woman like Fisher would probably have ended her life unknown to history, but her conversion altered her life in ways she could scarcely have imagined. She continued to travel and preach and was imprisoned over and over again. Her deep faith and willingness to suffer for her religion impressed her fellow Friends. When Thomas Aldam encountered her in prison in Pontefract, he wrote that "the Lord hath been elated to love her very faithfull. . . . [H]e doth put her in the power of his truth."[4]

Quakers listened carefully to their inner light, and the faithful strove to do whatever that compelling voice told them to do. The meeting to which a preacher belonged evaluated the preachers' "gift." Those with minor gifts might speak occasionally in meetings, but they would not be judged fit to travel and preach. Preachers like Fisher, whose gifts were powerful, would be given monetary support and letters to establish their credentials as they traveled. Friends felt themselves called to travel around Europe and throughout the Atlantic World. As one scholar observed, Quakers "viewed themselves as linked in one transatlantic community; no colonial religious group had closer transatlantic ties."[5]

That inner voice led Mary Fisher not only to travel and to preach across England but also to take a series of remarkable overseas journeys. In 1655, Fisher felt called to visit the West Indies and New England. She and fellow preacher Ann Austin sailed first to Barbados, where their message was well received. The lieutenant governor of the island converted under Fisher's preaching, and she called on George Fox (whom she addressed as "My deare father") to send other missionaries to the island, saying "if anney of our friends be free to com over they may be servisabell here. . . . [M]any convinced and many desires to know the way."[6]

The women may have enjoyed some success in Barbados, but the next stop on their journey, Puritan Massachusetts, was a more troubled one. They were the first Quakers ever seen in New England, and suspicious authorities refused to allow them to land and confiscated over one hundred books the women had brought to distribute. With evidence of their radical beliefs in hand, Boston's magistrates locked the women in the common jail. They were not allowed to have writing materials, the jailer took their bibles and bedclothes to pay his fees, and their bodies were searched for witch's marks. Ann Austin reported that she had not suffered as much in the births of her five children as she had at the hands of the Puritans. After five weeks in jail, the pair were deported. They aroused such intense fears that the Puritans began fining ship captains who brought Quakers into the colony and in 1658 passed laws that warned Quakers away from Massachusetts on pain of death. Half of the twenty-two charges of witchcraft made in New England between 1656 and 1664 were leveled against Quakers, and four Quaker preachers were executed, including one woman.[7]

In 1657 Fisher's inner light called on her to preach to the sultan of the Ottoman Empire, leading her to embark on the most remarkable journey undertaken by any of the Quaker preachers, male or female. She set out with a party that included one man and two other women. The little party reached Livorno, a port in Tuscany, where they preached for two weeks to the Catholics, Jews, and Englishmen who resided there. From there they traveled largely on foot to Smyrna, where the group became separated. Still on foot, Fisher made her way to Adrianople where Sultan Mehmed IV was encamped with his army. When the sultan's grand vizier heard that an Englishwoman had arrived with a message from God, he treated her as an ambassador and arranged for her to have an audience with the sultan. Mehmed IV listened with interest to her message through an interpreter and offered a military party to escort her to Istanbul, an offer she refused as she once again made her way on foot and alone. Back in England, she wrote to friends that she had endured "many tryalls such as I was never tried with before," but she added, "yet have I borne my testimony for our Lord before the King unto whom I was sent, and he was very noble unto me. . . . [H]e received the words of truth without contradiction."[8]

In the following decades, Fisher focused more on family and building a life in the colonies. In 1662 she married fellow Quaker preacher William Bayley, a former Baptist preacher and a shipmaster from Dorset, with whom she had a son and two daughters. Bayley died at sea in 1675. In 1678 she wed John Crosse, a cordwainer, and the couple moved to Charleston, South Carolina, with their family in 1680.

There is no record indicating why the family chose to move to Charleston, but several factors may have influenced that decision. Often regarded as the colony of a colony, Carolina owed much to Barbados, where Fisher had preached on more than one occasion. But there were important differences between the two colonies, including the fact that religious liberty was offered to prospective settlers to Carolina by the Lords proprietors. Mary Fisher had helped to plant Quakerism in Barbados, but the slave owners who governed the island soon grew suspicious of the Friends owing to their efforts to educate slaves, their call for humane treatment of the enslaved, their refusal to serve in the militia, and their refusal to swear oaths. By 1680 there were half a dozen Quaker meetings on the tiny island, comprising, all told, several hundred members. As their numbers grew, so did official efforts to rein them in; the Barbados Assembly imposed heavy fines for nonattendance at militia drills and for allowing slaves to attend worship services.[9]

The Carolina proprietors, especially Anthony Ashley Cooper, Lord Shaftesbury, who was most involved in the colony's early development, took a different view of Quakers. He actively encouraged Friends to migrate to Carolina, and in 1675 he asked his agent in Carolina, Andrew Percival, "to be very kind to them and give them all the assistance you can in the choice of a place or anything else that may conduce to theire convenient settlement, for they are people I have a great regard to and am obliged to care of." In keeping with his desire to facilitate the settlement of Quakers in Carolina, Friends were allowed to hold public office, and when taking an oath of office or appearing in court, they were permitted to affirm "according to the form of their profession" rather than being required to swear an oath. Indeed, the proprietors and the governors they appointed attempted to remove almost all restrictions that had so plagued the Quakers in Barbados. Many of the early Quaker migrants from Barbados to Carolina had been fined or otherwise persecuted for their faith, but in Carolina they prospered and even held public office. One of Carolina's early governors, John Archdale, was himself a Quaker, and, during his tenure, Friends could avoid military service by applying to the governor for certification.[10]

It is easy to imagine that Carolina would also have appealed to English Quakers like Mary Fisher, now known as Mary Fisher Crosse, who had suffered for their faith. Before the establishment of Pennsylvania in 1681, Carolina would have been the most tolerant colony for Friends who sought a new home in America. Significantly, Quakers who moved to Carolina in the colonial era tolerated slavery. South Carolina's dependence on slavery would alienate and drive out the last of the Quakers in the early nineteenth century, but in this period Quakers had no qualms about the institution. In fact, many Quakers in early Carolina owned slaves, including the Crosse family, who owned as many as ten slaves, both African and Indian. Other Quakers became wealthy planters and large slaveholders; Ralph Emmes, for example, owned fifty-three slaves, Thomas Elliott owned twenty-six, and James Stanyarne served as an agent for the purchase of Indian slaves.[11]

Mary Fisher Crosse played a major role in the growing Quaker community, whose members revered her as "Mother Crosse." By 1681 or 1682 the number of Friends in Carolina was large enough to establish a monthly meeting (the name for a local Quaker congregation). Although their numbers are uncertain, probably around one hundred Quakers lived in Carolina by 1700. At first they met in the homes of Friends, but in the mid-1690s Thomas Bolton left funds in his will to repair their burial ground and to build a meetinghouse, probably on the King Street lot where a meeting place later stood. The Charleston Monthly Meeting reported to the London Yearly Meeting, but given the distances between them, it usually functioned independently, though sometimes it reported to the larger Philadelphia Meeting. As the first generation of Quaker immigrants aged and immigration slowed, the Charleston Meeting struggled to survive.[12]

John Crosse died in 1695 and Mary Fisher Crosse died in 1698; their family's story thereafter illustrates the decline of the Quaker community. Quakers prohibited their members from marrying non-Quaker partners, but this rule was frequently violated, especially in places where the number of Friends was small. John and Mary Fisher Crosse had come to Charleston with Mary's son and two daughters born to her and her first husband. It appears likely that John and Mary's offspring remained faithful Quakers, but members of the next generation did not. For example, Mary's granddaughter, Rebecca Basden, became an Anglican when she married the Reverend William Guy, an Anglican priest. Susannah Bayley, Mary's youngest daughter, married Henry Wiggington, an Anglican, who was deputy secretary of the colony, but records of the Charleston Meeting reveal that Susannah Wiggington remained a Quaker. Her daughter Sophia, however, followed her father's Anglican faith.

In this respect, the Quaker experience can be usefully compared to the Huguenots, who immigrated at the same time as the Friends. In his study of the South Carolina Huguenots, Bertrand Van Ruymbeke found that at first the Huguenots married among themselves, but when the Charleston-born generation began to come of age, the majority married outside the faith. And the Huguenot population was probably five times larger than the Quaker group. These "out marriages," as the Quakers called them, reflected the difficulties of finding suitable marriage partners given the small size of the Quaker community as well as the growing integration of the Quakers into the economic, social, and political life of the colony. In the early eighteenth century the Church of England became the officially established church in South Carolina, a change that limited the rights of Dissenters, including the Quakers, to participate in the colony's government.[13] Like Huguenot politicians who found themselves in a similar situation, some Quakers practiced a "dual affiliation" by remaining Quaker but taking positions within the Anglican structure.[14]

In addition to these political problems, Quakers also faced growing criticism and persecution for their pacifism, which became even more of an issue as troubles intensified between the Carolina colony and its Indian neighbors. In 1703 the assembly enacted a new militia law requiring all men between the ages of sixteen and sixty to bear arms and attend militia drills without exception. In 1711 and 1712 the South Carolinians and their Yamasee allies successfully went to war against the Tuscarora Indians who had attacked white settlements in North Carolina. Tensions, however, developed between white settlers and the Yamasee over such issues as the deerskin trade, Indian slavery, and white encroachment on Indian lands. In 1715 these tensions erupted into open warfare when the Yamasee launched raids against white settlements in South Carolina. They were joined by other Indian tribes, and the South Carolinians were soon fighting for their very survival. Whites abandoned plantations and outlying settlements and fled to Charleston where starvation threatened the entire population. The tide turned only when the Cherokee decided to join the war on the side of the colonists, but by then about 7 percent of the white population had been killed, making this war one of the bloodiest in the history of colonial America. In this crisis, the Quakers' pacifism created widespread outrage, and Quakers were repeatedly fined for their refusal to bear arms.[15]

Under these conditions, it is hardly surprising that the Charleston Meeting apparently faltered and that many Friends left the fold. When Thomas Chalkley, a Quaker preacher from England, visited Charleston in 1713, he reported that the people were "generally loving," but he found "few Friends in this province." Thomas Kimberley, one of the Charleston Friends who was fined several times for refusing to bear arms, helped to revive the meeting shortly after or perhaps even during the Yamasee War. Another Charleston Quaker, William Piggott, wrote in 1719 that a few Friends had been meeting for about a year and a half when Kimberley convened a meeting at his residence to "consider the affares of the Church in a generall way." He noted that Kimberley "was the friend whose mouth the Lord had opened up amongst us." The Charleston Quakers resumed their monthly meeting, though apparently their meetinghouse had fallen into disrepair because they met at Kimberley's home. They assessed their finances, opened correspondence with other monthly meetings around the Atlantic World, and began to record births, marriages, and deaths. Among the faithful few who worked to revive the meeting was Mary Fisher's daughter Susannah Wiggington.[16]

Piggott explained that the number of Quakers had declined in Charleston "by reason of some going out of the Country, together with the Unfaithfulness of many of their Off Spring: the Number of those who workt in the Law of the Lord became verey Small."[17] It must have pained Susannah Wiggington that among those Quaker children who had strayed from the faith was her own daughter Sophia, born in 1701. Sophia later recalled:

> My Father was a Member of the Church of *England*, and educated me in that Way; and I well remember, I had a much warmer Side for his Opinion; not that I knew what was the essential Difference in their religious Sentiments, or at least that affected me any farther than that one allow'd me something more Liberty in Dress; whereas the other would tell me Plainness in Apparel was most agreeable to Christianity, and to the Divine Being, who hated Pride in his Creatures. To be sure I thought this Doctrine absurd, by the Reflection I remember I made at the Time, *That God, I believed, would not reject me, on the Score of wearing Lace, or a fine and gay Silk Gown.*[18]

The feelings of a young girl who loved her father, followed his teaching, and enjoyed wearing gay silks and laces can be easily understood. By the time Sophia came of age, Charleston was an elegant and wealthy place, one of the richest in the entire Atlantic World, and she was a daughter of privilege who could enjoy all the pleasures that the lively city had to offer. Balls, music, the theater, books, and the gentle arts thought suitable to a young woman of her station—the fine art of japanning, for example—occupied her thoughts and her time.[19]

Sophia made a suitable match when in 1721 she wed Robert Hume, a prominent lawyer, politician, planter, and land speculator. Hume served several terms in the assembly before being elected speaker in 1732. Soon after, however, his life and Sophia's took an unexpected turn when he hastily resigned his position and left for England, citing "personal business" as the reason for his sudden departure. The real reason was that news of his involvement in a financial scandal involving land in the Port Royal area was about to break, and Hume's reputation was soon ruined. He returned to Charleston after the scandal blew over but retired from public life and died in 1737. He left a large estate, a town house in Charleston, and over seven thousand acres of land. But the humiliating scandal and her husband's untimely death shook Sophia's world to its very foundations and led to a period of soul searching that caused her to renounce her former way of life. Sophia's spiritual writings offer unusual insight into the struggles she endured. She recalled:

I plainly perceived by that Light (he had placed in my Conscience, which enabled me to discern between Right and Wrong, the Precious and the Vile) that a Life of Pleasure and Diversion was inconsistent with the Life of a Christian; I found that to be thus carnally minded, has been Death to my Soul.

She warned:

You rich Men, weep and howl for your Miseries that shall come upon you; for you have lived in Pleasure on the Earth, . . . [w]eep for yourselves, and for your Children, . . . [f]or what is your Life! It is even as a Vapour, that appeareth for a little Time, and then vanishes away.

These spiritual battles clearly reflect the sudden reversal in her fortunes as she turned her back on the life she had once enjoyed.[20]

Sophia's trials led her back to the austere faith practiced by her mother and grandmother, and that dramatic conversion brought about a radical change in her dress and deportment, a transformation that her family and friends did not understand. Like other converts to Quakerism, Sophia renounced her old ways; she changed her behavior and appearance and refused to be governed by conventional gender expectations. The small band of Quakers still carried on their monthly meetings in Charleston in the mid-1730s during her time of troubles, and she began to attend them. She wrote that

being convinced of the Principles of the *People called Quakers*, I joined to that Society. Thus I became singular, and consequently despicable to my Children, and some of my Acquaintance and Friends; who not only profes'd a Dislike, but a Concern that I should appear in so contemptible a Manner, and so very different from what I usually had done. Here I had a Cross to bear.

Learned, literate, and well read, Sophia found guidance in the writings of prominent Quakers like Robert Barclay as she faced the criticism of her family and friends.[21]

Just as Mary Fisher's conversion led her to leave her home in Yorkshire and embark on journeys that would have been inconceivable before she joined the Society of Friends, Sophia's conversion led her to leave the comforts of her Charleston home for London. She left no explanation for her decision to leave Charleston, but the condemnation of friends and family may have been a factor. Perhaps, too, she sought a larger and more active Quaker community than Charleston could offer. She immersed herself in the Quaker community in London and lived a very different life from the one she had known in Carolina. Perhaps the most striking aspect of the London Meeting was the important role played by women preachers. Records indicate that well over eight hundred female preachers participated in the congregation between 1700 and 1799, a number equal to or greater than the number of male preachers. In addition, women had their own separate meetings, which one scholar has described as "an unprecedented inclusion of females in church government." In fact, Sophia was among the many women who worked to establish and maintain the separate women's meeting in London. She was one of over thirty women who signed a 1747 letter on behalf of the "women's meeting in London" in which they praised the "benefit, edification and comfort of such meetings." Sophia found great solace and spiritual growth among the London Friends. She wrote, "I had frequent and glorious opportunities of going up to the house or into the presence of God in sweet company and fellowship[.] . . . [T]hus happily exquisitely happy was I, as far as one engaged in Christian warfare can be."[22]

Despite the great distance Sophia had put between herself and her birthplace, Carolina continued to weigh on her mind and her heart. She felt "a concern I had often had for the inhabitants of my native country revived in my soul" and a desire "to call them from those things which I had been by the great love and power of God redeemed from." "This discovery," she wrote, "of the divine will gave me the greatest uneasiness I think I ever felt, the greatest cross I ever had to bear, which I long reasoned against and implored the Almighty if it was his Will to remove the burthen." But that burden was not removed; instead the call became more insistent: "I could have been contented to have lived alone as a sparrow upon the housetop, and have sat in silence and gone softly all my days for their sakes: but this was not the divine will concerning me; the word was gone forth, 'Obey my voice.'" She was forced to admit that there was no "block in my way but my unwillingness to become a fool, to go and abase myself in my native country where I have long lived in pride and exaltation of mind." She would go to Charleston, but this time in the role of a Quaker preacher, just as her grandmother had in the previous century.[23]

When Sophia, having been absent for nearly six years, arrived in her "native Country," the city's inhabitants did not exactly meet her with open arms. She found that "the Novelty of my religious Sentiments, and Meanness of my Appearance has . . . render'd me despicable in your Eyes." Nonetheless, she began to preach in the small Quaker meetinghouse. In the beginning, there was "some indecent Behavior of some rude People coming into the Meeting House when she was there." The reasons for such efforts to disrupt her services are not hard to find. She condemned all the elite pastimes that she saw as stumbling blocks on the road to salvation. She railed against the Charlestonians for attending "Assemblies once a Week, wherein you dance and game; Balls and Dancing at other

Times and Places, Card-playing at your own Houses, & c. And, suffer me to say, That I am sensible you . . . fail not to give your Attendance on every Occasion of Mirth and Jolity; and that you mimick *Great Britain* in every Foppery, Luxury and Recreation, within your Reach."[24]

Sophia was, of course, correct in her assessment that the Charleston elite made every effort to mimic Great Britain; this emulation is what has been referred to as the "Anglicization" of the Lowcountry. It was part of the quest of the elite to maintain their position and their authority in a slave society. As historian Edward Pearson has observed, "Deportment and dress, conversation and concerts all served as the vehicles by which the elite fabricated a sense of distinction that set them apart from others."[25] In large part, that effort to gain temporal wealth and power and the creation of distinctions based on class, gender, and race—in other words, the very foundations of colonial South Carolina—ran counter to the tenants of Quakerism. As Sophia told her countrymen, "Religious Minds despise and condemn all worldly Honour, and earthly preferment, seeking that only which comes from God." The central teaching of Quakerism was equality. As she put it, "I shall premise one Proposition, on which all I have to offer will greatly depend, *viz, That all Mankind have a Measure and Manifestation of the Light, Spirit, or Grace of God*."[26]

We know much about Sophia's 1747 ministry in Charleston because she published an essay entitled *An Exhortation to the Inhabitants of the Province of South-Carolina, to Bring Their Deeds to the Light of Christ, in Their Own Consciences.* It may well be the first work published by a native-born southern woman. She felt guided to write it, as she explained: "In the course of my continuing there a concern was laid on my mind to write a short account of the dealings of the Lord to bring me to himself, with an exhortation to the Inhabitants, and as I could not conveniently get it printed in Carolina in the time I proposed to stay there, I have brought it to Philadelphia in order to get it printed." Benjamin Franklin published the first edition of the tract, which went through at least six later editions in England, Ireland, and America. Israel Pemberton Sr., a prominent Philadelphia Quaker, wrote that her essay was popular among readers "not only of our Societ[y] but likewise of others."[27]

Once she was back in England, Carolina continued to weigh heavy on her heart. She published another tract entitled *An Epistle to the Inhabitants of South-Carolina* in London in 1754, an impressive work in biblical exegesis. She wrote and published several other religious tracts in the 1750s and 1760s.[28] And several other women preachers from London went to Charleston in the wake of her visit in an attempt to encourage the small meeting. In 1750, for example, Mary Weston of London visited Charleston with Elizabeth Nixon of North Carolina.

Weston was one of a group of Quaker preachers, many of them women, who sought to reform Quakerism and bring back the zeal of the early Friends. Records of the Charleston Meeting reveal that the two women "came to this town on a religious visit & after several meetings in town, . . . [t]hey returned to the Northwards." Mary Peisley of England and Catherine Payton of Ireland, two other leaders of the reform movement, visited America in 1753, and they began their trip in Charleston. They found a dwindling congregation and much disorder, which they tried to correct. Peisley noted that "the discipline was quite let fall and I found it my duty to endeavor to revive it. Herein I met with open opposition and evil treatment." The two women visited every Quaker family in the city and freely condemned any violations of discipline they found including "out marriages" and failure to use plain language ("thee" and "thou"). The women admitted that "we have driven several from the meeting, who could not bear sound doctrine," a necessary pruning that they expected would yield a healthier plant. As Peisley wrote, "Amen, to these leaving the profession, whose lives and conduct are a scandal to it." In 1761 Susanna Hatton of Ireland, another reformer, visited Charleston "in the work of the ministry."[29] Given the close-knit, transatlantic Quaker community, Sophia was no doubt aware of the efforts of her fellow female preachers to carry on the work in her hometown.

In 1767 Sophia felt a call to return to Charleston. Her fellow Quakers in London's Grace Church Street Meeting wrote, "We are Convinced on the Consideration of her advanced time of life [she was 65 at the time], and the Fatigues and Dangers she may probably have to Encounter, that no motives whatever could Enduce her to this service but the strongest persuasion of Duty and her love to Mankind; In becoming an Instrument to Publich the Glad Tidings of the Gospell of Life and Salvation by Jesus Christ."[30] By this time, her years in the ministry, her travels, and her publications had made her something of a celebrity. Her visit was announced in newspapers across the colonies; the *Virginia Gazette*, for example, noted her arrival and called her a "celebrated writer and preacher."[31]

Despite that warm welcome, the idea that a woman would preach still aroused considerable opposition, and some residents of the city said that "there [is] no defending this novelty, viz Women Preaching against the Prohibitions of the Apostles." To combat that view, the learned Sophia cleverly turned to John Locke, who defended the right of women to preach, noting that Locke's views had "been serviceable in obviating that objection in some." Others argued that "women may preach, pray, exhort, but not in a publick Place of Worship." But that, of course, is precisely what Sophia proceeded to do. The controversy very likely attracted more people to her meetings. She reported, "Our first day Meetings are pretty well attended the most of whom are Strangers the Meeting Place being small it will not admit above 80 Persons to sit unless we borrow Chairs, but at times I believe the generality of the Towns People have attended."[32] She continued her gatherings without interference. "Our Meetings are still often crowded with People," she observed, adding, "I have the Consolation now to meet with some of both Sexes, with whom . . . I feel the Unity of the Spirit in the bond of Peace and Love."[33] She noted that "I have been enabled to exhort the People for at least an Hour at a Time."[34]

Sophia found many problems among the Quaker community in Charleston. Like Peisley and Hatton, she was disturbed to find that many people who professed to be Quakers did not conform to discipline, and others, even some she considered friends, refused to attend meetings at all. She lamented that "to be . . . amongst false Brethren is harder to bear, than Persecution from them that are without."[35] Another problem confronting the Charleston Meeting was the status of its property. There was considerable confusion about the title and deeds to the King Street property, which included the meeting house and a house behind it. Since the Charleston Meeting had sometimes lapsed, one of the congregants, Joseph Shute, had taken over management of the property—he rented out the house and collected the rents, allowed someone to live in the meetinghouse itself, and claimed part of the property as his own. The Philadelphia Meeting tried to resolve the problem and asked Sophia to sort it out. She made every effort to do so; she met with various parties involved, and even called on her childhood friend Lieutenant Governor William Bull for his assistance, but she was unable to resolve the dispute. She wrote Israel Pemberton in Philadelphia, "I may just add with regard to the Meeting house that my short Continuance here will not admit my further Concern, especially as tis likely to be attended with Controversy."[36]

Another matter of controversy involved the institution of slavery. By the time of her second visit, more Quakers opposed slavery than had before. Historian Jon Butler has chided Sophia for her "dichotomous moralizing," criticizing Charlestonians for many of their pastimes but making no mention of slavery. It is true that Sophia's published works did not directly condemn slavery, but her letters paint a different picture. When she arrived in Charleston in 1767, rumors circulated that her purpose in visiting the city was not religious, as she claimed, but rather was to "recover an estate & gett possession of a Company of Negro Slaves." Those rumors reached Philadelphia, though Israel Pemberton assured her that "we are not so weak as . . . to believe thou would ever be concerned in continuing any of the Negro's in slavery which it may be in thy power to release."[37]

The charge was related to the estate of her deceased nephew, Robert Hume, though Sophia noted that she had planned her trip before she knew of his death, and that she had notified the London Meeting of the situation before her departure to avoid the appearance of conflict. Deeply distressed by these rumors, she wrote, "I had never any Thoughts or Intentions of having the least plausible Claim to any one Negro in the Province, But if I had, I am now so principled against the unchristian & wicked Practice & Traffick of dealing in & detaining any fellow Creatures in a state of Slavery, that if I know my own Heart, I should make no Such Claim." She admitted "this is now the state of my mind, yet in a time of more Ignorance 20 odd years ago I felt no such convictions when I sold several Negroes. But as I have observ'd that I would by no means have any Share in this unchristian Practice."[38]

Sophia shared Quaker antislavery tracts with people in Charleston, and although her acquaintances found the arguments compelling, she noted that they "think it impossible to carry on the Trades & Manufactures of the Province without Negroes—I don't observe this to discourage Friends in their Laudable Attempt, but I fear the Legislature at Home [in England] will hardly be persuaded to give up so large a Part of this Revenue."[39] Whether or not Sophia actually preached against slavery while in Charleston is unclear, though the fact that rumors about her own involvement in the institution—clearly intended to discredit her on this issue—reached as far as Philadelphia and London suggest that she did. And she was not one to withhold her views on the failings of her countrymen. In addition, some of the most ardent Quaker advocates of abolition were her close friends and regular correspondents, including Israel Pemberton, John Woolman, and Anthony Benezet.

The notice of Sophia's final departure from Carolina recorded in the April 1, 1768, minutes of the Charleston Meeting may be read in part as a vindication of her motives in coming to the city of her birth: "This Day our Antient and Worthy Friend Sophia Hume Sailed from hence in the Ship Called the London . . . Bound for London after Labouring in ye Ministrey Amongst us Neare Eight Months, and [we] are senisbly convinced that nothing Less Could induce her to this Service but the strongest perswasion of her Love and Dutey to Mankind, in becoming an Instrument in Publishing the Glad Tidings of the Gospel of Life and Salvation by Jesue Christ." Once back in London, she resumed her busy life among the London Friends. A painting of a service underway in Grace Church Street Meeting House around 1770 shows Sophia sitting in the raised preacher's gallery facing the congregation, her hand partly covering her face, a posture that Quaker preachers sometimes adopted when waiting for inspiration from their inner light. In 1773 she made out her will and "signified to several that she might go forth after suddenly, and chose to be in that prepared state."

She continued to attend meetings regularly; in January 1774, she "attended the morning meeting . . . [and] was then very particular in advice to ministers and elders." She sat through an afternoon meeting lasting several hours, slept at the house of a friend, and "breakfasted with usual health and spirits," but then she was suddenly "seized as some thought with a paraletic shock." She "languished but a few hours" and died. Her funeral drew the largest crowd ever seen at Grace Church for a burial. Two preachers—one male, one female—eulogized her "in the highest terms . . . that . . . could be bestowed." She requested a plain coffin made of unpolished elm and "no ornaments on the hearse, no wine or strong liquor handed about." When she was laid to rest in London, she had served as a dedicated preacher for over twenty-five years.[40]

What are we to make of the stories of these remarkable women? First, there can be no question that Quakerism radically transformed their lives. Mary Fisher, a thirty-year-old servant at the time of her conversion, would likely have lived a life of toil and obscurity in Yorkshire had she not become a Quaker. Her granddaughter, Sophia Hume, would have continued her life of ease as a Charleston society matron. These women would have been defined by their social station, but the Quakers judged them as individuals, recognized their powerful spiritual gifts, and nurtured and supported them in their ministerial roles. Guided by their inner light, these women embarked on inward spiritual journeys that then led them out of their small worlds into the wider Atlantic World and into public roles that would have been unthinkable before their conversion. Quakerism also opened up a rich social life for them and ushered them into a community of like-minded men and women who respected them as spiritual leaders. Like all Protestants, Quakers were people of the Book, and the literacy that was required to read the scriptures and the writings of the Quakers that were so fundamental to the Friends also brought these women into a world of letters and even authorship long before most southern women would have that opportunity. Quaker prohibitions against "outside marriages" also meant that their family lives reflected their religious lives. Mary Fisher's two husbands were themselves Quakers who respected her gifts and supported her public role, which called on her to preach and travel extensively. Sophia Hume was willing to face the ridicule and opposition from her family to answer the direction of her inner light. The women's faith enabled them to chart their own course, even in the face of opposition from friends and family and despite sometimes serious persecution. In a society that radically constricted women's legal and political rights and kept women silent in public and confined to the domestic sphere, the Quaker faith in the inner light led to a radical alteration in gender roles. It is also important to note that for these southern women, Quakerism was handed down through the female line from Mary Fisher Bayley Crosse, to her daughter Susanna Wiggington, to her daughter Sophia Hume.

It is difficult to exaggerate the symbolic importance of the Quaker vision of the equality of believers. No doubt many Charlestonians who came to hear the female Quaker preachers viewed them as objects of curiosity or even of derision, but they were *there*. It is important to note that the Church of England was the largest denomination in colonial Charleston and continues to be influential to the present day. The idea of a woman serving as an Anglican priest would have been unthinkable during Mary Fisher's and Sophia Hume's lifetimes, and even today it is not without controversy. The Episcopal Church in the United States did not ordain women until 1976, almost two centuries after Mary Fisher Crosse arrived in Charleston, and the Church of England did not follow suit until 1992. To this day, the Southern Baptist Church, the largest denomination in the state, does not ordain women. It is very likely that Charlestonians saw more female preachers in the eighteenth century than in the twentieth.

The doctrine of spiritual equality also led Quakers to campaign first for better treatment of slaves before they became more hostile to the institution later in the eighteenth century. Women preachers were at the forefront of that campaign. As we have seen, Sophia expressed her hostility to the institution, and other women preachers followed suit. When Mary Peisley and Catherine Payton preached in Charleston and other southern colonies in 1754 they condemned "the buying and keeping of slaves; which we could not reconcile with the golden rule of doing unto all men as we would they should do unto us." During her 1769 preaching tour Rachel Wilson warned southern Quakers "to keep thair hands Clear from purchasing Negroes as believing it never was intended for us to trafick [sic] with any part of the Human Species & if thair was no Buyer thair wo[ul]d be no Sell[e]rs."[41]

Quakerism might appear to be a rather minor footnote in the history of South Carolina, but it is important not to read backward into history. When the Quakers arrived in Charleston, they were a small but significant minority, and before the establishment of Pennsylvania as a Quaker haven, Carolina was the most welcoming place in colonial America for their settlement. In a colony that granted religious toleration, the Quakers joined a diverse religious community that included French Huguenots, Jews, and many small Protestant sects. They were a part of the marketplace of ideas in Charleston. Across British colonial America, Quakers composed the third largest religious group, and throughout the colonies they provided a compelling alternative to the prevailing culture. This was certainly the case in South Carolina where Quakers confronted a society grounded in inequality, patriarchy, violence, wealth, and racism. In some respects, their challenges to social norms—their insistence on simple dress in a society that aped the gaudy styles of Restoration and Georgian England; their use of the familiar "thee" and "thou" in a society based on class and rank; their refusal to swear oaths in a society where loyalty to state and crown were expected to be displayed; their condemnation of the theater, balls, and musical entertainments in a society where these leisure activities linked them to the elite pastimes of the metropole—might appear minor. Other aspects of their lives, however, represented a more obvious challenge, especially their pacifism, their insistence on the equality of believers, and their gender equality. And even when their numbers were small and their faith was weak, they provided a real alternative for women like Sophia Hume. The Charleston Friends continued to meet throughout the colonial period, still welcoming traveling preachers, including women, but by the early 1800s the meeting had disbanded.[42]

Imagine for a moment that the Quakers had survived into the antebellum period in Charleston and that women like Sarah and Angelina Grimké could have joined a society in their hometown rather than having to go to Philadelphia to find that community. Their voices were silenced in Charleston in a way that Sophia's was not, which meant that their message of equality and freedom was heard there in a different way. At the time of her death Sophia was writing a letter to her old friend Anthony Benezet, which read in part, "I cannot but mourn nor remain unmoved while our Tribes are in the Wilderness, surrounded by their enemies . . . for this my spiritual as well as natural bread, has been often mixed with tears." Through her tears, the elderly Sophia looked forward to a better day: "I want to see the time when the mountain of the Lord's house shall be on the top of every exalted mountain which poor unhappy mortals have raised to their own destruction. I want to see the people take the armour of God as it is graciously offered by the Captain of our Salvation[.] . . . I am thankful to the keeper of Israel. . . . [I]n my measure I am enabled to address the Father of mercies with strong cries, prayers, and many tears, that all Men may be blessed . . . and be saved from sin here and the dreadful penalty due to it hereafter."[43]

NOTES

The author would like to thank Alexandra Webber for assisting with research in London. The quotation in the title is taken from Sophia Hume, *A Short Appeal to Men and Women of Reason* (Bristol: E. Farley, 1750), 21.

1. The Lords proprietors adopted the Fundamental Constitutions of Carolina in March 1669. For an in-depth examination of them and religious toleration, see James Lowell Underwood, "The

Dawn of Religious Freedom in South Carolina: The Journey from Limited Tolerance to Constitutional Right," in *The Dawn of Religious Freedom in South Carolina*, ed. James Lowell Underwood and W. Lewis Burke (Columbia: University of South Carolina Press, 2006), 1–57.

2. See Fox's journal at http://www.strecorsoc.org/gfox/title.html (accessed September 11, 2008), chaps. 2–7; Rebecca Larson, *Daughters of Light: Quaker Women Preaching and Prophesying in the Colonies and Abroad, 1700–1775* (New York: Knopf, 1999), 14–26.

3. Mary Fisher to unnamed judge in York, n.d., A. R. Barclay Manuscripts, vol. 324, mss. 173, Library of the Society of Friends, London (hereinafter cited as LSF).

4. Aldam to Joan Killam, n.d., mss. portfolio 36:111, LSF.

5. Larson, *Daughters of Light*, 9, 64.

6. Jo Anne McCormick, "The Quakers of Colonial South Carolina, 1670–1807," (PhD diss., University of South Carolina, 1984), 28; Fisher to George Fox, January 30, 1655, LSF.

7. Larson, *Daughters of Light*, 232–33; Phyllis Mack, *Visionary Women: Ecstatic Prophecy in Seventeenth-Century England* (Berkeley: University of California Press, 1992), 258–60.

8. Mack, *Visionary Women*, 169–70; Fisher to Thomas Shillam, Thomas Aldam, and John Shillam "with your dear wives," January 13, 1658, LSF.

9. McCormick, "The Quakers of Colonial South Carolina," 20–24, 27–30.

10. Ibid, 20–33. Shaftsbury quoted on 20 and 40.

11. W. Scott Poole, "'Your Liberty in That Province': South Carolina Quakers and the Rejection of Religious Toleration," in *The Dawn of Religious Freedom in South Carolina*, 170.

12. Ibid., 29–30, 34–38; Larson, *Daughters of Light*, 261. When a local group of Quakers became large enough they formally organized as a "monthly meeting." The term is taken from the monthly business meeting held separately from the weekly services—also called a "meeting." The local monthly meetings or meetings reported to larger assemblies called "quarterly" "half year" or "annual" meetings, named after their geographic location. The Charleston Monthly Meeting officially reported to the London Meeting.

13. McCormick, "The Quakers of Colonial South Carolina," 29, 46; Larson, *Daughters of Light*, 224; Mabel L. Webber, ed., "The Records of the Quakers in Charles Town," *South Carolina Historical and Genealogical Magazine* 28, no. 3 (1927), 95.

14. McCormick, "The Quakers of Colonial South Carolina," 54–59; Bertrand Van Ruymbeke, "The Huguenots of Proprietary South Carolina: Patterns of Migration and Integration," in *Money, Trade, and Power: The Evolution of Colonial South Carolina's Plantation Society*, ed. Jack P. Greene, Rosemary Brana-Shute, and Randy J. Sparks (Columbia: University of South Carolina Press, 2001), 40.

15. McCormick, "The Quakers of Colonial South Carolina," 58, 63–64.

16. Chalkley, *A Journal or Historical Account of the Life, Travels, and Christian Experiences of that Ancient, Faithful Servant of Jesus Christ, Thomas Chalkley* (London: Luke Hinde, 1751), 71; McCormick, "The Quakers of Colonial South Carolina," 66–69, 67. For references to Wiggington see Webber, ed., "The Records of the Quakers in Charles Town," 95.

17. Piggott quoted in McCormick, "The Quakers of Colonial South Carolina," 46.

18. Sophia Hume, *An Exhortation to the Inhabitants of the Province of South-Carolina, to Bring Their Deeds to the Light of Christ, in Their Own Consciences* (Philadelphia: William Bradford, 1748), 30.

19. Ibid., 23–24; extract of copy of a letter to the Friends of Bromly Hall, portfolio 24:68, LSF.

20. William Roy Smith, *South Carolina as a Royal Province, 1719–1776* (New York: Macmillan,

1903), chaps. 2 and 3; McCormick, "The Quakers of Colonial South Carolina," 100; Hume, *Exhortation*, 48–49.

21. Webber, ed., "The Records of the Quakers in Charles Town," 97–98; Larson, *Daughters of Light*, 74–75; Hume, *Exhortation*, 77.

22. Larson, *Daughters of Light*, 31, 63, 228, 229; meeting manuscript 55, LSF; Sophia Hume (hereinafter cited as SH) to Hannah Hyam, June 1, 1748, Reynolds Mss., 319–24, LSF.

23. SH to Hannah Hyam, June 1, 1748, Reynolds Mss., 319–24, LSF.

24. Hume, *Exhortation*, 3; James Grame to John Kinsey, February 18, 1748, Quaker Collection, Haverford College Library, Haverford, Penn. (hereinafter cited as QC); Hume, *Exhortation*, 53.

25. Edward Pearson, "'Planters Full of Money': The Self-Fashioning of the Eighteenth-Century South Carolina Elite," in *Money, Trade, and Power*, 314.

26. Hume, *Exhortation*, 5.

27. SH to Hannah Hyam, June 1, 1748, Reynolds Mss., 319–24, LSF.

28. Pemberton quoted in Larson, *Daughters of Light*, 242. For a list of Hume's publications, including various editions of her works, see Joseph Smith, *A Descriptive Catalogue of Friends' Books . . .* (London: J. Smith, 1867).

29. Webber, ed., "The Records of the Quakers in Charles Town," 98; Larson, *Daughters of Light*, 198, 201, 203–6, 206–7; Webber, ed., "The Records of the Quakers in Charles Town," 99–101, 104.

30. Webber, ed., "The Records of the Quakers in Charles Town," 106.

31. *Virginia Gazette*, July 6 and August 6, 1767.

32. SH to Israel Pemberton (hereinafter cited as IP), March 1, 1768, QC; Henry Richard Fox Bourne, *The Life of John Locke* (New York: Harper and Brothers, 1876), 453.

33. SH to IP, March 1, 1768, QC.

34. SH to IP, June 1767, QC.

35. SH to IP, November 12, 1767, QC.

36. Ibid.; McCormick, "The Quakers of Colonial South Carolina," 87–91; SH to IP, March 1, 1768, C.

37. Butler, "Enlarging the Body of Christ: Slavery, Evangelism, and the Christianization of the White South, 1690–1790," in *The Evangelical Tradition in America*, ed. Leonard I. Sweet (Macon, Ga.: Mercer University Press, 1996), 108; IP to SH, July 30, 1767, QC.

38. SH to IP, August 21, 1767, QC; *South-Carolina Gazette*, January 3, 1735/36.

39. *South-Carolina Gazette*, January 3, 1735/36.

40. Webber, ed., "The Records of the Quakers in Charles Town," 178; Larson, *Daughters of Light*, 6; account of death of Sophia Hume in a letter from Will Foster to R. Dudley, Catchpool Mss. 1:151, L F.

41. Peisley, and Payton quoted in Larson, *Daughters of Light*, 220; Wilson quoted in Larson, *Daughters of Light*, 222; Hume, *A Short Appeal*, 29; David Brion Davis, *The Problem of Slavery in Western Culture* (Ithaca, N.Y.: Cornell University Press, 1966), and *The Problem of Slavery in the Age of Revolution, 1770–1823* (Ithaca, N.Y.: Cornell University Press, 1975).

42. Webber, ed., "The Records of the Quakers in Charles Town," 179–88; Poole, 174.

43. Part of a letter from Sophia Hume to Anthony Benezet, which was found unfinished after her death, 1774, Reynolds Mss., 329–32, LSF.

Mary-Anne Schad and Mrs. Brown

Overseers' Wives in Colonial South Carolina

LAURA ROSE SANDY

Historiographies of slavery in the colonial South claim that most plantation overseers were young and single. Those works that do acknowledge the married state of some overseers fail to explore their wives' roles on the plantation or their part in slavery.[1] Yet Plantation records reveal that many overseers in South Carolina had wives. Two such wives were Mary-Anne Schad and "Mrs. Brown," whose first name was not recorded.[2] Indeed, planters looking to recruit a new overseer often desired "one that ha[d] a wife."[3] This is not surprising, as overseers' wives undertook an array of important tasks on the plantation and were often commended by leading planters for their diligence in female-oriented work. The unique perspective these women provide on colonial South Carolina society, enmeshed as they were in a web of class, race, and gender relationships, is reason enough to rescue their memory from historical obscurity.

Within the wide-ranging historical scholarship on the eighteenth-century American South, the overseers charged with supervising slave labor have received little attention. Their central role in the economic and social development of the South has been marginalized, and they have been denigrated as little more than whip-wielding brutes. Their wives, scarcely mentioned by scholars, are the hitherto silent witnesses to eighteenth-century South Carolina's maturation as a slave society.

We know less about lower-class white women of the colonial South than we do about every other social group in that society. Women of the planter class figure prominently in the historical record. Even slave women are far more noticeable in colonial records than lower-class white women. Slave traders and slave owners meticulously recorded details about their human property in ledgers, account books, deeds of sale, hire contracts, inventories, wills, letters, and diaries. In contrast, people who were literate had next to no reason to write about the lower classes in colonial South Carolina with whom they had scant contact. The only lower-class whites who appear in the institutional record are those who either committed a crime or raised enough money to buy land or slaves. Lower-class women are rarely mentioned in the few sources in which their menfolk made a fleeting appearance. Their lack of personal wealth, their low social standing, the inferiority accorded to their gender, and their free status meant that no effort was spent on recording details about their lives. Furthermore, the vast majority of them were illiterate or barely literate, which resulted in a dearth of personal testimony.

Thus the evidence necessary to recreate a complete picture of the lives of lower-class white women in eighteenth-century South Carolina does not exist. One can, however, catch glimpses into the world of lower-class white women, women like these two overseers' wives who lived and worked on eighteenth-century plantations in the colony. These women were not so elusive that we cannot come to appreciate that they, too, shaped the multiracial plantation society in which they lived and worked.

Mary-Anne Schad and Mrs. Brown were not only wives and homemakers but also farmers, skilled craftswomen, nurses, midwives, supervisors of slaves, and business partners to their husbands. The two women put their skills and experience to practical use on the plantation and received praise as well as rewards from plantation owners for their work. However, their proximity to large numbers of slaves, combined with their lower-class status, often earned them the scorn and contempt of "respectable" white society.

The world in which these women lived was heavily influenced by South Carolina's distinct physical landscape and climate. The coastline was drained by the Pee Dee, Edisto, Santee and Savannah rivers, and the littoral zone itself was dominated by a number of small sea islands. Inland, though, much of South Carolina was marsh and swampland. The weather could reach extremes: in particular, temperatures rose very high in the summer months. The heat, combined with regular torrents of rainfall, produced conditions that were humid and oppressive, especially for those living on plantations.[4] The environment profoundly affected settlement patterns and agricultural practices in the eighteenth century and distinguished South Carolina and the Lowcountry from other regions in the South. Environmental factors governed planters' decisions about which crops to cultivate, and the precise location of the plantation and methods of cultivation were determined by the choice of crop. The agricul-

WANTED immediately, for the fubfcri-
ber's plantation near Bacon Bridge, an overfeer that un-
derftands fawing, making fhingles and rice ; one with a wife, to
mind a dairy and poultry, would be preferred, but none need. apply who is not well recommended ; any one properly recommended
and approved of, will meet with very good encouragement, from
Goofe-Creek, Sept. 17, 1765.   HENRY SMITH.

ADVERTISEMENT FOR OVERSEER AND
WIFE, *SOUTH-CAROLINA GAZETTE*
From the Charleston Library Society Collections, Charleston, S.C.

tural techniques that were implemented in turn determined the size and in-frastructure of plantations and the number of slaves assigned to work on each plantation.[5]

The conditions under which the colonists lived made life hard for them but were beneficial for plantation agriculture, especially rice production. The ex-tensive swamps, rich soils, abundant water supply, and predictable seasonal weather cycles made rice the preferred staple crop. In 1761, Governor James Glenn noted, "The Only commodity of any consequence produced in South Carolina is rice."[6] Historian Peter Wood has claimed that "no development had greater impact upon the course of South Carolina history than the successful introduction of rice."[7] Rice fashioned the lives of all those involved in its pro-duction on plantations. The introduction after 1745 of indigo as a staple did not radically affect the location, structure, and regimes on plantations during the eighteenth century.[8]

Rice production generally benefited from economies of scale, and this inevi-tably led to the dominance of sizable plantations in colonial South Carolina. The cost of setting up such plantations was huge, requiring an abundance of fertile land and a large labor force. On eighteenth-century rice plantations the minimum number of slaves laboring under the supervision of one overseer was twenty and, by 1720, half the plantations in South Carolina possessed twenty or more slave laborers.[9]

The harsh conditions, combined with the grueling nature of rice cultivation (and later of indigo), proved too trying for white indentured servants and de-terred landless free men from venturing to coastal South Carolina. Further-more, the hostile climate ensured that most planters and their families were ab-sentees for the greater part of the year. They chose to live instead in Charleston or in other towns and cities that were far safer and more entertaining than the swampy areas where their plantations were situated. However, the severe fevers and diseases that affected South Carolina's white population did not have the same lethal effect on African slaves, which is one reason they were desirable as plantation workers. The rise of South Carolina rice culture coincided with an increase in the number of Africans who were imported and the institutionaliza-tion of slavery. Thus, in South Carolina, the slave population rapidly multiplied while the white population grew slowly, resulting in a dramatic demographic imbalance.[10]

After the abortive slave insurrection of 1739 known as the Stono Rebellion, in which a contemporary source alleged that most of the conspirators were Angolans, slave owners began to extol the virtues of native-born slaves and took steps to encourage childbearing and rearing in the slave quarters. As a result, starting in the middle of the century, the slave population began to reproduce itself. The lack of indentured and free white laborers, the early presence of large numbers of imported slaves, and the natural increase of native slaves produced a population made up of a black majority in the eighteenth century.[11] Most of the slaves who made up this majority were worked in large groups on isolated plantations rather than being dispersed among the white population.[12] To control the increasing slave population, laws were introduced to regulate the number of white men present on large slave plantations.

Beginning in the early eighteenth century the law penalized slave owners who did not employ white overseers to supervise slaves living on plantations where owners were not residents. In 1712 the state passed a deficiency law that penalized the owners of plantations "wherein six negroes or slaves shall be employed without one or more white person living and residing on the same plantation." In 1726, and again in 1755, legislators rewrote the law, first to state that absentee masters with ten or more slaves were expected to hire at least one white man and then to rule that those with twenty or more slaves on their plantations were expected to have at least two white men in residence.[13] The Stono Rebellion precipitated the passing of a number of other strict laws regarding slaves, including one calling for a reduction in the number of "alien" slaves that were imported, as it was "new" Africans who had started the revolt. These laws, however, were deliberately ignored by many South Carolina planters. One commented, after visiting his plantation, that he had been alone among hundreds of slaves, apart from "a couple of overseers who are the only White Faces."[14]

In the early eighteenth century, overseers and their wives and families began to be categorized as belonging to a distinct "overseeing" class.[15] Although the law ordered planters to employ white men to supervise plantation slaves, planters prejudged any man who was willing to take the job. Sharing the negative perception of overseers, planters judged these men in relation to the reputation of the group as a whole rather than as individuals with different backgrounds and experience. Slave owners frequently claimed that overseers lacked morals, education, skill, or ambition. In some cases planters' negative feelings toward overseers and their families were warranted. The behavior of some overseers and their wives did indeed justify planters' censure and ill feeling. However, much of the negative stereotyping of overseers and their wives was undeserved and rooted in a marked and persistent class prejudice. The voices of more appreciative colonial planters have been drowned out by the cries of disgruntled, and often misogynistic, planters.

The reconstruction of the lives of Mrs. Schad and Mrs. Brown, however, suggests that in many cases, overseers' wives were highly valued members of the plantation community. Because of their work habits and domestic skills these women often received glowing reports from the planters they served, despite their low socioeconomic status in a world that was structured by class as well as race. Mary-Anne Schad was the wife of Abraham Schad. We do not know Mary-Anne's origins or when she married. However, it is clear that they were married before Abraham became a plantation overseer in 1763. Henry Laurens, a wealthy South Carolina slave merchant and planter, employed the couple to work on his Wambaw plantation. Though their ages are unknown, Laurens's fatherly advice to the couple regarding household affairs as well as plantation matters and his referring to Mary-Anne as Abraham's "young" wife suggests they had not been married long when they entered his employ.[16]

At this time Henry Laurens specifically sought married men as overseers. He, like many of his contemporaries, unreservedly condemned sexual relationships between slaves and overseers. Such relationships were not only considered a breach of contract but also viewed as extremely disruptive to plantation life. Some masters worried about their overseers harassing and abusing female slaves. More than this, planters wanted to prevent any potential upset that would disturb laborers and prevent them from carrying out their assigned workload. In 1763, on discovering a relationship between overseer James Lawrence and Hagar, one of the slaves under Lawrence's supervision, Laurens wrote to him that "I am now to inform you that I have provided a man to come and succeed you at Mepkin as Overseer there." He made clear to his overseer the grounds for his dismissal:

> The true reason of my taking this step is your familiarity with Hagar which besides being wrong & unwarrantable in itself must be extremely offensive to me and very hurtful to my Interest, as it must tend to make a good deal of jealousy and disquiet amongst the Negroes.[17]

According to Laurens, such a relationship was "foolish" and would cause a rivalry and resentment among the other slaves under Lawrence's control that had the potential to erupt into violence. Other planters who encountered similar relationships, whether consensual or not, between overseers and slaves no doubt viewed overseers with wives as a far more appealing and practical option. Although Laurens dismissed his overseer for having an affair, he promised not to reveal the details of his misconduct to anybody who enquired about the matter. Instead he offered to inform people only that he was to be discharged in favor of "a Man of more experience & one that has a wife."

A wife was clearly valued as a mechanism of control against white men's sexual desire toward slave women. Following this incident with James Lawrence, Henry Laurens only employed overseers with wives. Thus wives sometimes were critical to the employability of their husbands. Given Henry Laurens's recent experience with James Lawrence and the fact that Abraham Schad had relatively little experience in slave management, it is probable that Mary-Anne was an important factor in Laurens's decision to hire Schad as an overseer.

Apparently Laurens hoped Schad's young wife would encourage her husband to work diligently and return straight home to her and keep out of mischief. When Laurens experienced problems with another of his young and single overseers, Mr. Godfrey, who habitually absented himself from the plantation, he hoped marriage might remedy the problem. Irresponsible and negligent behavior was not usually tolerated for long by planters. However, Laurens considered the possibility that his overseer's recent engagement had necessitated more frequent visits to his fiancée to plan their marriage and was optimistic that although Godfrey was currently leaving the plantation more often than his contract stipulated, marriage would bring stability to the overseer's life. Laurens encouraged him to "make amends for past Delinquencies" and be "more at home" once his wife took up residence. After purposefully employing a number of overseeing couples, including Mr. and Mrs. Schad, the appearance of a "Mrs. Godfrey" evidently encouraged Laurens to give his overseer a second chance. Indeed, he trusted that Mrs. Godfrey would tame her husband into a "house cat."[18]

Many other eighteenth-century South Carolina planters favored married overseers, as advertisements in newspapers suggests.[19] They tied negligence on the plantation to bad habits such as drinking, gambling, womanizing, visiting friends, and entertaining unruly company, black and white, on the plantation. These bad habits were more generally associated with single men than married men. Thus, planters predicted that allowing white women to reside with their husbands would encourage them to settle down and reduce the risk of troublesome, wayward behavior. Planters hoped that overseers' wives would create an agreeable place of retreat for their husbands after a day's work and that family life would provide distraction and evoke a sense of responsibility in married overseers, thus increasing the overall stability of the plantation. Mary-Anne Schad did provide her husband with a home to return to after his labors, and the year after they moved onto the plantation she became pregnant. On October 16, 1765, she gave birth to a son and on January 17, 1767, she had a daughter.[20]

Beyond the social reasons that encouraged planters to favor overseers with wives, there were a number of other reasons it was practical to employ these white women alongside their husbands. Although some planters claimed that overseers' families were nothing more than extra mouths to feed, others realized that a wife added to, rather than wasted, plantation resources.[21] A wife like Mary-Anne Schad took care of all her husband's domestic needs. Overseers were expected to direct the slaves under their supervision constantly "and never stir from them during their hours of work."[22] This theoretically left them little time for anything else, so they needed someone to keep house for them.

Planters acknowledged the importance of fulfilling these basic domestic needs for overseers who were not married. They usually provided slave women to carry out domestic duties as a standard part of their compensation package. At the very least, "a single man" was provided "with his washing."[23] It remained a prerequisite for eighteenth-century unmarried overseers to be provided with domestic care and services that would not be deducted from their wages. The labor of a slave who was able bodied enough to do domestic tasks for an overseer was worth more than the cost of the provisions planters would need to provide for an overseer's wife. Thrifty planters recognized that overseers with wives saved them the cost of providing such services.

Even more indicative of the importance some planters accorded to overseers' wives was their willingness to reward them for their domestic labors. It was normal to provide board and provisions for wives as well as overseers who were required to live on the plantations, and planter-employers typically included such payments in their husbands' contracts. But some planters provided additional remuneration in the form of wine, cheese, and, occasionally, luxury items.[24]

Mary-Anne Schad had more to offer than just playing her traditional domestic role, however. Plantation owners also utilized the labor of wives to make plantations as efficient and cost effective as possible. In his correspondence with agents and overseers, Henry Laurens frequently expressed his hope that his overseers' wives would work hard and benefit the plantation. In his letters to the Schads, Henry Laurens outlined the tasks he expected Mrs. Schad to undertake. On one occasion he informed Mr. Schad that he was sending twenty-seven new slaves to the plantation and that he was placing them particularly in "your care & Mrs. Schad."[25] On another occasion he wrote to Schad, "Your own, Mrs. Schads, Mr Myers, & his wifes care and constancy at home will be all necessary now at this time of sickness & will the more oblige me."[26] Overseers' wives were expected to tend to injured or ill slaves and to prevent the spread of sickness and diseases such as typhoid and yellow fever. The climate and location of South Carolina plantations meant they were rife with mosquitoes that spread malaria, a problem that constantly affected the health and productivity of slave labor forces. Doctors would be called if necessary to tend to serious cases, but planters were extremely eager to avoid such costly visits.[27] Overseers' wives played a crucial role in slave welfare, battling against the effects of malaria and outbreaks of contagious illnesses that depleted the number of slaves well enough to work.

Overseers' wives took part in a number of other activities that aided the smooth running of the plantation. Daily necessities such as food, drink, and clothing were produced by women. In the seventeenth century the demographic imbalance between men and women meant there was a shortage of women to carry out these tasks. In fact, inventories reveal that most seventeenth-century farms and plantations lacked the equipment and individuals with the knowledge needed to carry out "labour that was traditionally defined by English women's work, and that was indispensable for the furnishing of goods and services for home consumption—dairying, brewing, baking of bread, poultry—keeping, spinning, and so forth."[28] However, by the eighteenth century more women inhabited the southern colonies, and they possessed the knowledge and skills as well as had access to equipment that allowed them to produce more of the everyday necessities of life. White women who lived on plantations in South Carolina produced cheese and butter, candles, soap, tailored clothing, wools, dyes, and sometimes shoes for the use of their families and for barter and sale.[29] Planters, who had previously viewed their slave plantations solely as commercial ventures and who had imported provisions and clothing, began to realize the value of producing food and making clothes on the plantation. Thus planters like Henry Laurens, who intended their plantations to be as self-sufficient as possible, expected the wives of their employees to help produce provisions for slave families and sometimes for their own households.[30] Henry Laurens informed Abraham Schad that "Mrs. Laurens is not very well & therefore cant make up such Cloaths but hopes your wife will do that part."[31] When slaves needed new clothes and other provisions, eighteenth-century planters looked first for a way to supply them using their own resources and their own workforce so as to avoid incurring the heavy costs bringing materials and laborers in from the outside. Overseers' wives, when called upon, also supervised groups of slave seamstresses and spinners or slaves who worked in the dairy, raised poultry, or cared for other domestic farm animals. No doubt, at the request of her employer Mrs. Schad took part in a number of activities on the plantation, most involving slave welfare but also in some cases ones that required supervising slaves in a manner similar to her husband's.

Planters consulted overseers' wives as well as their husbands on important issues concerning slaves and plantation matters. After the suspicious death of a slave named Chloe, Henry Laurens wrote that "Mr Schad & his wife are of the same opinion," namely that "they suspect that she reciev'd a portion [poison] from a jealous Sister at Hyde Park named Isabel, who came here on Saturday Night," as "Chloe was seized with the disorder that killed her on the next day." Here, Schad's wife's opinion seemed as important as her husband's.[32] Overseers' wives were considered part of the supervisory team, and their views were considered in a variety of matters relating to day-to-day plantation business. Mrs. Schad was not simply a housewife and appendage of her husband but was an equal member of an overseeing partnership. Her thoughts on various aspects of plantation business and slave-related affairs were highly valued.

Planters expected overseers' wives to play farmer, nurse, midwife, seamstress, and in some ways surrogate plantation mistress to the slaves, and they usually compensated them for their work. Plantation account books show small payments made to overseers' wives for performing various tasks. In particular, overseers' wives were regularly paid for acting as midwives at the births of black and white babies. One planter paid an overseer's wife four times in a short period for her midwifery and for her efforts in attending to pregnant slaves and preventing them from having miscarriages. Another overseer's wife was expected to "attend to sick negroes, raise the poultry, attend to the dwelling house & make butter," and help out with other jobs on the plantation.[33] Thus an overseer's wife could simultaneously play the part of homemaker, supervisor, nurse, and farmhand.

By taking part in activities that were traditionally associated with women but on a plantation-wide level and by assisting slaves and the planter's family, lower-class white women like Mrs. Schad not only provided additional plantation labor but also earned money and respect in their own right. This contributed to the upward mobility of their families. After six years in the employ of Henry Laurens, Abraham and Mary-Anne Schad left overseeing behind. In March 1769 Wambaw Plantation was broken up and divided between Laurens and the heirs of another planter, John Coming Ball. Mr. and Mrs. Schad had been granted a small plot of land in 1759 prior to their employment by Henry Laurens, and they owned at least one valuable slave when they left his employ. The couple petitioned for more land, and most likely they set up as small, independent farmers. There is little further information about what became of the Schads and their endeavors. In 1771 they sold a slave named Boston for 450 pounds to William Gibbons, and there are also a few documents detailing Abraham Schad's claims for compensation relating to his efforts during the American Revolution.[34] However, once outside of the confines of the plantation, Mary-Anne Schad disappeared into the obscurity that shrouds most of her contemporaries.

Mrs. Brown's life began in England and ended in South Carolina. In England, she met and married Stephen Brown, a rope maker by trade. Stephen Brown moved to America with the aim of setting himself up as an independent crafts-man. In contrast to many European men and women, the couple had enough funds to pay their passage across the Atlantic and thus did not need to indenture themselves or enter a servile position on arrival in order to move from the "Old" to the "New World."[35] On their arrival in South Carolina, the Browns attempted to set up independently in trade. However, their business failed to make a profit and Mr. Brown had to seek another occupation.[36]

It was at times difficult for white artisans to find employment in the colonial era, especially in South Carolina. When a Palatine weaver proposed moving from Pennsylvania to South Carolina, his friend predicted that

> his service will last probably no longer than until two negro slaves have learned the weaver's trade from him and can weave themselves. So it goes through all Carolina: the negroes are made to learn all the trades and are used for all kinds of business. For this reason white people have difficulty earning their bread there, unless they become overseers or provide themselves with slaves.[37]

Some tradesmen who moved to the region who could not find enough work in their own trade after relocation or a period of unemployment did indeed have little choice but to turn to overseeing to supplement their earnings. How-ever, other migrant-artisans, in particular those from Europe, took the initiative and applied for jobs as overseers, hoping to save money and make connections that would allow them to start up independently in their chosen trade or pro-fession or because they wished to learn about plantation management and then branch out into the sphere of farming. As with young men who were native to the region, indentured servants and other European migrants used overseeing as a means of education, networking, and resource accumulation so they could achieve their wider ambitions.

For example, Peter Horlbeck, an overseer for Henry Laurens, worked in England and Germany as a "master mason" before he moved to America. He initially pursued his trade in Charleston and was closely associated with the German community in South Carolina, where he met Catherine Fillhauer, who became his wife. To improve his circumstances, he took a job as an overseer for Laurens after he married. A few years later the Horlbecks left overseeing and were able to set up independently in the masonry trade. Their association with a leading member of South Carolina's planter elite benefited the couple's reputa-tion and gained them the financial support they needed to set up a business that eventually was profitable enough to allow them to buy slaves and land and run their own plantation.[38]

Another couple, Samuel Waddingham and his wife, friends of Mr. and Mrs. Brown, who, like them, had moved to America from England, had taken an overseeing position, progressed to management, and then were able to set themselves up as independent, small-scale slaveholders. They suggested that Mr. and Mrs. Brown follow their example. Stephen Brown took a job as an overseer for a local planter, then moved to a plantation owned by George Austin and run by another planter, Josiah Smith, in Austin's absence, who presumably offered him a better deal. Mr. Brown's friends thought that overseeing "would make him an able planter" and commented further that "a few more years experience, gained through overseeing" would provide the Browns with the means and skills to broaden their horizons and become planters in their own right.[39] Although it was generally felt that it was primarily the overseer who was learning to manage a plantation, their wives, who organized the dairy, the spinning, and other plantation activities, also gained experience in a number of aspects of plantation management.

In the colonial era, women who lived in northern cities such as New York, Boston, and Philadelphia, and even in a southern city like Charleston, South Carolina, could gain experience as apprentices to female artisans and then secure independence themselves, working in a trade or owning their own businesses.[40] The plantation economy in South Carolina meant there was little opportunity for the private enterprise of women outside of Charleston. However, the development of large slave plantations, which led to the need for overseers to supervise slave laborers, increased the number of economic opportunities for some women. Planters frequently specified in advertisements for overseers that they also sought a "wife that understands a dairy" or who "will superintend a dairy and turn it into the best and most profitable account the means on the estate will afford."[41] Josiah Smith was impressed with Mrs. Brown's endeavors and commented:

> The Overseers Wife at Ashpoo being very industrious, hath afforded me a tolerable supply of poultry & Butter from thence the past year but before then I scarce got any & from Perdee I very seldom got above 2 pair Turkeys in a season, with a pot of Butter now & then.[42]

Mrs. Brown undoubtedly received payment for her work in addition to the praise and separate mention in the planter's correspondence with her employer.

Living on plantations provided overseers' wives with the perfect opportunity to utilize their skills beyond providing for the daily needs of their own households and beyond the expectations of their grateful employers. Farmers' or small planters' wives had limited access to spinning, weaving, and dairy equipment. However, overseers' wives living on large slave plantations had access to a range of expensive equipment and resources that enabled them to produce goods on a large scale. Overseers' wives made use of their position, added to the productivity of the plantation, and gained respect and material rewards from their social superiors.[43] As a consequence, overseers' wives were able to take part in domestic manufacture on a larger scale than most lower-class white women. They put the skills they possessed, such as butter and cheese making, livestock rearing, spinning, weaving, and dyeing, to practical use for the greater good of the plantation and at the same time advanced themselves and their families.

One South Carolina planter gave his overseer's wife the "liberty to raise poultry" from his stock as long as she also supplied his "family in Town with some Poultry."[44] Like overseers, who were paid a share of the crop the slaves produced, some overseers' wives were paid a share of the produce that was made by slaves under their supervision. The wife of one overseer, Mrs. O'Brien, was included by name in her husband's contract, and her duties were detailed. Part of her role was to "superintend and take care of the said negroes, the dairy & poultry," for which she was to be paid with "a third of all poultry she raised" and a share of all dairy products.[45]

Some single women recognized the potential profit that could be made from working on a large slave plantation and placed advertisements in newspapers. One notice in the *South-Carolina Gazette* advertised "a single woman, with a child, would be glad of a place on a plantation, to take charge of a dairy, raise poultry, etc." Another presented herself as "a dairy woman who can make negro clothes [and who] wants work." Even a "single elderly woman experienced in the business" of looking after a dairy and attending to poultry sought employment on a slave plantation. Women with such skills were sought after and well rewarded. In 1769, one South Carolina planter advertised for a woman who could manage a dairy and raise poultry, offering "perquisites equal to £100 a year" to whomever he hired.[46]

A hardworking wife was an asset who allowed men of humble origins and moderate means to improve their material welfare and their position in society. Mrs. Brown proved to be an asset to her husband and a credit to the plantation. She was also a well-respected woman in her own right. Josiah Smith wrote to George Austin that Mrs. Brown was an industrious woman and that Mr. Brown "& wife will both save what money they get" and be able to buy "a couple of New Negroes on Credit" and progress into the world of independent, small-scale slaveholders. Both Mr. and Mrs. Brown impressed their employers so much that later Josiah Smith, on behalf of his client George Austin, lent the couple the money to purchase slaves, with the intention of facilitating their plans to become independent after a few years as overseers.[47]

Mrs. Brown's life was, however, cut short. In 1773, Josiah Smith wrote to George Austin and reported on the state of his plantations. He informed Austin that recent sickness had caused great suffering among the slaves and employees:

> Among the deceased are poor Mollineaux [an overseer] & Brown's Wife both in the month of November and within 10 days of each other. Brown himself has been very sick I believe not yet quite well, his Wifes death has been a great loss to him & also the plantation, as she appeared to me to be a very clever active woman, especially in the nursing way. Much Sickness also prevailed among your Negroes.[48]

Mrs. Brown was the second overseer's wife to die that month on George Austin's South Carolina plantations. Josiah Smith's comments indicate much about Mrs. Brown's character and perhaps that of the many overseers' wives, whose contributions to plantation life and South Carolina history have gone unnoticed. In the short time that she was an overseer's wife she greatly increased the productivity of the dairy, she raised far larger amounts of poultry than any of her predecessors, and was known to be a loyal wife and companion to her husband. Mr and Mrs. Brown had a successful overseeing partnership and it was Mrs. Brown whose achievements won the respect and plaudits of her social superiors.[49] After the couple proved their worth, they were able to purchase slaves on credit, which marked the beginning of their social and economic rise in white society.

The sudden and untimely death of Mrs. Brown highlights one more important point about the lives of overseers' wives: their residence on Lowcountry rice plantations, often near swamps "inhabited by insects, reptiles and mosquitoes, endangered their lives."[50] In South Carolina "overseers and poorer whites," just like the slaves they supervised "clearly, could not flee the countryside as easily as members of the planter elite," who "removed themselves from the worst dangers" while "the poor stayed behind to face them."[51] Many planters in South Carolina abandoned their plantations in the summer and autumn, but overseers had to remain on the plantation year round. Living in such a high-risk, disease-ridden environment, they often contracted serious illnesses. One planter admitted that new overseers and their families, especially those who had come from Europe and were unused to the climate and diseases so common to South Carolina, were easily susceptible to "Fevers and Agues" which would make "them unfit for Business & perhaps end only with their lives." Living in mosquito-infested areas and among large groups of slaves meant overseers' families were more likely to contract dangerous illness that would damage their health and diseases that would lead to their premature deaths. Letters among overseers, agents, and planters were filled with reports of diseases spreading quickly among residents of plantations and resulting in the deaths of members of overseeing families as well as slaves.

Furthermore, overseers' wives fell victim to dangers directly related to their racial and social situation on the plantation. Like their husbands, they were despised by the slaves they lived among, who associated them with forced labor and coercion. At the same time slaves recognized that overseers and their wives were socially inferior to their owners—low down in the chain of command that structured the whole of white society as well as plantation management. Not surprisingly then, slaves lashed out at overseers. It was no doubt a harrowing experience for overseers' wives to witness the conflicts and angry reactions of slaves to their bondage, especially if their husbands died at the hands of their charges. There are a number of recorded cases of slaves who attempted to poison their masters or overseers in the eighteenth century. Samuel Huey and his wife left their small plantation in South Carolina to take up residence as overseers on Richard Oswald's plantation in East Florida. A couple of years after the move, the slaves Mr. Huey was employed to oversee killed him. A short time after his murder, Laurens, a friend of Oswald's, hired the widowed Mrs. Huey as a housekeeper. Evidently the murder of her husband and the loss of her livelihood and place on the plantation had reduced Mrs. Huey to penury.[52]

Wives also ran the risk of death or injury at the hands of slaves. In a small number of recorded cases slaves who had been antagonized by an overseer's wife plotted their revenge. In 1735, a South Carolina planter named Silas Miles put forward a petition to the South Carolina Commons House of Assembly stating "the petitioner had the misfortune that one of his Negro Slaves (Primus) . . . [shot] his Overseers Wife." There is no mention of the events surrounding the shooting or whether the attack was provoked. However, as slaves' access to and use of guns was limited, and the slave in question absconded immediately after the attack, it is unlikely that the shooting was an accident.[53] What is clear from this incident and others like it is that overseers' wives' proximity to large groups of enslaved laborers and their distance from free white populations placed them in a vulnerable position. For slaves wishing to vent their anger and frustrations at their treatment and enslavement, overseers and their wives were the closest and most vulnerable targets.

The isolated and potentially dangerous lives led by these women usually earned them only the scorn of white society. The often undeserved ill repute of overseers that was circulated by some colonial planters in South Carolina encouraged the condemnation of all those involved in overseeing, including overseers' wives. However, the fragmentary evidence that remains of these women's lives demonstrates that lower-class white women, seemingly on the margins of colonial society, played a significant role on colonial slave plantations. Overseers' wives, like their husbands, were sneered at for their lowly origins, and as a "class," all were tarnished by the misbehavior and bad habits of some of their peers. For generations their lives have been portrayed in a distorted fashion. Such stereotypes have even found their way into popular culture—consider, for example, the portrayal of the overseers' wife in *Gone with the Wind* as a "white trash" woman of loose morals and no education. However, women like Mrs. Schad and Mrs. Brown defied social prejudice. Employers considered them to be trustworthy and praiseworthy.

The depiction of overseers and their families as characters with little agency and few options is unfounded. In reality, most overseers did their job as best they could under difficult circumstances and worked to improve their lot. Their wives went one step further. Many demonstrated remarkable resourcefulness by participating in a multitude of activities on the plantation that took them beyond the realm of family and home. Rather than occupying a servile and dependent position, in some ways women like Mrs. Schad and Mrs. Brown gained both agency and income, which allowed them to achieve a rough equality with their husbands as well as contribute to their family's position in colonial society.

Thus, the roles overseers' wives played helps dispel the assumption that all overseers and their wives were driven to work on slave plantations due to necessity born of their lowly origins, fecklessness, and poverty. In South Carolina it is apparent that choice and planning for a better future motivated many couples to move onto plantations as overseeing teams. Some planters were so appreciative of their efforts that they were willing to help them advance their careers and fulfill their ambitions, even if it meant losing them as employees. Investigating the lives of Mrs. Schad and Mrs. Brown and the part they played on slave plantations illuminates the unique position that free, white women who resided and toiled on slave plantations occupied. More broadly their lives demonstrate the numerous and important roles that many other lower-class white women were expected to perform in southern slave societies.

NOTES

1. See, for example, Philip Morgan, *Slave Counterpoint: Black Culture in the Eighteenth-Century Chesapeake and Lowcountry* (Chapel Hill: University of North Carolina Press for the Omohundro Institute of Early American History and Culture, Williamsburg, Virginia, 1998), 326.

2. Laura Rose Sandy, "Between Planter and Slave: The Social and Economic Role of Plantation

Overseers in Virginia and South Carolina, 1740–1790," (PhD diss., University of Manchester, 2006), 184–206.

3. Henry Laurens, *The Papers of Henry Laurens, 1746–1792*, ed. Philip Hamer, George Rogers, David Chesnutt, and C. James Taylor, 16 vols. (Columbia: Published for the South Carolina Historical Society by the University of South Carolina Press, 1968–2003), 3:248 (hereinafter cited as PHL).

4. Matthew Mulcahy, *Hurricanes and Society in the British Greater Caribbean, 1624–1783* (Baltimore, Md.: Johns Hopkins University Press, 2006).

5. For a detailed discussion of the South Carolina landscape and an analysis of the development of plantations in South Carolina in the eighteenth century, see S. Max Edelson, *Plantation Enterprise in Colonial South Carolina* (Cambridge, Mass.: Harvard University Press, 2006), 13–53 and 92–126.

6. Peter H. Wood, *Black Majority: Negroes in Colonial South Carolina from 1670 through the Stono Rebellion* (New York: W. W. Norton, 1975), 35.

7. Wood, *Black Majority*, 35.

8. Julia Cherry Spruill, *Women's Life and Work in the Southern Colonies* (Chapel Hill: University of North Carolina Press, 1938), 308–10.

9. Morgan, *Slave Counterpoint*, 39–41.

10. Kenneth Morgan, *Slavery and Servitude in North America, 1607–1800* (Edinburgh: Edinburgh University Press, 2000), 71.

11. Wood, *Black Majority*, 302, 314, 315; Morgan, *Slavery and Servitude*, 71.

12. Wood, *Black Majority*, 27.

13. Thomas Cooper and David McCord, eds., *Statutes at Large of South Carolina* (Columbia: A. S. Johnson, 1836–41), 363, 272, 125, 175.

14. Morgan, *Slave Counterpoint*, 298.

15. PHL, 4:503; Thomas Jefferson to William Wirt, August 14, 1814, Thomas Jefferson Papers, Library of Congress, Washington, D.C. (hereinafter cited as LC); George Washington to Antony Whitting, December, 16, 1792, *The Writings of George Washington from the Original Manuscript Sources, 1745–1799*, ed. John Fitzpatrick, 39 vols. (Washington, D.C.: U.S. Government Printing Office, 1931–44), 34:193; Lewis Gray, *History of Agriculture in the Southern United States to 1860* (Gloucester, Mass.: Peter Smith, 1958), 501–3.

16. PHL, 3:248; Mable Webber, "Parish Register of St. Santee," *South Carolina Historical and Genealogical Magazine* 17, no. 1 (1916): 42, 43, 76; PHL, 5:101.

17. PHL, 3:248.

18. Ibid., 8:89, 97.

19. Examples of advertisements placed in newspapers by planters who expressly wanted overseers with wives can be found in the *South-Carolina Gazette*, January 1736, August 1745, October 1748, September 1752, March 1753, December 1754, February 1755, March 1756, March 1757, October 1758, December 1758, September 1765, and November 1766, and the *Gazette of the State of South-Carolina*, October 1777.

20. PHL, 3:426.

21. Joseph Ball to Joseph Chinn, March 19, 1745, Joseph Ball Letter Book, TR 92, Rockefeller Library, Colonial Williamsburg Foundation, Williamsburg, Va.; *South-Carolina Gazette*, January 1752, June 1754, January 1755, October 1764, June 1765, January 1766, and December 1768.

22. Overseer agreement between George Washington and Burgess Mitchell, May 1, 1762, George Washington Papers, ser. 4, LC.

23. Overseer agreements between Robert Carter and John Hazebrig, Joseph Dozier, and William Wroe, August 22, 1778, Robert Carter Letter Book, 1775–80, part 2, 51, Manuscripts Department, William R. Perkins Library, Duke University, Durham, N.C.

24. Sandy, "Between Planter and Slave," 74–108 and 189.Overseers' wives often received separate mentions, by name, in contracts and account books, with regard to the duties they were expected to perform or had carried out and the payment, extra provisions, or other rewards they would receive for their role on the plantation, such as wine, cheese, household items, and small amounts of cash.

25. PHL, 4:598, 634, 666; 5:123.

26. Ibid., 4:598, 634, 666; 5:123.

27. Sandy, "Between Planter and Slave," 127–30.

28. Carole Shammas, *The Pre-Industrial Consumer in England and America* (New York: Oxford University Press, 1990), 52–69.

29. Gail Collins, *America's Women: 400 Years of Dolls, Drudges, Helpmates, and Heroines* (New York: HarperCollins, 2003), 49.

30. Edelson, *Plantation Enterprise*, 200–255.

31. PHL, 4:598.

32. Ibid., 5:123.

33. Overseer agreement between John Ewing Colhoun and Thomas Bone, February 18, 1797, John Ewing Colhoun Papers, box 1, ser. 2, folder 9, Southern Historical Collection, Manuscripts Department, Wilson Library, University of North Carolina, Chapel Hill (hereinafter cited as SHC).

34. PHL, 6:181; land plat for one hundred acres in Amelia County to be awarded to Abraham Schad and Mary-Anne Schad, 1759, South Carolina Department of Archives and History, Columbia (hereinafter cited as SCDAH); bill of sale for a slave named Boston, 1773, Miscellaneous Records, 2Q:10, SCDAH; audited accounts for Revolutionary War claims, Abraham Schad, file no. 6814, SCDAH.

35. For more information on indentured European migrants see; David Galenson, *White Servitude in Colonial America: An Economic Analysis* (Cambridge: Cambridge University Press, 1981); Kenneth Morgan, *Slavery and Servitude*; Warren Smith, *White Servitude in Colonial South Carolina* (Columbia: University of South Carolina Press, 1961).

36. Josiah Smith to George Austin, January 30, 1772, Josiah Smith Letter Book, SHC.

37. Carl Bridenbaugh, *The Colonial Craftsman* (Chicago: University of Chicago Press, 1961), 15–16; S. Max Edelson "Affiliation without Affinity: Skilled Slaves in Eighteenth-Century South Carolina," in *Money, Trade, and Power: The Evolution of Colonial South Carolina's Plantation Society*, ed. Jack P. Greene, Rosemary Brana-Shute, and Randy J. Sparks (Columbia: University of South Carolina Press, 2001), 217–55; Christine Daniels, "'WANTED: A Blacksmith Who Understands Plantation Work': Artisans in Maryland, 1700–1810," *William and Mary Quarterly*, 3rd ser., 50, no. 4 (1993): 743–67.

38. PHL, 4:575.

39. Josiah Smith to George Austin, January 30, 1772, Josiah Smith Letter Book, SHC.

40. Karin Wulf, *Not All Wives: Women of Colonial Philadelphia* (Ithaca, N.Y.: Cornell University Press, 2000); Patricia Cleary, "'She Will Be in the Shop': Women's Sphere of Trade in Eighteenth-Century Philadelphia and New York," *Pennsylvania Magazine of History and Biography* 109, no. 3 (1995): 181–202; Laurel Thatcher Ulrich, "Wheels, Looms, and the Gender Division of Labor in Eighteenth Century New England," *William and Mary Quarterly*, 3rd ser., 55, no. 1 (1998): 3–38.

41. *South-Carolina Gazette*, October 12, 1769; *South-Carolina Gazette*, December 22, 1738; *Gazette of the State of South-Carolina*, October 28, 1777, quoted in Jocyce E. Chaplin, *An Anxious Pursuit: Agricultural Innovation and Modernity in the Lower South, 1730–1815* (Chapel Hill: University of North Carolina Press for the Omohundro Institute of Early American History and Culture, Williamsburg, Virginia, 1993), 215.

42. Josiah Smith to George Austin, January 30, 1772, Josiah Smith Letter Book, SHC.

43. Mary Beth Norton, "The Evolution of White Women's Experience in Early America," *American Historical Review* 89, no. 1 (1984): 604.

44. Overseer agreement between John Ewing Colhoun and Benjamin Foster, November 10, 1790, John Ewing Colhoun Papers, box 1, ser. 1, folder 7, SHC, and overseer agreement between John Ewing Colhoun and Thomas Bone, February 18, 1797, John Ewing Colhoun Papers, box 1, ser. 2, folder 9, SHC.

45. Overseer agreement between John Ewing Colhoun and Joseph O'Brien, March 27, 1794, John Ewing Colhoun Papers, box 1, ser. 1, folder 9, SHC, and overseer agreement between John Ewing Colhoun and Thomas Bone, February 18, 1797, John Ewing Colhoun Papers, box 1, ser. 2, folder 9, SHC.

46. *South-Carolina Gazette*, November 5, 1764, September 12, 1774; *South-Carolina and American General Gazette*, January 16, 1769; *South-Carolina Gazette*, October 12, 1769, quoted in Spruill, *Women's Life and Work*, 311–12.

47. Josiah Smith to George Austin, February 25, 1772, Josiah Smith Letter Book, SHC.

48. Josiah Smith to George Austin, January 31, 1774, Josiah Smith Letter Book, SHC.

49. Josiah Smith to George Austin, July 22, 1773, and January 31, 1774, Josiah Smith Letter Book, SHC.

50. Morgan, *Slavery and Servitude*, 74.

51. Chaplin, *An Anxious Pursuit*, 97–98.

52. PHL, 6:583; Henry Laurens Account Book, 1766–73, Special Collections, Robert Scott Small Library, College of Charleston, Charleston, S.C., 347, 362.

53. *Journal of the Commons House of Assembly, November 21, 1752– September 6, 1754*, vol. 12 of *Journal of the Commons House of Assembly*, ed. Terry W. Lipscomb (Columbia: University of South Carolina Press, 1974), 114.

Eliza Lucas Pinckney and Harriott Pinckney Horry

A South Carolina Revolutionary-Era Mother and Daughter

CONSTANCE B. SCHULZ

Eliza Lucas Pinckney (1722–93) has long been one of the best-known figures in South Carolina history and in the history of the Revolutionary era United States. Much has been made of her skillful management of her absent father's South Carolina plantations and her successful cultivation of indigo, which made it one of the two most crucial crops in the development of South Carolina's eighteenth-century economic prosperity. All this she accomplished while still in her teens.[1] She later achieved further recognition as a much-celebrated "republican mother," known for rearing two sons, Charles Cotesworth Pinckney (1746–1825) and Thomas Pinckney (1750–1828), key southern military and political leaders in the Revolutionary and early national eras. For these accomplishments she was considered worthy of inclusion in textbooks from grade school to graduate school as a national heroine and female patriot—well before the upsurge in interest in women's history that accompanied the modern women's movement of the 1960s and 1970s.

The public aspects of Pinckney's career are well known, but her personal story is more obscure. After her marriage to Charles Pinckney (1699–1758) in 1744, she focused her energies on raising her children (she bore four, three of whom survived childbirth and infancy) and managing her husband's households in Charleston as well as on his nearby plantations. Then, from 1753 to 1758, the Pinckneys lived in England, where he represented South Carolina as a special agent to the Board of Trade. There she maintained through correspondence

HAMPTON PLANTATION, HOME OF HARRIOTT
PINCKNEY HORRY AND ELIZA LUCAS PINCKNEY
Courtesy of South Carolina State Parks historical staff, Columbia.

and visits an extensive social network among English aristocratic circles that complemented her husband's political and mercantile networks. The couple returned home to South Carolina with their daughter in May 1758 to supervise their properties, leaving their two sons behind to obtain an English education.

When Charles died of malaria in July 1758, Eliza once again found herself the chief administrator of a trans-Atlantic plantation business. It was an undertaking complicated by her grief and the necessity of supervising her sons' education from a distance of four thousand miles. When they returned to South Carolina as young men, her life story then became intertwined with theirs as they rose to political prominence in the years leading up to the American Revolution. Eliza offered refuge for their growing families during the chaos of early British attacks on Charleston and later the occupation of the city during the war for independence. The war interrupted and almost severed Eliza's ties with lifelong friends in England, but American independence brought major compensations—pride in the accomplishments of her sons as elected representatives and diplomats at the highest levels of the new republic. As the family matriarch, Eliza was surrounded by her daughter, daughters-in-law, and grandchildren, whom she knitted together into a close family circle that was connected to an extended kinship network.

Less well known are the contributions of Eliza Lucas Pinckney's daughter, Harriott Pinckney Horry (1748–1830), whose life and relationship with her mother shed light on the changing status and experiences of elite women in the early republic. The second of Eliza's three surviving children, Harriott married into an important South Carolina Huguenot family at the age of nineteen. Close in age and in affection to her younger brother "Tomm," she functioned as his domestic auxiliary support, providing encouragement, sending him news and gossip, responding to his frequent requests for provisions and personal necessities during the five years he served as an officer in the First Regiment of South Carolina before his marriage.[2]

Like her mother, Harriott became a widow while in her thirties and was left with the responsibility for raising two minor children and overseeing extensive plantation holdings. George Washington visited her successfully managed rice plantation in his 1791 presidential pilgrimage to the South. When Eliza was stricken with breast cancer in her seventieth year, Harriott Horry accompanied her to Philadelphia in an unsuccessful attempt to find a cure, and it is from her 1793 journal that we know of Eliza Pinckney's last months. A second more extensive journal recording Horry's travels northward from South Carolina to Portsmouth, New Hampshire, in the spring and summer of 1815 illustrates her own mercantile astuteness and descriptive powers as well as the public and private linkages between politically powerful families of the South and North.

The letters of both mother and daughter describe the economic and political events and people of their times from the perspective of women who were themselves managers of plantations and slave labor forces. The rich details of their lives and personal relationships, representative of the practical experiences of women of their class, speak eloquently of the crucial role elite southern women played in linking powerful families together and protecting their prerogatives.[3] Their lives thus create a bridge between traditional political, economic, diplomatic, and military history and a broad range of social history scholarship on the history of childhood, the family, and women.[4]

Telling the stories of the lives of these two women also helps us to draw distinctions between the roles and status of women in the British North American colonies in the pre-Revolutionary era and that of their daughters and granddaughters in the post–Revolutionary early American republic. Scholars have suggested a variety of labels to characterize women of each period. Laurel Thatcher Ulrich coined the term "deputy husbands" to describe those women in colonial New England who often seamlessly took over the responsibilities of businesses and farms in the face of widowhood or war that took their spouses away, although women only took on such duties temporarily. Daniel Blake Smith has portrayed elite women of the colonial Chesapeake as "kin specialists," whose contribution to the family economy was the maintenance of contact and thus cooperation among the members of increasingly complex extended family networks. Mary Beth Norton has pointed out that colonial women's lives in all geographic sections of English America revolved around their homes and families, and that within that domestic circle they enjoyed neither self-esteem nor any equality of status or autonomy. She argues that their lives were profoundly affected by the American Revolution. Women's role in the public sphere did not change, but their position "in [the] familial organization" did, as did their "personal aspirations [and] self-assessments," all of which are "more accurately revealed in . . . women's private writings than in . . . formal actions implemented by men."[5]

It was historian Linda Kerber who coined the term "republican motherhood" to describe these post-Revolutionary women, a term emphasizing the extent to which mothers in the new nation self-consciously undertook the responsibility to teach public as well as personal virtue and morality to their sons. These mothers understood and articulated that their teaching was critical in preserving the republic from corruption and failure. Her phrase set the stage for the now dominant interpretive understanding of the Revolution as the event that laid the basis for a civic role for women in the early nineteenth century. Jan Lewis expanded the notion of republican motherhood to encompass an ideology of women's influence over husbands as well as sons; in Lewis's account, the "republican wife" seduced her husband into mimicking (if not totally sharing) her virtuous qualities, which was an essential component of the survival of the American republican experiment.[6] Recent scholarly explorations of how these ideologies played out in the early national period suggest that women did not have to be either wives or mothers to contribute through their own sphere to the value systems that sustained public polity. One scholar has observed that a better label is "republican womanhood," one she applies to Eliza Pinckney.[7]

For the colonial period, then, the labels scholars have used to describe the roles that women saw themselves performing—"deputy husband" or "kin specialist"—derive from the fact that the family was the central unit to which women owed loyalty and responsibility. The generation of women after the Revolution continued to operate within the sphere of their families, but they understood that their domestic actions had implications for public benefit as well: they were "*republican* mothers." Although these labels have been widely used to forge a distinction between the two broad chronological categorizations of American women's experiences, for many individual women, exploring the intentions they expressed and the eventual outcome of their efforts are often as useful in understanding the values they lived by and activities they undertook as looking at the time period in which they lived.

The lives of Eliza Lucas Pinckney and her daughter, Harriott Pinckney Horry, illustrate the ambiguities of these labels. Pinckney as a young mother modeled many of the values later associated with republican motherhood, and her sons did become important political leaders in the American republic. She herself acted within the public economic sphere as well as in the domestic sphere. Yet when she extolled the virtues of Christian piety to her younger brother or urged her sons in England to study, to use their reason and control their passions, they were to do so for the sake of their families, not their country. Her daughter, who experienced motherhood during the chaos of revolution, was an active supporter of her brothers in their fighting for and building of the political structures of the new American republic. Yet her son rejected the republic for which his uncles had risked their own and their family's prosperity and future success, and the fruit of her activities as a republican mother did not ripen until the next generation in the successes of her daughter's children.

Eliza Lucas was born on December 28, 1722, into a wealthy and privileged English family on Antigua, one of the Leeward Islands of the British West Indies.[8] One of the largest sugar planters on the small island, her father, George Lucas, served frequently in the Antigua representative assembly and in 1739 reached the rank of lieutenant colonel in the Thirty-eighth Regiment of Foot in the West Indies. Little is known of Eliza's mother, Ann Mildrum, except that she bore four children with George Lucas, including Eliza. Although her daughter constantly worried about her poor health, when she died in 1759 Ann had outlived her husband and younger son.

Eliza Lucas was by birth a part of the English new world's privileged elite, an elite that had ties to persons of power and privilege in England as well as in Antigua. As the oldest child, Eliza was particularly close to her father, who may have been her earliest teacher. As was customary for young girls of her class, when she was ten George Lucas sent her to London, where she became part of the family of his friend Richard Boddicott, a sugar merchant for many of the Antiguan planters. From there she was sent to Mrs. Pearson's small boarding school to learn the accomplishments expected of daughters of the elite. When she returned to Antigua in early 1737 she left young and old friends behind her. Mrs. Boddicott figures in Eliza's correspondence almost as a mother; among her classmates were her cousin Fanny Fayweather and a Miss Martin, the daughter of a wealthy merchant and member of Parliament. For the first half of Eliza's life England was the "home" to which she and her family always expected to return permanently some day.

Early in 1738, Eliza began the agricultural experimentation for which she would become well known in her adulthood, encouraged by her father to "bring to perfection the plants of other Countries."[9] That summer Eliza may also have first undertaken plantation management responsibilities as "deputy husband"— or perhaps more accurately as "deputy daughter." George Lucas took his ten-year-old son Tommy to London to begin his schooling, leaving Eliza in charge with her mother and three-year-old sister Mary, called Polly by the family. By the time he returned to Antigua in late 1738, his economic troubles had deepened, his wife had fallen into ill health, and the international situation had deteriorated, and so he determined to remove his wife and daughters to the relative safety and better climate of South Carolina.

George Lucas and his father had accumulated a substantial amount of land in the Carolinas: Wappoo, a six-hundred acre plantation, six miles by water from Charleston; Garden Hill, a fifteen-hundred acre plantation on the Combahee River north of Beaufort; and three thousand acres of rice lands along the Waccamaw River near Georgetown. These Carolina properties offered George Lucas an opportunity for a fresh start. Unlike his heavily mortgaged Antigua properties, they were still unencumbered by debt, and the rice staple crop grown there required fewer slaves than sugar cane did to produce a profitable commodity. In late summer of 1739 Lucas sailed to Charleston with his wife, her niece Fanny Fayweather, and his two daughters. He planned to begin life anew as a South Carolina rice planter at Wappoo Plantation, but fate intervened. The declaration of war with Spain in October 1739 recalled him to his military duties in Antigua. When he left South Carolina in November he left his daughter Eliza, not quite seventeen, in charge of his plantations, promising to return. He never did. Appointed lieutenant governor of Antigua in 1742, then involved in military campaigns in the Caribbean against France in the War of Austrian Succession, he died in French captivity in Brest on January 11, 1747.[10]

For five years after her arrival in Carolina, Eliza Lucas performed admirably as a "deputy daughter."[11] She oversaw two plantations from a distance, consulting with and reporting to her father about the work of the overseers at Waccamaw and Garden Hill. She herself supervised the daily activities at Wappoo. "My time," she wrote in 1740, "is . . . imployed in business, of which my father has left me a pretty good share—and indeed, 'twas inavoidable as my Mama's bad state of health prevents her going through any fatigue."[12] Eliza quickly established a routine, which she described lightheartedly in some detail in 1742 to her young Charleston friend Mary Bartlett:

> I rise at five o'Clock in the morning, read till Seven, then take a walk in the garden or field, see that the Servants are at their respective business, then to breakfast. The first hour after breakfast is spent at my musick, the next is constantly employed in recollecting something I have learned least for want of practice it should be quite lost, such as French and short hand. After that I devote the rest of the time till I dress for dinner to our little Polly and two black girls who I teach to read, and if I have my Papa's approbation (my Mamas I have got) I intend [them] for school mistres's for the rest of the Negroe children. . . . The first hour after dinner as the first after breakfast at musick, the rest of the afternoon at Needle work till candle light, and from that time to bed time read or write.[13]

Her account ends with a list of how she varied this pattern with a special activity each day of the week and a playful description of her scheme to plant a "figg" orchard to make her fortune. The figs were but one of a number of agricultural experiments at Wappoo. Her father sent her seeds with almost every shipment from Antigua, and she reported to him late in the summer of 1740 on "the pains I have taken to bring the Indigo, Ginger, Cotton and Lucerne and Casadall [cassava] to perfection, and had greater hopes from the Indigo . . . than any of the rest of the things I had tryd."[14] Her father and her neighbors encouraged her in these experiments. By no means was she the first to attempt cultivation of indigo in North America, but where earlier plantings in Virginia and the Carolinas had failed, Eliza Lucas succeeded.

Eliza's success in growing indigo came at a most opportune time. The war with Spain in 1739 was a prelude to the resumption of the century-long struggle between England and France known collectively to Americans as the French and Indian Wars. The resumption of conflict cut South Carolina planters off from many European outlets for their bulky rice crop and deprived the growing textile industry in England of its supply of French West Indian indigo dye. Indigo proved to be an ideal complement to rice as a staple crop. Manufacture of the finished dye from the plant was highly labor intensive but fortunately the production cycle was such that the work had to be done at the points in the rice growing season when labor demands were relatively light, allowing planters to exploit more efficiently their heavy investment in slaves. Moreover, in the coastal lowlands indigo grew best in the unused lands between rice fields, on higher ground that could not be flooded for rice cultivation.

The problem that Eliza solved was not simply that of growing a crop from the seed; the manufacturing process of converting the green-leaved plant into dense cubes of intensely colored blue dye was also complex. The slaves who performed the labor during both parts of the process may have been an important source of expertise for Eliza as she attempted to cultivate indigo. We do not know the origins of her slave labor force, but Africans from the Cape Verde Islands and the Senegambia would have had experience both growing the plant and converting it into a dyestuff for textiles. Eliza was also assisted in her experiments by her French Huguenot neighbor, Andrew Deveaux, using the instructions of experienced dye makers who were sent by her father to help. Eliza was initially frustrated in 1741 when Nicholas Cromwell, the first instructor, "threw in so large a quantity of Lime water as to spoil the colour." The next year his brother Patrick Cromwell was more cooperative, and by 1744 the Wappoo plantation produced "17 pounds of very good Indigo" to ship to England as well as enough seed to distribute to all the neighbors. Its cultivation spread rapidly, encouraged by a bounty of a shilling a pound voted by Parliament in 1748. South Carolina exports of indigo peaked in 1775 at over a million pounds, and growers of indigo made great fortunes.[15]

Experimenting with new crops for her father's plantations, studying music, teaching her young sister and slaves to read and write, practicing French and shorthand, drawing up simple wills for her neighbors, writing regularly to her father and to his agents in London on business matters, and to her friends in London and her brothers in Antigua, Eliza still found time for a social life. She reported to Mrs. Boddicott that "Charles Town, the principal one in this province, is a polite, agreeable place. The people live very Gentile and very much in the English taste." Eliza spent as much as a month at a time there visiting her particular friends "Mrs. Pinckney and Mrs. Cleland."[16] The friendship with Mrs. Pinckney had an unexpected result, as Elizabeth Lamb Pinckney was the first wife of the man who would become Eliza's own husband.

The aunt of Eliza's friend Mary Bartlett, Elizabeth Pinckney had lived in London until her marriage to Charles Pinckney, grandson of one of the early English settlers in Charleston. An extensive landholder, a lawyer trained at the Inns of Court, a speaker of the Commons House of Assembly, Charles Pinckney was one of the leading men of the province. The couple was childless, and Elizabeth virtually adopted the teenaged Eliza as a daughter, encouraged by her husband, who became Eliza's advisor and mentor on legal and plantation matters. He teased her about her seriousness, but he loaned her books from his library by Plutarch, Virgil, and Malebranche and taught her shorthand.

Elizabeth Pinckney died in January 1744 after a prolonged illness. Within a short time Charles Pinckney applied to Eliza Lucas's father for permission to marry her. George Lucas had sent for his family to return to him in Antigua, but Eliza's mother and sister delayed their departure until after the wedding on May 27, 1744. Although at forty-five he was twice her age, Charles and Eliza Pinckney had for fourteen years what was clearly a happy marriage, based on affection and mutual respect. Eliza's dowry was the indigo crop on the Wappoo plantation; her new husband helped her to write a report on her agricultural successes, which he published in the *South-Carolina Gazette* under his own name. Within a month of their marriage, Eliza was pregnant with their first child. Charles took from her shoulders some of the responsibilities of settling the affairs of her father's Wappoo plantation, which had been sold to cover Lucas's debts. Although she corresponded affectionately with her father and continued to supervise some of the management of his remaining South Carolina properties, her years as "deputy daughter" had essentially ended, and a new phase of her life had begun.

The new Mrs. Pinckney was already familiar with her many responsibilities as a "plantation mistress." Her father had maintained a small house in Charleston, but now Pinckney built a grand brick home that came to be called Mansion House for her to manage on East Bay Street at Colleton Square, just above present-day Market Street and overlooking the busy harbor. There, and at his principal plantation, Belmont, five miles up the Cooper River from Charleston, she continued her supervision of household slaves, operating a dairy and a kitchen garden to supply both households with food. Her interest in agricultural and botanical experimentation remained unabated. At Belmont she grew flax and hemp and also planted mulberry trees in a continuation of her attempts at Wappoo to create a silk industry in the Carolinas. Though never successful on a large scale, in 1753 her silk cultivation efforts yielded enough thread to produce three elegant dresses, one of which she presented to the dowager Princess of Wales as a gift. She was already a skillful "kin specialist," writing regularly to her brothers in school in England and her Fayweather cousins as well as to her adoptive families in England. Now she added to her well-maintained networks of family and neighbors her Pinckney connections. Though she never would have claimed autonomy for herself, Eliza Pinckney clearly refutes historian Mary Beth Norton's assertion that colonial women enjoyed little or no self-esteem. Her satisfaction in the completion of her duties may have been a function of her class rather than of her gender, but her correspondence reveals a woman confident in the importance of her contributions to her husband and his enterprises.

Eliza also delighted in her roles as wife and mother. Her first child, Charles Cotesworth, was born in the newly finished Mansion House in February 1746 and given his County Durham paternal grandmother's family name. When he had reached the advanced age of three months, she wrote to Mary Bartlett in England, "I can discover all his Papa's virtues already dawning in him" and asked Mary's mother "to buy him the new toy . . . to teach him according to Mr. Lock's method (which I have carefully studied) to play himself into learning. Mr Pinckney himself has been contriving a sett of toys to teach him his letters by the time he can speak."[17] In the next four years, Eliza bore three more children. In June 1747, the shock of her discovery of a hidden letter telling of her father's death in captivity in January of that year led to the premature birth of a son, George Lucas, who lived only five days. Within a few months she was pregnant again; her daughter, Harriott, was born in August 1748. With the birth of a third son, Thomas, in October 1750, her childbearing ended abruptly just before her twenty-eighth birthday.

Most of her contemporaries bore many more children—or died young in childbirth—and we do not know whether her failure to have more children was the result of a decision deliberately made or whether it was a fortuitous accident. In a remarkably frank letter describing a visit to the royal family at Kew, Eliza confessed in response to a question from the Princess Augusta that she had not suckled her children. "I told her I had attempted it but my constitution would not bear it." Nursing was thus not for her a means of spacing her children. In the same visit, while discussing the education of Charles Cotesworth and Thomas, Charles Pinckney told Prince William that "he hoped to have another

[son] for the Sea."[18] Yet there is no evidence that Eliza had another pregnancy. All three of her surviving children reached adulthood, married well, and had children of their own. She devoted the remainder of her life to promoting their physical well-being, to their education, to their nurture in religious and civic virtue, to their development of civility and attachment to family.

That she regarded these responsibilities almost as a religious obligation is evidenced by a set of private resolutions she penned early in her marriage. A rational, pious, and orthodox member of the Church of England, she began with a litany of faith in God and "the rules of the Gospel of Christ" as a model for virtuous living. But the majority of her resolutions addressed not her own salvation but her responsibilities to others:

> I am resolved by the Divine Assistance to fill the several Stations wherein Providence has placed me to the best advantage.
>
> To make a good wife to my dear Husband in all its several branches; to make all my actions Corrispond with that sincere love and Duty I bear him. . . . [T]o be careful of his Health, of his Interests, of his children, and of his Reputation; . . . and next to my God, to make it my Study to please him.
>
> I am resolved to be a good Mother to my children, to pray for them, to set them good examples, to give them good advice, to be careful both of their souls and bodys, to watch over their tender minds, to carefully root out the first appearing and budings of vice, and to instill piety, Virtue and true religion into them. . . .
>
> I am resolved to make a good Sister both to my own and my Husband's brothers and sisters, to do them all the good I can, to treat them with affection, kindness, and good manners.[19]

Her resolutions conclude with pledges to be a good mistress to her servants and faithful to her friends and with a promise to "read over this dayly to assist my memory as to every particular contained in this paper." What is striking about the exercise is the way she represents her family in its entirety as the core of her obligations, not simply her husband and children.

When her children were small, Eliza lived and carried out her resolutions not in Charleston or the plantation at Belmont but back "home" in England. A combination of personal and political circumstances convinced Charles Pinckney to take his family to London in 1753. Charles Cotesworth was now seven and ready to begin more formal education. A hurricane in September 1752 severely damaged his Charleston properties, making coastal Carolina seem a vulnerable place to raise a family. Pinckney had been appointed to the royal council in 1750, and in 1752 Governor James Glen named him as interim chief justice of the colony subject to royal confirmation. The ministry in England, however, appointed instead Peter Leigh, a London politician who had been accused of electoral corruption but who was too powerful to dismiss even though he was an embarrassment to the government. Granting Leigh the distant colonial vacancy as a "placeman" solved the ministry's problems but put Charles Pinckney in an awkward position. He determined to leave Charleston before his rival arrived. His fellow councilors authorized Pinckney to act as a special agent representing the governor and the council to the Board of Trade in London. Governor Glen had been renting Mansion House in Charleston as his residence since 1749; Pinckney now arranged for his brother William to rent his other properties in order to generate sufficient income to support the family in England.[20]

On April 11, 1753, Charles and Eliza, their three children, their personal servants, and William Henry (1742–79) and Charles Drayton (1743–1820), the two young sons of John Drayton, a fellow councilor, sailed for Portsmouth on the *Edinburgh*. Although she reported to her Charleston friends that the weather was fine and the passage smooth, Eliza was miserably seasick on the twenty-five-day voyage. Their arrival at Portsmouth coincided with a virulent outbreak of smallpox there, and so the family proceeded on to London and immediately arranged to rent a furnished house in the nearby rural suburb of Richmond, Surry. There Eliza oversaw the extended process of immunizing all her young charges against the deadly disease. Called "variolation," essentially it involved inducing smallpox in healthy patients with live virus, then isolating them for several weeks while they endured a mild form of the disease. A small painting of Charles Cotesworth commissioned by his parents to capture his likeness should the treatment prove fatal survives to remind modern readers of the many dangers of an eighteenth-century childhood.[21] While Eliza, who had "taken the smallpox" herself as a student in England, nursed the sick, Charles traveled to County Durham to sell property he had inherited there from his grandmother Cotesworth.[22] Although he had intended to settle his family in a rented house on Craven Street near his business responsibilities at Whitehall, he instead used the proceeds of his inheritance to purchase a villa in Ripley, Surrey, where the Pinckney family was living by July 1753. There they remained for the next five years.[23]

Ripley was the ideal location for the complementary roles that Eliza and Charles played in representing South Carolina's interests. Eliza's schoolmate Miss Martin, who had married Sir Nicholas Carew in 1741, lived nearby at her husband's Beddington estate. The two friends frequently exchanged visits, and Eliza became part of Lady Carew's extended circle of country gentry and minor aristocracy. Eliza immediately reestablished connections with her other girlhood friends and with the scattering of South Carolina families residing in

London. Not quite twenty miles southwest of London, Ripley was close enough for Charles to attend regularly on the Lords of Trade and for Eliza to attend social and cultural events enjoyed by the elite, particularly the theater. The family legend recorded that "she never missed a single play when Garrick was to act."[24] Her correspondence sparkles with references to travel—to Bath, where she and Charles made an extended visit late in the summer of 1753, and to the west into Bristol and Wiltshire on a circular tour, visiting Studley, Stonehenge, and Salisbury Cathedral.

On one remarkable occasion in the summer of 1753 shortly after their arrival in England, Charles and Eliza took Harriott to visit the dowager Princess Augusta at Kew, where the next generation of the royal family was in residence. Augusta's husband, Frederick, the Prince of Wales, had died in 1751 while his father, George II, was still on the throne; her eldest son eventually became George III on the death of his grandfather in 1763. She lived with her nine children in the White House on the grounds at Kew where Frederick, a patron of the arts and of science, had begun to develop one of England's finest royal gardens.[25] A member of the Board of Trade effected an introduction for the Pinckneys. Her parents intended that five-year-old Harriott should make a gift of Carolina birds to the princes and princesses; the three youngest, four-year-old Princess Louisa, three-year-old Prince Frederick, and two-year-old Princess Caroline, were near her in age. They were welcomed by the entire family in a visit lasting two hours, Princess Augusta even taking small Harriott on her lap when she began to cry. While Prince William (then ten) took Charles aside to ask him about Carolina, Eliza conversed with Augusta "with as much ease . . . as with almost any of my acquaintance, such was her condescension and her affable engaging manner." Almost the same age, though separated by a great gulf in rank and status, the two mothers found topics of mutual interest: their children and their households. When Eliza spoke forcefully about keeping newborn infants at home, declaring "I told her we had Nurses in our houses, that it appeard very strange to me to hear of people putting their children out to nurse," the Princess "seemed vastly pleased" but "was suprized at the suckling blacks; the Princess stroakd Harriott's cheek, said it made no alteration in the complexion and paid her the compliment of being very fair and pretty."[26]

The vignette of a royal and a colonial family entertaining each other must, as Eliza exclaimed to the unknown Carolina recipient of her letter, "seem pretty extraordinary to an American." It is interesting to note that, in telling the story of meeting the future George III, Eliza for the first time referred to her correspondent—and herself—as "American." The incident as a whole tells us a great deal about the social world in which Eliza Pinckney and her family

circulated during their residence in London and, by extension, of the perme-
ability in those circles of the barriers between public and private connections
and influences. Though they never again met with royalty en famille at Kew,
Eliza's social connections were as important in the promotion of South Carolina interests as Charles's legal and mercantile connections. Eliza's letters to her
English friends might commiserate over a child's illness and then in the next
sentence refer to the earthquake at Lisbon, a battle on Lake George in New
York, or news of French and Indian attacks on the Carolina backcountry. Lord
Carew and Lord King passed on greetings to Charles through Eliza's correspondence with their wives; when Sir Nicholas Carew conversed with Charles
"at Guilford at the Sessions" he passed on news of his family's health for Eliza.[27]
An acquaintance from South Carolina, Peter Manigault (1731–73), reported to
his mother after a visit with the Pinckneys in Richmond that Mrs. Pinckney
was "a mighty good Sort of a Lady, though with all her Virtues she is a little
addicted to Scandal."[28] Young gentlemen might look on the news that women
exchanged as gossip and scandal, but it was an important part of the means of
civil discourse that characterized the mid-eighteenth century webs of personal
and civic relationships.[29]

Early in 1757 a number of events coalesced to change the Pinckneys' situation. Although appointed as a special agent without pay, Charles Pinckney had
in effect been functioning as South Carolina's official representative while the
assembly wrangled about whether to recognize him formally. In January 1757
news reached England that another man had been appointed commissioner
instead. The resumption of warfare between France and England in 1756 again
threatened both Carolina's trade on the high seas and the colony's western frontier. Pinckney also learned that his brother William had suffered a stroke and
was unable to manage Charles's property effectively. Much to Eliza's delight,
he resolved to remove permanently to England, necessitating a brief return to
Carolina to settle his affairs there. The house in Ripley would be rented out
furnished until their return; Charles Cotesworth and Thomas, now twelve and
seven years old, were placed in Camberwell, a small private school on the south
bank of the Thames in Surry. Early in March 1758 Charles and Eliza sailed for
Carolina with ten-year-old Harriott to tie up loose ends. In a letter of farewell,
blaming the French and the renewed war for her anxieties, Eliza challenged
Lady Carew to imagine "what I have suffered and do still suffer in the expectation of parting with my dear children for 2 or 3 years—considering the uncertainty of life, perhaps for ever!" but expressed the hope she would soon return
to England.[30] She never did.

The Pinckney family sailed into Charleston in mid-May 1758, where they were warmly welcomed by old friends and neighbors. They were dismayed, however, to learn that, though William Pinckney was partially recovered from his stroke, their properties had not recovered from his neglect. In late June Charles set out to inspect his plantations. Unused to the heat and mosquitoes of the Lowcountry after five years in an English climate, he contracted malaria. Eliza frantically moved him from the bustle of Charleston across the Cooper River to the home of Jacob and Rebecca Motte in Mount Pleasant in hopes of recovery, but to no avail. He died there on July 12, 1758, leaving Eliza a widow at the age of thirty-five. The shock of her loss plunged Eliza into prolonged mourning so deep that her friends worried for her health. Her Charleston house was still occupied by the governor, and her Belmont plantation was too full of memories, so for six months she sought refuge at the home of her friend Mary Butler Golightly in Saint Andrews Parish, writing anguished letters to her sons and her friends in England. Not until her brother George Lucas visited her in January 1759 with news from England of her sons did she begin to again take an interest in her surroundings.[31]

Eliza was roused from her grief for "the best and worthiest of men, the tenderest and most affectionate of all husbands, and best of Fathers to my children" by the need to care for those children. For the next decade, until Charles Cotesworth returned to South Carolina in 1769 to take up his role as head of the family, she shouldered again many of the same responsibilities she had shouldered as a young girl. Named by her husband as an executor of his will, she returned to Belmont to find "every thing and every way in bad order, with ignorant or dishonest Over Seers" so negligent that "it has gone back to woods again."[32] The estate had to be restored to support the expenses of her household and of her boys' education and, most importantly, to preserve it intact to pass on as their inheritance. Her letterbook was once again filled with the minutiae of crop management, shipping, and bills of exchange; of gifts of live turtles and ducks sent by any available ship to friends in England; and of directions regarding the education of her boys. Comments on the wars against France and against the Cherokee revealed her continued interest in civic affairs, at least as they affected her enterprises. Her correspondents now were George Morley, her business manager in London; the schoolmasters and friends looking after the interests of her sons; and the boys themselves, whom she urged to write whenever a vessel could carry their letters. Though she regretted their separation, she urged them to endure, "for though you are very young," she wrote to Charles Cotesworth in the spring of 1761 when he was fifteen, "you must know the welfair of a whole family depends in a great measure on the progress you make in moral Virtue, Religion, and learning."[33]

As in her girlhood, Eliza Pinckney had male advisors to call on, most nota-bly her husband's brother William (until his death in 1766) and his second son Charles (1731–82), who was already emerging as a powerful political figure in South Carolina and whose Snee Farm property was not far by water from Bel-mont. She divided her time between a small house in Charleston and Belmont, where she spent four or five months of the year.[34] Her companions at Belmont were her daughter, Harriott, who had grown tall, she reported to Lady Carew, and a good friend, Lady Ann Mackenzie, "a pious sensible young woman has been so good to stay chiefly with me since I came home," she wrote in 1760.[35]

Harriott Pinckney thus spent the formative years of her youth in a household of women. Like her mother, she quickly became a diligent correspondent, writ-ing to her friends and her brothers in England, especially to Thomas. There is no comparable list of her daily activities to the one Eliza had penned in 1742, but Harriott watched and assisted as her mother oversaw the domestic economy of several plantations where provisions for food, lodging, and health care had to be made for two or three hundred people. Meat had to be slaughtered and cured, a vegetable garden and fruit orchard tended, a dairy operated to produce butter and cream, the sick visited and remedies provided for their illnesses. Soap and candles had to be manufactured and clothing supplied, either by purchasing "negro cloth" or by supervising weaving by slave women.

Harriott had mastered the skills required to manage all of these activities by the time of her marriage to Daniel Horry (1738–85) on February 15, 1768. In March, Eliza wrote to her new son-in-law that "I am glad your little wife looks well to the ways of her household. . . . The management of a Dairy is an amuse-ment she has been always fond of, and . . . hers is perfectly neat. I find as you say she sends her instructions far and near. . . . She has people out gathering simples, different kinds of snake-roots and pink roots and is distilling herbs and flowers." [36]

At thirty, Harriott's new husband, the grandson of Huguenot émigrés who settled in the "French Santee" area near Georgetown, was still relatively young, although eleven years older than his bride. His first wife Judith Serre had died in October 1765, having borne two daughters who did not survive her, leav-ing him a childless widower. Judith Serre's dowry of extensive rice fields in the same region of the South Santee River where Horry's father and grandfather had developed their Hampton plantation made him one of the wealthiest rice planters in the province. He may have begun courting Harriott as early as 1766. Harriott's letters before her marriage reveal a young woman with a wide circle of friends, one who enjoyed but was not beguiled by the social activities in town, who was not averse to gossip, and who loved to read. Whereas her mother as a young woman had concentrated on cultivating indigo, Harriott tried to develop a silk industry at Belmont.[37] Even as she wrote discretely and obliquely of the attentions she received from "Mr. Horry," she reassured her friend "Miss R" who lived at Santee that "not only from what I have ever been taught but from my own little observation I am fully convinced that Virtue is the only solid foundation for happiness and if we can obtain that my friend in all its amiable Branches we are secure of it married or Single or whether Fortune smiles or Frowns."[38]

Harriott's marriage in February 1768 and her removal fifty miles north of Charleston to Hampton Plantation marked the beginning of a new life for Harriott and for her mother. Harriott's first child, named Daniel Huger Horry after his father, was born in August 1769. With the birth of a daughter, Harriott Pinckney Horry in October 1770, she too ended her childbearing years early, at the age of twenty-two. Eliza Pinckney was a frequent visitor at Hampton and cared for the Horry house and garden on Broad Street when she was in Charleston. Daniel, her first grandchild, delighted Eliza much as had her own firstborn. As soon as he was old enough to begin his education, she took him to stay with her in Charleston to study with a tutor. When his father took him to London for further study in 1781, Eliza became his steadiest correspondent. In part, she was freed to play the role of grandmother by the return in 1769 of her oldest son to take up his inheritance at Belmont. The Mansion House on East Bay, the residence of royal governors for nearly twenty years, now became Charles Cotesworth Pinckney's home in Charleston, and he took over from his mother the management of Belmont and his other properties.

Young Charles Cotesworth Pinckney was a son of whom his devoted mother could be proud. Educated at Westminster School and Christ Church College, Oxford, with English sons of the aristocracy, he had trained in the law under William Blackstone at the Middle Temple of the Inns of Court. He was called to the English bar in January 1769 before leaving for Charleston. During a tour of the Continent for his health in 1767–68, he had attended the Royal Military Academy at Caen, France. His sixteen years in England had not diminished his sense of identity as an American. During the height of the Stamp Act crisis in 1765–66, when he was still at Oxford, he commissioned a portrait for a college friend that represented him declaiming against parliamentary abuse of liberty. Within six months of his return to South Carolina, the St. Johns Colleton Parish elected him to a seat in the South Carolina Commons House of Assembly. Eliza saw him take his seat and the required oath of loyalty on December 5, 1769, and a year later, shortly before his twenty-fourth birthday, she reported with satisfaction his commission to practice law in South Carolina. One of his first political acts in the assembly was to vote for funds to defend John Wilkes, a journalist and member of Parliament imprisoned for criticizing George III. The Wilkes case became a symbol of resistance to tyranny and was an important milestone in the growing resistance of American colonial legislatures to parliamentary and royal authority.[39]

Despite his youth, Charles Cotesworth soon took a leading political and social role in South Carolina. He was active in the vestry of St. Philip's Church and in the Charleston Library Society, a founder of the Charleston Museum in 1773, and an eligible bachelor who patronized the balls and dinners of the annual February race week in Charleston. In September 1773 he married seventeen-year-old Sarah (Sally) Middleton, the youngest daughter of Henry Middleton of Middleton Place, further strengthening the links of the Pinckney family to the powerful planter and merchant world that dominated South Carolina. Sally's mother had died when she was four, and she became as much a daughter as a daughter-in-law to Eliza Pinckney. She bore five children in quick succession, although only three daughters survived infancy. Thomas Pinckney wrote fondly to his sister in 1777 of Sally's "Brats." The small Pinckney and Horry cousins grew up during the 1770s under the watchful eye of their grandmother.[40]

Eliza's second son Thomas did not return permanently to South Carolina until December 1774. Like his brother, he matriculated at Westminster School and Christ Church College, Oxford, studied law at the Middle Temple and military strategy at the Royal Military Academy at Caen, and was called to the English bar in November 1774. He briefly returned home to South Carolina in September 1771 after his twenty-first birthday to claim his inheritance and arrange for the management of his plantation at Aukland on the Ashpoo River. He lived with his mother at her small house on Colleton Square in Charleston and visited his sister at Hampton before returning to England in March 1773 to complete his legal training at the Middle Temple. He was more attached to the American cause even than his brother, leading his English schoolmates to dub Thomas "the Little Radical." His final months in London coincided with the height of parliamentary reaction against the Boston Tea Party, and he was so anxious to return home that in August he wrote his brother requesting funds to do so.[41] His mother proudly reported his admission to the South Carolina bar early in 1775, pleased to have learned from his cousin Charles Pinckney that he had argued his first case in court "extraordinarily well" and commenting to her daughter that "were he to Consult what became him he should wear no other dress but the Barr gownd—, it becomes him better than any thing he ever wore."[42] Her two sons were now poised to fulfill the wish expressed in their father's will that they pursue careers in the law. Instead, within a year both brothers were caught up in South Carolina military preparations to resist parliamentary authority.

For the next decade, the struggle for American independence dominated the lives of all Eliza and Harriott's immediate family. The Revolutionary War in South Carolina was particularly divisive and destructive, feeding on old rivalries between the wealthy and elite planter class along the coast, who controlled the province's political institutions, and the majority of white inhabitants, who lived in the interior areas known collectively as the backcountry. A civil and guerilla war between loyalists and partisans as well as a contest between colonial and British regular armies, the war destroyed, at least temporarily, the Pinckney family's fortunes and their homes.[43] It plunged Eliza and Harriott once again into the roles of "deputy husbands" as plantation managers and called on them to put to use their strengths as kin specialists. It elevated Charles Cotesworth and Thomas to national status as heroes but destroyed forever Daniel Horry's political power within South Carolina.

In the spring of 1775, Charles Cotesworth Pinckney and Thomas Pinckney, their cousin Charles Pinckney ("the Colonel") and his young son also named Charles ("the Signer"), and Daniel Horry all cast their lot with those in rebellion against the Crown, first as members of the state's provincial congress and then by taking up arms.[44] For the next five years they were on the move, recruiting and training troops for South Carolina's regiments and commanding units that built and then manned fortresses defending Charleston. Charles Cotesworth and Daniel traveled north in the fall of 1777 to meet with George Washington and his staff. Thomas Pinckney and his young cousin Charles Pinckney (1757–1824) participated in the unsuccessful siege of Savannah. Charles Cotesworth became a prisoner of war when Charleston fell to the British in May 1780; his brother-in-law Daniel Horry elected instead to accept protection from the British army and recommit his allegiance to Britain. Thomas Pinckney was wounded and captured at the Battle of Camden in August 1780. Both brothers were released on parole and eventually removed to Philadelphia until an exchange of officers could be arranged. They did not return until the liberation of Charleston in December 1782.

During the disruptive war years, the burden of managing plantations and households fell on Eliza Pinckney and Harriott Horry, even though the absence of their men was sporadic rather than constant, particularly before the British turned their full attention on the South in the fall of 1779. Charles Cotesworth Pinckney's young wife Sally, inexperienced and frequently pregnant, relied on her mother-in-law for help at Belmont. Both she and Eliza responded to Charles's requests for personal and military supplies from the plantation. Because Harriott's Hampton plantation was far removed from the military actions centered on Charleston, her home frequently became the refuge for women and young children fleeing the threatened British invasion. Eliza reported from Hampton to Thomas Pinckney in May 1779 that Harriott had "sent for Sally and the children upon the first appearance of Danger" and listed ten other women "with all their little ones" who had sought safety there. Sally had two small daughters to protect and was then pregnant with a son who was born in September.[45] When invasion was not imminent, the two women continued their seasonal travels between their plantation and Charleston homes, traveling by boat or overland by horse. When an outbreak of smallpox struck in the winter of 1779–80, they arranged for inoculation of their families and slaves; when drought threatened, they worried about the crops; when the British invaded, they arranged to move livestock and slaves inland to safety. Theirs was as important a contribution to the military effort as that of their men.

Until Thomas Pinckney married Elizabeth (Betsey) Motte on July 22, 1779, he relied on his sister Harriott to supply him with everything from clean underwear and brandy to "two or three Bear Skins which I am in want of" as well as provisions of meat for his regiment.[46] Brother and sister corresponded frequently. Mixed in with his descriptions of boredom at camp, the discomfort of traveling with the regiment, and accounts of military engagements, Thomas lightheartedly chided Harriott for her failure to send him better reports of her mastery of the assignments he had made her in Euclid! One wonders whether Harriott actually managed to focus on mathematical problems in the face of all her other responsibilities or whether she understood that her younger brother assigned himself the role of tutor to distract both of them from wartime demands and anxieties.

The British depredations in the South between 1779 and 1781 took a heavy toll on Pinckney properties. A threatened invasion of Charleston in the early spring of 1779 prompted the family to remove valuables from their several homes in town to the relative safety of Thomas Pinckney's plantation on the Ashpoo River, but on May 6, 1779, British troops moving northward from Savannah burned his house to the ground, plundering valuables, destroying all his father's papers, and carrying off the slaves. His mother proudly reported that Charles Cotesworth immediately offered to share his own inheritance with his brother, but shortly thereafter the British destroyed everything at Belmont, although they left the house standing. When Charleston fell, Charles Cotesworth, as one of the defending officers, was made a prisoner of war, exiled to Snee Farm with General William Moultrie, and his estates, including Belmont, seized. The cattle there were slaughtered to feed British troops and the trees harvested for firewood. Eliza's Charleston home was commandeered to house Hessian soldiers. In a letter written near the end of the war to a friend, Eliza apologized: "It may seem strange that a single woman, accused of no crime, who had a fortune sufficiency to live Genteely in any part of the world . . . should in so short a time be so intirely deprived of it as not to be able to pay a debt under sixty pound Sterling, but such is my singular case."[47] Quite literally the only home left to her was that of her daughter.

It was to prevent such loss that when captured as an officer in the fall of Charleston, Daniel Horry chose to become a "protectionist." He renounced his allegiance to the American cause and received permission to return to Hampton Plantation with his wife, Harriott, his mother-in-law, Eliza Lucas Pinckney, and his two young children. Within a year Horry left for London to enroll twelve-year-old Daniel at the Westminster school his Pinckney uncles had attended. While her husband was away, Harriott reputedly offered General Francis "Swamp Fox" Marion sanctuary and a dinner, then hid him and fed the dinner instead to British General Banastre Tarleton, who was pursuing Marion, thus allowing the latter's escape.[48] Her husband, Daniel Horry, returned to South Carolina in April 1782. By then the tide of battle in the South had turned. With British occupation of South Carolina ended, a punitive assembly met and included Horry's name on the list of seven hundred "protectionists" whose property should be confiscated. Only the intervention of her brothers in behalf of her husband saved Harriott's home. The assembly reduced Horry's punishment to an "amercement" of 12 percent of the value of his extensive holdings. Daniel Horry lived only three more years, dying of a fever on November 12, 1785. Widowed at the age of thirty-seven, Harriott invited her mother to make Hampton her permanent home. Her son, Daniel, never returned home from Europe, despite his grandmother's affectionate remonstrances to emulate his uncles in the practice of virtue and in loyalty to his country. After a youthful period of extravagance and dissipation in London, he traveled to France, where he married the niece of Lafayette. Perhaps out of shame at his father's political downfall, he changed his name from that of his father to Charles Lucas Pinckney Horry, honoring the family names of his grandmother and great-grandfather.[49]

The end of the British occupation of Charleston on December 14, 1782, shortly after the news that the American negotiators in Paris had reached a preliminary agreement of peace with Great Britain, led to a cessation of hostilities. It did not, however, restore the prewar prosperity enjoyed by Eliza Pinckney, Harriott Horry, and their families. When Charles Cotesworth and Thomas Pinckney returned home to the newly incorporated Charleston, they turned at last from bearing arms to practicing law, aware that they could no longer earn their living from their lands. Charles Cotesworth had loaned more than twenty thousand pounds to the South Carolina government to help fund its military efforts, but there was no immediate prospect of repayment. His estate at Belmont was almost beyond salvaging. Eliza's elaborate formal garden and the experimental mulberry trees so carefully tended by Harriott as a teenager were overgrown with weeds, the slaves were gone, the woods destroyed, and the house of Eliza's happy marriage destroyed by fire in February 1783. Although in 1779 Thomas had lost his inherited plantation house on the Ashpoo River, his marriage to Betsey Motte later that same year had brought him a new and extensive estate at Fairfield on the South Santee, not far from Harriott's home at Hampton, where his mother and sister now struggled to restore order.

The loss of British markets for rice and the end of the British bounty on indigo meant that the return of income from the state's staple crops would be slow. While the men rode the circuit, Eliza and Harriott continued their roles as "deputy husbands." Sally Middleton Pinckney, already suffering from consumption (tuberculosis), died of a fever at her brother's plantation in May 1784 while Charles Cotesworth was away arguing cases in the circuit courts; he immediately brought their three small daughters to Hampton for his mother and sister to raise. Within another year, Daniel Horry too was dead. Until Charles Cotesworth married Mary Stead in 1786 and took his daughters with them to Philadelphia while he attended the Constitutional Convention, Eliza and Harriott presided once again over a household of women and girls.[50]

In the aftermath of the war, the relationship of mother and daughter gradually shifted and reversed. Eliza celebrated her sixty-first birthday shortly after the liberation of Charleston. As she aged, her children took over many of the responsibilities she had carried out so well for so long. Harriott became the manager of extensive plantations, experimenting with and adopting the new system of tidal cultivation of rice with the encouragement of her brother Thomas. When the house at Belmont burned to the ground, Thomas wrote first to his sister Harriott with the news, not his mother. Eliza's chief pleasure was in her children and grandchildren, although at least one of the latter caused her concern. Word reached Hampton that Daniel, attending Cambridge University in England, was neglecting his studies for a life of indolence and indulgence; his fond grandmother renewed her efforts to instill in him the virtues of his uncles, reminding him that "an idle man is a burthen to society and to himself."[51] Of her own children, Eliza wrote to her friend in England, the poet George Keate:

> Outliving those we love is what gives the principal gloom to long protracted life. . . .
> I regret no pleasures that I can't enjoy, and I enjoy some that I could not have had
> at an early season. I now see my children grown up, and, blessed by God, see them
> such as I hoped. What is there in youthful enjoyment preferable to this? . . . Sincere

is my gratitude to Heaven for the advantages of this period of life, as well as for those that are passed.[52]

Others shared her pride in her children's accomplishments and admired her role in producing them. George Washington, on his travels into the South in the spring of 1791 to cement sectional support for the new national government under the Constitution, paid tribute to Thomas and Charles Cotesworth, who had served on his staff during the war, by dining at midday on May 1 at Hampton Plantation. Harriott and Eliza, flanked by Harriott's and Charles Cotesworth's daughters, greeted Washington wearing sashes painted with his likeness. Four days later both mother and daughter attended a ball in Washington's honor in Charleston. A planter at heart, Washington admired Harriott's rice and indigo fields and at the end of the visit sent Eliza a drill plow that, as he explained to his hostess, would improve the process of planting indigo seed.[53]

Two years later Eliza and Harriott saw the president again under less happy circumstances. In the spring of 1792, Eliza developed a cancerous tumor in her breast. After attempting more traditional cures—Charles Cotesworth sent his sister several shipments of leeches to apply to the tumor—her children decided to seek medical help for her in Philadelphia.[54] Accompanied by her daughter and three of her granddaughters (twenty-three-year-old Harriott Horry and Charles Cotesworth's teenage daughters Maria and Harriott), Eliza boarded a ship on April 10, 1793, and after a rough ten-day voyage sailed up the Delaware Bay past "a number of farms with fine fields of wheat and the fruit trees in bloom" to a stormy landing. "My Mother very sick," recorded Harriott in her diary. Despite her illness, the ladies and gentlemen of the federal government honored Eliza Pinckney with courtesy visits. Investigating the possibility that the surgeon Dr. Tate might provide relief for her mother, Harriott visited several patients who had had tumors removed surgically to ask "questions I chose of the pains &c which they suffered" and was impressed by Tate's results, but it was too late.[55]

Harriott recorded in her journal on May 26, 1793, "Dear mother continued to suffer extremely . . . and for several hours was in great agony when it pleased Almighty God to take her to himself." At his own request, Washington served as one of Eliza Lucas Pinckney's pallbearers. On May 27, she was buried in St. Peters churchyard in Philadelphia. Thomas, in London as minister to Great Britain, and Charles Cotesworth, attending court in Charleston, did not hear of her death until early in July.[56] "We have sustained my dear Harriott a heavy loss, the daily progress of the disorder to which you were a witness must have prepared you for it," Thomas wrote to his sister when he heard the news. "My apprehensions added to the accounts I received had in some measure effected the same with me. . . . [W]e my dearest sister have but to imitate her conduct & we may safely trust to the events."[57] Exhausted by the ordeal of caring for her mother and urged by her brothers to remain in the North to avoid the unhealthy summer season along the Carolina coast, Harriott Horry enjoyed the society of Philadelphia and spent a week in June traveling to visit the Moravian towns of Bethlehem and Nazareth before setting out overland to return to Carolina early in July. Thomas urged her to join him in London "as soon as the season will permit you to undertake the voyage," but she never did.[58]

Harriott Horry was now the matriarch of the Pinckney family. For thirty-seven years after Eliza's death until her own in 1830, she continued her seasonal migrations between her townhouse on Tradd Street in Charleston and her Hampton plantation on the South Santee. There she also kept on eye on her brother Thomas's nearby plantations, first Fairfield and later Eldorado. The three plantations, spread along a six-mile stretch of the south bank of the South Santee, afforded easy family communication by river and by road. Both Harriott and Thomas were keenly interested in implementing new scientific agricultural developments. They were among the first in their region to introduce a more efficient form of rice cultivation that involved investing heavily in canals and "rice trunks" to harness the tidal flow of the Santee and its numerous tidal creeks. Charles Cotesworth lived at a distance on his favorite plantation on Pinckney Island, near Hilton Head, where he grew sea-island cotton rather than rice. Like his siblings he was active in the South Carolina Agricultural Society. For the first decade after Eliza's death, Thomas and Charles Cotesworth were frequently away, deeply involved in the political and diplomatic affairs of the new American nation. Thomas was in Europe with his family from 1792 until 1796, first serving as minister to Great Britain and then negotiating a treaty in Spain. On his return, South Carolina elected him to Congress, sending him off to Philadelphia for much of the time between 1797 and 1801.[59] Charles Cotesworth too served in Europe as Minister to France between 1796 and 1798. Each in turn was selected by the Federalist Party to run for vice president or president in elections in 1796, 1800, 1804, and 1808.

It was Harriott who became the South Carolina anchor for the family. Like her mother, to her role as plantation mistress she added that of kin specialist, writing frequently to both her brothers of personal as well as public events in coastal Carolina and to correspondents in Philadelphia, New York, and Boston. Her son, Daniel, had made his home in Europe, and he never returned to live in the United States, although he did occasionally visit his mother. Her daughter, Harriott, remained at home with her at Hampton until her marriage in 1797 at the relatively late age of twenty-seven. Even then, the younger Harriott's husband, Frederick Rutledge, stayed at Hampton with his new family, and once again the plantation rang with the voices of small children watched over by a fond grandmother. Harriott Rutledge, unlike her mother and grandmother, bore many children, ten in all, despite her late start at motherhood. By 1802 the couple had four children. Thinking it was time to establish his own household, Rutledge purchased five hundred acres on the North Santee and began to build a plantation house named Tranquility. To be near them, in 1806 his mother-in-law Harriott purchased a rice plantation next to Thomas Pinckney's Eldorado plantation, and began another house called Harrietta. Hampton, however, became the Rutledge family's permanent home once it became clear that Daniel would never return to claim his inheritance and that Harriott and Frederick and their children would thus inherit the plantation. Upon her husband's death in 1821, Harriott Rutledge—like her mother and grandmother before her—became a widow while she still had young children at home. Until her death in 1858, she continued the family female tradition of efficiently managing a profitable rice plantation.

Harriott Pinckney Horry's interests in a wide variety of mechanical and agricultural innovations remained strong throughout her long life. The building of homes for her children and grandchildren led her to request Sarah Elliott Huger, a young kinswoman and frequent correspondent in New York, to investigate a brick-making machine whose promoter promised improved quantity and quality. Sarah's detailed description of the machine and its shortcomings revealed that both women knew their bricks as well as they knew the Duncan Phyfe furnishings that were the more usual subject of Harriott's requests and orders.[60] In 1815, two decades after the hurriedly arranged journey to Philadelphia seeking medical care for her mother, Harriott made another more extensive and leisurely five-month visit to the North. Traveling by coach rather than by sea, she was accompanied by her friend Elizabeth Martin, her niece Eliza, and her brother General Thomas Pinckney, only recently mustered out of military service as a commander of the Southern Division of the U.S. Army for the War of 1812. Setting out in May, the party saw firsthand much of the damage caused when the British burned Washington and attacked Baltimore. They reached Portsmouth, New Hampshire, in mid-July where they stayed two weeks to see how Harriott's seventeen-year-old grandson Edward Rutledge was faring in his naval training. She recorded in her diary, "I received much satisfaction in leaving Edward so much pleased with his situation and in hearing from some of the officers that they were well pleased with him."[61]

Harriott's interest in brick making had not abated. At almost every stop along the way, she inquired about and noted the local brick-making practices and the quality and cost, making special arrangements with her hosts to visit large brickyards in Virginia and New Hampshire. Manufacturing and technological innovation throughout the northern states fascinated her. She rode on Fulton's steamship up the Hudson, and she described knowledgeably an ironworks in Pennsylvania, indigo dyeing processes at a mechanized textile mill in Philadelphia, and an iced refrigerator box for chilling food in Virginia. Her brothers were both involved with the Santee Canal Company. One wonders whether Harriott anticipated that her native state would soon be trying to make manufacturing and technical innovations and, at the age of sixty-seven, was gathering the information that would permit her brothers, her children, and grandchildren to contribute to that effort.

Whatever her intent, her children and grandchildren followed a different course. Harriott outlived many of them. The final decade of her life was one of gradual loss for the family. A severe hurricane in September 1822 killed fifty slaves at Hampton and destroyed large sections of the diking that had reclaimed marshy lands from the delta.[62] In 1824, her son-in-law Frederick Rutledge died, leaving the two Harriotts to manage the continued rebuilding of the rice fields at Hampton. In March 1825, the three Pinckney siblings welcomed Lafayette to their homes on the Santee and in Charleston during the hero's triumphant American tour. Harriott Horry must have spoken to him then of her son, Daniel, his nephew by marriage, still living in France. By the end of that summer, Lafayette's Revolutionary War comrade-in-arms Charles Cotesworth Pinckney had died. Three years later, in 1828, Thomas Pinckney too was gone, and Harriott's son, Daniel, had perished in far-off France. Harriott Pinckney Horry had outlived her generation. With her death in December 19, 1830, the story of the founding family of Pinckneys came to a close.

That family's contributions to the national story were made possible by the closely linked roles of the first two generations of its women. Eliza Lucas Pinckney and Harriott Pinckney Horry do not neatly fit historians' labels of "republican mother" or "plantation mistress," although their lives illustrate some of the complexities of women's roles that those labels were coined to express. Eliza Pinckney lived in a world that valued distinctions of rank and saw family cohesiveness as a way to protect privileges of wealth and political power. The connections she assiduously and successfully cultivated with great charm and energy were with the old and new world's elite economic and political leaders. Large-scale agriculture and botanical experiments to improve its practice were her passions, and she mastered the complexity of international trade in its products with skill. She modeled many of the values of piety and virtue that became central to early nineteenth-century women's understanding of their role in a republic. Yet for most of her life the country in which she lived was not yet a republic, and her world valued those virtues for their contributions to different goals.

Eliza's daughter, Harriott Pinckney Horry, in spite of her childhood brush with royalty, lived her adult life in the republic that her brothers helped to found. Yet she too was hardly a republican mother, for her only son abandoned that republic at an early age. Harriott operated effectively in the masculine world, managing the business of modernizing and developing new technologies for her family's plantation holdings. Where her mother had used her epistolary skills to maintain connections across the Atlantic in England, Harriott used hers to bridge the ever-widening gaps between northern and southern society in the American republic. She welcomed visitors to Charleston from New York, Philadelphia, and Boston, sent to her by the extended network of young relatives and relocated South Carolinians, and exercised her curiosity about the emerging worlds of machinery that eventually divided the sections.

Historians have remembered the mother and forgotten the daughter. Both deserve to be remembered as women who transcended the "separate spheres" to which their gender might have confined them. Their long and full lives, thoroughly examined, tell us much about the varieties of women's experiences and about the history of South Carolina and the nation at a time when their family played an extraordinary role in both.

NOTES

1. Pinckney's contributions as the first successful South Carolina producer of commercial indigo were first described in David Ramsey, *The History of South Carolina, from Its First Settlement in 1670 to the Year 1808*, 2 vols. (Charleston, S.C.: David Longworth, 1809), 2:209. Ever since, she has received attention from historians and popular biographers, including Julia Cherry Spruill, *Women's Life and Work in the Southern Colonies* (Chapel Hill: University of North Carolina Press, 1938); Anne Firor Scott, "Self-Portraits: Three Women," in *Uprooted Americans: Essays to Honor Oscar Handlin*, ed. Richard L. Bushman et al. (Boston: Little, Brown, 1972); Frances Leigh Williams, *Plantation Patriot: A Life of Eliza Lucas Pinckney* (New York, Harcourt, Brace and World, 1967), a biography for young people; Constance B. Schulz, "Eliza Lucas Pinckney," in *Portraits of American Women*, ed. G. J. Barker-Benfield and Catherine Clinton (New York: St. Martin's, 1991); and Nancy R. Rhoden and Ian K. Steele, eds., *The Human Tradition in the American Revolution* (Wilmington, Del.: Scholarly Resources, 2000). The *South Carolina Historical Magazine* (hereinafter cited as SCHM), devoted its entire July 1998 issue to Eliza Lucas Pinckney.

2. Jack L. Cross, ed., "Letters of Thomas Pinckney, 1775–1780," SCHM 58, no. 1 (1957): 19–33, SCHM 58, no. 2 (1957): 67–83, SCHM 58, no. 3 (1957): 145–62, and SCHM 58, no. 4 (1957): 224–42.

3. See Darcy R. Fryer, "In Pursuit of Their Interest: Community Oversight of Economic and Family Life among the South Carolina Lowcountry Gentry, c. 1730–1789" (PhD diss., Yale University, 2001), for an extended discussion of this idea.

4. Sources for their lives include the *Journal and Letters of Eliza Lucas*, ed. Harriott Pinckney Holbrook (Wormsloe, Ga., 1850); *The Letterbook of Eliza Lucas Pinckney, 1739–1762*, ed. Elise Pinckney (Columbia: University of South Carolina Press, 1972) (hereinafter cited as *Letterbook*); and Harriott Horry Ravenel, *Eliza Pinckney* (New York: Charles Scribner's Sons, 1896). Harriott Horry kept a "receipt" or cookbook, published in a modern edition as *A Colonial Plantation Cookbook: The Receipt Book of Harriott Pinckney Horry, 1770*, ed. Richard J. Hooker (Columbia: University of South Carolina Press, 1984), which contains many of the entries from a similar receipt book kept by her mother.

5. Laurel Thatcher Ulrich, *Good Wives: Image and Reality in the Lives of Women in Northern New England, 1650–1750* (New York: Knopf, 1982); Daniel Blake Smith, *Inside the Great House: Planter Family Life in Eighteenth-Century Chesapeake Society* (Ithaca, N.Y.: Cornell University Press, 1980); Mary Beth Norton, *Liberty's Daughters: The Revolutionary Experience of American Women, 1750–1800* (New York: Little, Brown, 1980), xix.

6. Linda K. Kerber, *Women of the Republic: Intellect and Ideology in Revolutionary America* (Chapel Hill: University of North Carolina Press for the Institute of Early American History and Culture, Williamsburg, Va., 1980); Jan Lewis, "The Republican Wife: Virtue and Seduction in the Early Republic," *William and Mary Quarterly*, 3rd ser., 44, no. 4 (1987): 689–721.

7. Darcy R. Fryer, "The Mind of Eliza Pinckney: An Eighteenth-Century Woman's Construction of Herself," SCHM 99, no. 3 (1998): 218.

8. Principal sources for the information that follows on Eliza's experiences before she reached South Carolina, unless otherwise noted, are Carol Walter Ramagosa, "Eliza Lucas Pinckney's Family in Antigua, 1668–1747," SCHM 99, no. 3 (1998): 238–58, and Harriet Simons Williams, "Eliza Lucas and Her Family: Before the Letterbook," SCHM 99, no. 3 (July 1998): 259–79.

9. Eliza Lucas Pinckney (hereinafter cited as ELP) to Harriott Pinckney Horry (hereinafter cited as HPH), September 10, 1785, SCHM 17, no. 3 (1916): 101–2.

10. *Letterbook*, introduction, xvi, and 7. Williams, "Eliza Lucas and her Family," 268–76, convincingly documents a more accurate chronology for Eliza's arrival in Carolina than that provided by Elise Pinckney in the *Letterbook*.

11. Unless indicated otherwise, the narrative that follows is based on Eliza Lucas Pinckney's letters and memoranda in Elise Pinckney's edition of her *Letterbook*.

12. ELP to Mrs. Boddicott, May 2, 1740, *Letterbook*, 7.

13. ELP to Mary Bartlett, 1742, *Letterbook*, 35–36.

14. ELP, memorandum of letter to her father, July 1740, *Letterbook*, 8.

15. ELP to HPH, September 10, 1785, 101–2; ELP to George Lucas, 1744, in Ravenel, *Eliza Pinckney*, 104–5. On indigo cultivation in South Carolina, see David L. Coon, "Eliza Lucas Pinckney and the Reintroduction of Indigo Culture in South Carolina," *Journal of Southern History* 42, no. 1 (1976), 61–76, and John J. Winberry, "Reputation of Carolina Indigo," SCHM 80, no. 4 (1979): 242–50.

16. ELP to Mrs. Boddicott, May 2, 1740, *Letterbook*, 7–8.

17. Ravenel, *Eliza Pinckney*, 113.

18. Letter to unknown, n.d. (probably summer 1753), in Ravenel, *Eliza Pinckney*, 144–153; quotation on 151.

19. Ravenel, *Eliza Pinckney*, 117–18.

20. Frances Leigh Williams, *A Founding Family: The Pinckneys of South Carolina* (New York: Harcourt Brace Jovanovich, 1978) 13–15.

21. The portrait by an unknown English artist is in the collection of the South Carolina Art Association's Gibbes Museum of Art.

22. ELP to Mrs. Boddicott, May 2, 1741, *Letterbook*, 14.

23. Unless noted otherwise, the sources for the description of the Pinckneys' sojourn in England are Ravenel, *Eliza Pinckney*, 134–66, and *Letterbook*, 73–89.

24. Ravenel, *Eliza Pinckney*, 159.

25. The remarkable long letter describing this visit is printed in full by Ravenel in *Eliza Pinckney*, 144–53.

26. Ibid., 149, 152.

27. ELP to Lady Carew, May–June 1755, *Letterbook*, 85; ELP to Lady Carew, November 1755, *Letterbook*, 86; memorandum of a letter to Wilhelmina King, [January 1756?], *Letterbook*, 77; ELP to Lady Carew, February 7, 1757, *Letterbook*, 87.

28. Peter Manigault to Mrs. Gabriel Manigault, May? 29, 1753, SCHM 33, no. 1 (1932): 57 (date given as March in SCHM, but the Pinckneys did not arrive in Richmond until May).

29. See David S. Shields, *Civil Tongues and Polite Letters in British America* (Chapel Hill: University of North Carolina Press for the Omohundro Institute of Early American History and Culture, Williamsburg, Va., 1997), esp. chap. 4.

30. ELP to Lady Carew, February 7, 1757, *Letterbook*, 87–88.

31. ELP to "My dr. Children," February 1759, *Letterbook*, 110–11; "Your Uncle Lucas" reported that he had seen Charles Cotesworth (hereinafter cited as CCP) and Thomas (hereinafter cited as TP) in England and that they were well.

32. ELP to Mrs. Pocklington, May 1759, *Letterbook*, 114; ELP to Mr. Morley, March 14, 1760, *Letterbook*, 144; Ravenel, *Eliza Pinckney*, 189.

33. ELP to CCP, April 15, 1761, *Letterbook*, 167.

34. ELP to Mrs. Onslow in Sussex, February 27, 1762, *Letterbook*, 185.

35. ELP to Miss Varier, February 1760, *Letterbook*, 137.

36. ELP to Daniel Horry, March 9, 1768, in Elise Pinckney, ed., "Letters of Eliza Lucas Pinckney, 1768–1782," SCHM 76, no. 3 (1975): 144. Eliza's and Harriott's plantation activities are described in Ravenel, *Eliza Pinckney*, 191–93.

37. Letter to Dolly Golightly, July 20, 1763, Harriott Pinckney Horry letterbook, 1763–67, Harriott H. Ravenel Papers, 11/332/8, Pinckney-Lowndes Papers, South Carolina Historical Society, Charleston (hereinafter cited as HHR-SCHS); letter to "Miss R" in Santee, April 1766, January 14, 1767, and n.d. (probably spring 1767), 11/332/8, HHR-SCHS; letter to Becky Izard, December 20, 1766, and n.d. (probably late 1767), 11/332/8, HHR-SCHS.

38. Letter to Becky Izard, n.d., but probably early 1767, 11/332/8, HHR-SCHS.

39. See Marvin R. Zahniser, *Charles Cotesworth Pinckney, Founding Father* (Chapel Hill: University of North Carolina Press for the Institute of Early American History and Culture, Williamsburg, Va., 1967), chaps. 1 and 2.

40. TP to HPH, May 13, 1777, from Fort Moultrie, SCHM 58, no. 2 (1957): 80–81.

41. Williams, *A Founding Family*, 15–22, 40–41; Charles Cotesworth Pinckney, *Life of General Thomas Pinckney* (Boston: Houghton, Mifflin, 1895), 22–25.

42. ELP to HPH, February 17, 1775, and February 18, 1775, in Ravenel, *Eliza Pinckney*, 259–60.

43. Walter Edgar, *Partisans and Redcoats: The Southern Conflict that Turned the Tide of the*

American Revolution (New York: William Morrow, 2001); Walter Edgar, *South Carolina, A History* (Columbia: University of South Carolina Press, 1998), chap. 11.

44. The overview that follows is based on Williams, *A Founding Family*, chaps. 5 and 6; Pinckney, *Life of General Thomas Pinckney*, 26–80; and Zahniser, *Charles Cotesworth Pinckney*, 47–70.

45. Named Charles Cotesworth, the infant lived only a year (Pinckney, ed., "Letters of Eliza Lucas Pinckney, 1768–1782," 158–59; Williams, *A Founding Family*, 131–32).

46. TP to HPH, "Fort Johnson Sun: Morn," SCHM 76, no. 2 (1975): 73. Jack L. Cross edited seventy-eight of Thomas Pinckney's letters to his sister, Harriott, which appeared in the four issues of volume 58 of SCHM as "Letters of Thomas Pinckney, 1775–1780"; it is from these letters that this description is primarily drawn.

47. ELP to Dr. Alexander Garden, May 14, 1782, in Pinckney, ed., "Letters of Eliza Pinckney, 1768–1782," 168–70.

48. Ravenel, *Eliza Pinckney*, 285–86.

49. Williams, *A Founding Family*, 210, 332.

50. Ibid., 196–99; Ravenel, *Eliza Pinckney*, 306–7; Zahniser, *Charles Cotesworth Pinckney*, 80–81, 96.

51. ELP to Daniel Horry, n.d. (probably 1785), in Ravenel, *Eliza Pinckney*, 307.

52. ELP to George Keate, April 2, 1786, in Ravenel, *Eliza Pinckney*, 313–14.

53. Williams, *A Founding Family*, 292–93.

54. CCP to TP, August 27, 1792, quoted in Zahniser, *Charles Cotesworth Pinckney*, 114 n. 27.

55. HPH journal, April 10, 1793–May 4, 1794, entries for Friday, April 19, and Thursday, May 9, 1793, 11/332B/13, HHR-SCHS.

56. HPH journal, April 10, 1793–May 4, 1794, entry for May 26, 1793 (mistakenly stated as June 10 in typescript), 11/332B/13, HHR-SCHS. See also Williams, *A Founding Family*, 447–48, and Ravenel, *Eliza Pinckney*, 316–17.

57. TP to HPH, July 9, 1793, 11/332, HHR-SCHS.

58. Ibid.

59. Pinckney, *Life of General Thomas Pinckney*, 97–147 and 151–81.

60. See for example Sarah E. Huger to HPH, March 17, 1812, and October 15, 1812, HHR-SCHS.

61. HPH journal, entry for September 2, 1815, HHR-SCHS.

62. Elias Bull, "Storm Towers of the Santee Delta," SCHM 81, no. 3 (1980): 95–101.

Rebecca Brewton Motte

Revolutionary South Carolinian

ALEXIA JONES HELSLEY

Rebecca Brewton Motte was a remarkable woman who lived at a remarkable time. Her life and sacrifices during the American Revolution were the stuff of legend. In the war for independence as in the Civil War, there was considerable suffering among civilians and much loss of property in South Carolina, but no other woman in the state's history is known to have willingly agreed to the burning of her own home to secure a victory for her cause.

Born in 1737 to a family of privilege and prominence, Rebecca Brewton married into another such family when she wed Jacob Motte Jr. in 1758. During the war, however, she lost both her husband and brother, and struggled to maintain her family and property on her own. By war's end she had suffered considerable losses both personal and material. Before her death in 1815 she managed to settle her debts and become a successful rice planter. Motte is best known for her wartime sacrifice. Yet her devotion to her family and her struggles as head of her household during the dark days of war had much in common with those of other elite white women in South Carolina who continued to carry out their pre-war responsibilities as wives and mothers while taking on many unfamiliar and unwanted duties.

On the eve of the American Revolution, elite women in South Carolina and the other colonies had many privileges and many duties but few rights. In South Carolina, a married woman, a *feme covert*, could not manage her property, engage in business, or write a will without her husband's consent. Under English common law as adopted in the colonies and the colony of South Carolina in particular, upon marriage a husband gained control of all real and personal property of his wife. A small percentage of women, often those from the planter and merchant classes, profited from prenuptial agreements. These marriage

REBECCA BREWTON MOTTE

From Elizabeth F. Ellet, *The Women of the American Revolution* (New York: Baker and Scribner, 1848).

settlements not only protected the woman's property from despoliation by her husband but also could specify the rights the woman would retain after marriage—such as the right to make a will or manage the property she owned at the time of the marriage. Generally, a widowed woman had more property rights and greater latitude in exercising them. But whether she was single, married, or widowed, a woman's life in colonial South Carolina, like that of most women in the thirteen colonies, was one of legal limitations and well defined social roles.[1] The family was the key component that determined and shaped colonial society. Within the family, a married woman occupied a "position of crucial significance."[2]

Like other wives and mothers, Rebecca Motte was responsible for rearing her children and for the smooth operation of her household. By 1780, the year her husband died and the British seized Charleston, she had her hands full with three young daughters and was concerned for their care, their education, and their marriage. As a widow she was also compelled to take responsibility for the management of her property and the settlement of her husband's estate—while at the epicenter of the Revolution in South Carolina.

Even before the war, South Carolina women faced uncertainties and dangers from the natural environment in which they lived. In the Lowcountry these included natural disasters such as hurricanes and floods, but perhaps nothing had a greater impact on their daily lives than disease. Colonists suffered particularly from insect-borne illnesses including yellow fever and malaria, from smallpox, and from cholera and similar illnesses bred by poor sanitation. Children died from measles, whooping cough, dysentery, tetanus, and a myriad of other childhood diseases. Women facing childbirth knew that there was always the chance that they and their babies would not survive.

The American Revolution brought still more uncertainty. The cauldron of revolution would challenge established roles and legal conventions and exacerbate the tensions of daily life. When the Declaration of Independence was signed in 1776, men and women living in the thirteen former British colonies had to make difficult choices between maintaining their allegiance to King George III and pursuing the dream of a new nation independent from Great Britain. The vicissitudes of war, uncertainties on the home front, and doubts about the ability of the new nation to survive led people to waver in their allegiances.

Initially, many Lowcountry planters pushed for independence. On the other hand, in the backcountry, loyalists such as Thomas Fletchall controlled the militia regiments. In December 1775, an early military expedition known as the Snow Campaign led by Colonel Richard Richardson and William Thomson brought an uneasy truce to the backcountry. However, with the fall of

Charleston to British forces in 1780, war engulfed South Carolina. Some former patriots shifted their allegiance from the patriot cause to the British, including Henry Middleton, Gabriel Manigault and Colonel Charles Pinckney (father of the Charles Pinckney who fought in the Revolution and was later governor of the state and a signer of the United States Constitution).[3] There were few places for the undecided to hide. Patriot and Tory militia in turn terrorized the countryside and preyed on farms and plantations including those managed by women like Rebecca Motte. Plantation agriculture was disrupted as hundreds of slaves sought freedom behind British lines. The British confiscated others from Lowcountry plantations, and still others were away providing support for the patriots' military undertakings.

British officers including Lieutenant Colonel Banastre Tarleton and Major James Wemyss harassed patriots, burned homes and dissenting churches, and raided farms and plantations for supplies. Tarleton earned particular opprobrium in Granville County by outfitting his dragoons with prized Lowcountry horses. Both Tarleton and Wemyss were regular British army officers who frequently fought with large numbers of ancillary Tory troops. The looting, burning, and persecution of noncombatants by British and Tory forces as well as patriot militia made the Revolution in South Carolina a bloody civil war. In places, the destruction was so widespread that there was neither food for the inhabitants nor fodder for their livestock. Neither side was blameless in this war of scorched earth and intimidation, but historian Walter Edgar has credited the policies of Charles, Lord Cornwallis, and the British occupying forces of 1780 with setting the tone for how the war in South Carolina was conducted.[4]

For the elite men who led the independence movement in South Carolina, the task of creating a new government and providing for the defense of a new state were challenging in the extreme. They agonized about these crucial decisions, argued among themselves, and grew weary of the seemingly endless conflict. Those who took up arms in defense of the state led demanding lives that necessitated long periods of time away from home. Communication was difficult even if the correspondents were literate, and most South Carolinians were not. The threat of disease, injury, and death mingled with the boredom of long periods of inactivity. The occupying British paroled many captured patriots but they imprisoned other patriot leaders and confiscated patriot property. And as the war dragged on, patriot leaders faced increased pressure to serve with the British despite initial reassurances that they would not have to. Many men died from wounds and disease and women on the home front faced new demands as they sought to play the three roles of wife, mother, and household mistress.[5]

Existing public records only hint at the role women played during the American Revolution, with the exception of the National Archives Revolutionary War pension applications and the accounts audited for Revolutionary service in South Carolina. The accounts audited, held by the South Carolina Department of Archives and History, document the activities of South Carolina women who furnished supplies to feed and clothe the state militia. Petitions to the South Carolina General Assembly also offer poignant tales of personal sacrifice and buried dreams of patriot and loyalist women. The story of the Revolution in South Carolina also includes many stories of heroic women who risked their lives to further the patriot cause, some of which live on mainly in family lore. Emily Geiger and Dicey Langston reputedly carried important messages for patriot commanders. Others endured British harassment and intimidation, notably Dorcas Richardson whose husband was serving with the American forces and trying to avoid capture. Mary Cantey Richardson is famous for refusing to reveal the hiding place of General Francis Marion, South Carolina's celebrated "Swamp Fox," even when British flogged her in a vain attempt to learn the whereabouts of the guerilla leader who harassed their supply trains.[6] But far more typical of South Carolina women were the women who, like Rebecca Motte, supported the war effort while remaining on the home front, coping with shortages and threats to home and family. Many elite South Carolina women managed households, farms, plantations, and businesses, their routines challenged by scarcity, enemy depredations, and a diminishing workforce.

Rebecca Brewton Motte, born June 15, 1737, lived a privileged life before the Revolution, growing up in Charleston. According to research by historian Mary Beth Norton, "City daughters from well-to-do homes were the only eighteenth-century American women who can accurately be described as leisured." Such women did not have to spin cloth or perform other domestic chores as did women in rural or less prosperous families. Wealthy homes had servants to assist mothers with managing their households. Elite young women were often educated and had the luxury of sleeping late, socializing with family and friends, and studying music.[7]

Rebecca was the daughter of Robert Brewton and Mary Griffith, his second wife. Robert Brewton (1698–1759) was the son of a Barbados goldsmith named Miles Brewton who immigrated to Charleston. Robert Brewton also worked as a goldsmith and served in the Commons House of Assembly, the elected house of South Carolina's colonial legislature. In addition, Brewton held a number of public offices. He served as powder receiver, churchwarden of St. Philip's Parish, commissioner of fortifications for Charleston, justice of the peace, and colonel in the Berkeley County Regiment of Militia. Brewton was a wealthy and influential leader in colonial affairs. His Charleston single house at 71 Church Street, built around 1730, is still standing.[8]

Prior to the American Revolution, Rebecca's brother, Miles Brewton, a merchant, was one of the wealthiest men in the province. Not only was Miles Brewton one of South Carolina's most important slave traders, but he also invested in ships and land. For example, he had an interest in eight sailing vessels. Among other properties, Brewton owned thousands of acres on the Congaree, Pacolet, and Savannah rivers. These lands included several plantations—Greenwich and Mount Joseph on the Congaree River and Marianna and Somerton on the Savannah River. Brewton also had extensive holdings on the Georgia side of the Savannah River, including Twickerham Plantation. His crowning jewel was an elegant town house constructed on King Street in Charleston in 1769 at an expense of 8,000 pounds sterling. In 1773 Josiah Quincey of Massachusetts dined with Brewton and commented on "the grandest hall I ever beheld."[9] An architectural historian termed the house, which still graces King Street in Charleston, "the finest townhouse of the Colonial period."[10] In addition, Brewton had an interest in cultural and educational matters. According to his will, if his children died, certain funds would be left to the College of Philadelphia, and he bequeathed 1,000 pounds sterling to support a similar institution in South Carolina.

Active in public affairs, Brewton served several terms in the Commons House of Assembly. When tensions with the British arose, risking his wealth and commercial connections and at great personal expense, Brewton supported the Non-Importation Association, an organization that protested the Townshend duties by refusing to import enumerated goods. He also served in the first provincial congress and on the Council of Safety. Elected to the second provincial congress, Miles Brewton's promising career ended abruptly. On August 24, 1775, Brewton and his family perished as they sailed from Charleston to Philadelphia. Fearing the outbreak of armed hostilities, Miles was trying to take his family to safety but all were lost at sea.[11] At Brewton's death, his wealth and properties passed to his surviving family including his sisters Frances Brewton Pinckney, the wife of Charles Pinckney (president of the provincial congress), and Rebecca Brewton Motte. Rebecca inherited Mount Joseph, a thirteen-hundred-acre plantation, and the Miles Brewton town house on King Street in Charleston.

In 1758 Rebecca Brewton married Jacob Motte Jr. (1729–80) in a match that strengthened the financial standing of both families. Jacob was the son of Jacob Motte and his first wife, Elizabeth Martin. Jacob Motte Sr. was treasurer of South Carolina and a business partner of James Laurens.[12] Prior to their marriage, the senior Jacob Motte executed a four-part agreement conveying to trustees for the benefit of Rebecca Brewton upon her marriage with Jacob Motte Jr. a low water lot with a wharf or bridge on the Cooper River with "houses, outhouses, stores, warehouses, scale houses[,] . . . privileges, fees, Wharfages, Customs, Tolls." Rebecca and Jacob had the use and benefit of the property during their marriage; after their deaths, the property would pass to their heirs. The agreement also mentioned that this transaction was in addition to whatever property Robert Brewton settled on Jacob Motte Jr. at the time of the marriage. The four parties to the agreement were Jacob Motte Sr., Robert Brewton, Rebecca Brewton, and Jacob Motte Jr. The two trustees were Miles Brewton and Benjamin Smith.[13]

Jacob Motte Jr. began his political career in 1761. That year, voters in St. Marks Parish chose him to represent them in the Commons House of Assembly. He served in several sessions of the Commons House and the first, second, and third general assemblies of the newly independent state of South Carolina. Between his wife Rebecca's inheritances from her father and brother and what he had inherited from his father, Jacob Motte was able to become a successful planter. At his death, he owned over two hundred slaves.

Jacob and Rebecca Motte had a number of children, but only three daughters lived to maturity—Elizabeth (1762–94), who married Thomas Pinckney; Frances (1763–1843), who married John Middleton and, after his death, married her late sister's widower, Thomas Pinckney; and Mary (born c. 1768), who became the second wife of William Alston who had extensive holdings on the Waccamaw River.

Like many in South Carolina, Rebecca and her husband supported the patriot cause. Prior to his death in 1780, Jacob Motte Jr. furnished pork, beef, rice, and corn to the troops. Jacob, and later, Rebecca provided supplies for Continental and militia forces under such prominent South Carolina military leaders as General Thomas Sumter, General Andrew Pickens, and Colonel Richard Winn. At the end of the war, the state of South Carolina appropriated over 600 pounds to settle accounts with Jacob and Rebecca Motte.[14]

Jacob Motte Jr. died in January 1780. Within a few months Charleston fell to the British who occupied the city. The British occupation of Charleston was a major setback for the patriot cause. On May 12, 1780, Major General Benjamin Lincoln, commander of the American forces in the South, surrendered not only the city of Charleston but also the major patriot forces in the South—6,684 men. The British made Lincoln and his Continental troops prisoners of war. However, most of the American troops were exchanged within a few months. Many of the militia who surrendered eventually took British parole. In time, the British would imprison a number of patriot leaders in the basement of the Exchange Building and in St. Augustine, Florida.[15]

To her dismay, the British occupation brought Rebecca Motte unwanted houseguests as Sir Henry Clinton, the British commander, chose the handsome home she had inherited from her brother as his headquarters. The house was close to the water and easily the most imposing home in Charleston. As a result, the recently widowed Motte was gently pressed into service as the unwilling hostess of the British high command. South Carolina patriot General William Moultrie remembered being received by Sir Henry Clinton "at Mrs. Motte's house in the drawing room upstairs."[16] The drawing room was significant because here Lord Rawdon, the supreme British commander in South Carolina, refused to grant clemency for Colonel Isaac Hayne, who was hanged to deter other paroled South Carolinians from taking up arms against the British. It had the opposite effect, however. The death of Hayne became a rallying cry as South Carolinians refocused their efforts to drive the British from their borders.

Rebecca Motte, now in her forties and the mother of three, found herself in a difficult situation. She and her family remained in the house after the British occupation. Neither Clinton nor his successor Lord Rawdon ejected her from the property. Rather, they "requested" that she stay and generally considered themselves her "guests." Rebecca Motte understood the polite fiction and the subtle ironies of her predicament. So, she dined with them and played well her role as hostess. Her uninvited guests complimented her on her management of the household and her gracious demeanor. She had mastered the skills society expected of her. Yet, she "kept her three pretty daughters" (Elizabeth, Frances, and Mary—now ages eighteen, seventeen, and twelve) safely secured in the attic of the house. She did not trust them to the society of the British officers. The story is told that when Rawdon finally agreed to let Motte and her family leave the city for her country house, Rawdon thanked her for her hospitality and lamented that "he had not been permitted to make the acquaintance of her family."[17]

The oldest of the daughters, Elizabeth, was by that time a married woman and expecting her first child, a situation that added to her mother's concerns during the occupation. On July 22, 1779, Elizabeth had married Major Thomas Pinckney (1750–1828) of the First South Carolina Continental Regiment. (The younger daughters did not marry until after the British evacuated Charleston.) At the time of their wedding, Thomas Pinckney was twelve years older than his not quite seventeen-year-old bride. According to family correspondence, he had been interested in Elizabeth, "the adorable Miss Betsey," since 1775. In 1778 he had written his sister, Harriott Pinckney Horry, that "If Chance should throw my Charmer in your way I charge you make strong Love for me." In Charleston for a meeting of the general assembly, Pinckney pushed for the wedding despite his military responsibilities, the war with Great Britain, and the uncertainties of life in South Carolina. The families of the bride and groom approved the match. The marriage of Thomas Pinckney and Elizabeth Motte cemented connections between two of South Carolina's leading patriot families. Elizabeth's paternal grandparents, the Jacob Mottes Sr., had been close friends of Thomas's parents, Charles and Eliza Lucas Pinckney. Charles Pinckney, father of Thomas, had even died in the Motte's home at Mount Pleasant. Also, Rebecca Motte's sister Frances had married another Charles Pinckney. Frances and Charles Pinckney were the parents of a number of children, including yet another Charles Pinckney who earned the sobriquet "Constitution Charlie" as one of South Carolina's delegates to the Constitutional Convention.[18]

Though placed in the awkward situation of hosting British officers, Rebecca Motte and her daughters were at least spared one humiliation when General Lincoln surrendered Charleston to the British. Major Thomas Pinckney was not part of the surrender. A short time before that fateful day, Lincoln had dispatched Pinckney out of the city with information for Governor John Rutledge and then directed him to facilitate the arrival of expected reinforcements from North Carolina and Virginia. Rutledge and other South Carolina state leaders had left Charleston as the military situation deteriorated. When Pinckney heard the news of the surrender, he escaped to the North, hoping to offer his services to George Washington.[19] Understandably, the pregnant Elizabeth Pinckney preferred to remain in Charleston with her mother. It was a number of months before Elizabeth saw her husband again.

Thus, within a few months, Rebecca Motte — despite her family connections and great fortune — found herself a refugee with several younger women to maintain and protect. When Lord Rawdon allowed her to leave Charleston, Rebecca moved her family to Mount Joseph, her plantation in Orangeburg District that she had inherited from her brother Miles Brewton. At Mount Joseph, she oversaw a household that included her three daughters and her nephew's widow, Mary Weyman Brewton. Mary's husband, John, a captain of the Charleston militia, had died in 1777.[20]

Unfortunately Rebecca soon found that the British were again interested in her property. Mount Joseph, Rebecca Motte's country home, sat "on a commanding hill" near the junction of the Wateree and Congaree rivers that forms the Santee River. The site overlooked McCord's Ferry, an important crossing of the Congaree River. This property had great strategic value for both British and patriot forces as it sat astride the principal British supply route that ran from Charleston to Camden.[21] At some point during their occupation of the interior of South Carolina, the British fortified Mount Joseph.

The British erected a stockade around her "new and spacious mansion" on Buckhead Hill, converting Mount Joseph into "Fort Motte," "one of the links in the chain of fortified posts" the British established in an attempt to secure control of the hinterlands of South Carolina and protect communication and supply routes. The British built the fortification by digging a deep trench, or "fosse," around the property and erecting a "strong and lofty parapet" along the inside rim of the trench. Lieutenant Donald McPherson of DeLancey's Corps commanded a garrison of 155 men at Fort Motte. Once British troops had fortified the property, Rebecca again found herself unwillingly sharing her new house with the enemy—a house that, ironically, she may have modeled after the Miles Brewton town house in Charleston.[22]

These were trying times indeed for Motte and her household but they were not the only ones struggling with the effects of the war. A letter written by Eliza Lucas Pinckney, mother of Rebecca Motte's son-in-law, captured the altered conditions under which elite South Carolina women lived and the particular challenges they faced, their once comfortable lives now disrupted by war. Pinckney wrote an acquaintance in England:

> I have been rob[b]ed and deserted by my Slaves; my property pulled to pieces, burnt and destroyed; my money of no value, my Children sick and prisoners.
>
> Such is the deplorable state of our Country from two armies being in it for near two years; the plantations have some quite, some nearly, ruined—and all with very few exceptions—their Crops, stock, boats, Carts gone, taken or destroyed.[23]

A letter from Elizabeth Motte Pinckney to her mother-in-law suggested other concerns as well. She reported the specter of smallpox rampant in the neighborhood and mentioned the difficulty of keeping and feeding livestock with the British in the area.[24]

In August 1780, still at Fort Motte, Elizabeth, gave birth to a son named Thomas. A few weeks later, on August 16, the baby's father, Major Thomas Pinckney, was critically wounded at the Battle of Camden and captured by the British. Pinckney's leg was shattered and amputation was a serious threat. His survival was in doubt. At this point, a series of unforeseen circumstances conspired not only to save Pinckney's life and his leg but also to reunite him with his wife and infant son.

Captain Charles Barrington McKenzie, a British officer with the Seventy-first Regiment, had attended Westminster School in England with Thomas Pinckney. McKenzie found the wounded Pinckney and intervened to save his life. He had Pinckney transported to Camden to the home of Ann Clay who "had been ordered by the British to take wounded into her house." McKenzie also arranged with Lieutenant Colonel Banastre Tarleton of the British Legion to send a British regimental surgeon to examine Pinckney.[25] According to Pinckney's grandson, Tarleton not only allowed medical care for Pinckney but even "offered to restore Mrs. Motte's horses, four fine bays that he had impressed from her stables."[26]

Pinckney survived the compound fracture of his leg, but endured a long and painful convalescence. On August 18, 1780, he wrote General Horatio Gates that his injury was "in the same part of the Leg in which Genl Lincoln receivd his; & tho' the bone is entirely shattered, I have hopes of retaining my Leg." On August 24, he again wrote Gates, informing the general that his "treatment has been humane, Politic & attentive from the British officers into whose Hands I have fallen."[27]

Pinckney's good care continued, and in September he learned from Major John Money, aide-de-camp to Cornwallis, that Cornwallis had approved his request to continue his recuperation at the Motte home at Fort Motte. Despite Cornwallis's approval, the move was difficult to orchestrate. Pinckney had to locate his clothes, papers, and other belongings, and the Mottes had to arrange transportation. As a result, his move to Fort Motte did not occur until October. Mrs. Robert Brewton, a relative of the Mottes, traveled to Camden and brought Pinckney to Fort Motte in a "springless cart."[28] Given the condition of his leg, Pinckney must have endured excruciating pain.

Once at Fort Motte, Pinckney's recovery proceeded slowly and there were new challenges for Rebecca Motte. Not only did she have the care of her wounded son-in-law, but smallpox afflicted Elizabeth and her infant son. By October 26 Pinckney wrote his nephew, Daniel Horry, "Your aunt has got rid of her Fever, tho' she is still so week that she fainted two days ago in extracting a small Piece of bone from the wound in my Leg; as she has been for a Fortnight past my only Surgeon."[29] Pieces of bone continued to work out of the damaged leg for months. In time, Rebecca's nursing skills paid off and Pinckney recovered sufficiently to join a group of captured American officers the British sent to Philadelphia to await exchange. His wife and infant son joined him there. After he was exchanged, Pinckney met the Marquis de Lafayette in 1781 while recruiting in Virginia. Later, he served with Lafayette at Yorktown.

With Thomas Pinckney and his family gone, the Motte household was smaller and quieter. Rebecca Motte continued to coexist with her British "guests" at Fort Motte. The British permitted Motte and her family to live in the main dwelling house. However, in 1781, General Nathanael Greene, a Rhode Island Quaker who was now in charge of the Continental Army in the South, dispatched Lieutenant Colonel Henry to work with General Francis Marion to harass enemy supply lines and take Fort Motte. In light of the pending conflict, in early May 1781 the British moved Motte to her "overseer's residence."[30] Other accounts simply referred to the building as an "old farmhouse."

On May 8, 1781, patriot troops commanded by Brigadier General Francis Marion and Lieutenant Colonel Henry "Lighthorse Harry" Lee surrounded Fort Motte. Marion was a South Carolina partisan leader feared by the British for his guerilla tactics. Lee, a Virginian, was a member of the Continental Army whose success in raiding enemy supply trains gained the attention and admiration of General George Washington, commander in chief of the American forces.

Shortly before the patriots deployed their forces, Captain Neil Campbell reached the fort with a British supply convoy. Lee and his troops camped on a hill north of Fort Motte—the site of the overseer's house inhabited by Rebecca Motte and her family. Marion and his patriots camped on the eastern side of Buckhead Hill—the site of Fort Motte. Marion and Lee moved swiftly to prevent the convoy from leaving or the British troops from escaping. General Greene had detailed Major Eaton with cannon to shore up the American position at Fort Motte. Marion then constructed a mound possibly fifteen feet tall and positioned the cannon so that its fire would rake the northern face of the British parapet. On May 8, they began firing on the fort.

With their prey hemmed in, Marion and Lee planned to dig siege lines and attack the fort from the front under cover of their trenches. The valley between the two hills enabled American troops to approach within four hundred yards of Fort Motte. On May 10, having begun operations, the American commanders asked the British to surrender. McPherson refused to consider surrender. So, Marion and Lee planned an extended trench assault and devoted three days to digging approach trenches.

External forces conspired to abort these plans. Marion and Lee received intelligence that Lord Rawdon and his forces were on the Nelson's Ferry Road, east of the Wateree River. Rawdon and his men were retreating from Camden, South Carolina. According to William Dobein James, "On the night of the 10th, the defenders of Fort Motte could see the fires of lord Rawdon's camp on the Santee hills." With the possibility of reinforcements in the area, a speedy end to the siege was essential. Consequently, Marion and Lee conferred and determined that the only way to force the British troops from the fort was to set fire to Rebecca's recently constructed Motte mansion that sat in the center of the fortifications.

Marion and Lee knew the loyalty of Rebecca Motte, the patriotic work of her deceased husband, and the valor of her son-in-law, then a British captive. Knowing the hardships Rebecca had already faced, the decision to set fire to her home was a difficult one. Lee "had daily experienced her liberal hospitality," which she extended not only to him and his officers but also to the wounded and sick. In his memoirs, Lee fondly remembered the "antiquated relics of happier days"—Rebecca Motte's sideboard with the "best wines of Europe." The decision reached, the commanders were reluctant to tell her about their plans.[31]

Rebecca Motte surprised them. With "a smile of complacency," Motte replied to their suggestion "that she was gratified with the opportunity of contributing to the good of her country, and that she should view the approaching scene with delight."[32] Motte's demeanor never wavered. Her reported actions reflect a determined, competent, and coolheaded woman. Rebecca Motte also gave Marion and Lee combustible arrows reputedly imported from India and given to her by her brother Miles Brewton.

On May 12 the patriot forces had trenched within firing range of the Motte house. Marion again sent a flag to McPherson informing him of the plans to fire the house and offering him and his men a chance to avoid the conflagration. McPherson again adamantly refused. Then, at about noon, according to family sources and Lee's memoirs, patriot soldiers fired the combustible arrows from rifles, not bows. Two ignited. A biography of Marion recounted that one of Marion's men, Nathan Savage, used a ball of rosin and brimstone to set the roof on fire. As British soldiers climbed on the roof to extinguish the flames, the fire of American sharpshooters and the cannon drove them back into the house. In short order, McPherson hung out a white flag and surrendered. Rawdon reported that the fire "obliged his men to throw themselves into the ditch and surrender at discretion." McPherson's force included 135 regular army and 45 militia troops. The patriots had captured not only the strategically important Fort Motte but also the British supply convoy and a carronade. The American forces under Brigadier General Francis Marion numbered 591.

With the fighting behind them, the soldiers from both sides joined in a successful effort to save the Motte house, although ironically the house burned a number of years later. With the Americans in control, Rebecca Motte later hosted a "sumptuous" dinner for the American and British officers. Her demeanor during the meal particularly impressed Lee. He marveled at the "ease, vivacity, and good sense" she exhibited. However, all was not well between the victorious Americans and the captured British. Americans, according to one report, hanged two of the captured men who were loyalists from Rebecca Motte's gate. Francis Marion, however, intervened to save a third man, a local loyalist named Levi Smith from a similar fate. That evening, Marion paroled the British soldiers and allowed them to return to Charleston. Not long afterward, Greene, eager for news of the siege and information about the location of Rawdon, arrived with a detachment of cavalry. As the siege had been "prosperously" concluded, he detailed Marion and Lee to other South Carolina locations.[33]

The capture of Fort Motte was a major coup for American forces in South Carolina. Not only did the Americans begin to seize control of the interior of South Carolina but British fortunes in the state as a whole took a turn for the worst. The same day that Fort Motte surrendered, General Thomas Sumter captured the British fortification at Orangeburg and on May 15, he took Fort Granby. Key British positions were then in American hands.[34]

Despite her personal bravery and contribution to the patriot victory, Rebecca Motte faced hard economic facts in the postwar years. The departure of many slaves decimated her workforce and her assets were depleted. According to some accounts, her husband had stood surety for the debts of others, and Motte resolved to honor the debts even at the cost of her own property.[35] Rebecca Motte worked to settle her debts and build a new life in postwar South Carolina. In June 1784 she purchased four hundred acres on the Santee River at a cost of 150 pounds sterling. At the age of forty-seven, Rebecca Motte embarked on new enterprise in the parish of St. James Santee. She named her new plantation Eldorado and became a successful small rice planter. Her property adjoined two tracts of land acquired by her son-in-law John Middleton.[36]

According to records of the Court of Common Pleas of Charleston District, Motte was the defendant in a number of debt cases between 1781 and 1814. Several cases involved two lots of bricks purchased by Motte in 1788. The court found for the plaintiffs and Motte eventually satisfied those creditors. Another case was more complicated. This case concerned Mary Drayton's interest in the estate of Jacob Motte Sr. and Rebecca Motte's efforts as the executor/administrator of the estate of Jacob Motte Jr. At the request of William Drayton, Jacob Motte Jr. had signed as a surety for a joint bond between William Drayton, William Henry Drayton, and Benjamin Smith in 1765. The court rendered a judgment in the case June 11, 1814. This judgment probably was one of the debts that Motte specified should be paid from her estate.[37]

On a personal level, Rebecca faced more tragedy. Her eldest daughter Elizabeth, the wife of Thomas Pinckney, died in England in 1794. Thomas had been elected governor of South Carolina in 1787, and in 1791 President George Washington appointed him minister to the Court of St. James. The appointment was confirmed in January 1792 and Pinckney took his family to Great Britain. There Elizabeth died at the age of thirty-two. On October 23, 1797, Pinckney married Frances, the middle Motte daughter, becoming a double son-in-law to Rebecca Motte.[38] Rebecca's youngest daughter, Mary, became the second wife of Colonel William Alston, a veteran of the Revolutionary War. Alston was also a highly successful Waccamaw rice planter who owned three hundred slaves and over twenty-six thousand acres.[39] During George Washington's trip through South Carolina in 1791, Mary Alston entertained the new country's first president. Washington arrived at Clifton, the Alston estate, on April 29, 1791, which he described as "large" and "elegantly furnished."[40]

Rebecca Motte lived a long and productive life. According to the 1790 census, she lived in St. James Santee Parish, probably on her Eldorado plantation, with seventy-one slaves.[41] In 1800 the number of her slave workers had increased to eighty-two. By 1810, her household included a white male between twenty-six and forty-four years of age, possibly an overseer.[42] Rebecca Motte died at Eldorado on January 12, 1815. Her will mentioned her two remaining daughters—Frances Motte Middleton Pinckney and Mary Motte Alston. Her son-in-law Thomas Pinckney qualified as the executor. She left Eldorado to Frances and Thomas Pinckney. Ever the woman of business, her will specified that the slave workforce should be kept intact until after the crop was harvested. Rebecca Mott was a woman of her times. Her will included no touching manumission of favorite slaves. She was a successful plantation owner with no apparent questions about the slave system so essential to profitable harvests.

At her death Rebecca Motte was again a wealthy woman. The inventory and appraisement of her estate dated July 1, 1816, indicated that she cultivated rice at Eldorado; owned a large slave workforce that included field-workers, house servants, and craftsmen such as carpenters and a blacksmith and few livestock (hogs and a mule); and had furnished her home with mahogany furniture. Her wine closet held four dozen bottles of Madeira. The inventory showed a large, well-appointed house with a hall, parlor, four chambers, two dressing rooms, two passages, a library, housekeeper's room, pantry, nursery, linen closet, wine closet, and kitchen.[43]

The story of Rebecca Motte and her act of patriotism has been told and retold, though few textbooks include an account of it. In 1852 Elizabeth Ellett asked the South Carolina legislature to support the publication of her "domestic history," as she wanted the state's school children to know more about the war in the South Carolina including the heroism and sacrifices of women like Rebecca Motte.[44] One group that remembered Motte and her actions was the Rebecca Motte Chapter, National Society Daughters of the American Revolution. In 1903, this chapter honored Rebecca Motte by erecting a tablet in her memory in the vestibule of St. Philip's Church in Charleston.[45]

Rebecca Motte certainly deserves recognition as a patriot of the American Revolution. She and her family contributed to the Revolution in even more ways than the story of Fort Motte indicates. She and her husband supported the war financially. Their daughters all married veterans who actively supported and fought for American independence. Rebecca maintained her dignity through trying times and proved her competence as wife, mother, and household man- ager, as did many women of her time and place. She protected her children and provided a refuge for other family members including her critically wounded son-in-law. Working within the confines of occupation, depleted resources, and enemy depredations, she maintained her equilibrium. And then, at the crucial moment, she was willing to sacrifice her home to further the cause of American independence.

Rebecca Brewton Motte's story is unique in its public nature. Few South Carolina women have left such a documented history of their wartime sacrifice and heroic acts. Yet her story is indicative of the experiences of many women of the plantation class as well as a reminder that the American Revolution took a tremendous toll in the state of South Carolina in human and economic terms. Motte's story also demonstrates dramatically that privilege did not ward off ad- versity and that gender did not preclude patriotism.

NOTES

1. For a more detailed discussion of women's property rights and the use of marriage settlements in South Carolina, please see Marylynn Salmon, "Women and Property in South Carolina: The Evi- dence from Marriage Settlements, 1730–1830," in *Women's America: Refocusing the Past*, ed. Linda K. Kerber and Jane Sherron De Hart, 3rd ed. (New York: Oxford University Press, 1991), 74–84.

2. Mary Beth Norton, "Eighteenth-Century American Women in Peace and War: The Case of the Loyalists," in *A Heritage of Her Own: Toward a New Social History of American Women*, ed. Nancy F. Cott and Elizabeth Hafkin Pleck (New York: Simon and Schuster, 1979), 136.

3. Walter J. Fraser Jr., *Patriots, Pistols and Petticoats: "Poor Sinful Charles Town" during the Ameri- can Revolution*, 2nd rev. ed. (Columbia: University of South Carolina Press, 1993), 134.

4. Walter Edgar, *Partisans and Redcoats: The Southern Conflict That Turned the Tide of the Amer- ican Revolution* (New York: William Morrow, 2001), 136.

5. Linda K. Kerber, *Women of the Republic: Intellect and Ideology in Revolutionary America* (Cha- pel Hill: University of North Carolina Press for the Institute of Early American History and Culture, Williamsburg, Va., 1980), xv.

6. Edgar, *Partisans and Redcoats*, 134; South Carolina recognized the needs of some of the many women widowed during the war and granted them pensions. Other women would eventually col- lect federal pensions, but for many, life was a lonely daily struggle without male breadwinners or federal or state assistance.

7. Mary Beth Norton, *Liberty's Daughters: The Revolutionary Experience of American Women, 1750–1800* (Ithaca, N.Y.: Cornell University Press, 1996), 23.

8. Walter B. Edgar and N. Louise Bailey, *The Commons House of Assembly, 1692–1775*, vol. 2 of *Biographical Directory of the South Carolina House of Representatives*, ed. Walter B. Edgar (Colum- bia: University of South Carolina Press, 1977), 98.

9. Ibid., 95–97; George C. Rogers, *Charleston in the Age of the Pinckneys* (Norman: University of Oklahoma Press, 1969), 70.

10. Thomas T. Waterman, *The Dwellings of Colonial America* (Chapel Hill: University of North Carolina Press, 1950), 81–85.

11. *The Commons House of Assembly, 1692–1775*, 95–97.

12. South Carolina Wills, book RR, 1767–71, 468–74. South Carolina Department of Archives and History (hereinafter cited as SCDAH).

13. South Carolina Deeds, book 3–E, 391–93. SCDAH.

14. Alexia Jones Helsley, *South Carolinians in the War for American Independence* (Columbia: South Carolina Department of Archives and History, 2000), 65; "Col. Miles Brewton and Some of His Descendants," *South Carolina Historical and Genealogical Magazine* 2, no. 2 (1901): 151.

15. Helsley, *South Carolinians in the War for American Independence*, 17–18, 87.

16. Harriette Kershaw Leiding, *Historic Houses of South Carolina* (Philadelphia: J. B. Lippincott, 1921), 6.

17. Harriott Horry Rutledge Ravenel, *Charleston: The Place and the People* (New York: Macmillan, 1912), 276; Leiding, 5–6.

18. Frances Leigh Williams, *A Founding Family: The Pinckneys of South Carolina* (New York: Harcourt Brace Jovanovich, 1978), 115–16, 136–37; "Col. Miles Brewton and Some of His Descendants," 144–45.

19. Charles Cotesworth Pinckney, *Life of General Thomas Pinckney* (Boston: Houghton, Mifflin, 1895), 73.

20. "Col. Miles Brewton and Some of His Descendants," 152.

21. Helsley, *South Carolinians in the War for American Independence*, 65; Pinckney, *Life of General Thomas Pinckney*, 81.

22. Terry W. Lipscomb, "South Carolina Revolutionary Battles—Part Six," *Names in South Carolina* XXV: 28-29.

23. *The Letterbook of Eliza Lucas Pinckney, 1735–1762*, ed. Elise Pinckney (Chapel Hill: University of North Carolina Press, 1972), xxiii–xxiv.

24. Williams, *A Founding Family*, 160.

25. Ibid., 168.

26. Pinckney, *Life of General Thomas Pinckney*, 80.

27. Walter Clark, ed., *The State Records of North Carolina*, 26 vols. (Goldsboro, N.C.: Nash Brothers, 1886–1907), 14:560, 575.

28. Williams, *A Founding Family*, 170.

29. Ibid., 170–71.

30. Pinckney, *Life of General Thomas Pinckney*, 81.

31. Henry Lee, *Memoirs of the War in the Southern Department of the United States* (1812; rpt., New York: New York Times, 1969), 345–49; *The Papers of Nathanael Greene*, ed. Richard Showman et al., 13 vols. (Chapel Hill: University of North Carolina Press for the Rhode Island Historical Society, 1972–2005), 8:68, 246, 252–53; Lipscomb, "South Carolina Revolutionary Battles," 28–29; William D. James, *A Sketch of the Life of Brig. Gen. Francis Marion* (Marietta, Ga.: Continental Book Company, 1948), 120–21; Charles B. Baxley, "The Siege of Fort Motte, May 8–12, 1781," *Southern Campaigns of the American Revolution* 2, no. 4 (2005), 15–21; "Lord Rawdon to Earl Cornwallis," May 24, 1781, in *Documentary History of the American Revolution*, ed. R. W. Gibbes, 3 vols. (New York: Appleton, 1853), 3:77–80; National Register Files, SCDAH; Levi Smith, "To the Printers of the Royal Gazette," *Royal Gazette* (Charlestown), April 13–17, 1782.

32. Smith, "To the Printers of the Royal Gazette."

33. Ibid.

34. Baxley, "The Siege of Fort Motte," 16.

35. Elizabeth F. Ellett, *The Women of the American Revolution*, 3 vols. (1848–50; rpt., Williamstown, Mass.: Corner House Publishers, 1980), 2:74–75.

36. Charleston District, Register of Mesne Conveyance, deeds, book K-5, 358–64; deeds, book L-5, 261–70, SCDAH).

37. For an overview of Motte's legal difficulties, see Charleston District, Court of Common Pleas, judgment rolls, 1791, nos. 444A and 445A; 1801, nos. 364A and 365A; 1803 no. 461A; 1814 no. 280A, SCDAH.

38. Mabel L. Webber, "The Thomas Pinckney Family of South Carolina," in *South Carolina Genealogies: Articles from the South Carolina Historical (and Genealogical) Magazine*, 5 vols. (Spartanburg, S. C.: Reprint Company, 1983), 3:299–300.

39. "Col. Miles Brewton and Some of His Descendants," 144–45; Ravenel, *Charleston*, 354.

40. Terry W. Lipscomb, *South Carolina in 1791: George Washington's Southern Tour* (Columbia: South Carolina Department of Archives and History, 1993), 10–11.

41. U.S. Department of Commerce and Labor, Bureau of the Census, *Heads of Families at the First Census of the United States Taken in the Year 1790* (Washington, D.C.: U.S. Government Printing Office, 1908), 37.

42. U.S. Department of Commerce and Labor, Bureau of the Census, *1800 Population Schedule, St. James Santee, Charleston District*, National Archives Microcopy M32 roll 48, p. 51; *1810 Population Schedule, St. James Santee, Charleston District, South Carolina,* National Archives Microcopy M252, roll 60, p. 447.

43. Charleston District, South Carolina Wills, book E, 1807–18, 524–26, SCDAH; Charleston District, South Carolina inventories of estates, book E, 1807–19, 323–25, SCDAH.

44. State of South Carolina, Records of the General Assembly, petitions, 1852, no. 39. SCDAH.

45. Leiding, *Historic Houses*, 6; *Tablet to Mrs. Rebecca Motte Erected by Rebecca Motte Chapter of the Daughters of the American Revolution Ceremony of Unveiling at St. Philips Church, Charleston, S.C. May 9th, 1903* (Charleston, S.C.: Daggett Printing Co., 1903).

Dolly, Lavinia, Maria, and Susan

Enslaved Women in Antebellum South Carolina

EMILY WEST

It is difficult to piece together the stories of Dolly, Maria, Lavinia, and Susan and the enslaved women of South Carolina, whose lives and times they represent. Evidence about the lives of female slaves in the American South is scarce, and for women enslaved in South Carolina there exist no published autobiographies such as the now famous one written by Harriet Jacobs, a slave in Edenton, North Carolina.[1] Source materials left by white slave owners, male and female, including advertisements they placed in attempts to recapture runaway slaves and their correspondence with one another, reveal a lot about the lives of the women they held in bondage. They do not, however, convey the perspectives of enslaved women themselves. Fortunately sentiments of the latter can be found within the testimony ex-slaves gave to Works Progress Administration (WPA) interviewers in the 1930s and in the rare letters of South Carolina enslaved women who were literate and corresponded with their owners. Thus historians of women slaves in South Carolina must draw from a variety of different primary sources. From bits of evidence offering "snapshots" of female slaves' lives at particular points in time, broader life experiences can be teased out and the evidence used to make suggestions about the life cycles and typical experiences of enslaved women within the state.

One unusual piece of evidence is the notice that Louis Manigault penned in April 1863 about his runaway female slave, Dolly, for the Charleston police station. It was unusual for runaway slave advertisements in that it included an image of Dolly at a time when the enslaved were rarely photographed. Manigault appears to have cut out Dolly's image from a photograph and pasted it onto

When Received.	Conveyance.	No. of bush. Rough Rice.	No. of bbls. Clean Rice.	No. of bus. to the bbl.	Price.	Date of Sales.	Gross Amount of Sales.	Nett Amount of Sales.

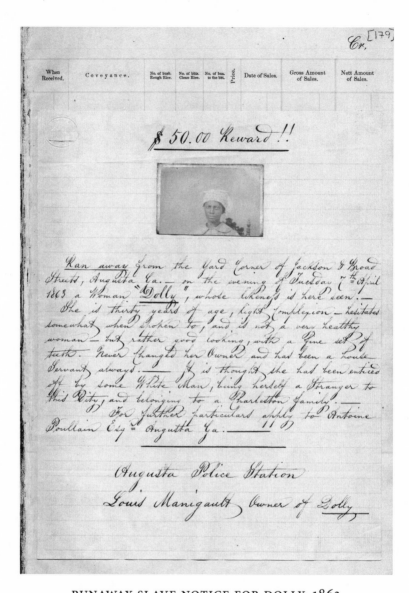

$ 50.00 Reward !!

Ran away from the Yard Corner of Jackson & Broad Streets, Augusta Ga. — on the evening of Tuesday 7th April 1863 a Woman "Dolly", whose likeness is here seen. — She is thirty years of age, light complexion — hesitates somewhat when spoken to, and is not a very healthy woman — but rather good looking, with a fine set of teeth. Never changed her Owner and has been a house Servant always. — It is thought she has been enticed off by some White Man, being herself a stranger to this City, and belonging to a Charleston family. — For further particulars apply to Antoine Poullain Esq. Augusta Ga. — " "

Augusta Police Station

Louis Manigault, Owner of Dolly

RUNAWAY SLAVE NOTICE FOR DOLLY, 1863

Courtesy of the Southern Historical Collection, Manuscripts Collection,
Wilson Library, University of North Carolina, Chapel Hill.

the advertisement. As often happened, Manigault offered money—"fifty dollars reward!!"—for the return of his slave, who was described as follows:

> She is thirty years of age, of small size, light complexion, hesitates somewhat when spoken to, and is not a very healthy woman, but rather good looking with a fine set of teeth. . . . Never changed her owner, has been always a house servant, and no fault ever having been found with her. It is thought she has been enticed off by some white man and likely has gone towards Charleston, South Carolina, to which place she belongs.[2]

Manigault's speculation about Dolly's motives is interesting, as it denies her own volition or agency and instead suggests she was enticed away. Just as likely, however, is that her unhappiness at the failure of her marriage to another Manigault slave named Hector who lived and worked on another of Manigault's plantations led her to flee. Dolly resided at Gowrie, a large rice plantation on Argyle Island on the Savannah River, where she lived and worked in the Big House as a cook and washer to the Manigault family. Hector was a field hand at East Hermitage, an adjacent plantation.[3] Dolly and Hector may have split up for any number of reasons, but it would not have helped their relationship that they were forced to spend much of their time apart in a marriage that crossed plantations.

Marriage among the enslaved of the antebellum South was, of course, not legally recognized. Nonetheless, it was the custom for slaves to choose a partner, to undergo some sort of ceremony, and to thereafter regard themselves as partners in wedlock. They also strove to marry someone of their own choosing regardless of ownership or place of residence. Bondage rendered matrimony for purposes of wealth or status moot for the enslaved, so their marriages were instead based upon companionship, attraction, love and affection. Thus in a sense slaves pioneered in the concept of marriages based on romantic love, which differentiated their own unions from those of some nineteenth-century white Americans and of those in precolonial West Africa.[4] Further, the high incidence of marriages that crossed plantations, in which slaves received none of the benefits from owners that they would receive if they married a slave on the same plantation (such as better quality housing, a small patch of land or garden, and improved rations), suggests that the enslaved were marrying for love, not practical gain.

For slaveholders, the benefits of encouraging wedlock were obvious—happy and contented slaves made better workers and were more likely to reproduce. Yet, the lack of a legal infrastructure also absolved owners of any responsibility for the maintenance of enslaved marriages. Because their marriages were not recognized by law, owners could separate married slave couples through sale without ramifications. Owners did not, then, take enslaved marriages as seriously as those of whites.

Because of the incentives for owners, this more informal, flexible system of wedlock mostly permitted the enslaved a good deal of choice in their marriage partners. House servants, for example, were allowed to "marry" field hands. Testimony from South Carolina ex-slaves interviewed by the WPA suggests that house servants marrying field hands was common, despite the claims of one respondent, Rosa Starke, of Winnsboro, who professed to believe that "a house nigger man might swoop down and mate wid a field hand's good lookin' daughter, now and then, for pure love of her, but you never see a house gal lower herself by marryin' and matin' wid a common field-hand nigger. Dat offend de white folks, 'specially de young misses, who liked de business of match makin' and matin' of de young slaves."[5] Starke's insistence that the enslaved tended not to marry those from different labor categories for fear of "offending" whites, however, was atypical: other evidence makes it clear that most slaves married whom they wanted to, regardless of their job, although at a practical level, those who worked together may have had more chance to mix with each other. Starke's comments, therefore, tell us more about what white owners wanted to believe about the social structure of slave communities than about the actual social structure itself.[6] The notion of a "divide" between those who labored in the field and domestics was one largely created by slaveholders in their desire to believe their house slaves were more similar to themselves.[7]

Slaves' choices regarding marriage partners, however, were limited, especially on large plantations with many slaves. The Manigaults, in fact, were a fairly atypical slaveholding family in that their wealth enabled them to restrict the marriage patterns of their slaves by imposing rules and regulations about spousal choice. Like many large slaveholders, they discouraged off-plantation marriages (also known as cross-plantation or "abroad" marriages). They did not like to allow their enslaved men to visit wives and children belonging to others because they believed it suggested they lacked control. Cross-plantation unions, which usually meant Saturday night visits at the very least, would, it was feared by owners, lead to more movement among and perhaps a greater degree of independence for their slaves. Yet, whites were forced to recognize that both social custom and their desire to see their slaves reproduce demanded that abroad relationships be permitted.

It was quite common for owners to show concern about cross-plantation arrangements in their plantation books. In his "Rules for Government of Plantation," for example, Sumter slave owner John B. Miller wrote:

Negroes:

To be kept in good order and at home and not to leave plantation without a ticket and that to express the place they are to go to and how long to be absent and not to be for any greater distance than a few miles without my express orders, except to the nearest church. Tickets to be given alone by me, wife or son. . . . No negro but those connected to my negroes and of good character to be allowed on plantation and they must have a ticket for that purpose from their owners to be brought to me except them that have a wife or husband on the plantation.[8]

Miller's rules illustrate well how owners sought to reconcile accepted customs and the need for a reproductive workforce with the desire to control the freedom—especially the geographic movement—of their chattel.

Plantation rules found in the papers of the South Carolinian Conway-Black-Davis family also refer indirectly to the inconvenience of cross-plantation links. Overseers were advised to "prevent night visits in the week, and put an end to late hours. Let 'early to bed and early to rise' be the word."[9] Rested workers would presumably be more productive. Similarly, Charleston planter Andrew Flinn worried about night visits and the mobility of his property, writing that slaves were not to be allowed out of their houses after nine o'clock at night in summer and eight o'clock in winter.[10] Since those in cross-plantation families were more desirous of geographical mobility, a minority of owners simply banned abroad marriages.

Social norms therefore superseded the law when it came to enslaved marriages. For example, Marion County ex-slave Nancy Washington, who had an abroad marriage, would have been forced to look for a partner away from her quarters since her master, Giles Evanson, only owned her, her siblings, and her mother.[11] For masters who owned only a handful of slaves, too, allowing abroad marriages was often the easiest way of ensuring a reproductive labor force.[12] Evidence from antebellum South Carolina suggests that cross-plantation marriages accounted for approximately one-third of enslaved households and that they were far from weak and nominal relationships.[13] Instead—like same-residence unions—wedlock of this kind was usually vigorously supported by the slaves who had taken the vows.

Wealthy slaveholders who owned more than one plantation, however, could and often did limit their slaves' choice of marriage partner to those slaves they owned. James Henry Hammond only permitted cross-plantation marriages on his Beech Island lands such as Silver Bluff if he owned both slaves. He wrote in his plantation diary that "negroes living on one plantation and having wives at the other can visit them only between Saturday night and Monday morning" and stated that "no marriage will be allowed with negroes not belonging to the master."[14] The Manigaults, who owned Dolly and Hector, took the same position. During the 1840s, Charles Manigault (Louis's father) simply dictated that "I allow no strange negro to take a wife on my place" in a letter to his overseer.[15] Manigault probably felt that the large size of his rice plantation meant he did not need to "indulge" his slaves, and so he simply denied the privilege of abroad wedlock. However, because he owned various tracts of lands and plantations, many of his slaves' marriages, including that of Dolly and Hector, operated in practice in exactly the same way as cross-plantation unions; they visited each other only on weekends.

That the marriage of Dolly and Hector failed to survive reveals the stresses and strains that these abroad marriages placed on enslaved couples and the tension and dissatisfaction they caused within enslaved communities. There could be benefits, in that these women and men were spared witnessing the abuse or punishment of their partners.[16] However, cross-plantation marriages also caused anguish for spouses, who had to spend much of the working week apart. Louisa Davis, one of the few WPA respondents who had been married while a slave, told her interviewer:[17]

> My husband was a slave of de Sloans and didn't get to see me as often as he wanted to, and of course, as de housemaid then, dere was times I couldn't meet him, clandestine like he want me. Us had some grief over dat, but he got a pass twice a week from his marster, Marse Tommie Sloan, to come to see me. . . . Sam was a field hand and drive de wagon way to Charleston once a year wid cotton, and always bring back something pretty for me.[18]

It may have been, as Manigault thought, that Dolly had fled to meet someone. Historians have recently suggested that runaway slaves were often running to someone rather than away from an abusive master, mistress, or overseer.[19] Many slaves, then, were placing primary importance on their ties of affection as they made decisions to leave as well as decisions to stay. Yet, to whom, if anyone, Dolly may have been running to and what made Manigault assume that she was participating in an interracial relationship is not known. It is possible that Manigault, who displayed other typically paternalistic ideas about the enslaved in the runaway notice, sought to deny Dolly agency to reassure himself and save face. Further, in claiming that an external influence was at work in her desire to escape, Louis Manigault could convince himself and others that Dolly had not fled because she was abused at the hands of the his family.

The harshness of slavery is also revealed in the runaway notice. Manigault described Dolly as being of "light complexion" and "rather good looking, with a fine set of teeth." These attributes would have increased Dolly's monetary value: in mentioning them Manigault was conveying just how valuable this attractive slave was.[20] Manigault's indicating that Dolly "hesitates somewhat when spoken to" also reveals much about his and other slaveholders' ideas about what was desirable in a slave. It is likely that Dolly was "hesitant" only in her conversations with those who owned her, reserving her more open character for private moments within the remit of her broader enslaved community. But presenting a hesitant, quiet front had broad benefits for the enslaved, who were less likely to feel the wrath of their owners or other whites if they did nothing to antagonize them. This reticence was often, therefore, a tactic employed by enslaved people anxious to avoid conflict: a mask worn to cover true emotions and sentiments. However, that so many slaves assumed a quiet, hesitant, and reserved manner gave slaveholders ammunition in their claims for black racial inferiority and for slavery as a positive good in "civilizing" inferior peoples.[21]

We cannot be sure that Dolly ran away owing to the distress caused by her separation from Hector; without a record of her words, the reason for her absconding remains elusive. It has been suggested by historians that, for various reasons, enslaved women were less likely to run away than were men. Pregnant women were physically in no state to escape their homes, and the care and nurture of children as well as women's emotional attachments and fears that the children would not survive if taken along also served to tie them to their farms or plantations. Women were also less likely to be assigned to carry out forms of labor that permitted them to be away from their place of residence, which meant that the sight of an enslaved female away from the plantation would have been more notable to patrollers or other whites than that of a slave man.

Historians have also noted that the love for a spouse was a strong deterrent against running away. Scholars John Hope Franklin and Loren Schweninger have argued that it was mostly young, single male slaves who attempted flight.[22] There were rare instances in which South Carolina enslaved couples in love sought escape together. It was, of course, very risky. The minutes of the Ebenezer Baptist Church of Florence County detail the case of a slave, Philip, who in 1829 absconded from his master. A fellow slave, London, informed the church that Philip had told him was going to Charleston from where he planned to leave South Carolina by sea in the hope of obtaining his freedom. However, the captain of the boat refused to take Philip's wife, and Philip was unwilling to leave her. They therefore decided to return home together.[23]

Dolly, however, does not appear to have had any children and was separated from her husband. Apparently she was not bound to the Manigault household through ties of affection to either a spouse or children. However, the fact that she and her husband were forced to conduct their marital life across plantations and the subsequent breakdown of the marriage suggest possible explanations for her unhappiness and willingness to make the momentous and dangerous decision to flee.

A letter written by a slave woman, Lavinia, in 1849 and found within the papers of the Lawton family of Allendale also reveals much about the experiences of enslaved women and their perspectives on slave life. This letter is a rare find, as it was illegal for slaves to read or write, though a few did master these skills.[24] In the letter written to her "missus," a highly distressed Lavinia wrote: "I am tormented. My conscience is bruised, my feelings are vex." The source of this anxiety was the separation of Lavinia's daughter, Aggy, from her husband, Jimmy. Lavinia begged her mistress not to allow Jimmy to set up home with an unnamed woman, who, she claimed, was "worse than Mary Magdalene."[25]

In the letter Lavinia was appealing to her mistress for some empathy and solidarity on the grounds that they were both religious women and mothers. Although South Carolina enslaved women and their mistresses were divided by their race and status, this letter suggests that women held in bondage at times sought the support of their masters' wives, invoking shared values and appealing to the white woman to regard slave women in the same way that they would if they were white, equal, or even family. Referring to separations in enslaved marriage, she wrote, "Do you think it rite in the site of God? What God put together for mankind to broke asunder." Later she pleaded that her mistress "view the matter as you would if they were your own children. Have they not souls as well as white people? Do not allow such adultery." She described the woman who enticed her son-in-law away as "a devil" who with "her sparkling black eye" attracted "other wimmin's husbands" and suggested that such behavior threatened not only her daughter's marriage but possibly other slave marriages as well.

The letter also reveals that this was not the first time that Lavinia had made a powerful plea for her mistress's intervention. She wrote: "Dear Missis can't you take pity on Aggy and use your influence in stopping this wretched business. I can't sleep all nite for hearing Christmus's groans and sighs about the hard lot of his daughter. You stopped my husband going to Mrs. Winburn Lawton's by your pleading and prayers."[26] Lavinia's marriage was therefore also saved by the mistress, who used her influence with the master on Lavinia's behalf.

In the correspondence between white members of the Lawton family, there is no mention of Lavinia or her family, and her highly unusual letter is all we have to guide us. Lavinia's role on the plantation is unknown, although her familiarity with the mistress suggests she may have been a domestic who labored in the Big House. Neither do we know the outcome of her plea. However, the letter makes it clear that Lavinia expected that a slave woman acting in a promiscuous manner might well be sanctioned and that she had no qualms about appealing to a white woman in her efforts to help her daughter and herself. Significantly, she asked her mistress to "use your influence." It is unlikely that South Carolina enslaved women would have felt confident about approaching masters directly; shared gender and perhaps a close relationship between Lavinia and her "missus" meant that approaching another woman was the easier option. Clearly Lavinia assumed that her mistress had at least some influence over the decisions made by her husband.

Historians have long debated what relations were like between enslaved women and the women in the families who owned them. It has been suggested that black and white women formed close relationships along gendered lines, across the divisions created by race and class. Historian Catherine Clinton has argued that "wives and daughters would often plead with planters for the humane treatment of slaves. Slaves understood this role of white women and would often appeal directly to the mistress to intercede with the master on his or her behalf."[27] On the other hand, Elizabeth Fox-Genovese has emphasized the gulf that racism created between mistresses and female slaves. She makes the point that white women could complain about slavery without necessarily opposing it as a social system. They did not accept the bourgeois claims of the (mostly northern) feminists about female universality across class and race lines.[28]

More recently, in a study of elite plantation women in South Carolina, Marli Weiner has claimed mistresses did seek to help their female slaves, most notably by intervening in cases of physical punishment. Such women interpreted the prevalent ideology of domesticity as justifying concern for the personal lives of those they held in bondage; they wanted to see themselves as good mistresses, as representing ideal womanhood. However, as Wiener points out, although they genuinely cared for their slaves, identifying with them on issues such as childbearing, the fact that they could not imagine a world without slavery meant that even if mistresses had reservations about slavery and interracial sexual liaisons, they expressed those reservations only in private.[29] In this Weiner concurs with an opinion expressed by historian Anne Firor Scott in 1970 that many southern women were actually "private abolitionists." Yet other evidence illustrates how South Carolina mistresses occasionally treated their enslaved women with brutality and also that a plea to a mistress did not always generate the anticipated outcome.[30]

A lengthy letter by Elizabeth Franklin Perry of Greenville, South Carolina, to her husband, the South Carolina politician Benjamin Perry, is perhaps representative of the kind of troubling relations that could obtain between mistresses and slave women and their families. Elizabeth was disturbed about a case of alleged domestic abuse by her slave Jim of his wife Maria.[31] Slaveholders and their wives often became involved in their slaves' marital disputes and discussed these affairs in their correspondence, journals, or diaries. They believed they knew "what was best" for those they held in bondage, and as slaveholders, they were in any event keen to maintain harmony in the quarters.[32]

Elizabeth informed her husband that she had had a tearful visit from Maria's mother, Winnie, who belonged to a Mr. Couble. Winnie explained to Elizabeth how Jim had beaten Maria. He had apparently "beat her, broke her head, cut her face." Elizabeth then went to Jim and Maria's cabin where she found that "Jim's abuse of her had been exaggerated. Maria was alone[,] . . . [and] everything about her [was] filthy, the floor not even swept, the beds, pails etc.[,] . . . all dirty[.] [S]he showed me a scar on her neck, where Jim had struck her, I talked to her and gave her some good advice about doing better." Perhaps Elizabeth thought that Maria was to blame for her domestic misfortune because she was a poor housekeeper. She then asked Jim for his interpretation of events, and he explained that he did not mind admitting that he had "struck Maria about three blows." In fact, he claimed "that it was not half she deserved, that she was the worst creature that ever was[,] . . . that he felt when he married her that he was doing wrong[,] . . . that she is obstinate . . . and lazy and dirty, that she will not clean the house, wash his clothes or mend them, or even wash hers, that their meals she would give them in dirty plates, with peas all sticking to them, that often he had to neglect his work in the field to clean the home and wash the dishes."

Elizabeth reported that Maria's mother, Winnie, had indicated that her owner, Mr. Couble, Maria's former owner, would be happy to take her back. However, on approaching Mr. Couble, Elizabeth discovered this was not the case. "Nothing would induce him to take Maria back, not if he were given five negroes along with her." Winnie may have made this claim in desperation, seeking, like Lavinia, to help and protect her daughter. Interestingly, in this case Elizabeth Perry directed her anger at her husband, because Mr. Couble had apparently described Maria's perceived "laziness" to Benjamin Perry at the time of purchase.[33] Elizabeth wrote, "I think it was astonishing you should think of buying her. . . . I want her sold to the first drover [slave trader] who passes[.] . . . [Y]ou are not strict enough with your servants, you can't make them work, and Mr. Couble says you are not a good manager of servants, and I have always said that. Now I have done with Maria, hoping you will sell her as soon as possible."[34]

Elizabeth Perry's letter points to other issues aside from the alleged domestic abuse of Maria by her husband and the efforts of a slave mother to help her daughter by turning to her daughter's mistress for help. Significantly, the violence toward Maria was seen as justifiable because she was not an adept homemaker. The bulk of domestic work fell on enslaved women, and a failure to conform to expected gender conventions could have significant consequences, as illustrated by Perry's lack of sympathy for Maria's plight. Because she failed to perform her perceived "duties" in her own home, Maria became the victim of a gendered discrimination not unique to slavery.[35]

The testimony of an ex-slave from South Carolina named Susan also enlightens us concerning relationships between enslaved women and their white mistresses. In the late 1930s, the WPA set up a program under which elderly ex-slaves were interviewed about their early lives. The majority of the interviewers were white, but there were a few African Americans who interviewed ex-slaves. Susan, who had been enslaved in Charleston, was the only South Carolina informant who testified to both a black and a white interviewer—to an African American man, Augustus Ladson, and to a white woman, Jessie Butler. This makes Susan's testimony particularly important, as historians today believe that when interviewed by whites in the harsh racial climate of the 1930s, former slaves often tailored their responses to white expectations.[36]

Susan, who had lived in Charleston, used to belong to Edward Fuller, president of the First National Bank of Charleston. Her evidence offers a unique perspective on the lives of enslaved girls in an urban setting. Unlike the other South Carolina slave women explored here, we have an approximation of Susan's surname (Jessie Butler described her as "Susan Hamlin" and Augustus Ladson as "Susan Hamilton" and it is not clear by which name she wished to be addressed).[37]

In contrast to Lavinia's letter, which suggested she profited from close ties with her mistress, Susan's testimony concerning life in antebellum Charleston made it clear that relationships between enslaved women and their mistresses could be fraught with tension and sometimes result in violent confrontation. Susan recalled to Ladson how one of Edward Fuller's other slaves, Clory, described as "a mulatta with beautiful hair she could sit on" and as the family's washer, had been whipped severely. Clory apparently threw her mistress out of the laundry room when the latter criticized Clory's work. Mrs. Fuller was pregnant, and "less than two hours [later] de baby wus bo'n." Susan elaborated no further, and so we don't know whether the child lived or died, but she described Clory's punishment for her display of aggression. "Dey whip 'er until dere wusn't a white spot on her body. Dat wuz de worst I ebber see a human bein' got such a beatin'. I t'ought she wus goin' to die." Clory recovered, and her master insisted she be hired out. "She willingly agree' since she wusn't 'round missus."[38]

We do not know how Clory's mistress felt about Clory remaining with the family: it is somewhat unusual that she was not sold. But slaveholding men had the final say about those they held in bondage, despite the efforts of women such as Elizabeth Perry to sway their husbands' decisions. Ultimately mistresses, as the slave woman Lavinia put it herself, could only use their "influence." Edward Fuller realized, most likely, that he could make more profit in the long run through hiring out Clory than he could by selling her. This practice was more common in urban environments where the majority of labor performed by the enslaved was domestic.[39] Susan conveyed to her white interviewer that she had been hired out to a Mr. McDonald on Atlantic Street, where she cared for his children.[40]

Interestingly, in her conversations with the white interviewer, Jessie Butler, Susan did not relate the story of Clory. Instead, she emphasized the positive attributes of Edward Fuller and his family, perhaps conveying what she thought Jessie Butler would want to hear. She thought Butler was from the welfare office and perhaps wanted to give a good impression of herself and her relations with whites. "I don't know about slavery but I know all the slavery I know about, the people was good to me. Mr. Fuller was a good man and his wife's people been grand people, all good to their slaves."[41] Susan also played down the significance of punishments and sales within the Fuller household in her conversations with Butler, describing separations vividly but in a general way: "Sometimes chillen was sold away from dey parents. De Mausa would come and say 'Where Jenny', tell um to put clothes on dat baby, I want um. He sell de baby and de ma scream and holler, you know how dey carry on." However, Susan was then quick to convey how "Mr. Fuller didn't sell none of us."[42]

Similarly, when Butler probed her about whether most masters were kind, Susan answered: "Some was kind and some was mean. . . . I see some wickedness and I hear 'bout all kinds of t'ings but you don't know whether it was lie or not. Mr. Fuller been a Christian man."[43] Susan suggested slaveholders were indeed brutal yet distanced both herself and her former owner from that brutality. Describing the darker side of bondage in a rather generalized way was a common tactic of the WPA interviewees, who were reluctant to talk about the harshness of the slave regime with white interviewers.[44]

The image of South Carolina enslaved mothers screaming for their absent children is a harrowing one, yet in the interview conducted with the African American interviewer, Augustus Ladson, Susan described the agonies of sale and punishment in stronger language. "All time, night an' day, you could hear men an' women screamin' to de tip of dere voices as either ma, pa, sister, or brother wus take without any warnin' an' sell. Some time mother who had only one chile was separated fur life. People wus always dying frum a broken heart. One night a couple married an' de next mornin' de boss sell de wife."[45] Equally distressing is her description of how slaves were punished: "W'en any slave wus whipped all de other slaves wus made to watch. I see women hung frum de ceilin' or buildin's an' whipped with only supin tied 'round her lower part of de body, until w'en dey wus taken down, dere wusn't breath in de body. I had some terribly bad experiences." She also confided to Ladson that her brother William was the son of Edward Fuller.[46]

In their comparison of the testimony Susan gave to her black and white interviewers, historians James West Davidson and Mark Hamilton Lytle concluded that "it would be difficult to conceive of a more strikingly dramatic demonstration of how an interviewer can affect the responses of a subject."[47] It was in her testimony to Augustus Ladson that Susan conveyed the harsh realities of sale, separation, physical punishment, and interracial sexual contact for women enslaved in South Carolina.

Susan's interviews also reveal much about the everyday lives of women enslaved in the state. Indeed, the WPA evidence is often most valuable for what it tells us about less private or less controversial issues. Susan provided helpful accounts of everyday occurrences in the lives of "ordinary" rank-and-file enslaved women in South Carolina, including a description of work patterns and "hiring out." Like Dolly and her husband, Hector, Susan's parents lived in a cross-plantation marriage, her father residing on Edisto Island. In recounting slave wedding ceremonies, she emphasized the extent to which both whites and blacks participated in them. "All slaves wus married in dere master house, in de livin' room where slaves an' dere missus an' mossa wus to witness de ceremony. Brides use to wear some of de finest dress an' if dey could afford it, have de best kind of furniture. Your master nor your missus objected to good t'ings."[48]

The four small pieces of evidence considered here together tell us much about the lives of enslaved women in South Carolina. We learn about the lives of younger and older female slaves; those who were single, married, and separated; those who were happily and unhappily married. The sentiments of slave children, childless women, and enslaved mothers can be traced as can the lives of those living on plantations or in their owner's house in both urban and rural environments. While some South Carolina slave women had close relationships with their mistresses, others were the victims of violence at their hands. The evidence of South Carolina slave women also reveals much about enforced separations, the hazards of running away, cross-plantation marriages, physical punishment, domestic abuse, and the difficulties of interracial relationships. We can never know as much as we want to know about the lives of these women who suffered the vicissitudes of slavery in antebellum South Carolina and their efforts to make it as bearable as possible for themselves and their families, but these four pieces of evidence, used with other sources of a less personal nature and placed within a broader context, allow us to come closer to understanding their lives and times.

NOTES

1. Harriet Jacobs, *Incidents in the Life of a Slave Girl* (Cambridge, Mass.: Harvard University Press, 1987).

2. Notice for runaway slave by Louis Manigault, 1863, Manigault Family Papers, Southern Historical Collection, Manuscripts Collection, Wilson Library, University of North Carolina, Chapel Hill (hereinafter cited as SHC).

3. Rachel Hall, "Missing Dolly, Mourning Slavery: The Slave Notice as Keepsake", *Camera Obscura* 21, no. 1 (2006): 76. See also William Dusinberre, *Them Dark Days: Slavery in the American Rice Swamps* (New York: Oxford University Press, 1996), 5. For more on Manigault's plantations, see Jeffrey R. Young, "Ideology and Death on a Savannah River Rice Plantation, 1833–1867: Paternalism amidst 'a Good Supply of Disease and Pain,'" *Journal of Southern History* 59, no. 4 (1993): 673–706.

4. Emily West, *Chains of Love: Slave Couples in Antebellum South Carolina* (Urbana: University of Illinois Press, 2004), 23–24.

5. *South Carolina Narratives*, vol. 2, pts. 1 and 2, and vol. 3, pts. 3 and 4, of *The American Slave: A Composite Autobiography*, ed. George P. Rawick (Westport, Conn.: Greenwood Press, 1972), 3.4.148.

6. West, *Chains of Love*, 103.

7. Ibid., 85–87. See also Paul D. Escott, *Slavery Remembered: A Record of Twentieth Century Slave Narratives* (Chapel Hill: University of North Carolina Press, 1979), 61, and Eugene Genovese, *Roll, Jordan, Roll: The World the Slaves Made* (New York: Vintage, 1974), 328–29.

8. "Rules for Government of Plantation," Cornhill Plantation Book, 1827–73, [plantation of John B. Miller], McDonald-Furman Papers, Manuscripts Department, William R. Perkins Library, Duke University, Durham, N.C. (hereinafter cited as WRPL).

9. List of plantation rules, February 1815, Conway-Black-Davis Family Papers, Manuscripts Division, South Caroliniana Library, University of South Carolina, Columbia (hereinafter cited as SCL).

10. List of plantation rules, Andrew Flinn Plantation Book, SCL.

11. *South Carolina Narratives*, 3.4.184–87.

12. Genovese, *Roll, Jordan, Roll*, 473, Richard Steckel, *The Economics of U.S. Slave and Southern White Fertility* (New York: Garland, 1985), 229.

13. See West, *Chains of Love*, chap. 2.

14. Quoted in Orville Vernon Burton, *In My Father's House Are Many Mansions: Family and*

Community in Edgefield, South Carolina (Chapel Hill: University of North Carolina Press, 1985), 163 n. 50, 169 n. 69.

15. Charles Izard Manigault to Mr. J. F. Cooper, January 10, 1848, Letterbook, 1846–48, Charles Izard Manigault Papers, SCL.

16. Deborah G. White, *Ar'n't I a Woman? Female Slaves in the Plantation South* (New York: W. W. Norton, 1985), 154.

17. I found five South Carolina WPA respondents married during the days of slavery. See West, *Chains of Love*, 46.

18. *South Carolina Narratives*, 2.2.300.

19. John Hope Franklin and Loren Schweninger, *Runaway Slaves: Rebels on the Plantation* (New York: Oxford University Press, 1999), chap. 3.

20. For more on the physical attributes of slave women in relation to sales, see Walter Johnson, *Soul By Soul: Life inside the Antebellum Slave Market* (Cambridge, Mass.: Harvard University Press, 1999), chap. 4.

21. For more on the idea of "masks" worn by the enslaved, see John Blassingame, *The Slave Community: Plantation Life in the Antebellum South*, rev. and enl. ed. (New York: Oxford University Press, 1979), chap. 6.

22. Franklin and Schweninger, *Runaway Slaves*, 210.

23. See minutes of Ebenezer Baptist Church, entries for March–July 1829, Florence County, South Carolina Department of Archives and History (hereinafter cited as SCDAH), and West, *Chains of Love*, 57.

24. See Janet Duitsman Cornelius, *"When I Can Read My Title Clear": Literacy, Slavery and Religion in the Antebellum South* (Columbia: University of South Carolina Press, 1991).

25. Lavinia to "Missus," 1849, Lawton Family Papers, SCL.

26. Ibid. See also Wilma King, "'Rais Your Children Up Rite': Parental Guidance and Child Rearing Practices among Slaves in the Nineteenth Century South," in *Working Toward Freedom: Slave Society and Domestic Economy in the American South*, ed. Larry E. Hudson Jr. (New York: University of Rochester Press, 1994), 154.

27. Catherine Clinton, *The Plantation Mistress: Woman's World in the Old South* (New York: Pantheon, 1982), 187

28. See Elizabeth Fox-Genovese, *Within the Plantation Household: Black and White Women of the Old South* (Chapel Hill: University of North Carolina Press, 1988), 338.

29. See Marli F. Weiner, *Mistresses and Slaves: Plantation Women in South Carolina, 1830–80* (Urbana: University of Illinois Press, 1998), 76–80, 93–96.

30. Anne Firor Scott, *The Southern Lady: From Pedestal to Politics, 1830–1930*, exp. ed. (Charlottesville: University Press of Virginia, 1995), 51.

31. For more on the Perry marriage, see Carol K. Bleser, "The Perrys of Greenville: A Nineteenth Century Marriage," in *The Web of Southern Social Relations: Women, Family, and Education*, ed. Walter J. Fraser Jr., R. Frank Saunders Jr., and Jon L. Wakelyn (Athens, Ga.: University of Georgia Press, 1985), 72–89.

32. On owners' involvement in the cross-plantation unions of their slaves, see Emily West, "Masters and Marriages, Profits and Paternalism: Slave Owners' Perspectives on Cross-Plantation Unions in Antebellum South Carolina," *Slavery and Abolition* 21, no. 1 (2000): 56–72.

33. Elizabeth Perry to Benjamin Franklin Perry, May 11, 1846, Benjamin Franklin Perry Papers, SCL.

34. Ibid. It is not clear from later letters whether Maria was eventually sold or not.

35. Fox-Genovese, *Within the Plantation Household*, 338.

36. Interview with Susan Hamilton by Augustus Ladson, in *South Carolina Narratives*, 2.2.233–36; interview with Jessie Butler by Augustus Ladson, in *South Carolina Narratives*, 2.2.226–32.

37. On the "Hamlin-Hamilton" naming debate, see James West Davidson and Mark Hamilton Lytle, *After the Fact: The Art of Historical Detection*, 2nd ed. (New York: Knopf, 1986), 196–97.

38. *South Carolina Narratives*, 2.2.234–35.

39. For more on the practice of hiring out, see Jonathan D. Martin, *Divided Mastery: Slave Hiring in the American South* (Cambridge, Mass.: Harvard University Press, 2004), and Peter J. Parish, *Slavery: History and Historians* (New York: Harper and Row, 1989), 105–6.

40. *South Carolina Narratives*, 2.2.226.

41. Ibid., 2.2.227–28.

42. Ibid., 2.2.231–32 and 2.2.235. See also Davidson and Lytle, *After the Fact*, 191–201.

43. *South Carolina Narratives*, 2.2.229.

44. Writings on methodological issues associated with use of the WPA narratives are extensive. See, for example, John Blassingame, "Using the Testimony of Ex-Slaves: Approaches and Problems," *Journal of Southern History* 41, no. 4 (1975): 473–92; Charles T. Davis and Henry Louis Gates Jr., eds., *The Slave's Narrative* (New York: Oxford University Press, 1985); and Donna J. Spindel, "Assessing Memory: Twentieth-Century Slave Narratives Reconsidered," *Journal of Interdisciplinary History* 27, no. 2 (1996): 247–61.

45. *South Carolina Narratives*, 2.2.235.

46. Ibid., 2.2.233, 2.2.235.

47. Davidson and Lytle, *After the Fact*, 201.

48. *South Carolina Narratives*, 2.2.234.

The Bettingall-Tunno Family and the Free Black Women of Antebellum Charleston

A Freedom Both Contingent and Constrained

AMRITA CHAKRABARTI MYERS

In 1842, Barbara Tunno Barquet became ensnared in the legal battles of a wealthy South Carolina couple. That year, Elizabeth Heyward Hamilton, a member of a powerful planter family, sued her husband, James, for violating their marriage contract.[1] State laws throughout the antebellum United States dictated that when a woman married, any property she owned prior to her marriage passed to the control of her husband. South Carolina, however, allowed couples to enter into marriage contracts by which a woman could put the property she brought to her marriage in a separate trust estate to be administered by special trustees for the woman's "sole and separate use."[2] Elizabeth brought an estate worth 100,000 dollars into her marriage, and she and her husband agreed to place this property in a trust estate. By law, James could not use the entrusted property to guarantee or to pay his debts. But he did just that. A land speculator and gambler, James, who somehow had himself appointed guardian of his wife's estate, nearly bankrupted the trust. In 1842, with creditors closing in, Elizabeth initiated a lawsuit to remove her husband as guardian of the trust. She also named several of her husband's creditors, all of whom were seeking payment out of the trust, as codefendants in her suit. Seven of these debts were mortgages James had taken out on his wife's entrusted real estate. The holder of one such mortgage, in the amount of 5,178 dollars, was Barbara Tunno Barquet, a free black woman from the city of Charleston.[3]

How did Barbara Barquet, an affluent black woman, get caught up in the affairs of Elizabeth and James Hamilton, members of South Carolina's white

BROWN FELLOWSHIP SOCIETY GRAVEYARD
(LATER CALLED CENTURY FELLOWSHIP SOCIETY),
CHARLESTON, S.C., CIRCA 1905,
WHERE BARBARA TUNNO WAS BURIED

Holloway scrapbook. Courtesy of Avery Research Center for African American
History and Culture, College of Charleston, Charleston, S.C.

plantation elite?[4] Considering the Old South's racial and gendered hierarchies of power, how do we make sense of a court case wherein a powerful white man was financially indebted to a free black woman? Finally, what does the lawsuit teach us about Barbara as an individual and about the broader experiences of free black women in Charleston and throughout the antebellum South? To answer these questions, and provide a broader historical context for the suit in question, we must step back from the 1842 legal action and examine the women in Barbara's family, including her mother, Margaret Bettingall, and her half sister, Hagar Cole.

It is important to note that Margaret, Hagar, and Barbara were different from the majority of Charleston's free black women. Wealthier than most of the city's free women of color, all three owned real estate and were slaveholders. Additionally, they were members of a racially mixed family and had access to white men of influence. The family also left records allowing us to resurrect their stories, fragmented though the documents may be. Finally, these women navigated an unjust social landscape in startling ways and acquired certain privileges thought to be outside the reach of both free blacks and women. They are thus worthy of study partly because their lives were, in some ways, exceptional. Rather than providing an example of the experiences "common" among free blacks, their stories reveal more fully the range of black female life and behavior in the Old South and challenge assumptions about what it meant to be a typical free black woman during the slave era. Indeed, the desire to define the "typical" free black experience obscures the complexity of the world in which antebellum black women lived, a complexity these women's lives illuminate in important ways.

Though these three women were exceptional in some ways, the constraints they faced in their quest for a life of their own design, and the strategies they utilized to survive and succeed, were representative of those faced by most of the city's black women. In particular, Charleston's women of color understood that men were both a hindrance to and a help in their efforts to secure greater liberty for themselves. The circumstances of black women's lives meant that men were the gatekeepers to the expanded freedom they sought, so they engaged in a myriad of relationships with black and white men in order to attain the privileges these affiliations offered them, even as they struggled against the constraints these same men placed on them. Thus the records of this one family allow us to delve into issues ranging from interracial sexual relations to black female wealth, autonomy and power, and the access black women had to justice in the Old South. In particular, these women's stories illuminate how Charleston's social, economic, and legal structures were designed to limit the liberty of black women and how black women worked from within this inequitable system and reshaped it to better fit their own definitions of freedom and justice.

For Charleston's black women, freedom was more than just legal manumission. It meant securing the freedom of their loved ones and living with them; marrying and/or living with the domestic partner of their choice in their own home; pursuing an occupation that paid them enough to live with dignity; being exempt from race-based taxes; acquiring property and being able to protect it; obtaining an education for their children; attending the church of their choice; and creating the social networks through which they could raise their families in a manner of their own choosing. Additionally, they sought the protections of the law that white South Carolinians enjoyed as their birthright, appealing to the courts and the legislature in an effort to obtain these protections and further their quest for liberty. To this end, they signed petitions seeking to abolish unjust taxes and filed lawsuits to protect their property rights.

The story of this family begins with Margaret Bettingall. Much of Margaret's early history remains a mystery, including where and when she was born and when she arrived in Charleston. We do know that by the early 1800s, Margaret was involved with a white man named Adam Tunno, a wealthy Scottish merchant. An importer of Madeira wine, Tunno was wealthy and well respected. Known for hosting elegant wine and dinner parties, he was also actively involved in the St. Andrew's Society, one of Charleston's most illustrious benevolent organizations, whose membership included government officials, affluent merchants, and skilled artisans. Adam's social circle thus included men of power and influence, and his wealth and prominence enabled him to build a house on Charleston's East Bay, a home he shared with Margaret Bettingall and their children: a daughter named Barbara and a son who died in infancy. Margaret also had a daughter from a previous marriage named Hagar who lived with her mother and stepfather until she married.[5]

Margaret and Adam lived together for almost forty years in a relationship that, to many, looked like a marriage. Margaret ran Adam's home, bore his children, and helped prepare the elegant wine parties for which he was famous. Black friends and neighbors referred to Margaret as Adam's wife and considered them to be a married couple. White contemporaries referred to her as the "mistress of Adam's house-hold" or the "head and front" in charge of his premises. Regardless of what they called her, however, they all agreed that Margaret lived with Adam in the mansion on East Bay, oversaw the work of the many slaves who lived in small dwellings scattered about the couple's yard, and carried the keys to the estate on her belt. These testimonials, when viewed alongside Adam's and Margaret's wills, reveal that Margaret and Adam had an enduring conjugal relationship. These same documents refer to Margaret as "brown," a "Negro" or a "black woman," allowing us to identify her conclusively as a woman of color.[6]

Legally a person of color, Margaret was not a typical black woman owing to her wealth and social connections. In other ways, however, her life reflected the larger black female community of which she was a part. Like most black women in the Old South, Margaret was illiterate and left no records in her own hand: the only document directly attributable to her is her last will and testament, a document she signed with an "x."[7] This lack of firsthand materials has long been used to deny women, the poor, and racial minorities a place in the history books, the claim being there is not enough evidence to inform scholarship about these groups. The stories of women like Margaret can be told, however, if scholars diligently seek out all the available records and, when necessary, make a series of informed assumptions about what the documents tell us. Historians in search of black female voices thus find themselves engaged in detective work, unearthing small fragments of black women's lives that allow us to fill in portions of a canvas, much of which remains frustratingly blank.

Faced with the evidentiary obstacles, it is not surprising there are unanswered questions about Margaret Bettingall, beginning with her status as a legally free woman. That Margaret was a free person is suggested by the fact that she owned real property, which enslaved people were forbidden from doing, and by the fact that she left a will in which referred to herself as a "free woman of color." What is not clear is whether she had been born a slave. On the one hand, no manumission records have been recovered for her, and her contemporaries stated she had never been enslaved. Further, Margaret's daughter Hagar paid taxes as a free person of color, and no manumission records appear in Hagar's name, suggesting Margaret was free when Hagar was born.[8] On the other hand, on August 20, 1803, the legal emancipation of a child named "Barbary" was recorded in Charleston's manumission books: Barbary's guardian was listed as Adam Tunno.[9]

The evidence thus suggests that Margaret was enslaved when Barbara was born and that she lived her life as a de facto free person. Fugitive slaves, persons who were illegally freed, and those hired out as enslaved urban laborers to Charleston's business owners all lived within the city's black community as quasi-free people. Indeed, de facto manumission was widely accepted and rarely challenged in South Carolina prior to 1820, when the free black population was smaller and thus considered to be less threatening. Living unsupervised by whites, these blacks—whether free by the intention of their owners or by their own initiative—began taking advantage of the opportunities the city afforded them. They married, attended church, found jobs, purchased homes, bought and sold property, and paid the taxes required of free blacks. It was in this manner that Lydia Weston came to be listed on the federal census as a free black woman. Illegally manumitted and allowed to live as a free woman of color, Lydia found work, paid her taxes, and conducted herself as a free woman in kind and so became one in fact. Margaret Bettingall may well have done the same thing.[10]

In addition to the speculation surrounding her free status, there are questions about the legality of Margaret's marriage to Adam. No marriage certificate has been found for the couple, although records indicate Margaret attended St. Philip's Episcopal Church, along with many other elite blacks and wealthy whites. Acquaintances confirm she was a communicant at St. Philip's, which she could not have been were she not Adam Tunno's wife since the Episcopal Church did not extend membership to anyone leading a "wicked" life.[11] In short, had Margaret been "living in sin" with Adam, she would not have been allowed to commune at St. Philip's. Family history states that Margaret, known for her piety, was distressed when the rector of St. Philip's refused to administer the sacraments to her for this very reason. This led Margaret to ask Adam to provide her with a letter stating she was his wife. Apparently Margaret then presented this document to the rector and was henceforth allowed to commune at St. Philip's.[12]

Whether the white community regarded Margaret and Adam as being legally married, however, is debatable. Black Charlestonians referred to Margaret as Adam's wife on the grounds that since she acted like his wife, managed his household like a wife, and bore his children like a wife, she ought to be treated as such. The laws of the state upheld this belief: South Carolina did not forbid interracial marriage as long as both parties were free, and state law decreed that marriage was a civil contract requiring no written document or ceremony for its manifestation but only the agreement of the parties in good faith. Additionally, state courts ruled that relationships became legal unions once the parties had cohabited for more than thirty years. Under South Carolina law then, if she were legally free, Margaret and Adam's union would have qualified as a legal marriage at the time of his death, by which point the pair had lived together for almost forty years. White Charlestonians may not have agreed with the state's definition of a legal marriage, however, and they may not have regarded Margaret as Adam's wife, but they certainly knew the couple lived in the same house, engaged in a long-term sexual relationship, and had children together.[13]

The issues surrounding her freedom and marital status indicate that Margaret's liberty, like that of other antebellum black women, was both contingent and insecure. To live according to her vision of freedom and secure the manumission of her children, Margaret had to maintain a relationship of goodwill with a wealthy, well-connected man. And, despite her position in Adam's household and the apparently consensual nature of their partnership, Margaret would have lost the financial benefits she gained from her alliance with Adam had the couple separated. Additionally, if Margaret were not legally free, Adam could have sold her away from her children or turned her over to the authorities as a fugitive slave. No matter the scenario, Margaret's status, and that of her daughters, would have instantly changed. At best, such concerns would have meant Margaret strove to keep Adam happy in order to safeguard her family's freedom. At worst, it could have kept her in the relationship beyond the duration of any affection she may have had for Adam. Unlike a legitimate wife, women in partnerships that had not yet achieved the status of common-law marriage had little legal recourse if their partners left them. Realizing their liberty was tenuous and that they could not afford to upset their "protectors," they had to daily walk a fine line in their quest for a freedom of their own design.

The fears that plagued free black women were only too real. Margaret's main concern would have been the freedom and financial security of her children, particularly Hagar, who was not Adam's biological child. Hagar lived with Margaret and Adam until she married one Thomas Cole, a free man of color with whom she had at least two children: a son named William and a daughter, Mary. Hagar's husband was almost certainly the same Thomas Cole who in 1819 resided at 13 Maiden Lane and was a carpenter by trade. In all likelihood, Hagar's husband, a Charlestonian by birth, was the son of Thomas Cole Sr., a free black man and bricklayer or brick maker. If so, he was a member of one of the city's oldest free families of color.[14]

It appears, then, that Hagar married into one of Charleston's most prominent free black families. This is significant considering the questions surrounding her mother's free status and the fact that Hagar was not Adam's biological daughter. Charleston's affluent free blacks were careful whom they married. As free blacks were deeply concerned with respectability, marriage among them was as much a matter of maintaining their wealth and free status as it was about love or companionship. That Hagar was able to marry into the Cole family despite her hazy lineage thus testifies to the strength of her family's position. Whatever complications Thomas's marriage to Hagar may have created for the Cole family, especially if her own freedom was uncertain, it still connected them to Adam Tunno, a powerful man who left Hagar a significant inheritance as proof of his affection for her.[15]

What we know about Hagar is limited by the fact that she, like her mother, did not leave any personal papers. According to public records, Hagar resided on Archdale Street from 1821 to 1823 and paid her annual "head" taxes. She did not, however, reappear in the capitation books until 1840, when she was excused from any further payments because she was "overage."[16] It is possible Hagar did not appear in the capitation books for sixteen years due to recording errors. She was listed in the federal census of 1830, however, which suggests it is more likely that Hagar deliberately did not pay her "head" taxes.[17] Certainly other free blacks in Charleston avoided paying these taxes without being fined, jailed, or reenslaved.[18] Like them, Hagar's connection to a powerful white man likely enabled her to avoid paying a tax that penalized her simply for being black. That Hagar paid her city property taxes, dues collected from all property owners and calculated at the same rate, regardless of race or gender, supports this conclusion.[19]

The issue of capitation taxes again attests to the constraints free blacks faced and the contingency of their freedom. Free people of color were burdened by head taxes they often could not afford to pay, and the penalties for nonpayment were severe (a free person of color could, for example, be "temporarily" reenslaved). Some women responded to these threats against their freedom by petitioning the state to repeal race-based taxes. "Helpless females," they claimed, ought not to be "sold into bondage on account of their poverty."[20] Others utilized relationships with men of influence to avoid payment or ducked the tax collectors. Certainly not every woman who did not pay her capitation tax was as fortunate as Hagar Cole. When Hetty Barron failed to pay her 2-dollar capitation tax in 1838, the sheriff of Charleston was directed to find Barron, take her into custody, and "sell her services" to recoup the money "necessary to pay the said Capitation Tax."[21] Clearly, Charleston's economic and legal structures were designed to limit the freedom of black women. Equally apparent is that black women were politically savvy actors who engaged in various tactics of negotiation, from filing legislative petitions to forging alliances with men of stature, to acquire a broader freedom than the one envisioned for them by white southerners.

Hagar's desire, and ability, to create a freedom of her own design ran deep. According to the city's public records, Hagar Cole, despite her marriage, was in charge of her own business affairs and conducted herself as a *feme sole*.[22] For example, it was Hagar, not her husband, who was listed as the head of the Cole household in the 1830 federal census, although Thomas was alive in 1830 and may have been living as late as 1860.[23] Hagar also inherited real and moveable property from family members, property "free from the debts and liabilities of her husband, Thomas Cole," and she paid taxes on real estate held in her own name.[24] Although no formal sole trader deed has been found for Hagar, state law mandated a husband's "tacit consent" was enough to allow a wife to act as a sole trader. That Hagar owned her own property, paid taxes separately from her husband, and was listed by census takers as the head of her own household all suggest Thomas "tacitly" agreed to treat Hagar as a *feme sole*.[25]

Hagar Cole exercised significant control over her finances without the oversight of her husband, a situation outside the norm for most married American women of the era, white or black.[26] Her ability to live as a *feme sole* stemmed in large part from the fact that she had wealth and power of her own. Certainly her marriage to Thomas strengthened her social standing in Charleston, but Hagar was not financially dependent on her husband since she had her own money, given to her by her mother and stepfather. Additionally, Hagar also had an elevated social status because she was Adam's stepdaughter. In all likelihood, then, Hagar was able to oversee her own affairs, regardless of whether Thomas "tacitly consented" or not, because of the position she occupied and wealth she acquired as a result of her mother's long-term relationship with a powerful white man of means.

The same could be said of free black hotelier Eliza Seymour Lee. When Eliza's mother, free woman of color Sarah Seymour, passed away, she left the bulk of her estate to her daughter. This estate was acquired in large part from her white lover, most likely Eliza's father. The inheritance allowed Eliza and her husband, the free black man John Lee, to open the Mansion House, one of Charleston's finest hotels. The success of this venture in turn enabled Eliza to purchase the city's other premier hotel, the Jones Hotel, by 1838. Considering she began her days as a pastry cook and then ran a boardinghouse before obtaining the funds to purchase a hotel, it is fair to say Eliza worked long hours cooking and cleaning for other people in order to become a successful entrepreneur. Equally important, however, was the inheritance she received from her mother. It not only allowed Eliza to open the Mansion House more quickly than if she and John had had to depend on their savings alone; it also permitted her to oversee her own business affairs, independent of her husband, and to eventually hire her own financial advisor.[27]

Barbara Tunno Barquet proved to be as independent as her half sister, Hagar, and hotel owner Eliza Lee. Barbara grew up with her parents in their mansion on Charleston's East Bay and was educated at a school for free blacks in the city, an education her father paid for. She thus improved on her mother's situation and died a literate woman, evidenced by her ability to sign her name to her last will and testament. Barbara was also openly acknowledged by Adam and other members of his extended white family as his daughter: Adam's nephew John referred to her as his "Cousin Barbara," and Barbara carried her father's last name until she married. She also inherited a large part of Adam's estate when he died. Barbara, then, by virtue of her mother's careful negotiations and her father's money, was a free black woman of high social position.[28]

Barbara's status was reinforced by her choice of a spouse. On July 6, 1814, Barbara married an artisan from Saint Domingue (today the island of Haiti) named Jonathan Pierre Barguet/Barquet.[29] If wealth and white lineage could lead to freedom and status for black women, light skin color and the practice of a skilled trade could do the same for black men. John came to Charleston from the Caribbean, was well educated, spoke French, and was an umbrella maker by trade. His status as a skilled artisan and his French background elevated his standing among Charleston's free blacks and made him eligible for membership in the Brown Fellowship Society (BFS) in 1807. The BFS was Charleston's premier benevolent order for light-skinned free men of color. Thus Barquet's membership placed him firmly within the ranks of Charleston's free black elite.[30]

The Barquets set up house at 113 Meeting Street and had seven children together, all of whom spoke both English and French. The young Barquets attended St. Philip's Episcopal Church with their parents and lived in an environment of material comfort, the bulk of their family's wealth coming from the Tunno side of the family. Adam helped Barbara maintain a comfortable lifestyle for her family, giving her gifts of cash, slaves, and real estate over the years. He was also involved in the lives of his grandchildren. Barbara's son, Liston, spent a fair amount of time at his grandparents' home and remembered his grandfather fondly. According to Liston, Adam paid his tuition at Thomas S. Bonneau's renowned school for free black children and ensured the boy was fed on the days he visited his grandparents after school.[31]

Thanks to her mother's relationship with Adam, by 1830, Barbara was a woman of means. That year, Barbara headed up two households in Charleston: one the house in which she lived in Ward 3, the other a house in Ward 4. Between both dwellings she oversaw the lives of twenty-two men, women, and children, thirteen of whom were free persons of color. Nine of these free people included Barbara and her family, but the identities of the other four, all of whom lived in the house in Ward 4, are unknown. These persons may have been relatives or boarders who brought in extra income for the family—taking in boarders was a common practice among free blacks in Charleston and elsewhere. The remaining nine residents of Barquet's homes were enslaved. Affluent and well connected, Barbara Tunno Barquet was also a slaveholder.[32]

Like Hagar, Barbara, not her husband, was listed as the head of these households. And while no *feme sole* deed was recorded in Barbara's name, she appears in a variety of public records under her own name and seems to have exercised significant personal authority.[33] For example, she purchased property, loaned out money, managed her own investments, and hired out her enslaved laborers for profit. As was the case for her half sister, the key to this authority was Barbara's personal wealth and status, derived from her position as the daughter of Adam Tunno. Not beholden to John Barquet for her economic security, her social position and family money made Barbara one of the most autonomous married women in Charleston, black or white.

Barbara's business sense, honed by years of managing her own money and renting out her slaves, enabled her to run her husband's umbrella shop after his death in 1831. This business sense might explain why Barbara's position as a widow did not negatively affect her social or economic status, as it did many antebellum women. Indeed, while many antebellum widows quickly remarried, as much out of a need for financial security and protection as for love and companionship, Barbara remained single. Already prosperous, she was now a business owner as well, and remaining a widow allowed her to utilize the title of "Mrs.," with all its attendant virtues of respectability, while continuing to act as a *feme sole*, which a new marriage could have prevented. Barbara likely wanted to remain a *feme sole* since her financial position was strengthened shortly after her husband's demise when her father also died. After battling the effects of heart disease for over a year, Adam Tunno passed away on December 27, 1832, at the age of seventy-nine, with Margaret and their daughter at his bedside.[34]

Adam's estate included slaves, cash, stocks, household goods, real estate, and more, and he was generous in his bequests to his black family. Margaret, "with her daughter Hagar Cole and children," received 2,500 dollars in cash, and Barbara Barquet received another 2,500 dollars in cash. This sum was enough to purchase a brick home in an affluent neighborhood in Charleston or two solid, wooden homes in respectable working-class neighborhoods. Additionally, all of Tunno's household goods, including his clothing, house linens, furniture, dishes, glasses and silverware, were to be distributed evenly among his servants, "with Mrs. J. Harrison, Mrs. Burguit, and Hagar's family to be considered as sharing in the distribution of these articles." Since his estate was worth between 300,000 and 400,000 dollars, the value of these household items added significantly to the money Adam left his daughter and stepdaughter.[35]

Of the three black women in Adam's family, it was Margaret Bettingall whose life changed the most after Adam's death. She not only lost her companion of almost forty years; she also had to relocate to a new residence at 19 Archdale Street. The mansion on East Bay, her home for over thirty years, was sold in order to liquidate Adam's estate and fulfill the cash bequests he made in his will.

Thus Margaret, like many antebellum widows, simultaneously experienced the emotionally taxing losses of death and physical dislocation. Unlike many widows, however, Margaret did not have to rely on her children or another man to help her out or take her in. She purchased a new home for herself and she, like Barbara, never remarried.[36]

For Barbara, life continued on much as it had before her father's death. Already affluent, Barbara became wealthy after she received her legacy from Adam's estate.[37] She continued to live at 113 Meeting Street and to run her late husband's umbrella business, a venture in which she likely employed some of the slaves she owned. Barbara also rented out several of her slaves to augment her monthly income and, understanding the benefits of slave labor, passed others on to her children in order to help further their quest for financial stability. In 1835, she sold a twenty-year-old man named Peter to her daughter, Margaret Humphries, for 1 dollar. The sum indicates Peter was a gift, one Barbara hoped would help her daughter and son-in-law, Joseph, build their tailoring business. The gift appears to have done the trick: by 1840 the Humphrieses owned four laborers, including Peter, and their business was booming.[38]

Hagar Cole also remained in Charleston after her stepfather's death. She, like Barbara, inherited a substantial legacy from Adam, but things were not as secure for Hagar as they were for her half sister. In May 1834, Hagar appeared in court to request that Edward Frost, a local white attorney, be appointed legal guardian of her children, William and Mary Cole, "minors entitled to a personal estate within this state." Thomas Lehre, judge of the Court of Ordinary, upheld Cole's request and made Frost responsible for the maintenance and education of the two children and for the management of their estate, "for the better securing of the said estate for the benefit of the said minors."[39]

This document is surprising. Why would Hagar terminate her husband's parental rights, and her own, and ask Edward to become her children's legal guardian? A *feme sole* with her own wealth, Hagar was quite capable of looking after her children's interests, so why would she seek a white male guardian for them? The only clue we have is that William and Mary were "minors entitled to a personal estate." This "estate" would have been the inheritance left them by Adam Tunno. It is possible, then, that Hagar wanted to ensure her children's estates were not accessible to their current guardian (their father) or to any creditors he may have had, so she gave Frost guardianship of her children. The courts would not have given Hagar herself legal guardianship of the children since her husband, their father, still lived. Fathers received guardianship of their children automatically at their birth. Indeed, one wonders what Thomas Cole's reaction was to this loss of his paternal rights. It is unclear if he even had a say in the matter: his name appears nowhere in the guardianship records and the transfer request was filed in Hagar's name alone.[40]

Hagar likely still had substantial control over her children's lives considering Edward Frost was also her guardian.[41] Why Hagar had a guardian is unknown: only free black men were required to have guardians. Perhaps she believed fewer people would try taking advantage of her if they knew she had a white lawyer to speak on her behalf. It is also possible that as a woman of means, Hagar hired Edward as a financial advisor. Regardless, the man was evidently someone Hagar trusted with her own affairs and with her children. Still, she took a risk placing her children's lives in Frost's hands. Had he been unscrupulous and bled their estates dry, Hagar would have been hard pressed to fight the man in court. With the problems Hagar and her children may have faced from Thomas and his creditors, however, giving Edward guardianship of the children might have been Hagar's best option.

As Hagar strove to protect her children's future by allying herself with a white man, Hagar's half sister, in contrast, had no such concerns. A wealthy widow, Barbara had no husband to threaten her financial independence. Indeed, Barbara became the guardian of four free children of color in 1838, all of whom had inherited under her father's will in 1832.[42] Barbara assumed guardianship of the children shortly before her mother's death, after the parents of all four had died. Margaret's will, written in May 1838, stated she was leaving "To Barbara Barquet, in trust for Sarah and Margaret Reid, children of Margaret Cooper, deceased, $1000. To Barbara Barquet, in trust for Eliza and Alexander, children of Matilda Lesesne, deceased, $1000." These children required a guardian now that their mothers were deceased, and Margaret evidently wanted to ensure the guardian would be someone she could trust to protect their inheritances. Barbara thus assumed guardianship in August 1838, three months after Margaret wrote her will.[43]

It is not clear when Margaret Bettingall passed away. Her will was proven in probate court on January 13, 1840, so she likely died early in 1840, but the exact date and cause of death are unknown. Her passing meant that her daughters and several other free blacks received substantial inheritances for the second time in six years. Margaret, it seems, not only knew how to run a household; she also had a head for finances and investments, dying with an estate appraised at just under 7,500 dollars. A sizeable sum, this amount does not take into account one of the four houses she owned or four of her eleven enslaved laborers. These goods were passed onto her children, and so their value was not included in the assessment of her estate.[44]

Margaret was certainly unique: the city's tax lists indicate that only two other free black women acquired real property holdings in excess of 10,000 dollars.[45] Furthermore, black women in Charleston who reached the ranks of propertied taxpayers were a minority among free black property owners, free blacks in general, and the propertied class as a whole. Indeed, black female taxpayers were as rare as rich women were among all women.[46] It is important to note, however, that black wealth was a pittance when compared to the holdings of Charleston's white elite: free people of color possessed estates worth an average of 5,400 dollars, white property holders, 54,000 dollars. And while 20 percent of white Charlestonians were worth 10,000 dollars, only 1 percent of the city's free blacks ever attained such financial heights. Finally, free blacks comprised 15 percent of the city's population but controlled only 1 percent of the city's total wealth. Only within the black community, then, were property holders like Margaret "elite," for they were never the financial or social equals of the white elite whose wealth and position always surpassed their own.[47]

Elite or not, both of Margaret's daughters benefited handsomely under the terms of their mother's will. Barbara inherited 600 dollars in cash, two enslaved laborers named Henry and Joe, and a share of her mother's furniture and clothing, while Hagar received 100 dollars in cash, her mother's house and lot on Pitt Street, a slave man named Nelson, and a share of her mother's furniture and clothes. Finally, all of Margaret's grandchildren were left sizeable cash trusts.[48] On January 23, 1840, Margaret's estate was liquidated at auction and the proceeds from the sale of her houses, lots, and slaves went toward creating the trusts her will mentioned.[49]

Margaret built up an estate that was admirable for any person of her time, male or female, black or white. The construction of her will also reveals she never forgot how tenuous life was for free blacks in Charleston: she instructed that the money she left her legatees be used to buy her descendants houses and property. Money could be spent unwisely and stocks could become worthless. Real estate, however, was a solid investment, the purchase of which would provide ongoing financial security for Margaret's family and increase their net worth. It would also improve their social standing, since antebellum southerners placed their wealth in land and houses and held in high esteem those who owned real estate.[50]

Margaret was a product of her time in other ways as well: a slaveholder, she bequeathed some slaves to her children and sold others in order to make her descendants' lives more secure. Her concern was for her family's well-being, and she knew that owning slaves would guarantee their financial security. Like other free blacks, Margaret also realized her freedom was dependent on the goodwill of elite whites, who viewed free blacks with a modicum of distrust. Owing to the contingent nature of their freedom, free blacks could not openly denounce slavery, nor could they manumit their slaves after South Carolina changed its manumission laws in 1820. Instead, they sought to protect their own freedom, and their financial interests, by owning slaves and expressing no outward concerns about it. Black slave ownership thus provided whites with evidence of free black loyalty, retained for free blacks the white patronage their small businesses needed to prosper, and provided many free people of color with the means necessary to acquire wealth and upward social mobility.[51]

Realizing that free blacks walked a fine line in antebellum Charleston, Margaret also understood how tenuous life was for free women of color. Her will indicated a desire to ensure that the actions of men did not destroy the security of her family. First, she wanted Barbara to take guardianship of the four orphaned black children who inherited under her will, aware that if Barbara was not named trustee, the courts would appoint whomever they wanted, including white men of standing who may or may not have acted in the children's best interests. Even more telling was how Margaret strove to protect the inheritance of her daughter, Hagar, from Hagar's husband. Twice Margaret stated that "the portion of this property to which Hagar Cole will be entitled to be free from the debts and liabilities of her husband Thomas Cole." Margaret Bettingall was no fool: she knew how easily men could wreak havoc on a woman's financial security.[52]

Antebellum women in general understood that their status derived from their connections to men. Women of color also knew they lived in a society that discriminated against both women and blacks. To combat the constraints of a system both racist and sexist, black women thus bound themselves to the very persons responsible for creating this inequitable system: men, particularly white men. They never forgot these relationships were double-edged swords, however. They used their ties to men to obtain the privileges of liberty, but black women realized these same men could make their freedoms disappear. Thus Margaret, who acquired her power from her connection to Adam, worked to ensure that what she had labored to gain would not be squandered by other men. And Hagar, who attained social prominence by marrying Thomas, sought to protect her children's estates from their father by turning them over to the guardianship of a white man, although she risked losing control of her children in so doing. Such risks illuminate the contingent nature of liberty for antebellum black women: full freedom was out of their reach, their agency daily constrained by the society in which they lived. Limited in their choices, they thus did the best they could with what they had.

In retrospect, Margaret Bettingall left her descendants more than just a share

of healthy estate. She was wise with her money, she understood the social climate of her time, and she shrewdly worked within the system to ensure the best
possible outcome for herself and her family. She knew what it meant to be a free
black woman in a society dominated by white male slaveholders, and although
she engaged in some of the practices of this racist and sexist society, including
slave ownership, she did not accept others, as evidenced by her efforts to protect
her family from the patriarchal authority of men, both black and white. Using
all the tools available to improve the condition of her family, Margaret was, on
her death, still the same woman who, so many years before, had worked to acquire the right to commune at St. Philip's Church. It was this legacy of agency,
wisdom, and strategic negotiation Margaret left her family, a legacy that would
stand her younger daughter in good stead in the near future.

The years after Margaret's passing were tumultuous ones for Barbara, for this
was when she was dragged into the legal battles of Elizabeth and James Hamilton. The link between Barquet and the Hamiltons was James G. Moodie. A
friend of her father's, James became Barbara's financial advisor after Adam's
death and helped manage her inheritance. One of the properties she acquired
on his advice was the mortgage on Rice Hope, property Barbara thought belonged to James Hamilton, but which was actually part of Elizabeth's trust
estate. Thus it was that a free black woman came to loan money to an elite,
white male plantation owner. It may also have been at Moodie's suggestion that
Barbara hired Alexander Mazyck to represent her in responding to Elizabeth
Hamilton's "Bill of Complaint." And, though all the defendants hired attorneys,
Barbara alone asked that the debt owed to her be paid out of James's personal
funds rather than from the trust estate. According to court records, Barbara
stated since the debt was James's, not Elizabeth's, any repayment should come
from his assets, not hers.[53]

Hamilton v. Hamilton played out in a number of stages over several years. In
1843, the court finally ruled that Rice Hope was, indeed, part of a trust estate.
James had illegally used that estate to pay off his debts and defrauded his creditors by not informing them they were purchasing mortgages on property held
in trust. The trust was thus removed from James's control and placed in the
hands of a new trustee, who was charged with managing the estate for Elizabeth's sole and separate use. Finally, while the trust was not to be held liable for
James's personal debts, the mortgages on Pennyworth and Rice Hope plantations were upheld. This was of small comfort to Elizabeth: she was unable to
pay the mortgages, and both properties went into foreclosure. The court then
ordered both estates to be sold at auction and stipulated that the proceeds were
to be distributed to the mortgage holders in order of the dates of their liens.[54]

James Hamilton then arranged for the Bank of Charleston to buy Rice Hope at auction. The deal was that the bank would then extend enough credit to the Hamiltons' two grown sons to enable them to take title of the plantation. The sons agreed to pay off the loan with profits from future rice sales. What happened next was fraud, plain and simple. To prevent excessive bidding, the bank bought the first two mortgages outstanding on Rice Hope and promised the wealthy holders of the large fifth mortgage that they would be paid back before the holders of the smaller third and fourth mortgages. The bank was thus able to purchase a plantation worth 60,000 dollars for only 11,000 dollars, and Barbara, who held the third mortgage on Rice Hope, was swindled out of 5,178 dollars. Her response to this injustice was not surprising, considering her family history. Financially savvy, connected to influential people, head of her own household, legal guardian of several children, a businesswoman and a slaveholder, Barbara Tunno Barquet followed the examples her mother and sister had set for her: she worked from within the system to demand justice and protect her rights by filing a motion asking the courts to overturn the fraudulent sale of Rice Hope.[55]

We can only imagine the reaction of white Charlestonians when they heard a free woman of color had challenged one of the most prestigious combinations of bankers, planters, merchants, and lawyers in the state. It would have been seen as an attack on the southern social system, a system that openly professed to place all women under the authority of men and all black people, enslaved or free, no matter how wealthy or how light-skinned, under the control of whites. If Barbara won her case, what would that do to the legitimacy and public image of the South's supposedly rigid racial and gendered social hierarchy? Equally troubling was the possibility that if a free black woman, even one as wealthy or well connected as Barbara, won a case against an elite white man in open court, other free blacks might get ideas about "their rights."

These very concerns may have led the first judge who heard the case, William Harper, to dismiss Barbara's motion. A political crony of James Hamilton, Harper believed the "African negro [sic] . . . was an inferior variety of the human race" and "peculiarly suited" for enslavement. People of African descent, said Harper, could never exercise power in civilized society. As for women, Harper felt they suffered from an "infirmity, unsuitableness of character, or defect of discretion" that also made them unfit for the exercise of public power. In Barquet, then, Harper faced a plaintiff both black and female and thus, by his standards, an individual who was doubly unfit to exercise power (i.e., undeserving of the rights of citizenship) in "civilized society." It is safe to assume that both racism and sexism influenced Harper's decision.[56]

Undeterred, Barbara appealed William Harper's ruling to the next rung of the judicial system. Upon receiving an equivocal decision from the Court of Appeals, Barbara continued her quest for justice and took her case to the superior constitutional court of the state, the Court of Errors. It was here, four years after the original suit began, that Barbara finally won her case. The South Carolina Court of Errors ruled the first sale of Rice Hope had, indeed, been fraudulent and ordered a new auction be held. Early in 1846, Rice Hope Plantation sold for almost 56,000 dollars and Barbara Tunno Barquet finally received her money. Elizabeth Heyward Hamilton's sons managed to purchase most of the Rice Hope property on credit and held it in a trust for their mother's use and benefit.[57]

Winning her suit likely gave Barbara a deep feeling of pride. She, a free woman of color, had been vindicated in her demand for justice against a major financial institution and a family of elite white plantation owners. Her victory would have been another example to her descendants of their progenitors' determination, proving yet again that they came from a line of women who never ceased fighting for their rights and freedoms. Barbara had little time to enjoy her victory, however. Physically unwell, shortly after the case was settled she wrote out her will and in February 1846, at the age of fifty-three, Barbara Tunno Barquet died from a thickening or enlargement of the heart, also known as "hypertrophy of the heart." She was buried in the Brown Fellowship Society cemetery in Charleston.[58]

The only document we have in her own hand, Barbara's will gives us some insight into her private thoughts. First, it reveals that Barbara, like Margaret, wanted to protect her daughter from the meddling of men. Barbara left her daughter, Caroline, "for her sole and separate use, my servant Phebe, not subject to the debts or contracts of her present or any future husband." Just as Margaret strove to protect Hagar's inheritance from Thomas Cole, and Hagar, in turn, gave guardianship of her children to Edward Frost to safeguard their estates, Barbara tried to protect Caroline from any man who might try to take advantage of her. Barbara learned an important lesson from the women in her family and from her experiences in the equity courts. Seeing what James Hamilton did to his wife and realizing the courts did not always protect a woman's interests, even the interests of a white woman of privilege, Barbara strove to ensure that Caroline's inheritance was protected from potential male predators.[59]

Barbara also owned enslaved people and she, like her mother, viewed her laborers as goods to be disposed of in the best interests of her family. Barbara named ten slaves in her will and divided seven of the ten amongst three of her children without regard to maintaining the family ties if any of the enslaved persons. She also instructed the remaining three slaves be left to all her children equally and stated they could be sold in order to facilitate such a division. Estate papers indicate the slaves in question were auctioned off five months later for 1,350 dollars and that the proceeds from the sale were divided amongst Barbara's children to fulfill the terms of the will. Any qualms Barbara may have had about the bondage of black people (and it does not appear as if she had any) were, then, overridden by her desire to ensure her children's security.[60]

Barbara's children benefited handsomely from her death. Even without the seven slaves she willed to them, Barbara left an estate valued at over 6,000 dollars. This included her home on Meeting Street, appraised at 2,500 dollars, several mortgages and bonds, five shares in the State Bank, two shares in the Charleston Bank, laborers Diana, Bella and Isaac, and 140 dollars in household goods. Except for her silverware, some clothes, a few sentimental tokens and the aforementioned seven slaves, Barbara's estate was left to her children and to her granddaughter, Mary Louisa McKinlay, in equal shares, McKinlay inheriting in place of her dead mother.[61]

Barbara's death closed a significant chapter in the history of her family. The story of the Bettingall-Tunno women illuminates how southern black women navigated a series of obstacles first to obtain their freedom and then to negotiate that freedom on a daily basis, each right wrenched from a system designed to deny them access to the full fruits of freedom. Black women understood freedom did not grant them unfettered access to equality and that blacks and whites had differing ideas about what freedom should look like for black people. Battling to shape the contours of their lives to better fit their own vision of freedom, black women thus engaged in a variety of personal acts to further their political agency. Regularly allying themselves with men and working within the system, black women took lovers, owned slaves, married for upward social mobility, found guardians, and hired financial advisors and attorneys. Such tactics bound women of color to the individuals who were their greatest obstacles to true liberty, but they simultaneously improved black women's abilities to fashion a freedom of their own design.

The lives of the Bettingall-Tunno women reflect both their agency and the constraints on that agency and reveal that no matter how industrious they were, much of what free black women attained in their lives resulted from their negotiations with men. Margaret Bettingall's forty-year partnership with Adam Tunno allowed her to acquire wealth, power, and perhaps even freedom. She ran Tunno's home, owned real estate and slaves, and attended the most prestigious church in the city. Despite her social standing, however, Margaret's legal status as a free woman and a wife were never confirmed, and, unlike white women of comparable status, she went to her grave illiterate.

Hagar Cole used her mother's relationship with Adam Tunno to make significant gains for herself. She married a man from an elite free black family, inherited property from her mother and stepfather, became a slaveholder, and apparently used her position as Adam's stepdaughter to avoid paying her capitation taxes and to live as a *feme sole*. Despite her wealth and power, however, Cole retained a white male guardian to protect her legal interests and transferred guardianship of her children to that same man in order to safeguard their estates. Additionally, we do not know if Hagar was literate. No documents with her signature have been recovered and being his stepdaughter may not have been enough to encourage Adam to send Hagar to school, although white women of comparable social and economic position would have received some type of education.

Barbara benefited the most from Margaret's relationship with Adam. In addition to receiving a top-notch education, paid for by her father, Barbara inherited a substantial portion of Adam's estate upon his death. It was her education, wealth, and social position that enabled her to marry a high-status free artisan of color and live as a *feme sole*. As a wealthy widow, Barbara became legal guardian to several free black children, owned slaves, ran a successful business, engaged the services of both a white financial advisor and a prominent white attorney, and won a major lawsuit against both the Bank of Charleston and a white man from a prominent plantation family. Her children grew up in an affluent home, attended an elite church, were well educated, and inherited substantial property upon their mother's death.

Despite her prestige, however, even Barbara did not live a life wholly free from constraints. Like all free black women in the Old South, she was hedged in by both time and place and understood she could never be completely free. Instead, her freedom, like those of other women of color, entailed never-ending compromise with the men who dominated the society in which she lived. Consider the lawsuit Barbara filed near the end of her life. Unlike white men who found themselves involved in similar litigations, Barbara had to hire a white male attorney to both file her legal documents and speak for her in court: in the nineteenth century, the state of South Carolina, like most others, did not permit either women or free blacks to testify on their own behalf in a court of law.[62] White men, then, quite literally became the voices of women and people of color, both of whom were legally silenced. Barbara's foray into the South Carolina court system, and her eventual victory, is thus one more example of how Charleston's social, economic, and judicial structures were designed to limit the agency and freedom of black women and how black women worked from within an inequitable system to make their voices heard and create lives that better fit their own definitions of freedom and justice.

NOTES

1. For a detailed examination of this lawsuit see Virginia Glenn Crane, "Two Women, White and Brown, in the South Carolina Court of Equity, 1842–1845," *South Carolina Historical Magazine* (hereinafter cited as SCHM) 96, no. 3 (1995): 198–220.

2. On marriage and property see Norma Basch, *In the Eyes of the Law: Women, Marriage, and Property in Nineteenth-Century New York* (Ithaca, N.Y.: Cornell University, 1982); Richard Chused, "Married Women's Property Law: 1800–1850," *Georgetown Law Journal* 71, no. 5 (1983): 1359–1425; Carol Jenson, "The Equity Jurisdiction and Married Women's Property in Antebellum America: A Revisionist View," *International Journal of Women's Studies* 2, no. 2 (1979): 144–51; and Mary-lynn Salmon, "Women and Property in South Carolina: The Evidence from Marriage Settlements, 1730–1830," *William and Mary Quarterly*, 3rd ser., 39, no. 4 (1982): 655–85.

3. Most of the information in this essay comes from the Langdon Cheves Legal Papers (hereinafter cited as LCLP), South Carolina Historical Society, Charleston (hereinafter cited as SCHS). In this collection are seven folders devoted to the Tunno family lawsuit from which my material is drawn. See also *Elizabeth M. Hamilton per pro ami Henry D. Cruger v. General James Hamilton*, in *Hamilton v. Hamilton*, Charleston Court of Equity, Bill #105, 1843, South Carolina Department of Archives and History, Columbia (hereinafter cited as SCDAH); and William Harper's report, Court of Equity Reports, 1839–45, March 3, 1842, 40, SCDAH.

4. Throughout this piece, individuals are described as black, brown, persons of color, negro (sic), mulatto, or yellow according to how they are referenced in the historical record. When discussing larger groups, I use "free blacks" or "free people of color." Both terms were used in the antebellum era by free blacks when referring to themselves and by whites referring to free blacks. Finally, I refer to people as free if they were listed in the historical record as free people, referred to themselves as free people, lived or behaved as free people, or were viewed by others to be free people, and thus were de facto free.

5. See Thomas N. Holmes and Theodore E. Mitchell, LCLP, F3, SCHS, and Liston W. Barguet, LCLP, F4, SCHS. See also James H. Easterby, *History of the St. Andrew's Society of Charleston, South Carolina, 1729–1929* (Charleston, S.C.: St. Andrew's Society, 1929), 21, 30, 34.

6. Holmes and Mitchell, LCLP, F3, SCHS; Barguet, LCLP, F4, SCHS; Margaret Bettingall, will books of Charleston County (hereinafter cited as WBCC), 1839–45, 42:67–69, SCDAH, and Adam Tunno, WBCC, 1826–34, 39:1239–43, SCDAH.

7. Margaret Bettingall, WBCC, 1839–45, 42:67–69, SCDAH.

8. For manumission documents see Miscellaneous Records of the Secretary of State, 1729–1825, Charleston County index to manumission books, 1801–48, SCDAH, and WBCC, SCDAH. See also Margaret Bettingall, WBCC, 1839–45, 42:67–69, SCDAH; Holmes, LCLP, F, SCHS; and Hagar Cole, state free negro capitation tax books, Charleston, South Carolina, 1811–60, 1821–23, 1840, SCDAH.

9. Barbary, Charleston County index to manumission books, 1801–48, 1:51; Barbara's marriage certificate also refers to her as Barbary (marriage of John P. Burget and Barbary Tunno, 1814, Parish Registers of St. Philip's, 1810–40, SCDAH).

10. For more on de facto free blacks and the opportunities free people of color had in Charleston, see Larry Koger, *Black Slaveowners: Free Black Slave Masters in South Carolina, 1790–1860* (Columbia: University of South Carolina, 1985), 35–36; Bernard E. Powers Jr., *Black Charlestonians: A Social History, 1822–1885* (Fayetteville: University of Arkansas, 1994), chap. 2; and Marina Wikramanayake, *A World in Shadow: The Free Black in Antebellum South Carolina* (Columbia: University of South Carolina, 1973), 33–34, 41.

11. Holmes and John Gregg, LCLP, F3, SCHS, and Frederick Dalcho, *An Historical Account of the Protestant Episcopal Church in South Carolina* (1820; rpt., New York: Arno, 1972), 246, 585.

12. See Holmes and Langdon Cheves, LCLP, F3 and F1, SCHS.

13. See Holmes, LCLP, F3, SCHS. See also *Powers v. McEachern*, in Thomas Cooper and David J. McCord, eds., *The Statutes at Large of South Carolina*, 10 vols. (Columbia: State Co., 1836–40), 7:290, 7:293–94; *Fryer v. Fryer*, in ibid., 9:85, 92; and *Johnson v. Johnson*, Court of Chancery, 1 DeSaussure (1800), 595–96, SCDAH. On the views of white Charlestonians toward the relationship see Cynthia Kennedy-Haflett, "Moral Marriage: A Mixed-Race Relationship in Nineteenth-Century Charleston," SCHM 97, no. 3 (1996): 206–26.

14. On Thomas Cole, see Margaret Bettingall, WBCC), 1839–45, 42:67–69, SCDAH; James W. Hagy, ed., *Charleston, South Carolina, City Directories for the Years 1816, 1819, 1822, 1825, and 1829* (Baltimore, Md.: Clearfield, 1996), 37; Koger, *Black Slaveowners*, 15, 142–43; and Loren Schweninger, *Black Property Owners in the South, 1790–1915* (Urbana: University of Illinois Press, 1997), 20–21, 247–48.

15. If Margaret were not legally free, Hagar, and her future children, would be enslaved as well. For more on free blacks and marriage, see Powers, *Black Charlestonians*, chap. 2, and E. Horace Fitchett, "The Free Negro in Charleston, South Carolina," (PhD diss., University of Chicago, 1950). See also Adam Tunno, WBCC, 1826–34, 39:1239–43, SCDAH.

16. From 1756 to 1865, South Carolina required all free persons of color to pay an annual tax on their persons. In 1801, legislators determined only free persons of color between fifteen and fifty years of age would be held liable for the tax. The note "overage" means, then, that Hagar was over the age of fifty in 1840. See Hagar Cole, state free negro capitation tax books, Charleston, South Carolina, 1811–60, 1821–23, 1840, SCDAH; Acts of the General Assembly, Early State Records, SCDAH; Cooper and McCord, eds., *Statutes at Large*, 9:265, 9:540; and Barguet, LCLP, F4, SCHS.

17. The 1830 census lists Hagar Cole in ward 4 heading up a household of thirteen people (Carter G. Woodson, *Free Negro Heads of Families in the United States in 1830* [Washington, D.C.: Association for the Study of Negro Life and History, 1925], 156, and Carter G. Woodson, "Free Negro Owners of Slaves in the United States in 1830," *Journal of Negro History* 9, no. 1 [1924]: 41–85, esp. 72).

18. Jehu Jones, a free black hotelier, was able to avoid paying his capitation taxes as a result of the influence of his white guardians, John L. Wilson and William Lance (petition of Jehu Jones, Papers of the General Assembly [hereinafter cited as PGA], ND00 01871, 1823 00130, 1823 00138, and 1827 00102, SCDAH).

19. See Hagar Cole, *A List of Taxpayers of the City of Charleston, 1859* (Charleston, S.C.: Walker, Evans, 1860), 386.

20. Richland County petitions and committee reports, PGA, 003 ND00 01808, 003 ND00 01809, 003 ND00 01885, 004 1806 00090, and 004 ND00 00781, SCDAH; petition of sundry free people of color from Charleston, Richland County petitions and committee reports, PGA, 004 1809 00129, SCDAH; and petition of sundry free women of color from Charleston, Richland County petitions

and committee reports, PGA, 004 1841 00069, SCDAH. That many women could not pay their head taxes is borne out by the fact that the notation "destitute" is written next to their names. See state free negro capitation tax books, Charleston, South Carolina, 1811–60, SCDAH; capitation tax book for Charleston's free people of color in the lower wards, 1859, SCHS; and city of Charleston tax book for free persons of color, 1861.

21. See arrest warrant of Hetty Barron, Miscellaneous Documents, Avery Research Center, College of Charleston, Charleston, S.C. (hereinafter cited as ARC).

22. In the antebellum era, upon marriage a woman became a *feme covert* who ceased to exist as a separate legal entity apart from her husband. She could not own property, buy or sell goods, enter into contracts, sue or be sued, or transact any business unless her husband permitted her to become a *feme sole*, usually through the execution of a written deed. A *feme sole* could pursue her own business interests, her husband could not interfere in those affairs, and her assets could not be seized to pay husband's debts (Marylynn Salmon, *Women and the Law of Property in Early America* [Chapel Hill: University of North Carolina, 1986], 45–49).

23. See n. 17. Return of interments in the city of Charleston, 1819–61, Charleston County Public Library, Charleston, S.C. (hereinafter cited as CCPL); Margaret Bettingall, WBCC, 1839–45, 42:67–69, SCDAH; Thomas Cole, *A List of the Taxpayers of the City of Charleston for 1859*, 386; Thomas Cole, *A List of the Taxpayers of the City of Charleston for 1860* (Charleston: Walker, Evans, 1861), 317.

24. "Real property" was defined by the city as real estate, slaves, and horses. See *A List of the Taxpayers of the City of Charleston for 1859* and *A List of the Taxpayers of the City of Charleston for 1860*. See also Alexander Forrester, WBCC, 1851–56, 46:280, SCDAH; Hagar Cole, *A List of the Taxpayers of the City of Charleston for 1859*, 386; Hagar Cole, individual tax returns for free people of color in St. Philip's and St. Michael's Parishes, 1860, SCDAH; and Margaret Bettingall, WBCC, 1839–45, 42:67–69, SCDAH.

25. See sole trader deeds, Miscellaneous Records of the Secretary of State, 1729–1825, SCDAH.

26. Basch, *In the Eyes of the Law*; Chused, "Married Women's Property Law"; Jenson, "Equity Jurisdiction"; Salmon, "Women and Property"; Salmon, *Women and the Law of Property*.

27. See Sarah/Sally Seymour, WBCC, 1818–26, 36:1008, SCDAH, and Eliza Lee Papers, Rutledge-Young Collection, SCHS. See also Frances A. Kemble, Records of a Later Life, vertical files: negroes, SCHS; Powers, *Black Charlestonians*, 42, 44; Harriott Horry Rutledge Ravenel, *Charleston: The Place and the People* (New York: Macmillan, 1931), 461; Schweninger, *Black Property Owners*, 84, 115–16, 132; and Wikramanayake, *World in Shadow*, 81, 103–6, 111.

28. See Barbara Barquet, WBCC, 1845–51, 44:23, SCDAH; John C. Tunno, LCLP, F1, SCHS; Barguet, LCLP, F4, SCHS; Holmes, Mitchell, and Reverend John Johnson, LCLP, F3, SCHS; marriage of Burget and Tunno, 1814, Parish Registers of St. Philip's, SCDAH; and Adam Tunno, WBCC, 1826–34, 39:1239–43, SCDAH.

29. See n. 28; Johnson and Mitchell, LCLP, F3, SCHS. John likely came to Charleston during the Haitian Revolution. For more on Haitian independence and the subsequent influx of émigrés to the United States see Ira Berlin, *Slaves without Masters: The Free Negro in the Antebellum South* (New York: New Press, 1974), 35–36, 58; Michael P. Johnson and James L. Roark, *Black Masters: A Free Family of Color in the Old South* (New York: W. W. Norton, 1984), 33; Powers, *Black Charlestonians*, 28; and Wikramanayake, *World in Shadow*, 18, 159.

30. Mitchell, LCLP, F3, SCHS; Barguet, LCLP, F4, SCHS; Hagy, *Charleston, South Carolina, City Directories*, 1, 33, 70, 137; rules and regulations of the Brown Fellowship Society, Brown Fellowship Society Papers, ARC; James B. Browning, "The Beginnings of Insurance Enterprise Among

Negroes," *Journal of Negro History* 22, no. 4 (1937): 417–32; Robert L. Harris Jr., "Charleston's Free Afro-American Elite: The Brown Fellowship Society and the Humane Brotherhood," SCHM 82, no. 4 (1981): 289–310.

31. See Hagy, *Charleston, South Carolina, City Directories*, 70; Mary Louisa Enburg, LCLP, F3, SCHS; and Barguet, LCLP, F4, SCHS.

32. Woodson, *Free Negro Heads of Families*, 156; Woodson, "Free Negro Owners of Slaves," 71–72. On free black slave owners see Michael P. Johnson and James L. Roark, eds., *No Chariot Let Down: Charleston's Free People of Color on the Eve of the Civil War* (New York: W. W. Norton, 1984), 128–30; Koger, *Black Slaveowners*, 98, 166, 170, 214–18; and Wikramanayake, *World in Shadow*, 73, 80, 87, 94.

33. See sole trader deeds, SCDAH.

34. See Barguet, LCLP, F4, SCHS; Adam Tunno, WBCC, 1826–34, 39:1239–43, SCDAH; Adam Tunno obituary, *Charleston Courier*, December 28, 1832, in LCLP, F5, SCHS; and John C. Tunno, LCLP, F1, SCHS.

35. See n. 46 and Adam Tunno, WBCC, 1826–34, 39:1239–43, SCDAH.

36. See James W. Hagy, ed., *Directories for Charleston, South Carolina, for the Years 1830–31, 1835–36, 1836, 1837–38, and 1840–41* (Baltimore, Md.: Clearfield, 1997), 2.

37. "Wealthy" refers to persons who possessed property valued at over 10,000 dollars, "affluent" or "prosperous" to those whose estates were assessed between 1000 and 9999 dollars. See nn. 46 and 47.

38. Hagy, *Directories for Charleston, South Carolina*, 32, 73; Koger, *Black Slaveowners*, 94–95.

39. Letter of guardianship, Records of the Probate Court of Charleston County, vol. 2, subsection B (May 27, 1834), 39, SCDAH.

40. See n. 39. On free blacks and guardianship, see Berlin, *Slaves without Masters*, 215; Powers, *Black Charlestonians*, chap. 2; and Wikramanayake, *World in Shadow*, 42–44, 55, 59, 65, 151. See also Adam Tunno, WBCC, 1826–34, 39:1239–43, SCDAH.

41. That Frost was Cole's guardian is mentioned in Margaret Bettingall, WBCC, 1839–45, 42:67–69, SCDAH.

42. Letter of guardianship, Records of the Probate Court of Charleston County, vol. 2, subsection C (August 6, 1838), 35; Adam Tunno, WBCC, 1826–34, 39:1239–43, SCDAH.

43. Margaret Bettingall, WBCC, 1839–45, 42:67–69, SCDAH.

44. Ibid; Margaret Bettingall, Charleston County inventories and appraisals, 1839–67 (hereinafter cited as CCIA), 1839–44, A:47, A:570, SCDAH.

45. Had the final house and additional four laborers been included in the assessment of her estate, Margaret's real property holdings would almost certainly have surpassed 10,000 dollars. Jane Wightman and Maria Weston also controlled real property in excess of 10,000 dollars. See *A List of Taxpayers of the City of Charleston, 1859*, 403 and 404; *A List of Taxpayers of the City of Charleston, 1860*, 332 and 333; and city of Charleston tax book for free persons of color, 1861.

46. Few free people of color were prosperous. If the cost of a brick home in Charleston, 2000 dollars, is used as a benchmark for economic stability, only 117 free blacks could claim financial security. If you include those who owned either 2000 dollars in real estate or at least one slave, one-sixth of Charleston's free blacks were affluent. Numbering 120 individuals (500 if you include family members), this group comprised 3 percent of the city's free black population. See Leonard Curry, *The Free Black in Urban America, 1800–1850: The Shadow of the Dream* (Chicago: University of Chicago, 1981), 43; Johnson and Roark, *Black Masters*, 204–7; Johnson and Roark, *No Chariot*,

6–7; and Jane H. Pease and William H. Pease, *Ladies, Women, and Wenches: Choice and Constraint in Antebellum Charleston and Boston* (Chapel Hill: University of North Carolina, 1990), 105.

47. Johnson and Roark, *Black Masters*, 205; Johnson and Roark, *No Chariot*, 6–7; Schweninger, *Black Property Owners*, 98–99.

48. Margaret Bettingall, WBCC, 1839–45, 42:67–69, SCDAH.

49. Margaret Bettingall, CCIA, 1839–44, A:47, A:570, SCDAH.

50. For more on landownership see Koger, *Black Slaveowners*; Schweninger, *Black Property Owners*; and Wikramanayake, *World in Shadow*.

51. See Margaret Bettingall, WBCC, 1839–45, 42:67–69, SCDAH, and Margaret Bettingall, CCIA, 1839–44, A:47, A:570, SCDAH. See also Act of 1820, in Cooper and McCord, *Statutes at Large*, 7: 459–60.

52. Margaret Bettingall, WBCC. See also Salmon, *Women and the Law of Property*.

53. Answer of Barbara Barquet, *Hamilton v. Hamilton*.

54. Johnson decree, *Hamilton v. Hamilton*, March 25, 1843.

55. Affidavits of Alexander Mazyck, *Hamilton v. Hamilton*, January 2, 1844, and January 25, 1844.

56. Harper's decree, *Hamilton v. Hamilton*, June 27, 1845; William Harper, "Memoir on Slavery," in *The Ideology of Slavery*, ed. Drew Gilpin Faust (Baton Rouge: Louisiana State University Press, 1981), 79–135.

57. J. S. G Richardson, *Report of Cases at Law Argued and Determined in the Court of Appeals and Court of Errors*, 15 vols. (Columbia, S.C.: A. S. Johnston, 1845–69), 2:355–67; Equity Report Books, 1843–44, 15–17, SCDAH; Equity Report Books, February 1845–July 1846, 142–43, SCDAH; South Carolina Court of Appeals, January 28, 1845, SCDAH; Equity Decree Book, April 1843–February 1844, 112–13, SCDAH.

58. Barbara Barquet, WBCC, 1845–1851, 44:23, SCDAH; Barbara Barquet, Return of interments in the city of Charleston, 1819–61, February 1846, CCPL; and rules and regulations, Brown Fellowship Society Papers, ARC.

59. Barbara Barquet, WBCC, 1845–1851, 44:23, SCDAH.

60. Ibid; Barbara Barquet, CCIA, 1844–50, B:207–8, SCDAH; Koger, *Black Slaveowners*, 94–95.

61. See Barbara Barquet, WBCC, 1845–51, 44:23, SCDAH, and Barbara Barquet, CCIA, 1844–50, B:207–8, SCDAH.

62. See Crane, "Two Women."

Angelina Grimké

Abolition and Redemption in a Crusade against Slavery

CHARLES WILBANKS

As July 1835 came to a close much of the nation was gripped in a maelstrom of violence against abolitionists. In the fall, the violence would ensnare William Lloyd Garrison, the famed editor of the antislavery newspaper the *Liberator*, as a mob assaulted and manhandled him through the streets of Boston. His only crime was to have urged his fellow citizens to listen to the words of British abolitionist George Thompson and to allow him to speak unmolested. An earlier public appeal by Garrison and escalating threats of violence against him and other abolitionists came to the attention of Angelina Grimké, a native South Carolinian then living in Philadelphia, who received the news with dismay and alarm.

Grimké was an unlikely abolitionist. She was the daughter of a former South Carolina Supreme Court justice, John Faucheraud Grimké, and the heir to a large estate built with slave labor. Angelina's thirteen siblings included Benjamin, a prominent Charleston physician; Thomas, a state legislator; and an older sister Sarah, to whom she was especially close. Yet Angelina Grimké and her sister Sarah had rejected slavery and their large and prominent family's slaveholding and had moved to Philadelphia. By the summer of 1835, Angelina had become concerned that the abolition movement could not protect its crusaders, and she worried that soon antislavery reformers would shrink from the threats and the abuse they faced. She wrote a letter to Garrison that summer and in it, for the first time, made a public commitment to act on behalf of emancipation. Grimké urged abolitionists to stand their ground. She wrote: "If persecution is the means which God has ordained for the accomplishment of this great end, EMANCIPATION; then . . . I feel as if I could say, LET IT COME."[1]

Something else bothered Grimké that July. There had been a near riot in her native Charleston over the receipt of antislavery literature. The *Charleston Courier* reported on July 30, 1835, that this inflammatory literature represented nothing less than an "assault on Southern Institutions." The newspaper protested that "a repetition of it will, in all probability, so influence public indignation as to render the U.S. Mail unsafe, at least in this quarter."[2] Later that night a mob broke into the post office and burned the literature. The crowd dispersed only after it succeeded in burning effigies of William Lloyd Garrison and other notorious abolitionists as well.[3] Grimké no doubt read accounts of the melee and noted the vitriol that the Charleston newspapers exhibited in reporting the incident. Shortly after the confrontation, the *Courier* predicted ominously that "the exposure of U.S. Mail and Post Offices to mob violence, which however temperate now, may ultimately fall into its usual and dangerous excesses, is an evil of serious magnitude and general concern and one that ought not to be thus wantonly provoked."[4]

Grimké was no doubt uncertain whether members of her family and former friends had participated in the violence. She may have worried that someone close to her had taken part in the very actions that she had resolved to address personally. Both that disturbing possibility as well as the reality of her slave-holding family focused and energized her abolitionist efforts. In 1836, the following year, she made her first great contribution to the cause of emancipation, her *Appeal to the Christian Women of the South*, a book also publicly burned in Charleston. This was a work deeply rooted in evidence from scripture and directly aimed at gaining the eternal salvation of her slaveholding "sisters in Christ" in South Carolina.

Angelina Grimké is widely recognized as one of the nineteenth century's most eloquent and effective advocates for emancipation. As a southerner, she offered a compelling voice for the cause of abolition. Together with her sister Sarah she challenged others to examine their hearts and actions on matters of religion and morality. They joined hands in protesting the practice of segregation in worship services of the Society of Friends. For several months in 1837 they toured the Northeast speaking to audiences made up of both men and women about the evils of slavery. On February 21, 1838, Angelina became the first woman to address a meeting of a state legislature when she spoke to the Massachusetts Legislature on abolition. And on May 17, 1838, just a few days after marrying fellow abolitionist Theodore Weld, Angelina addressed an overflow crowd at

ANGELINA GRIMKÉ

Courtesy of the Library of Congress, Washington, D.C.

Philadelphia's newly constructed Pennsylvania Hall, delivering one of the most dramatic antislavery speeches ever given by anyone.

The Grimké sisters quickly became famous as abolitionists, which led many to protest the fact that women were assuming such a public role. In 1837, the General Association of Congregational Churches of Massachusetts issued a famous "Pastoral Letter" denouncing the behavior of women "who so far forget themselves as to itinerate in the character of public lecturers and teachers." It insisted that Congregational churches throughout the state deny them a venue for their speeches—an act that only enhanced their notoriety and swelled their audiences. Grimké also wrote a series of letters that were initially published in Garrison's *Liberator* in which she forcefully rebutted fellow abolitionist Catherine Beecher's contention, proffered in her *Essay on Slavery and Abolition with Reference to the Duties of American Females* (1837), that women ought not to engage in matters outside their sphere. Many other abolitionists likewise objected to their activism, fearing that the participation of women in their movement would hurt their cause. They worried that the political argument that the Grimké sisters were making about the rights and power of women would undercut the effectiveness of the religious and moral justification for abolition. This resistance led Angelina and Sarah to become advocates of women's rights as well as opponents of slavery, and they are famous in American history as pioneers in both the antislavery and women's movements.[5]

Less well known is Angelina Grimké's concern about her own family as slaveholders and the challenge she offered to them concerning religion, morality, and slavery. The Grimké sisters had high hopes that their beloved brother, Thomas Grimké, who remained in South Carolina and was involved in the American Colonization Society, would become an abolitionist, but he died in 1834 and with him their closest link to their Charleston family. None of their other brothers and sisters shared their antislavery sentiments, to say the least, nor did their mother, Mary Smith Grimké. After moving to the North, the sisters never saw their mother again: when Angelina's *Appeal* was published, Mrs. Grimké was warned by Charleston police that if Angelina returned home she would be arrested and sent North. But until her death in 1839 Mrs. Grimké maintained a warm and loving correspondence with her exiled daughters. Their other sisters also maintained a respectful and somewhat friendly correspondence, though they were very hostile to their sisters' antislavery views and activism.[6]

Angelina's *Appeal* was directed not just to her family members, however, but to all southern women. Angelina hoped they could be reached by one of their own and be persuaded to use their influence on southern male slave owners to bring an end to the evil institution at the heart of their society. In her eloquent

Appeal, she stated that she knew southern women did "not make the laws," yet they were "the wives and mothers, the sisters and daughters of those who do." She urged them to read and pray about slavery and then to act—freeing slaves if they could, petitioning for emancipation, and, at the very least, violating the law against teaching slaves to read. She implored each reader: "Try to persuade your husband, father, brothers and sons that slavery is a crime *against God and man.*" This was, above all, a moral issue.[7]

Many recent treatments of Angelina Grimké's antislavery rhetoric have argued that social reform was in large part the aim of her efforts. It is undeniable that her immediate goal was to end slavery. It was not just public policy that she wanted to reform, however. It was even more important to her to reclaim the soul of the slave owner.

Grimké participated in a crusade that not only was significant in political terms but was nothing less than a grand "redemption drama."[8] At times, she aimed her argument at a northern audience that heard or read it; more importantly, she targeted a southern audience she hoped would read it. Grimké acknowledged the validity of the regional values her southern kinsmen held, but she argued that these values could not justify the perpetuation of slavery. In other words, she used proslavery values to undermine the *virtue* of slavery. By turning one fundamental aspect of her hearers' identity against another, she offered her audience a clear path to redemption. She was more a redeemer than a reformer.

Angelina had been deeply disturbed by slavery when she lived in Charleston and appalled by her own family's participation in its cruelties. In one instance she had personally intervened to save one of her brother's slaves from a beating.[9] Of that incident she wrote that the sounds of such beatings "went like daggers to my heart, & this was done too in the house of one who is regarded as a light in the Church. O Jesus where is thy meek and merciful disposition to be found now, are the works of discipleship changed or where are thy true disciples."[10] The burden of living in a land of slavery, indeed, of living in a house of slavery, became too heavy for her. She left her native Charleston and comfortable home to escape the horrors of an oppressive society and the debilitating effects it had on her soul. Almost without exception, however, despite her words and her actions, the members of her family remained mired in what she considered to be the sinful practice of slaveholding.

Grimké found a degree of solace in Philadelphia that she could not hope to find in South Carolina. She found comfort and acceptance among her Quaker brethren. In fact, Angelina utilized much scriptural support in the *Appeal,* seeking, perhaps, to justify her new militancy to her Quaker community and perhaps to her sister Sarah. A more likely aim, however, was to win the redemption of all her spiritually wayward "sisters." Grimké's position was clear. Her rhetoric explicitly articulated her fear for the souls of her family. She wrote in the *Appeal*: "It is because sin is imputed to us just in proportion to the spiritual light we receive. Then, the prophet Amos, in the name of Jehovah, You only have known of all the families on earth: therefore I will punish you for all your iniquities."[11] To Grimké there were consequences for the actions people take, consequences that have eternal implications. She feared for the ultimate salvation of her family.

In the *Appeal* and in her subsequent antislavery rhetoric, Grimké was primarily concerned with saving the souls of the slave owner. While other antislavery crusaders sought to deliver the oppressed from the oppressor, Angelina worked to save the oppressors from themselves and from eternal damnation. She fashioned herself as a redeemer, and the public discourse that she produced was likewise the rhetoric of redemption.

Grimké argued that slave owners violated the laws of God, the natural order, and the sacred principle of the new nation, which was the unassailable primacy of the individual. "We [abolitionists] say," she wrote, "that all the laws which sustain the system of slavery are unjust and oppressive—contrary to the fundamental principles of morality, and therefore, null and void."[12] She then identified republican values, the values of the nation's founders, as the values that informed the fundamental principles of morality:

> We hold that all slaveholding laws violate the fundamental principles of the Constitution of the United States. In the preamble of that instrument, the great objects for which it was framed are declared to be "to establish justice, to promote the general welfare, and to secure the blessings of liberty to us and our posterity." The slave laws are flagrant violations of these principles.[13]

More importantly, Grimké specifically identified Christian beliefs (even perhaps the meaning of the creation story itself) as under assault by proslavery advocates. She wrote that slavery should be immediately ended because "liberty is due every American citizen according to the laws of God and the Constitution of our country; and a fair recompense for his labor is the right of every man."[14] In her *Appeal*, Grimké also cited the Declaration of Independence's underlying principle of individualism. She argued that

> it is even a greater absurdity to suppose a man can be legally born a slave under our free Republican government, than under the petty despotisms of barbarian Africa.

If then, we have no right to enslave an African, surely we can have none to enslave an American; if it is a self-evident truth that all men, everywhere, and of every color are born equal, and have an inalienable right to liberty, then it is equally true that no man can be born a slave, and no man can ever rightly be reduced to involuntary bondage and held as a slave, however fair may be the claim of his master or mistress through wills and title-deeds.[15]

The argument was brilliantly constructed. It struck at the heart of the southern justification for slavery that had been put forth since the eighteenth century. The argument that slavery was a "positive good" because slaves were "better off" had taken deep root. But, by the same token, in the early republic, the principle of individualism had been infused into the nation's psyche and its politics. The Revolution was fought and won on the inalienable right of human beings to pursue their own happiness. The "positive good" justification for the continuation of slavery was at odds with this new national philosophy. Slave owners would have to oppose either slavery or the primacy of the individual. It was a difficult dilemma for the slave owner, and Grimké knew it.

Grimké understood the dialectical bind in which proslavery advocates found themselves. Her approach, however, was not shared by all abolitionists. For example, Catharine Beecher (Harriet Beecher Stowe's older sister), with whom Grimké participated in an ongoing public debate about abolition principles and women's public activism, chose a fundamentally different political strategy. Beecher, as well as other moderate abolitionists, aimed their efforts at alleviating the suffering of the slave. Because Beecher was convinced that total and immediate emancipation could not possibly be achieved peacefully she argued for a more measured approach than Grimké and other like-minded abolitionists were willing to advocate. Beecher wrote that "the wisdom and rectitude of a given course depend entirely on the probability of success."[16] It is likely that Beecher saw the problem of slavery more as a political one, unlike Grimké, who regarded it as a spiritual or moral challenge. To Beecher, reproaches and rebukes would not end slavery but rather would worsen the conditions under which the slaves lived. She argued:

The best way to make a person like a thing which is disagreeable is to try, in some way, to make it agreeable; and if a certain class of persons is the subject of unreasonable prejudice, the peaceful and Christian way of removing it would be to endeavor to render the unfortunate persons who compose this class, so useful, so humble and assuming, so kind in their feelings, and so full of love and good works, that prejudice would be supplanted by complacency in their goodness and their pity and sympathy for their disabilities.[17]

In one of her celebrated letters, Grimké responded to Beecher's pragmatic proposal in the starkest terms:

> So then, instead of convincing a person by sound argument and pointed rebuke that sin is sin, we are to disguise the opposite virtue in such a way as to make him like that, in preference to the sin he had so dearly loved. We are to cheat a sinner out of his sin, rather than compel him, under the stings of conviction, to give it up from deep-rooted principle. . . . Or, in other words, if one person is guilty of a sin against another person, I am to let the sinner go entirely unreproved, but to persuade the injured party to bear with humility and patience all the outrages that are inflicted upon him, and thus try to soothe the sinner into complacency with their goodness in bearing all things, and enduring all things.[18]

Grimké's argument was aimed at what she saw as the destruction of the natural moral order, and it allowed for no compromise. On its face, Grimké's argument required her audience to radically change its perspective, and it provided a large dose of moral clarity. It changed the nature of the debate. To Grimké the dispute was not about the physical well-being of the slave as much as it was about the spiritual well-being of the slave owner. But slavery's defenders did not submit easily. In response to Grimké's moral argument, proslavery advocates turned the debate again to focus on the slave. Their strategy was to dehumanize the slave—effectively to deny that the slave had an equal place in creation and to reject the idea that the slave was an inheritor of the new nation's freedom.

The Revolution's republican roots led to America's declaration of the inalienable rights of the individual. The national commitment to this ideal was so strong that it ultimately led to our almost reverential regard for individual rights. Even in the early nineteenth century, this national commitment to individual rights made it difficult, on a rational level, for the southern slave owner to justify slavery. The belief in human equality mandated the search for commonalities, not the differences on which the justification for slavery had been built. Individual rights became so important to the nation's political philosophy that the very identity of the country was defined by it. Individualism took on almost religious significance; certainly, it became spiritual in character.[19] As the practice of slavery persisted in the South, a new social and moral order based on a growing national solidarity with respect to the issue of equal rights was emerging, one that was utilized effectively by Grimké when addressing her southern "kinsmen" about the evils of slavery.

Even before the Revolution, there had been debate about the morality and the wisdom of slavery. Eighteenth-century slaveholders had viewed the kinship community in which they lived as populated with people who each had their own responsibilities and obligations. The slaveholding patriarchs took the position—one that was clearly not egalitarian and certainly not consistent with the individualism that grew out of the Revolution—that their responsibility to the free and unfree members of their plantation communities was like that of a father to his children. Slaves were seen as obligated to labor in exchange for their masters' protection and provision, allowing the enterprise to prosper and the community to be strengthened.

As the final years of the eighteenth century loomed, antislavery rhetoric began to reflect the new principle of individualism. In 1791, for example, Jonathan Edwards Jr., the son of the great revivalist preacher, spoke to the Connecticut Society for the Promotion of Freedom and for the Relief of Persons Unlawfully Holden in Bondage. He suggested that the Revolution had universalized, or nearly so, the acceptance of the value of individual freedom, the fundamental concept of republicanism, and that the ideal was inconsistent with the perpetuation of slavery. Edwards stated it plainly. He argued that slavery "is unjust in the same sense, and for the same reason, that it is, to steal, to rob, or to murder. It is a principle, the truth of which hath in this country been generally, if not universally acknowledged since the commencement of the late war, *that all men are born equally free.*"[20] Edwards reasoned that to keep slaves would be the same as stealing from them or even murdering them.

As did Grimké, Edwards pointed to the philosophical dilemma that the southern slaveholder had had to face since the successful conclusion of the Revolution. It appeared that the slaveholder's paternalism could no longer survive the growing (and in Edwards's words, almost universal) acceptance of the ideal of individual and natural rights. Edwards was eloquent in juxtaposing these two positions and exposing the contradiction between them. It seemed that white southerners must choose, that they must abandon either the new national identity or support for slavery. Edwards further clarified the dilemma by arguing that "there are indeed cases in which men may justly be deprived of their liberty and reduced to slavery, as there are cases in which they may be justly deprived of their lives. But they justly can be deprived of neither, unless they have by their own voluntary conduct forfeited it. Therefore still the right to liberty stands on the same basis as the right to life."[21] These ideas ushered in by the Revolution and so eloquently articulated by Edwards, and later by Angelina Grimké, represented a frontal assault on both the eighteenth-century justification of slavery and the more brutal rhetoric of subsequent generations. The notion of the rights of the individual was newly applied to slavery by speakers such as Edwards, but the application of natural law had long been a common rhetorical vehicle for slavery's opponents.

Seventeen years before Edwards's sermon, John Wesley, the founder of Methodism, had written of the inconsistency between slavery and moral law. Wesley proclaimed, "But waving, for the present, all other considerations, I strike at the root of this complicated villainy; I absolutely deny all slaveholding to be consistent with any degree of natural justice."[22] While Edwards focused on the right of slaves to enjoy freedom, Wesley touted justice and mercy as natural rights. Wesley argued that "all slavery is as irreconcilable to justice as to mercy."[23] Justice, to Wesley was tied to the right to liberty; therefore denying it was an injustice. He wrote that "liberty is the right of every human creature, as soon as he breathes the vital air; and no human law can deprive him of that right which he derives from the law of nature."[24] For Wesley, these natural rights had a near biblical or spiritual basis. In a passage that may best summarize his assault against slavery, Wesley wrote:

> May I speak plainly to you? I must. Love constrained me; love to you, as well as to those you are concerned with. Is there a God? Then there must be a state of retribution; a state wherein the just God will reward every man according to his works. Then what reward will he render to you? O think betimes! Before you drop into eternity! Think now. "He shall have judgment without mercy that showed no mercy."[25]

Wesley seemed to connect the political ideas of freedom and justice to the fate of one's soul. Natural rights arguments that were utilized by Wesley and others prior to the Revolution were universalized, which led to a growing reverence for the individual. This burgeoning republican movement undermined the justification for slavery. So the argument connecting slavery to the destruction of both the social and moral order had been well established by the 1830s when Grimké refined it further.

By this time there had been an unlikely reframing of the proslavery argument, a reframing intended to render it consistent with republican values. After the rise of the new ideal, proslavery rhetoric abandoned the "positive good" arguments of the previous generation and attempted instead to dehumanize the slave and outrightly appropriate republican values. After this rhetorical transformation, slavery advocates could proclaim allegiance to the natural human right to freedom and support slavery at the same time. They could appear to be consistent with republicanism by denying that the slave had individual worth.

One such attempt was made by a South Carolina academic named Thomas Cooper, who wrote in 1835 that "if the known laws of human nature have anything to do with the rights of man, then it is a known law of human nature, from the very commencement of historical records, throughout the whole surface of the globe, that the black race has been inferior to and held in bondage by the white race."[26] Cooper did not reject the force of natural law but argued that natural law logically led one to redefine the republican notion of universal equality. To Cooper, "universal" freedom did not apply to blacks and whites alike. The arguments utilized by Cooper and his proslavery cohorts, however, did not rely exclusively on historical claims to dehumanize the slave. They also attempted to reduce the humanity of slaves by denigrating their physical, intellectual, and spiritual attributes. If slavery's apologists could successfully argue that blacks were less than human, then they could argue that the republican mandate of natural human rights would not apply to them. Cooper offered "scientific" support for his effort to dehumanize blacks. He wrote that "the Blacks may be of the same species, for the mixed progeny will breed. But they are an inferior variety of the animal, man. . . . Let any man draw an imaginary line on a black's head from the centre of one ear to the centre of the other, and he will find the mass of brains *behind* in the black, and *before* in the white."[27]

Cooper went on to describe and compare the physiology of the white man and the black man. He reasoned that if blacks were *by nature* so inferior as to be incapable of freedom, then it was improper for even republicans to grant it. Cooper in essence argued that the natural right of freedom that all humans enjoy (proclaimed in the Declaration of Independence and institutionalized as a result of the success of the Revolution) did not apply to the slave because of deficiencies *intended by nature*. So, proslavery advocates argued, slavery was consistent with republican values after all.

The racism that characterized proslavery rhetoric in the nineteenth century, however, did not manifest itself only in the attempt to dehumanize slaves by identifying physical and intellectual deficiencies. Others argued that there was scriptural support to establish the inferiority of blacks on spiritual and moral grounds. For example, George Freeman of North Carolina proclaimed in 1836:

[Slavery] may be regarded as one of the penal consequences of sin—an effect of that doom pronounced upon the human race in consequence of the disobedience of our first parents, whereby perpetual labour was entailed upon man as the only means of sustaining life—"Cursed is the ground for thy sake; in sorrow shalt thou eat of it all the days of thy life. In the swat of thy face shalt thou eat bread till thou return unto the ground." Though this sentence was passed upon mankind generally, it was not to be expected, that its effects would continue for any length of time to be felt by all alike. There would of necessity, very soon arise an inequality among men.[28]

Freeman's position was not dehumanizing in the same way as that of other pro-slavery advocates, not in the same sense as Cooper, for example, but it did deni-grate the spiritual worth of the slave, which is perhaps a more insidious form of racism. Later, Freeman was more direct in his denigration of the morality of Africans. He preached:

> The country from whence the slaves of this continent have been derived, it is agreed by the most learned and judicious authors, is that assigned in the division of earth, to the descendants of *Ham*, the reprobate, or at least, the *grievously offending* son of Noah; upon whom and his posterity, the patriarch, guided by inspiration, pronounced the memorable sentence, recorded in the ninth chapter of Genesis.[29]

Thus to Freeman, the servant class suffered as it did because people were being punished by God. There was not only a natural reason for their condition but a moral one as well. Although Freeman advocated religious instruction of slaves, he clearly indicated that the necessity was not as urgent, nor would it be as effec-tive as such instruction directed toward others in the community. While Free-man suggested that salvation was open to all people, he repeatedly described the natural state of the African as more "debased in intellect, in knowledge, in the moral perceptions, and in the perceptions of the heart, than the lowest of this class here."[30] Although Freeman's racism appears to be less brutal than that of others, he nonetheless argued that the differences between the two races were significant and comprehensive.

Presumably, the proslavery argument was that if men moved to free slaves, they would be acting against common sense, against nature, and against God. Cooper summarized the position with clarity: "We talk a great deal of nonsense about the rights of man. We say that every man is born free, and equal to every other man. Nothing can be more untrue. No human being ever was, now is, or ever will be born free."[31] Cooper seemed to believe that human rights applied only to certain men as nature determined. The conclusion he came to was that nature, not man, had assigned the slave his inferior status. The dehumanization and spiritual devaluation of slaves allowed nineteenth-century proslavery ad-vocates to argue that they were republicans, slaveholders, and good Christians without contradiction.

Even one of Angelina's brothers rejected her argument. Frederick Grimké echoed the sentiment of the master class, that the slave was unworthy of free-dom: "The black race do not appear to have possessed even the faculty of imi-tating, so as to build up any institutions resembling those which were trans-ported to their soil. This race still continues wrapped up in that immovable state

of barbarism and inertia which existed four thousand years ago."[32] Frederick
Grimké took his argument to another level, however. He not only maintained
that the "black race" was barbarous but also that the distinction was a perpetual
condition, suggesting that it was naturally intended. He wrote that

> according to all the laws which have hitherto governed civilization, Africa should
> have been civilized as early as Europe. We can give no further account why it has
> not been, than that there is an inherent and indelible distinction between the two
> races, which retains one closely within a certain limit, and permits the other to
> spring far beyond it. To deny the distinction is not a mark of philanthropy, but
> rather a defiance of those laws which have been imposed by the Deity, and which
> are no more inconsistent with his benevolence, than innumerable physical and
> mental differences which exist among individuals of the same race.[33]

In the minds of many nineteenth-century slaveholders, as long as slavery
produced equality among whites, then the institution promoted republicanism.
Jefferson Davis articulated that very argument before the Senate in 1859:

> To propose that we should change our industrial system, that we should bring the
> negroes up to a level with the white man, would be such an offense that the lec-
> turer who would come to teach such philosophy would be fortunate indeed if he
> should escape without some public indignity. One of the reconciling features in the
> existence of that particular institution called domestic slavery of African bonds-
> men, is the fact that it raises white men to the same general level, that it dignifies
> and exalts every white man by the presence of a lower race. I say it in no terms of
> disparaging comparison with others. I say but what has been with me a deliberate
> conviction, that is promotive of, if not essential to, the preservation of the higher
> orders of republican civilization.[34]

To Davis and other proslavery advocates, slavery was not only consistent with
republican values, but its continuation ensured the preservation of those ideals.
Proslavery rhetoric included more far-reaching claims, however. Since slavery
preserved republican ideals, southern slaveholders argued that abolitionism
threatened the unity and stability of the nation. This position helps to explain,
perhaps, why the Charleston mob, in the summer of 1835, felt so threatened by
the arrival of antislavery pamphlets at the post office. South Carolina's John C.
Calhoun made the argument that "the constitution is stable. It is a rock. On it
we stand, and on it we can meet our friends from the non-slaveholding States.
It is a firm and stable ground, on which we can better stand in opposition to
fanaticism, than on sifting sands of compromise."[35] Frederick Grimké offered a
slightly different logical path to the same conclusion:

Now if we suppose that the American negroes, on being emancipated, will fall into the inert and sluggish habits which characterize their race throughout Africa, in Jamaica and Hayti; that they will be content with a few acres of ground, upon which to seat themselves, and to vegetate in a condition little above that of the brutes, we cannot make the same calculations as if the country were peopled by the white race alone.[36]

To proslavery advocates, slavery supported republicanism generally and the Constitution specifically. If slavery could be preserved, national unity and stability would follow.

The circularity of these arguments is breathtaking. In an effort to respond to the eloquently articulated position of Angelina Grimké and like-minded abolitionists, the institution's advocates first dehumanized the slave, effectively marginalizing him from the fruits of the new republic. Then the proslavery camp appropriated and celebrated republicanism itself.

Although the rhetoric of Grimké and other abolitionists was met with resourceful, if fanciful, discursive contortions, it succeeded in transforming the national debate about slavery. It forced slave owners to consider their own souls and their own eternal survival. It forced Grimké's former neighbors and even her family to face the challenge that the young republic required of them. Of all the abolitionists of her day, Angelina Grimké was perhaps the most effective. Her unique perspective and rhetorical objective certainly gained her a wide constituency.

Angelina Grimké provided a brand of abolitionism unique in the 1830s. Her rhetoric was primarily directed at redemption. Grimké's efforts were aimed less at emancipation of the slave than at the salvation of the slave owner. As she explained to Catharine Beecher:

In the work in which abolitionists are engaged, they are compelled to 'walk by faith;' they feel called upon to preach the truth in season and out of season, to lift up their voices like a trumpet, to show the people their transgressions and the house of Jacob their sins. The success of this mission, they have no more to do with, than had Moses and Aaron, Jeremiah or Isaiah, with that of theirs. Whether the South will be saved by Anti-Slavery efforts, is not a question for us to settle—and in some of our hearts, the hope of its salvation has utterly gone out.[37]

Grimké left the question to individual slave owners and their God. "The result of our labors is hidden from our eyes," she insisted. But the preaching of "anti-Slavery truth" was quite simply her duty.[38]

Angelina Grimké died on October 26, 1879. But she never ceased to care about her South Carolina family and its participation in the institution of slavery. And she cared about *all* of her family. That she and Sarah stood out among Americans of the nineteenth century—including abolitionists—for their abhorrence of race discrimination as well as slavery became clear when they welcomed into their home and family three young men who were sons of their brother Henry by a slave, Nancy Weston. With the aid of their aunts, two of the young men, Francis James Grimké and Archibald Henry Grimké went on to Princeton Theological Seminary and Harvard Law School, respectively, and to become leaders in the movement for the rights of African Americans.[39]

Historian Stephen Howard Brown has written that "Angelina Grimké lived her life in the spaces between, in the gaps and fissures that separated her from what was left behind and from a more perfect future."[40] It was her role as redeemer, however, that connected her to what she left behind, and it was her steadfast belief that redemption was possible for all people, even slave owners, that kept her gaze and her hopes fixed on a more perfect future.

NOTES

1. Angelina Grimké, *Slavery and the Boston Riot* (Philadelphia: American Anti-Slavery Society, 1835).

2. *Charleston Courier*, July 30, 1835.

3. Gerda Lerner, *The Grimké Sisters from South Carolina: Pioneers for Women's Rights and Abolition* (New York: Oxford University Press, 1998), 93.

4. *Charleston Courier*, July 31, 1835.

5. Lerner, *The Grimké Sisters from South Carolina*, 131–34.

6. Ibid., 75, 76, 98–101, 188, 189.

7. Ibid., 95, 96.

8. See Kenneth Burke, *Rhetoric of Religion* (Berkeley: University of California Press, 1970), 208–22. For an excellent analysis of Burke's redemption drama see David A. Bobbitt, *The Rhetoric of Redemption: Kenneth Burke's Redemption Drama and Martin Luther King Jr.'s "I Have a Dream" Speech* (Lanham, Md.: Rowman and Littlefield, 2004).

9. Charles Wilbanks, ed., *Walking By Faith: The Diary of Angelina Grimké, 1828–1835* (Columbia: University of South Carolina Press, 2003), 39.

10. Ibid., 37–38.

11. Angelina Grimké, *Appeal to the Christian Women of the South*, in *The Public Years of Sarah and Angelina Grimké: Selected Writings*, ed. Larry Ceplair (New York: Columbia University Press, 1989), 56.

12. Angelina Grimké, *Letters to Catharine E. Beecher* (Boston: I. Knapp, 1838), 9.

13. Ibid., 9.

14. Ibid., 11.

15. Angelina Grimké, *Appeal*, 37.

16. Catharine Beecher, *An Essay on Slavery and Abolitionism with Reference to the Duties of American Females* (Philadelphia: H. Perkins, 1837), 47–48.

17. Ibid., 26–27.

18. Angelina Grimké, *Letters*, 42–43.

19. For a more in-depth discussion of making the individual sacred, see *Durkheim on Religion: A Selection of Readings with Bibliographies*, ed. W. S. F. Pickering, trans. Ephriam Fischoff (London: Routledge and Kegan Paul, 1975), 62.

20. Jonathan Edwards, *The Works of Jonathan Edwards* (Andover, Mass.: Allen, Morrill and Wardell, 1842), 76.

21. Ibid., 76.

22. John Wesley, *Political Writings of John Wesley*, ed. Graham Maddox (Bristol, U.K.: Thoemmes Press, 1998), 97.

23. Ibid., 97.

24. Ibid., 105.

25. Ibid., 103.

26. Thomas Cooper, "Slavery," *Southern Literary Journal* 1, no. 3 (1835): 188–89.

27. Ibid., 192.

28. George W. Freeman, *The Rights and Duties of Slaveholders: Two Discourses Delivered on Sunday, November 27, 1836, in Christ Church, Raleigh, North Carolina* (Charleston, S.C.: A. E. Miller, 1837), 5.

29. Ibid., 14.

30. Ibid., 18.

31. Cooper, "Slavery," 189.

32. Frederick Grimké, *Considerations Upon the Nature and Tendency of Free Institutions* (Cincinnati, Ohio: H. W. Derby, 1848), 329.

33. Ibid., 329–30.

34. Jefferson Davis, *Jefferson Davis Constitutionalist: His Letters, Papers, and Speeches*, comp. Dunbar Rowland, 10 vols. (Jackson: Mississippi Department of Archives and History, 1923), 4:49.

35. John C. Calhoun, *The Essential Calhoun: Selections from Writings, Speeches, and Letters*, ed. Clyde N. Wilson (New Brunswick, N.J.: Transaction Publishers, 2000), 388.

36. Frederick Grimké, *Considerations*, 335.

37. Angelina Grimké, *Letters*, 55–56.

38. Ibid., 56.

39. Lerner, *The Grimké Sisters from South Carolina*, 257–62; Betty L. Fladeland, "Sarah Moore and Angelina Emily Grimké," in *Notable American Women, 1607–1950: A Biographical Dictionary*, ed. Edward T. James, 3 vols. (Cambridge, Mass., Harvard University Press, 1971), 2:97–99.

40. Stephen Howard Browne, *Angelina Grimké: Rhetoric, Identity and the Radical Imagination* (East Lansing: Michigan State University Press, 1999), 1.

Elizabeth Allston Pringle

A Woman Rice Planter

CHARLES JOYNER

The Allston family had been long settled in the Georgetown District of South Carolina. The family was a large one, and the residence of one branch was at Chicora Wood Plantation on the Pee Dee River, where for many generations its members had engaged in planting thousands of acres of rice. The rice fields lay just along the river. They were originally cypress swamps that were cleared and drained by slave labor. The fields could be flooded or drained, as needed, by a system of canals and small floodgates called trunks and trunk docks. West of the rice fields was a belt of upland covered with live oaks. Here the provision crops of rye, peas, corn, oats, and potatoes were grown. And here too were the fabled Big Houses of the rice planters, situated at the end of avenues of moss-draped live oaks. The rice planters considered their plantations, for all their profitability, to be unhealthy places during the summers. "No white person could remain on the plantation," according to Elizabeth Watie Allston, called Bessie, "without danger, of the most virulent fever, always spoken of as 'country fever.'" It was commonly believed that "to remain here a Summer will be Suicide." So each summer rice plantation households "migrated to the sea" and did not return until early November, "by which time cold weather had come and the danger of malarial fever gone." Bessie described the Allston summer home at Pawleys Island as "only four miles to the east of Chicora as the crow flies, but was only to be reached by going seven miles in a rowboat and four miles by land." It was there that Bessie was born, May 29, 1845. "To me it has always been intoxicating," she would later write of Pawleys Island, "that first view each year of the waves rolling, rolling; and the smell of the sea, and the brilliant blue expanse; but then I was born there and it is like a renewal of birth."[1]

In Bessie's self-consciously aristocratic plantation world, family pride

achieved a remarkable strength and vitality. It was through family ties that
land, wealth, and power were channeled from generation to generation. It was
through family ties that members of the slaveholding class were inculcated with
the patriarchal code of honor. Every element of life was affected by the values of
duty, paternalism, and family pride inherent in the southern ethic. The Allston
family stood at the very center of the antebellum plantation aristocracy of large
slaveholders. The Allstons possessed a strong sense of family purpose based
on traditions of patriarchal accomplishment, traditions that became the standard by which later generations measured themselves and their place in history.
Each generation was expected to achieve additional success, to bring additional
honor on the family.[2]

The master of Chicora Wood was a singular man. Holding title to 630 human
beings, Robert F. W. Allston was one of the South's largest slaveholders and one
of the region's most conspicuously successful planters. After serving in the state
legislature for twenty-eight years, he was governor of South Carolina from 1856
to 1858. He was also widely known across the region for his articulate publications on rice culture and seacoast crops. The mistress of Chicora Wood was
wealthy and well connected in her own right. The beauty and grace of Bessie's
mother (if not her bloodlines) met the exacting standards expected of a plantation mistress. Adele Petigru Allston was born on a modest Upcountry farm into
a Scotch-Irish family with distant French Huguenot ancestry. Her brother, the
noted Charleston lawyer and outspoken Unionist James Louis Petigru, changed
the family name from Pettigrew "back" to its supposed French original. Their
mother's Gibert family was Huguenot, and a Huguenot name was thought to be
of social advantage in South Carolina. Another brother, Thomas Petigru, a U.S.
Navy captain, married Robert F. W. Allston's neighbor Mary Ann LaBruce and
acquired a rice plantation on Sandy Island.[3]

Bessie Allston's world was circumscribed by a web of race, class, and gender
that can be understood only within the context of patriarchal society. Women
were expected to exemplify the "feminine virtues" of nurturing and self-sacrifice.
In theory women were not expected to voice their own wants or needs, to think
for themselves, or to speak their own minds. In reality the situation was more
complex. Within the plantation household, women might possess considerable
residual power to influence family life or even political opinion, but only if
they exercised it with public circumspection. Nevertheless the power to influence was not the power to govern. If husband and wife held differing opinions,
the wife could see her wishes overruled. If males were so inclined—and most
were—then they remained firmly in charge. Adherence to such gender and
family conventions was enforced by community pressures. These conventions

MRS. PRINGLE AT CHICORA WOOD.
Photograph by Amelia M. Watson.

ELIZABETH ALLSTON PRINGLE WITH AN UNIDENTIFIED
AFRICAN AMERICAN WOMAN AT CHICORA WOOD

Courtesy of the South Caroliniana Library, University of South Carolina, Columbia.

offered little to women beyond the prestige accruing from their proximity to powerful husbands or fathers.[4]

Although women in the Old South were proscribed from speaking out in public, when displeased many of them raised objections privately. Bessie's mother, Adele, was a woman who voiced her frustrations, which her husband saw as a lamentable example of insubordination. The problem, as he perceived it, was simply "an error of belief" on Adele's part. He added ominously that it was an error "which must prove fatal to our peace unless corrected." Robert grumbled that "on the least difference between us you impute to me 'unkindness'. . . . If Providence has endowed me with some judgment & firmness in the management of affairs," he wrote to her, "you certainly have enjoy'd the benefits, common to my family, derived from their exercise. They may be entitled to some respect from you in common with the rest."[5]

It fell within the mother's sphere to instruct the young in proper codes of behavior. She might use that responsibility to make a daughter subservient to patriarchal authority. Or she might use that responsibility to teach a daughter to think for herself. When Adele required Bessie to keep "a journal of all that had taken place the day before," ostensibly as a writing exercise, she could not have been unaware that the act of writing in itself might very well promote contradictory feelings on Bessie's part. With few exceptions, southern ladies were expected to accept male opinions without question, but writing necessitated thinking for one's self. Whatever Adele's motivation, Bessie acquired the writing (and thinking) habit while still a very young girl.[6]

Despite Adele's efforts and example, it was to her father rather than her mother that Bessie looked for the embodiment of southern virtue, with its propensity to exalt the "manly virtue" of control—control over one's slaves, over one's self, and over one's wife and children. The patriarchal culture encouraged daughters to look to their fathers as authority figures to be obeyed without question and helped to assure that women upheld the male-centered order. Bessie saw her father as a man of great courage and personal rectitude, a strict but fair disciplinarian. She had never known him to "show a trace of weakness or indecision," she would later write, never known him to be "unjust or hasty in his judgment of a person," had never seen him "give way to temper or irritation, though I had seen him greatly tried," and had never seen in him any "sign of self-indulgence, or indolence, or selfishness." He was "the only person in the world in whom I had absolute faith and confidence." In his daughter's eyes, Robert F. W. Allston was society's "ideal type."[7]

Bessie was tutored by an English governess at Chicora Wood until she was nine, when she joined her older sister at Mme. Acelie Togno's boarding school in Charleston, with its gracefully curving balconies overlooking Meeting Street. There she studied arithmetic, diction, English, French, history, music, and singing. Mme. Togno placed special emphasis on the fine arts, reinforced by frequent outings to concerts and the theater. The language of instruction was French. It was difficult at Mme. Togno's "to find a place where one could dream in peace," Bessie wrote. "There were girls everywhere jabbering bad French." But she eventually found a refuge where she could indulge her writing habit. "It was a great relief to write journals and pour out my woes to these safe confidants," she would recall. "When the outside world was too hard and unfeeling," she slipped away to her private retreat—under the dining table—"and wrote and wrote until my griefs were assuaged, then rolled up my treasure and returned to the outer world refreshed."[8]

Even in the summers, which she spent on Pawleys Island with her family, Bessie had to study and practice her music daily before she would be allowed to play on the beach. Bessie read French and English history. "It is delightful," she wrote in her journal at the age of sixteen, "to know something of the private life of those persons named in history and who took part in the great events on which the fate of all Europe depended." The Victorian passion for history tended to legitimate the experience of men as history's proper subject, relegating women's experience to the margins of history. But this lesson was at least partly offset by the influence of the Swedish traveler Frederika Bremer. Bessie poured over Bremer's account of her travels in America, including her visit to White House Plantation a few miles down the Pee Dee from Chicora Wood.[9]

When Bessie's father was elected governor of South Carolina in 1856, he bought the historic Nathaniel Russell House on lower Meeting Street in Charleston as a residence for official entertaining. One day Bessie's mother allowed the high-spirited girl to treat three of her friends to a ride through the streets of Charleston in the governor's open carriage. When the little group became rather more boisterous than befitted their station and began to sing, the family coachman stopped the carriage. Aleck Parker, who according to Bessie "always sat as straight as if he had been trained at West Point," commanded considerable deference within the Allston family. He turned around sternly. "'Miss Betsy,'" he said, "'if unna [second-person plural] kyant behave unna self, I'll tek yu straight home! Dis ain't no conduk fu de Gubner karridge!'" Bessie silently fumed. Another male, this time a slave, was telling her what to do. How far did male dominance extend?[10]

As the secession crisis deepened into a long war, South Carolina aristocrats found it increasingly difficult to maintain their lifestyle. Bessie wrote in her diary that she had endured "some hardships." The fare at Mme. Togno's school "has been poor," she wrote. "We always have meat once a day; our supper consists of a huge tray of corn dodgers which is brought into the school-room and placed on the table, that we may help ourselves and the tray goes back empty." Nevertheless, she felt "rather proud to feel that we are sharing, at a very safe distance, some of the hardships borne by our brave soldiers." By the end of May 1863, she was ready "to leave school today never to return! I suppose I am grown up! The war is raging, but we, shut up here with our books, and our little school tragedies and comedies, have remained very ignorant of all that is going on outside."[11]

Despite the war Bessie endeavored to remain "bright and cheerful." She saw a great many soldiers in Charleston. "The men are so charming," she wrote, "and look so nice in their uniforms." On June 20, 1863, she confided to her diary that she had been to "a most delightful dance in Fort Sumter. The night was lovely and we went down in rowing boats." Cannon balls were piled up in all directions and sentinels paced the fort's ramparts. Within the fort's walls, she described "pretty, well dressed women, and handsome well-bred men dancing, as though unconscious that we were actually under the guns of the blockading fleet." She found it "a strange scene." She considered it her first real party. "The strange charm of the situation wove a spell around me; every man seemed to me a hero—not only a possible but an actual hero! One looks at a man so differently when you think he may be killed tomorrow!"[12]

Bessie's father, bitterly disappointed at being passed over by the Confederacy for both civil and military posts, sullenly continued to manage his rice plantation at Chicora Wood. With the appearance of Union gunboats on the Pee Dee River, however, Robert F. W. Allston sought a safer refuge for his family. He removed them from Chicora Wood to Crowley Hill, a farm in Darlington County some eighty miles inland, while he stayed behind at Chicora Wood, venturing inland from time to time to visit his family for a few days. As the war ground on, the "manless little family" learned to improvise, to substitute, and to do without. They planted a garden to keep food on the table, but other supplies became increasingly scarce. They set up a loom in the kitchen, on which Bessie learned to weave, "and we knit, knit, knit all the time." They cut carpets into blankets and thick damask curtains into coats. The Civil War, fought partly to preserve the patriarchal system, inevitably undermined the false image of female helplessness on which the system had rested. Surviving and overcoming hardships by their own efforts gave Bessie and her mother a new sense of confidence in their own abilities.[13]

Bessie's own self-confidence was also bolstered by an exchange with her father shortly before he died in 1864. He had asked her to do something. She had answered that she could not, because she did not know how. He placed his hand on her shoulder and spoke to her very quietly and very solemnly. "Don't ever say that, my daughter. God has given it to you that whenever you put your whole self to accomplish anything you will succeed. When you fail it will be because you have not tried hard enough. Don't forget this; it is a great responsibility. Never say you cannot do a thing!" Perhaps Robert F. W. Allston was, at the last, recognizing the newly demonstrated ability of women to manage without men. More likely, he was merely making an exception to the prevailing gender conventions by applying the patriarchal values of duty, strength, and family pride to his daughter. In any event, Bessie never forgot his words. "Many times in my life when things have risen up before me which have seemed quite beyond my strength and capacity and endurance," she would later write, "I have remembered that conversation and gone ahead, only to find that he was right."[14]

The day her father died, Bessie was kneeling on the floor of his bedroom fervently praying for him. "I would kneel beside the bed and take his hand and he would press mine in a grip which showed his pain, and at last as I knelt there I gave him up and prayed God to relieve him from his agony." Finally, when she felt the end must be near, "he lifted his right hand with a powerful sweep and said in a strong voice, 'Lord, let me pass!' And it was all over in a few seconds, with no struggle or distress." He was buried on April 8, 1864, in the family plot at Prince Frederick's Episcopal Church in Pee Dee, not far from his beloved Chicora Wood. His death, which came just a month short of his sixty-third birthday, left Bessie with a "sense of terrible desolation and sorrow." For the rest of her life Bessie was seriously affected by her father's enduring presence.[15]

At his death Robert F. W. Allston left to each of his children a plantation and a hundred slaves. The task of managing them until the estate could be settled fell upon his widow. Bessie saw that her mother "was crushed not only by her grief but by the feeling that she was utterly inadequate to the task before her." But Bessie found it "perfectly wonderful to see how she rose to the requirements of the moment, and how strong and level her mind was." Despite Bessie's father's bequests, his children would receive no such inheritance. Robert F. W. Allston's estate was deeply encumbered by debt, and emancipation would eliminate property rights in slaves. The end of the war found his estate insolvent.[16]

In the meantime, conditions in Bessie's corner of the Confederacy went from bad to worse. In March 1865, foragers from General William Tecumseh Sherman's advancing legions ransacked Crowley Hill in search of firearms and liquor. Their arrival was preceded by news of the destruction that had accompanied Sherman's march. Bessie, her mother, and her sister sat up all night in the parlor, fully dressed, their most cherished valuables stuffed under their petticoats. Mrs. Allston read calmly while Bessie wrote in her journal and her sister Della slept on the sofa. "I never fully understood terror until now," Bessie wrote. "They delight in making terrible threats of vengeance and seem to gloat over our misery." She quoted a Union captain, who, in response to some suggestion about answering for one's sins, said "Oh I know what you mean[,] you mean the Almighty, but the Almighty had nothing to do with this war!" Bessie wrote in her journal that "such blasphemy silenced me completely."[17]

A messenger from Chicora Wood soon arrived at Crowley Hill to announce that "'a Capting from de Yankee A'my kum en a kerridge en tell de people dem is free en ebry ting belongst to dem. No wite people 'ill neber kum back, en den him 'stribute ebery ting,'" Bessie recalled. So she and her mother set out at daybreak for the two-day trip to Georgetown to consult with federal officials. Adele requested that Colonel P. P. Brown send a detachment of troops to take the barn keys from the former slaves and give them to her. "I acquiesce readily in the freeing of the negroes," she told him, "but surely our property should not be taken from us." He replied that he could do nothing for her until she took the oath of allegiance to the United States. Once she had done so, Brown wrote a note ordering the former slaves to deliver the keys to her. But she would have to enforce the order herself. He would not send even a single soldier with her.[18]

It was clear that the former slaves would not accept her authority easily. With the arrival of Union forces and the reality of emancipation, the newly freed slaves had plundered the most visible symbols of their former masters' power—the Big Houses, provision barns, store rooms, and smokehouses—and had divided the livestock among themselves. "The conduct of the negroes in robbing our house, store room[,] meat house etc. and refusing to restore anything," Adele commented subsequently, "shows you they think it right to steal from us." What Adele saw as thievery, however, the former slaves considered overdue payments for years of involuntary servitude.[19]

Down the road, the dust settling, Bessie and Adele returned in their carriage. The Big House seemed not to get nearer but just to float there in front of them, increasing slowly in size like something in a dream. By midmorning the sun was well forward in the sky. Normally the line of trees in the distance was a gray silhouette a little darker than the sky, but this morning the line was almost black. Behind it the March sky glared livid white.

At last the two women reached the Big House. As they drove into the yard, hundreds of armed and angry former slaves assembled to meet them. Adele leaned forward, shading her eyes from the piercing sunlight with her hand. Her pale sharp glance had already passed over everyone in the yard. A huge coffee-colored man came slowly forward. Adele spoke pleasantly with him, asking about his family and the old people on the plantation. "And now, Mack," she said finally, "I want the keys to the barn." The foreman did not seem to hear her at first. He smiled absently and stood looking at her. At length he replied, "De officer give me de key, ma'am, en I kyant gie um to yu." She raised her eyebrows in mock wonder and said, "I have here the officer's order to you to give the key to me." As he looked at the paper, a murmur arose from the crowd. A sullen and threatening young man brandished a sharp stone and aimed it at the two women. Then, as though to intimidate them, he came nearer and leaned on the wheel of the carriage. Bessie watched with a dazed stare as her mother stepped out into the midst of the former slaves, looking at them with her arms folded across her chest. Bessie wanted to grab her mother's coat and hold on like a child. But Adele quietly told her to stay in the carriage. The March day grew warmer, and the older woman walked slowly up and down among the former slaves, stopping to speak to each by name, inquiring after their children. Bessie said that her mother "showed no irritation, no impatience, only friendly interest, no sense that they could possibly be enemies." Soon the tension abated. The foreman gave Adele the keys without interference from the others, and the two women left.[20]

Despite the grudging respect won by Adele's show of courage, such assertiveness and independence on the part of blacks frustrated planters' desire for a disciplined and subordinate labor force. The conflict that followed was inevitable and went to the very heart of Reconstruction.

Bessie's older brother, Benjamin, returned from Confederate service. Before the war Ben had resisted his father's desire that he become a rice planter, choosing a military career instead. Now that the decisive Confederate defeat appeared to have foreclosed that alternative to him, he determined to plant rice on the Pee Dee. When he appeared before the United States provost marshal in Georgetown to swear his loyalty to the United States, however, the marshal refused to administer the oath to him. Allston, a graduate of the United States Military Academy at West Point and a former officer in the United States Army, would have to apply for a special pardon. He acknowledged in a letter to President Andrew Johnson that he had served as a colonel in the Confederate army. "I felt in honor bound to bear my part with the people of my state and section," he wrote. "I believed that we had right and justice on our side." But the political, social, and economic questions, he conceded, had been decided by the outcome of the war. Benjamin Allston received his pardon.[21]

Now Ben set out to plant rice with a free labor force. Under the careful supervision of the U.S. military, he negotiated labor contracts with his father's former slaves. According to the 1866 contracts he was to furnish mules, wagons, and farm implements. The laborers were to keep his fences and ditches in good repair. After the harvest he could deduct one-fifth of the rice and provision crops to cover plantation expenses. The balance would then be shared equally by landlord and laborers. When freedmen balked at the terms, U.S. army general Daniel Sickles ordered them either to sign the contracts or get off the plantations within ten days. Within a month Ben was already complaining to Union authorities that the former slaves at Chicora Wood had repudiated their contracts.[22]

Many Lowcountry planter families had abandoned their plantations for inland safety during the war and had left their slaves behind to work the land. Bessie's father had remained at Chicora Wood until his death in April 1864, but after that, it was another year before an Allston was in residence on any of the family's coastal plantations. At the end of the war the former slaves believed that the land and the crops should remain in their hands. Land ownership was, next to freedom itself, a priority. In the first year after emancipation blacks made an extraordinary effort to acquire land. To former slaves land was the symbol of a new status; to former masters land was the symbol of their old status. Blacks had to occupy the land in order to gain it; whites had to occupy the land in order to retain it.[23]

On the rice plantations of the Lowcountry, the central conflict of Reconstruction was between former masters and former slaves over the appropriation of the plantations' surplus product. Unhappily for former slaves, they had access to neither land nor credit. Limited in their economic choices, they found "free labor" disillusioning. But trying to strike out on their own seemed even less promising. Ben Allston and other former masters were only marginally better off. Their plantations lay in ruins, their livestock had been slaughtered or driven off, tools were worn out or missing, their capital was exhausted, and their own access to credit was limited. What Ben and other planters felt they needed was an assured labor supply. All that the freedmen had to negotiate with was their ability to work. Thus former slaves and former masters were again thrown together, this time in a landlord-tenant relationship. Although the plantations survived the Civil War, they operated in a distinctly different context. Like many once mighty planter families, the Allstons came out of the war with most of their resources destroyed. The prospects for poverty and ruin were very real.[24]

Ben Allston wanted to use the lash on recalcitrant former slaves. With federal authorities overseeing the labor contracts, however, he could no longer beat blacks with impunity. When he struck a freedman named Brutus, Ben was brought up on charges of assault and battery. As before the war, freedmen could be punished if they did not work. But now punishment for violation of contracts would be meted out by military courts rather than by former slaveholders. In an October 1865, letter to Lieutenant Colonel A. Willard, Ben tried to get federal authorities to force the former slaves to continue ditching on his plantation after the crop was already in. But the Union commander was unwilling, and probably unable, to force them to do the work. He had in his command only three noncommissioned officers and twenty enlisted men to supervise an equitable division of the crops.[25]

Accustomed to instant obedience as a slaveholder and as a military officer, Ben Allston was unable to cope with the difficulties of a labor force that refused to be intimidated. His mother, writing from Charleston, urged acceptance of the inevitable. "Negroes will soon be placed upon an exact equality with ourselves," she wrote him, "and it is in vain for us to strive against it." Emancipation and enfranchisement made slaves into voters and undermined the politics of deference that had allowed the planter class to dominate antebellum politics. Blacks constituted nearly 90 percent of the population of Georgetown District, and their right to vote was now guaranteed by the Fifteenth Amendment to the Constitution.[26]

Ben Allston found the prospect of racial equality appalling. He considered the prospect of former slaves voting even more intolerable. A well-meaning northern friend urged Ben to "make yourself popular with them and get their votes, [since] the color of the votes is of little consequence so long as good sensible white men are elected by them." His friend assured him "the people at the North are not more desirous of being ruled by the nigger than you are in the South, but you are surrounded with them and the sudden outburst of popular feeling against them evinced at these late elections may have a tendency to make the darkey uneasy." But Ben was too rigid to consider even such democratic hypocrisies as cultivating black support. He thought of moving to California, but his northern friend dissuaded him with the pointed question, "Do you think by going West you are to get rid of the Negro?" By 1867 Ben could take it no longer. At a time when northern journalists, novelists, and dramatists were depicting emasculated southern men, spiteful and unruly southern women, and a southern culture thoroughly and utterly feminized, Ben felt his own manhood impaired. He filed for bankruptcy in federal court and moved to Texas. He failed there, too, and entered the Episcopal ministry.[27]

Unlike Ben, Bessie accepted the end of slavery with equanimity. "Slavery was in many ways a terrible misfortune," she acknowledged. "I myself am truly thankful that slavery is a thing of the past." Perhaps her sympathy for the slaves was part of the "veiled liberalism" of southern women, prompted by what she called her "sensitive temperament and fierce Huguenot conscience." But it seems clear in context that Bessie considered slavery a misfortune mainly for the masters. She was grateful "that I did not have to take up the burden of the ownership of the one hundred people my father left me in his will (all mentioned by name)." Unlike her sister Carolinians Sarah and Angelina Grimké a generation earlier, Bessie made no connection between the condition of the slaves and the condition of southern white women. The Grimké sisters saw an opportunity to use the intimate relationship between patriarchy and slavery—and thus between sexism and racism—as a means of redefining both gender roles and southern society. But Bessie remained loyal to a social ideal based on subordination and hierarchy. That social ideal accorded her status and insulated her from the drudgery of manual labor. She never challenged it.[28]

In an attempt to put her life back together, Adele decided to convert the Nathaniel Russell House in Charleston into a boarding school. She wanted Bessie to help by serving as an instructor of French, literature, and piano. Struggling to retain at least part of her husband's estate, Adele hoped she might be able to save enough money from the enterprise to make needed repairs at Chicora Wood and to feed her family. But Bessie rebelled. "Mamma, I cannot teach," she complained. "Don't ask me to do it. I just hate the thought." Bessie had been socialized into the role of the "southern belle," schooled in all the "social graces." She expected the period between childhood and marriage to be one of fun and frivolity, a whirlwind of balls and beaux. Her mother pointed out that that world no longer existed. Now she must help support her family.[29]

Not yet twenty at the end of the war, Bessie mustered her courage and resolved to confront her devastated world. To her great surprise, she not only found that she "delight[ed] in teaching" but also that her "little class learns amazingly." The Allston school consisted of ten boarding students from all over the state plus a number of day students, including the daughter of General Daniel Sickles, the commander of the Union occupation forces. The school turned out to be a great success. Adele and Bessie operated it profitably for nearly three years.[30]

By 1869 social life was reviving in Charleston. "The last year we were in Charleston," Bessie wrote, "the St. Cecilia Society began to revive, and determined to give two balls." Bessie admitted to an "intense love of pleasure" in her youth. "I go into society, and enjoy myself fiercely." She would later regard her short career as a southern belle as "very trivial and very silly," but when she was in the midst of Charleston's social whirl she was less than enthusiastic about returning to the plantation. Nevertheless, by 1869 the house had been sufficiently repaired for the family to move back to Chicora Wood.[31] Eventually

Adele was forced to dispose of most of her inheritance at public auction. Under South Carolina law, all that could be claimed of the 4000 acres of land planted by Robert F. W. Allston before the war was the widow's dower—the 890 acres of Chicora Wood.[32]

There was as exaggerated an emphasis on marriage after the war as before. The institution of marriage was used to enhance a family's social position. Families continued to supervise their daughters' social contacts carefully. Now more than ever they felt it desirable for their young women to make good matches. Thus a central concern was the social position of a prospective spouse and the reputation of the spouse's family, a concern that tended to limit marriage choices to the sons of families who lived close by and occupied a similar social position. To preserve or enhance a family's reputation and honor, parents did not hesitate to make their wishes known as to whom their son or daughter should choose as a marriage partner.[33]

Before the war Robert F. W. Allston had advised his son Ben that an army daughter, no matter how talented or beautiful she might be, would make an unsuitable wife for a rice planter. It was simply assumed that a man of his social prestige would marry into money. Writing to console Ben upon his having been "unfortunate in a tender passion" while serving as an army officer in the West, the senior Allston quoted the folk proverb "If you wish your wife to be contented, and wish to be contented with your wife, marry your neighbor's daughter."[34]

Ben did not take his father's advice, but Bessie applied her father's advice to herself. The "bonds of matrimony" could be quite literal for women, but they were not easily avoidable, as spinsterhood was widely regarded as a form of social death. In Bessie's world the roles of wife and mother were the most important ones in life. Marriage extended family connections and childbirth perpetuated the patriarchy. Connections newly formed by marriage could also strain old ones based on blood, since a bride became part of her husband's family and was expected to take up residence on her husband's estate. Bessie—socialized from birth to think of her identity in terms of the Allston family's traditions of honor, patriarchal accomplishment, and collective purpose—avoided that dilemma by marrying her neighbor's son.[35]

Bessie caught the eye of John Julius Pringle after his return from the war in 1865. Pringle, scion of the family that owned White House and Greenfield plantations, twelve miles down the Pee Dee River from Chicora Wood, became a frequent visitor to the Allston residence during the summer and fall of 1865. He came nearly every day to visit and read aloud to Bessie. She and Julius sat shyly looking at each other across the windowsill. She confided to her diary, "I sit inside the window and sew on my ingenious remakings of old things and he sits outside the window and reads." She found the arrangement to be "perfectly delightful for me, it is so much easier than talking." They were dismally afraid of each other. She found it "disagreeable" that "the village is all saying we are engaged. I know he is hearing it all the time, as I am, and it is so awkward for both. I thought it would be easier if I referred lightly to it, so this morning, sewing very fast, pricking my first finger brutally, I said, 'Last evening I was walking in the village and heard something so absurdly ridiculous.' I got no farther, for in a solemn, hurt voice, from across the window sill, there came, 'I'm sorry it seemed so ridiculous to you. It did not seem so to me.'" She "took refuge in immoderate laughter" and asked him to proceed with his reading.[36]

John Julius Pringle attempted to restore rice culture on his own family's plantations. So during the time she was teaching in Charleston, she only saw him on rare occasions. Caught up in Charleston's social whirl, Bessie had what she called "a very gay time" even though "my own special friend" was so busy working in the country that "he did not very often get to town." Somehow she "always knew when I entered a ballroom if he was there, without seeing him, by a queer little feeling." But "I always treated him with great coolness and never gave him more than one dance in an evening, for there were two kind of people I could not bear to dance with—the people whom I disliked and those I liked too much, and he was the only one in the second class." Furthermore, John Julius, who had learned to dance while studying at Heidelberg, "shot about the floor in an extraordinary manner, which endangered the equilibrium of the quiet couples, and that made me furious."[37]

When Bessie returned to Chicora Wood in the summer of 1869, their courtship intensified, and their feelings for each other blossomed. On April 26, 1870, Bessie married John Julius and went to live at White House, his family's nearby plantation. It had once been the showplace plantation of planter-politician-diplomat Joel Roberts Poinsett. "Never was a girl more blessed than I in her marriage," she recalled in her memoirs. "Too happy to live, I often felt." She described the six years she and her husband lived at White House as a period of "passionate happiness." But their marriage was burdened with debts that exceeded the plantation's productivity. And it was cut short by the death of John Julius from malarial fever on August 21, 1876, in the last year of Reconstruction. Years later, Bessie would recall vividly how she took strength the moment she first saw her husband after his death: "I made the terrible journey to Charleston and stood on tiptoe to look down into the ice-packed coffin where he lay—instead of crying out and fainting as they thought I would, my whole being broke into a smile! Then & there I held communion with the great loving heart of the man I loved, and his spirit calmed and filled mine as it had never succeeded in doing before, his brave and faithful soul permeated mine, his strong courage passed into me, and from that hour my nature was changed—I was not afraid of anything."[38]

With neither husband nor children in a world that considered the roles of wife and mother the most important ones in a woman's life, the young widow, not yet thirty years old, returned to Chicora Wood in 1876 to help her mother with the duties and management of the plantation. In 1879, when an unexpected bequest from a distant relative enabled her to make a down payment, Bessie purchased White House on credit from the Pringle heirs. Reared in an elite environment in which honor and family identity were at least partly defined by possessions, Bessie felt a strong desire, she wrote, to purchase the plantation of her married happiness. It was there under the live oaks at White House that Bessie and her husband used to stroll on summer evenings. In 1885 Bessie began to manage White House herself from Chicora Wood.[39]

When Adele died in 1896, once again the Allston estate had to be divided. Chicora Wood, which Bessie's father had inherited from his grandfather, was to be sold. None of the Allston family could afford to buy it. A syndicate seemed the most likely purchaser. Bessie determined to purchase Chicora Wood herself "and devote the rest of my life to keeping it in the family, and perhaps at my death some of the younger generation would be able to take it." The decision to carry on in the old way, she felt, "would condemn me to a very isolated existence, with much hard work and anxiety; but, after all, work is the greatest blessing, as I have found." Bessie acted, she said, from an impulse of the heart rather than the head in buying Chicora Wood. Years later, she would attempt to explain the depth of her attachment to the land. "There are no rich people at the South now," she wrote in 1898, "and both branches of the Allston family have shared the common lot, but they retain their love of land and of horses and their high spirit has carried them through the evil days." She planted rice and provision crops at both White House and Chicora Wood until 1918, uncertain whether she would ever be able to pay off her mortgages on the two plantations. But she never regretted her decision. "With my horses, my dogs, my books, and piano, my life has been a very full one."[40]

It was Bessie's practice to arise before dawn. In the cool bright mornings, as she drove her buggy down the dirt road between Chicora Wood and White House, the lifting fog's revelation always brought her a vague longing for times past, when values seemed clearer. Sweet bay, cypress, and live oak made a dense wall beside the road. On frosty mornings the sun would seem to follow her buggy at a respectful distance, then climb fast through the gray clouds as it sought to overtake her. In the late morning, she would disembark from her buggy to a boat for the six additional miles to the rice fields. Beyond the old blue waters of the rice fields stretched the distant shore. Each day Bessie inspected the growing crop. Walking carefully over her two hundred acres, looking from side to side as if she were in a strange country, she alternately chastised and commended the workers. Each day she made an appeal to the workers' self-interest, to their pride in hard honest work. But she did not hesitate to mete out punishments to workers when she deemed it necessary. And on most days she deemed it necessary. Still she always brought with her some little present—a pear, a biscuit, a piece of candy to give to the workers as they came up and spoke with her. In the late afternoon Bessie would again board the small boat. Surrounded by the pale blue sky of the Pee Dee, carrying a load of rice or field equipment, she would recross the river.

Bessie's efforts to maintain rice culture were part of an unsuccessful effort to stem the long-term economic decline of agriculture in the South Carolina Lowcountry. Before the Civil War, producing rice for the European market with slave labor made the Lowcountry one of the wealthiest areas in the world. But after the war it lost much of its market to cheaper rice from Asia as well as from Texas and Louisiana. By the dawn of the twentieth century the once flourishing rice district had become what historian Peter Coclanis terms "one of the poorest parts of one of the poorest states." When it left the Union in 1860, South Carolina had the third highest per capita income in the United States. By 1929, it had fallen to dead last. The problems of rural Carolinians were compounded by malnutrition, inadequate housing, and illiteracy.[41]

For the next quarter century, Bessie planted rice. Managing a rice plantation before the war had demanded of her father judgment, organizational ability, and self-control. How much greater were the demands that confronted her as a woman in a man's world. She was doing what had been considered a man's work on the plantation but without the control that slavery had given the master, without a man's traditional authority. Relationships between Bessie and her tenants, who carried out the physical work, were not always smooth and harmonious. Each had different ideas about how plantation resources should be distributed. But both Bessie and her tenants profited to some extent from their uneven partnership. In the first year the tenants earned enough money to buy a yoke of oxen or perhaps a horse and buggy of their own. And Bessie earned enough money to be able to pay off her mortgage on Chicora Wood, though White House remained mortgaged.[42]

But Bessie's effort to meet her payrolls and pay her taxes was a constant struggle. She rented White House as a hunting lodge, advertising it in *Field and Stream*. On one occasion she borrowed money from her cook, Clarinda

Lance, writing a note for the loan at 6 percent interest. In 1901 she wrote to her sister that a syndicate "proposed to buy up all the rice lands in the country." The syndicate was organized by the Atlantic Coast Lumber Company and local rice planters James Louis LaBruce, Samuel Mortimer Ward, Louis Claude Lachicotte, Francis W. Lachicotte, St. Julien M. Lachicotte, and Albert A. Springs. "Their object is to control the labour and they do not wish anyone to have land to plant. It might interfere with their control." She found it "quite astonishing the number of planters who have consented to sell[,] . . . nearly every one." The syndicate proposed to use machinery to build "an immense bank around the whole island from Thoroughfare [Cut] to the point below the White House." That might be good for the syndicate, but "if they made their bank below this," Bessie noted, "it would be ruin to this place." Bessie believed the syndicate "made me a very liberal offer, as things go now." She anticipated that Chicora Wood would scarcely bring in a 100 dollars that year, but expenses were expected to be higher than ever, since the rice banks had been badly damaged by continental freshets. The syndicate offered her 5,000 dollars for Chicora Wood and 10,000 dollars for White House, leaving her the houses on both places, plus ten acres of land at White House and more at Chicora Wood. Bessie estimated that her income from White House was greater than the interest on 10,000 dollars would be, but she also knew that her expenses were growing annually, "and I suppose I would be wise to let it go at that." If she sold her rice lands, she decided, she would "need only three servants, which would cut her expenses considerably." The offer seemed "providential" to her, she wrote to her sister. "And then again," she continued, "I feel sorry to think that Papa's life work is to be broken up by the altered conditions of things. . . . I have more to occupy my mind than it can hold."[43] On reflection she declined the syndicate's offer. On another occasion Bessie considered selling out to the South Carolina-born financier Bernard M. Baruch. But once again, somehow she managed to hold on.[44]

Before the Civil War young Bessie had shared the genteel, paternalistic racism of the rice coast aristocracy. Her father had believed, deeply and sincerely, that black Africans were inherently inferior to white Europeans and that slavery was their proper condition. But Robert F. W. Allston had also believed that masters had a responsibility to treat their bondsmen with fairness and kindness, that slaveholders would have to answer to God for the condition of their slaves' souls and bodies. Allston had tried, mostly successfully, to be what according to his standards was a "good" master. After the Civil War, however, and accelerating by the end of the century, a cruder, more aggressive, and more virulent kind of racism swept North and South alike as the estranged sections reunited to take up the "white man's burden" in the Spanish-American War: perhaps the ugliest manifestation of the new racial extremism was a sharp increase in white mob violence against black victims. This was the period of which Lillian Smith would write, in *Killers of the Dream*, "One day, sometime during your child-hood or adolescence, a Negro was lynched in your county or the one next to yours." In the first decade of the new century, lynchings increased until a black victim was lynched somewhere in the South almost every other day. Whites justified the savagery of lynching by asserting that blacks were reverting to savagery—regarded as their natural African state now that they were no longer restrained by the beneficent bonds of slavery.[45]

Elizabeth Allston Pringle was not immune to the new racial spirit. As the old century faded and a new century dawned, her correspondence began to be peppered with such epithets as "darkeys" and "nigs" and complaints about ste-reotypical lying and stealing blacks. "The nigs are fatalists and never cast down," she wrote her sister in 1901, "but they are stealing more than usual. The little rice made here is stacked and being threshed out steadily everyday. They know they cannot pay their rent and think it only wisdom to get all they can before it gets into the barnyard." She described theft on the plantation as rampant. "I will have to dismiss Stephen," she wrote her sister on another occasion. "He brings in only about half the milk. As soon as I went away the quantity he brought was greatly diminished. . . . Last autumn, he openly fed his hogs on corn out of the field, carrying home a large pile every evening!" But theft was only one example of what she saw as the blacks' reversion to savagery. "Stephen made a violent attack on Clarinda, threatening her with a stick because he thought she had told Billy he had stolen potatoes from the bank—she did not know he had taken them so had not told, but he no doubt had done so, or he would not have been so angry. . . . Last night I told him he must go April 1." A nephew replied to one of her jeremiads, "Your letter came yesterday and the detailed account of the once-faithful helpers is a sad tale. The spirit of gain and greed seems to have invaded the quiet hovels of the darkey if not the weather stained residences of their old masters." Her nephew's contrast was overdrawn. Both blacks and whites were engaged in a losing struggle for economic survival in the Lowcountry's long-term agricultural decline. It is hardly surprising that in such circumstances former masters and former slaves had different, and equally self-serving, ideas about the distribution of plantation resources.[46]

In March 1903, in a desperate attempt to find a supplemental source of in-come, Bessie wrote letters of inquiry to several northern newspapers. Typical was her letter to William M. Laffan, editor of the *New York Sun*, asking if he would "like to have a weekly letter from a South Carolina Rice plantation and what you wd [would] pay for such letters." She acknowledged that she had "never undertaken such a thing" but it seemed to her that there might be some general desire "to know what the conditions really are at the South." The fact that "I am managing two rice plantations myself," she wrote, "gives me the ability to describe things as they are."[47]

Bessie later wrote to Ambrose Gonzales, editor of South Carolina's capital city newspaper, *The State*, that she had chosen the *Sun* because it "was read little at the South, indeed I thought not at all, but everywhere among the most bigoted at the North." Its editor was known as "an ultra-conservative," whom she expected to be sympathetic. She had expected "to write freely," she explained to Gonzales, "telling of the grinding poverty & heroic endurance & self control of the white people" as contrasted with what she considered "the idle ways of the untrained negro free from all control and constraint." She was dismayed when her very first letter was reprinted in Charleston's *News and Courier* and, despite her use of a pseudonym, "all my friends recognized me at once." She wrote to Laffan that she would be unable to write a weekly letter under the circumstances "as the being recognized made all the difference." She complained to her sister that her newspaper articles were "read all through the country now even by the darkeys."[48] But the letters continued through 1912. In that year the Macmillan Company offered to publish a book of her *Sun* letters, with an introduction by her friend Owen Wister and illustrations by her cousin, the Charleston artist Alice Ravenel Huger Smith.[49]

Bessie tried to write every day, whenever and wherever she could. In the mornings she worked on her correspondence. But it was difficult to find time. She always carried a satchel containing her diary or a small pad of writing paper with her on her plantation rounds. She wrote while directing the hay harvest before an impending storm. She wrote while tallying corn in the barn. She even wrote while being rowed across the Waccamaw River in a storm, scribbling blindly in the rain until her note pad became too soaked for her to continue.

After supper the candles were lighted and Bessie wrote in her diary. Out in the night, beyond the singing of the frogs, the wake of a passing boat lapped upon the shore. From somewhere on the river, the hum of voices and movements out of the past came back to her, borne into the house on the steady draft that blew in through the open windows and around her head. Faces floated in and out of her consciousness. So many sights and sounds flooded in on her that at times she hardly knew what she was writing. Blessed—or cursed—with an excess of memories, she could dream that time had stood still, dream that history had not happened, dream that here, at Chicora Wood, she could cut off the future's thrust and will herself by name back into a hard, clear, undefeated past, a "super-present" past that embodied the "frozen speed at the heart of things." Finally she would get up from the writing desk, get ready for bed, say her prayers, and go to sleep.[50]

Bessie's *New York Sun* letters were published as the book *A Woman Rice Planter* in 1913. It purported to be a straightforward factual diary. Early reviewers regarded the work as autobiographical, and Pringle's own comments seem designed to assure readers that her intentions were purely historical. But appropriate classification is considerably more complex. The book is actually the product of a process of writing and rewriting in three very different modes. First, Bessie wrote almost daily in her private diary, often as she drove her buggy or was rowed from one plantation to another. Second, in her study she revised the private diary into the *Sun* letters. Finally, she "surgically reconstructed" the *Sun* letters, as she put it, transforming their leisurely pace into the tighter structure of a book. Not only did Bessie write under the pseudonym Patience Pennington; she also disguised the identity of many of the people and places described in the book. Chicora Wood, for example, becomes Cherokee, White House becomes Casa Bianca, Plantersville becomes Peaceville, and Georgetown becomes Gregory. Likewise Chloe is the pseudonym for Clarinda Lance, Napoleon for Billy Grice, and Jim for Joe Addison. Despite its appearing to be a chronological diary of the four years from 1903 to 1906, *A Woman Rice Planter* depicts events that actually occurred over the eleven years from 1901 to 1912. Like the so-called diaries of Mary Boykin Chesnut, *A Woman Rice Planter* embodies both literary and autobiographical impulses. Like Chesnut, Pringle was simultaneously novelist, journalist, social satirist, memorialist, and autobiographer. Like Chesnut, Pringle used self-taught fictional techniques to set scenes and round out characters. Like Chesnut, she relied on her own instincts for structure and metaphor. *A Woman Rice Planter* retains the diary form, but it is preeminently a literary achievement. And like Chesnut's well-known work, it serves not so much as a record of events as an opportunity for discourse about them. Anne Montague Blythe, after a careful comparison of Pringle's book with her *New York Sun* letters, pronounces *A Woman Rice Planter* "a very carefully wrought work of art" and its author "an artist growing, changing and perfecting her craft." Blythe finds each version "more experimental, more dramatic, more polished, and more skillfully crafted than its predecessor." What emerged, then, from Bessie's telescoping and rearranging, her expanding some episodes and eliminating others, is "a different literary form altogether; one closer to fiction than to autobiography."[51]

Elizabeth Allston Pringle, like her contemporaries Thomas Nelson Page, Joel Chandler Harris, and Ambrose Gonzales, used her writing to make an important contribution to a new national consensus on race relations, a consensus that made possible reconciliation of the white people of the estranged North and South at the expense of black people. Pringle's conception of the character of black folk is most memorably depicted in her account of two stereotyped black orphans whom she calls Rab and Dab. They are based on Jesse and Robert Spivey, two black orphans at Chicora Wood. Their story is embedded in *A Woman Rice Planter*. As Bessie portrays them, Rab and Dab are glib liars who would rather tell a falsehood than the truth. For them, temptation is less something to be resisted than an opportunity to be seized. They sneak out of bed at night to steal chickens, bite their necks to kill them, and roast them beneath the house. They break into the pantry to have a clandestine feast. They steal eggs to eat, sell, or bury. Rab and Dab are chronic truants from school. They love to fight and to frolic. They delight in frightening horses to make them bolt and in shooting roman candles at jackrabbits. Pringle decided to continue their story in another book, writing again under the pseudonym Patience Pennington. It was serialized in three parts as "Rab and Dab: A Woman Rice Planter's Story" in the *Atlantic Monthly* in November 1914 and January 1915. It did not, however, appear in book form until 1984. In the meantime Pringle sent the Spivey brothers to the Jenkins Orphanage in Charleston.[52]

Pringle's descriptions of black folk at Chicora Wood give her readers little hint of the richness or uniqueness of the Gullah culture they and their ancestors had created. In the Lowcountry of South Carolina and Georgia cultural roots ran deep into Africa. Modern scholars have discovered striking African continuities in the creole language created by the slaves. Although language was only one element in the transformation from a variety of African cultures to a particular African American culture, Gullah continued to be the language in which that culture was passed down to posterity. Far from the African context of their sacred world, Gullah-speaking slaves blended the heritage of Africa with the European version of Christianity to create a folk religion that retained the earliest "shouting" styles of singing spirituals. The African religious phenomenon of spirit possession remained vividly manifest in Gullah prayers, music, and body movement. The slaves sang their hauntingly beautiful spirituals in the traditional African call-and-response style. Spiritual singing combined with ecstatic shouts and the soaring rhetoric of prayers to provide a release from the travails of slavery. African patterns of naming persisted on the Lowcountry plantations, and slave proverbs reflected the African preference for speaking by indirection. Black storytellers blended African elements with elements of the American historical experience in tales of the audacious animal trickster Buh Rabbit and of the no less audacious slave trickster John. Talented Lowcountry artisans created beautiful sweetgrass baskets, strip quilts, and wrought-iron work. Folk medicine of both the pharmaceutical and psychological varieties healed the sick, comforted the afflicted, and offered advice to the troubled. Thus, whenever they spoke, told stories, worshiped, sang, cooked, quilted, built houses, or made baskets and pottery, Lowcountry slaves manifested not only African continuities but also African creativity. Out of African traditions as well as American circumstances they created a new language, a new religion, indeed a new culture. That new culture not only helped them to endure the collective tragedy of slavery but also to bequeath a notable and enduring heritage to generations to come.[53]

Following publication of *A Woman Rice Planter*, Pringle had "a great desire to put the picture of my father and mother and their life in an enduring form." Continuing her disciplined writing habits, she "put in very many intimate foolish details of my own life taken from diaries of which I have had the habit all my life" in order, as she said, "to catch the popular reader." But she insisted that her sole aim was "a true picture of my parents." By the summer of 1920 she was ready to contact Scribner's publishing house. Charles Scribner Jr. responded, expressing regret that her inquiry had arrived during the absence of his vacationing editor Maxwell Perkins. "Though perhaps you may," Bessie replied to him, "I do not regret the absence of Mr. Perkins. I have always preferred, when possible to draw from Fountain Head." Scribner was most interested, but some revisions were necessary. Bessie pressed for an early publication. "It will be a very great blow to me if the book cannot appear this season," she wrote him, "for it is most likely I will never see it if it does not—Pardon a little personal detail here—I am seventy-five, with such a feeble overstrained heart, that many doctors have told me that I could not possibly live on.—It has been a great disadvantage in the preparation of this sketch." As it turned out, publication was delayed because of her health, and Pringle was still making revisions on her deathbed. She died in December 1921, in the very month Scribner's began actual composition of the book. It was published in the spring of 1922 as *Chronicles of Chicora Wood*. In the introduction Pringle assumes another literary persona. Now she is the philosopher looking back over "years as dark and tragic as that leaden storm-bank at the horizon's edge, but redeemed from utter despair by a courage and a sacrifice equal in splendor to its illumined summits."[54]

A Woman Rice Planter was Elizabeth Allston Pringle's response to the crumbling of her privileged world in the traumatic years of Civil War, Reconstruction, and their aftermath. These upheavals rendered many of the old definitions inoperative, including, certainly, traditional conceptions of gender roles. Because Bessie was articulate and because she had an astute understanding of her society, her book illuminates experiences shared by many women of her class and station.

A Woman Rice Planter appeared at a time of crisis and transition from the

Victorian world to the beginnings of modern feminism. Throughout the nineteenth century the central symbol of southern culture had been the southern
lady on her pedestal, representing all that seemed lovely about the South—she
was physically delicate, sexually pure, submissive, sacrificial, and, of course, silent. It may be that the dawn of the twentieth century, when many women's
issues were first articulated, embodied the dawn of a distinctively feminist consciousness. This was certainly a period in which many southern women began
to question Victorian concepts of separate spheres, began to question their own
shadowy role in southern culture, perhaps began to question gender conventions themselves. Bessie's cousin Susan Petigru King had earlier stripped the
veil of southern womanhood from the heroines of her novels to make plain the
connections between gender and southern society. Similarly, Bessie put herself
at the center of *A Woman Rice Planter* as an assertive, intellectual, questioning
woman who challenged gender roles and struggled heroically to succeed at what
had been considered "men's work" in the rubble of a patriarchal society. Elizabeth Allston Pringle was the daughter of a patriarchal culture who nonetheless created a persona that both disrupted patriarchal structures and subverted
models of narration based on literary hierarchy. In *A Woman Rice Planter* she
represented herself as "the indestructible woman" succeeding in a man's world,
imposing control over men and events and establishing for herself a new order
of financial security and personal happiness. And she subverted conventional
literary discourse by creating a female active voice within the patriarchal tradition, removing woman from the passive role.[55]

Elizabeth Allston Pringle took her place within an established tradition of
southern women writers. She may have felt more comfortable in writing than
women working within a shorter tradition. But the patriarchal society of the
South did its own kind of disservice to the literary profession. The South relegated belles lettres to the category of a frill and equated fiction with beauty,
women, and irrelevance.[56] Bessie also wrote in part *because* she was southern,
because she grew up in a patriarchal society in which her intelligence was both
encouraged and discouraged, *because* she was compelled to feel and think her
way through issues, *because* the Allston family pride achieved such remarkable
strength and vitality. As she sat at her writing desk the past vied with the present over which would be the ghost world. The South provoked Bessie to think
and feel her way—however gropingly and imperfectly—beyond hypocrisy toward truth.

In a time of crisis, Bessie, no less than the males of her time and place, sought
inspiration in heroic images that could override negative circumstances and
help restore to her people a sense of wholeness and identity within a realiz-

able destiny. The most important was the heroic image of the genteel patrician, an image she found embodied in her father. This was the ideal she sought to emulate herself. A second image was that of the artisan, who took pride in work and valued personal independence. Bessie sought, with variable success, to promote that image among the former slaves. A third image was that of the aggressive self-made man, the man at center of the new postwar culture, preoccupied with power and force, imposing his will on the world because he feared being crushed by it, as her brother Ben had been. Bessie abhorred this role, but ultimately she came to adopt it for herself—even as she extolled her father's patrician values. Elizabeth Allston Pringle never quite freed herself from her early socialization in patriarchal thinking, nor did she wholeheartedly affirm female autonomy. She did not express sympathy for emerging feminist positions, nor did she discuss women's issues in her writings. Her writing about her own efforts to expand gender roles is as fascinating as they were courageous. But her efforts remained personal rather than social; they remained efforts in her own behalf rather than in behalf of women in general.[57]

Ultimately, however, Elizabeth Allston Pringle must be seen as a transitional figure, a woman suspended between two worlds, one inviting the pursuit of female autonomy, the other instilling economic and emotional dependence on men. She perceived clearly the collapse of the old patriarchal society, but in attempting to construct something in its place she built on a foundation of patriarchal values, the patriarchal values taught her as a young girl. She struggled with the social codes for her gender and class as she attempted to redefine herself by emulating her father and the qualities she so admired in him. If she had any concern for the gender asymmetry that frustrated her mother, she certainly never mounted any direct challenge to it in her writing. She seems not even to have considered the possibility of a transformation of the structure of gender. She was sometimes superficial, occasionally coquettish, often materialistic, and increasingly racist. But in her carving out a niche of personal freedom, however precarious, in life and in literature, she took a giant step toward becoming a modern woman.[58]

NOTES

This essay is a revised version of the author's introduction to *A Woman Rice Planter* by Elizabeth Allston Pringle (Patience Pennington), first published in cooperation with the Institute for Southern Studies and the South Caroliniana Society of the University of South Carolina. It is published here with the permission of the University of South Carolina Press.

1. Elizabeth Allston Pringle, *Chronicles of Chicora Wood* (New York: Charles Scribner's Sons,

1922), 67–73; William Allston to Robert F. W. Allston, June 19, 1838, in Allston Family Papers, South Carolina Historical Society, Charleston (hereinafter cited as AFP-SCHS).

2. Sociologist Daniel R. Hundley, writing in 1860, noted that "in the South the family is a much more powerful institution than in other portions of the Republic." See his *Social Relations in Our Southern States*, ed. William J. Cooper, Jr. (Baton Rouge: Louisiana State University Press, 1979), 74. Key studies of family relations among the patriarchal southern plantation aristocracy include Anne Firor Scott, *The Southern Lady: From Pedestal to Politics, 1830–1930* (Chicago: University of Chicago Press, 1970); Michael P. Johnson, "Planters and Patriarchy: Charleston, 1800–1860," *Journal of Southern History* 46, no. 1 (1980), 45–72; Catherine Clinton, *The Plantation Mistress: Women's World in the Old South* (New York: Pantheon, 1982); Bertram Wyatt-Brown, *Southern Honor: Ethics and Behavior in the Old South* (New York: Oxford University Press, 1982); Jan Lewis, *The Pursuit of Happiness: Families and Values in Jefferson's Virginia* (New York: Cambridge University Press, 1983); Jane Turner Censer, *North Carolina Planters and Their Children, 1800–1860* (Baton Rouge: Louisiana State University Press, 1984); Orville Vernon Burton, *In My Father's House Are Many Mansions: Family and Community in Edgefield, South Carolina* (Chapel Hill: University of North Carolina Press, 1985); Walter J. Fraser Jr., R. Frank Saunders Jr., and Jon L. Wakelyn, eds., *The Web of Southern Social Relations: Women, Family, and Education* (Athens, Ga.: University of Georgia Press, 1985); Jean E. Friedman, *The Enclosed Garden: Women and Community in the Evangelical South, 1830–1900* (Chapel Hill: University of North Carolina Press, 1985); Elizabeth Fox-Genovese, *Within the Plantation Household: Black and White Women in the Old South* (Chapel Hill: University of North Carolina Press, 1988); Stephen M. Stowe, *Intimacy and Power in the Old South: Ritual in the Lives of the Planters* (Baltimore: John Hopkins Press,1987); Jane H. Pease and William H. Pease, *Ladies, Women, and Wenches: Choice and Constraint in Antebellum Charleston and Boston* (Chapel Hill: University of North Carolina Press, 1990); and Carol Bleser, ed., *In Joy and In Sorrow: Women, Family, and Marriage in the Victorian South* (New York: Oxford University Press, 1991). Cf. Natalie Zemon Davis, "Ghosts, Kin, and Progeny: Some Features of Family Life in Early Modern France," *Daedalus* 106, no. 2 (1977): 97.

3. Margretta P. Childs, "Elizabeth Allston Pringle," in *Notable American Women 1607–1950: A Biographical Dictionary*, ed. Edward T. James, 3 vols. (Cambridge, Mass.: Harvard University Press, 1971), 3:100–101; Charles Joyner, *Down by the Riverside: A South Carolina Slave Community* (Urbana: University of Illinois Press, 1984), 31; *The South Carolina Rice Plantation as Revealed in the Papers of Robert F. W. Allston*, ed. J. Harold Easterby (Chicago: University of Chicago Press, 1945), 11–16, 43–46. Among Robert F. W. Allston's publications are his *Memoir of the Introduction and Planting of Rice in South Carolina* (Charleston, S.C.: Miller and Browne, 1843), subsequently published in *DeBow's Review* 1, no. 4 (1846): 320–57; and his "Sea-Coast Crops of the South," *DeBow's Review* 16, no. 6 (1854): 589–615, also published separately (Charleston, S.C.: A. E. Miller, 1854). Allston won prizes for the high quality of his rice at the Paris Exposition of 1855 and others. See *The South Carolina Rice Plantation*, 92, 123, 149. On the Pettigrew/Petigru family, see James Petigru Carson, *Life, Letters and Speeches of James Louis Petigru* (Washington, D.C.: W. H. Lowdermilk, 1920), and Clyde N. Wilson, *Carolina Cavalier: The Life and Mind of James Johnston Pettigrew* (Athens, Ga.: University of Georgia Press, 1990), 1, 50.

4. Southern society, according to Anne Goodwyn Jones, constituted "a rigid southern patriarchy that subjected women, blacks, children, and non-slaveholding white men to the control and authority of the slaveholding men" (*Tomorrow Is Another Day: The Woman Writer in the South, 1859–1936* [Baton Rouge: Louisiana State University Press, 1981], 43). See also Scott, *The Southern Lady*, 3–44;

Clinton, *The Plantation Mistress*, 36, 179; Fox-Genovese, *Within the Plantation Household*; Edward Ayers, *Vengeance and Justice: Crime and Punishment in the 19th-Century American South* (New York: Oxford University Press, 1984), 13, 29; Johnson, "Planters and Patriarchy," 45–72; and Wyatt-Brown, *Southern Honor*, 226–53.

5. Robert F. W. Allston to Adele Allston, June 2, 1856, AFP-SCHS. He also chastised her for resisting what he called "the imagined tyranny" of his subjecting her to "my arbitrary will." Adele, according to him, had always overrated his will.

6. Pringle, *Chronicles*, 137–38. Cf. Jones, *Tomorrow Is Another Day*, xi. One notable exception was Elizabeth McCall Perry, wife of South Carolina's Unionist politician Benjamin Franklin Perry. See Carol Bleser, "The Perrys of Greenville," in *Web of Southern Social Relations*, 79–84. For others, see Eugene D. Genovese, "Toward a Kinder and Gentler America: The Southern Lady in the Greening of the Politics in the Old South," in *In Joy and In Sorrow*, 125–34.

7. Pringle, *Chronicles*, 36, 63–65, 78, 210–11. Cf. Bertram Wyatt-Brown, "The Ideal Typology and Antebellum Southern History: A Testing of a New Approach," *Societas* 5, no. 1 (1975): 1–29.

8. Madame R. Acelie Togno to Adele Petigru Allston, July 17, 1854, AFP-SCHS; Pringle, *Chronicles*, 123–38. See also Steven M. Stowe, "The Not-So Cloistered Academy: Elite Women's Education and Family Feeling in the Old South," in *Web of Southern Social Relations*, 90–106.

9. Elizabeth Allston journal, July 16, 1861. There are also fragmentary entries in 1862 and 1865 in the Allston-Pringle-Hill Papers, South Carolina Historical Society, Charleston (hereinafter cited as APH-SCHS); Pringle, *Chronicles*, 137–38, 176–83; Frederika Bremer, *Homes in the New World: Impressions of America*, trans. Mary Howitt, 2 vols. (New York: Harper, 1853), 1:289–90.

10. Pringle, *Chronicles*, 167–68; Joyner, *Down by the Riverside*, 77.

11. Esther Alden (pseud. of Elizabeth Allston Pringle), "Diary of Esther Alden," in *Our Women in the War: The Lives They Lived; The Deaths They Died* (Charleston, S.C.: *News and Courier* Book Presses, 1885), 354–63.

12. Ibid., 363. For a perceptive discussion of the role of parties in the Old South, see Stowe, *Intimacy and Power in the Old South*, 71–72.

13. Pringle, *Chronicles*, 189–96. Gail Godwin uses the term "manless little family" to describe her own childhood. See her "Becoming a Writer," in *The Writer and Her Work*, ed. Janet Sternberg (New York: W. W. Norton, 1980), 231–33.

14. Sternberg, "Becoming a Writer," 200–201.

15. Adele Petigru Allston to Benjamin Allston, April 13, 1864, AFP-SCHS; All Saints Waccamaw, parish register, April 8, 1864, SCHS; Pringle, *Chronicles*, 200–210.

16. Pringle, *Chronicles*, 9–11, 209–12; *The South Carolina Rice Plantation*, 43–49.

17. Elizabeth Allston journal, March 8, 1865, APH-SCHS; Pringle, *Chronicles*, 218–42. For a rewritten version, see her "Fun in the Fort," published under the pseudonym Esther Alden in the *Charleston Weekly News and Courier*, 1884–85, reprinted in *Our Women in the War*, 354–63.

18. Pringle, *Chronicles*, 251–65; Adele Allston to Colonel P. P. Brown, March 1865, AFP-SCHS.

19. Pringle, *Chronicles*, 251–65; Adele Allston to Benjamin Allston, September 10, 1865, AFP-SCHS; Joyner, *Down by the Riverside*, 227–29.

20. Pringle, *Chronicles*, 265–75, esp. 265–67.

21. *The South Carolina Rice Plantation*, 18; Benjamin Allston to Andrew Johnson, July 3, 1865, Amnesty Papers, S.C., RG 94, National Archives, Washington, D.C. (hereinafter cited as NA)

22. Ben Allston, labor contract, February 1866, RG 105, NA; Ben Allston to Lieutenant Colonel B. H. Smith, January 30, 1866, RG 98, NA. A freedman named Ancrum, who had been one of the

Allston slaves at Chicora Wood, described his contracts with Ben: "The fust contract was; you fu'nish land and seed and animals an' get two-thirds, I fu'nish wuck and get one-third. Eery day I didn't wuck was deduct' from my share. . . . Now Mauss Ben he done puty [pretty well] by me; I had nine head [children] to feed, an' Mauss Ben say he feed them all fo' my wuck, so Mauss Ben feed my family fu' dat year, and feed dem well, an' we mek fine crop o' rice." See Pringle, *Chronicles*, 366.

23. Joyner, *Down by the Riverside*, 234–35.

24. Pringle, *Chronicles*, 268–69. "The white man does not need the negro as litterateur, statesman, ornament to society," a southern spokesman wrote. "What he needs is agricultural labour" (Myrta Lockett Avary, *Dixie After the War: An Exposition of Social Conditions Existing in the South, during the Twelve Years Succeeding the Fall of Richmond* [New York: Doubleday, 1906], 394]. See also Eric Foner, *Reconstruction: America's Unfinished Revolution, 1863–1877* (New York: Harper and Row, 1988), 104, 597. Rodney Hilton, in his *Class Conflict and the Crisis of Feudalism* (New York: Hambledon Press, 1990), calls a somewhat similar conflict the "prime mover" of the feudal social order.

25. Brutus, sworn statement, January 11, 1866, RG 98, NA; Ben Allston et al. to Lieutenant Colonel A. Willard, October 20, 1865, RG 96, NA.

26. Adele Petigru Allston to Benjamin Allston, December 27, 1866, APH-SCHS.

27. Oliver H. Kelley to Benjamin Allston, September 6, 1867, AFP-SCHS; Oliver H. Kelley to Benjamin Allston, October 10, 1867, AFP-SCHS; Oliver H. Kelley to Benjamin Allston, November 30, 1867, AFP-SCHS; Nina Silber, "Intemperate Men, Spiteful Women, and Jefferson Davis: Northern Views of the Defeated South," *American Quarterly* 41, no. 4 (1989), 614–35; Sandra Gilbert, "Soldier's Heart: Literary Men, Literary Women, and the Great War," *Signs: Journal of Women in Culture and Society* 8, no. 3 (1983): 423; Benjamin Allston, petition in bankruptcy, United States Courts, S.C. District, Bankruptcy Records, Act of 1867, in George C. Rogers, *History of Georgetown County, South Carolina* (Columbia: University of South Carolina Press, 1970), 454; Benjamin Allston to James R. Sparkman, March 18, 1870, Sparkman Family Papers, South Caroliniana Library, University of South Carolina, Columbia (hereinafter cited as SCL).

28. "Veiled liberalism" is the term used by Anne Goodwyn Jones to describe the indirection of southern women writers when speaking out on issues of the day (*Tomorrow Is Another Day*, 45). Pringle, *Chronicles*, 7–8; Gerda Lerner, *The Grimké Sisters of South Carolina: Rebels against Slavery* (Boston: Houghton Mifflin, 1967).

29. Pringle, *Chronicles*, 289–90; Clinton, *The Plantation Mistress*, 62.

30. Elizabeth Allston diary, December 1, 1865, APH-SCHS; Pringle, *Chronicles*, 307–13, 316–30.

31. Pringle, *Chronicles*, 9–11, 209–311; *The South Carolina Rice Plantation*, 22, 43–49. Cf. Suzanne D. Lebsock, "Radical Reconstruction and the Property Rights of Southern Women," *Journal of Southern History* 43, no. 2 (1977), 195–216.

32. Burton, *In My Father's House Are Many Mansions*, 116.

33. Ibid.

34. Ibid.

35. Cf. Censer, *North Carolina Planters and Their Children*, 78; Bleser, "The Perrys of Greenville," 84; Johnson, "Planters and Patriarchy," 65; Clinton, *The Plantation Mistress*, 37, 44; Wyatt-Brown, *Southern Honor*, 229–39.

36. Elizabeth Allston diary, September 3, 1865, APH-SCHS; Pringle, *Chronicles*, 291–92.

37. Pringle, *Chronicles*, 332–33. Cf. Susan Petigru Bowen, "A Coquette," in *Sylvia's World: Crimes Which the Law Does Not Reach* (New York: Derby and Jackson, 1859), 294–95; Stowe, *Intimacy and Power in the Old South*, 71–72; Censer, *North Carolina Planters and Their Children*, 78.

38. Pringle, *Chronicles*, 118, 268–69; *Charleston News and Courier*, August 22, 1876, 4; August 23, 1876, 3; August 24, 1876, 4. Susan Lowndes Allston, "White House Plantation," *Charleston News and Courier*, Sunday, November 16, 1930; Elizabeth Allston Pringle to Owen Wister, January 15, 1914, Wister Collection, Library of Congress (hereinafter cited as LC).

39. Patience Pennington (pseud. of Elizabeth Allston Pringle), *A Woman Rice Planter* (New York: Macmillan, 1913), 1; Georgetown deed book F, 397, Georgetown County Courthouse; draft of letter from Elizabeth Allston Pringle to William Laffan, n.d., [1903], APH-SCHS; Childs, "Elizabeth Allston Pringle," 100. Cf. Wyatt-Brown, *Southern Honor*, 72.

40. "Death of Mrs. R. F. Allston, Wife of the Late Gov. R. F. W. Allston, of South Carolina," newspaper clipping, n.d., 1896, in Mary Motte Alston scrapbook, Allston Family Papers, LC; Elizabeth Allston Pringle to Lionel Cresswell, May 24, 1898, APH-SCHS; Elizabeth Allston Pringle to W. D. Morgan, January 30, 1907, W. D. Morgan Papers, SCL; Pennington, *A Woman Rice Planter*, 5. Elizabeth Allston Pringle leased White House to L. S. Parnell in 1918 and to her nephew Elias Vanderhorst in August 1919. She sold White House to LeGrande Guerry in April 1920, after the Big House had burned (Vanderhorst Papers, APH-SCHS).

41. Peter A. Coclanis, *Shadow of A Dream: Economic Life and Death in the South Carolina Low Country, 1670–1920* (New York: Oxford University Press, 1989) 155; Charles F. Kovacik and John J. Winberry, *South Carolina: A Geography* (Boulder, Colo.: Westview Press, 1987); Rupert B. Vance, *Human Geography of the South: A Study in Regional Resources and Human Adequacy* (Chapel Hill: University of North Carolina Press, 1932), 214–19; Gilbert C. Fite, *Cotton Fields No More: Southern Agriculture, 1865–1980* (Lexington: University Press of Kentucky, 1984).

42. Deed book F, 397, December 2, 1879, Georgetown County Courthouse; Elizabeth Allston Pringle to William Laffan, April 12, 1903, APH-SCHS; Pennington, *A Woman Rice Planter*, 3; Childs, "Elizabeth Allston Pringle," 3: 100.

43. Elizabeth Allston Pringle, Georgetown, to Adele Petigru Allston, Highlands, N.C., September 1, 1893, APH-SCHS; Charles Petigru Allston, Georgetown, October 17, 1893, to Adele Petigru Allston, Highlands, N.C., APH-SCHS; A. H. Smith, Lohorsville, Iowa, to Elizabeth Allston Pringle, December 29, 1906, APH-SCHS; Elizabeth Allston Pringle to Jinty [Jane Allston Hill], November 16, 1901, APH-SCHS; Phoebe Apperson Hearst to Elizabeth Allston Pringle, August 17, 1917, Hearst Papers, Bancroft Library, University of California, Berkeley; Pringle, *A Woman Rice Planter*, 149–50; Pringle, *Chronicles*, 17; Duncan Clinch Heyward, *Seed from Madagascar* (Chapel Hill: University of North Carolina Press, 1937), 221–48. Cf. Rogers, *History of Georgetown County*, 487–89, 498–502, 506, 510.

44. Draft, Elizabeth Allston Pringle to Bernard M. Baruch, February 15, 1907, APH-SCHS.

45. Robert F. W. Allston, quoted in Ulrich B. Phillips, "Racial Problems, Adjustments, and Disturbances," in *The South in the Building of the Nation*, ed. Julian A. C. Chandler et al., 13 vols. (Richmond, Va.: Southern Historical Publishing Society, 1909–13), 4:20; Joel Williamson, *The Crucible of Race: Black/White Relations in the American South since Emancipation* (New York: Oxford University Press, 1984), 5–8, 111–39, 459–522; Lillian Smith, *Killers of the Dream*, rev. ed. (New York: W. W. Norton, 1978), 97; Charles Crowe, "Racial Violence and Social Reform-Origins of the Atlanta Riot of 1906," *Journal of Negro History* 53, no. 3 (1968): 234–56; and Charles Crowe, "Racial Massacre in Atlanta, September 22, 1906," *Journal of Negro History* 54, no. 2 (1969): 150–75.

46. Elizabeth Allston Pringle to Jane Allston Hill, November 16, 1901, March 29, 1901, APH-SCHS; R. F. W. Allston to Elizabeth Allston Pringle, September 9, [1906] APH-SCHS.

47. Elizabeth Allston Pringle, Chicora Wood, to William M. Laffan, editor of *New York Sun*,

March 16, 1903 (draft), APH-SCHS. Cf. Elizabeth Allston Pringle to editor of the *New York Tribune*, March 16, 1903; Elizabeth Allston Pringle to editor of the *New York Herald*, March 16, 1903; Elizabeth Allston Pringle to editor of the *Philadelphia Press*, March 16, 1903.

48. Elizabeth Allston Pringle to Ambrose E. Gonzales, November–December, 1906, APH-SCHS; *New York Herald*, November 20, 1909; Elizabeth Allston Pringle to Jinty, December 11, 1908, APH/SCHS.

49. Elizabeth Allston Pringle to Frederic Bancroft, June 24, 1912, Bancroft Collection, Columbia University Library, New York; R. F. W. Allston (nephew of Elizabeth Allston Pringle) to Elizabeth Allston Pringle, September 9, [1906], APH-SCHS; George R. Brett [?], Macmillan Company, to Elizabeth Allston Pringle, November 14, 1912, APH/SCHS Owen Wister to Elizabeth Allston Pringle, December 9, 1908, Wister Collection, Mss. Division, LC; Alice R. Huger Smith to Elizabeth Allston Pringle, July 24, 1913, APH-SCHS.

50. The terms "super-present" ("sur-present") and "frozen speed" ("vitesse glacee") are Jean-Paul Sartre's. See his essays "Sartoris" and "On The Sound and the Fury: Time in the Work of Faulkner," in *Literary and Philosophical Essays*, trans. Annette Michelson (London: Radius Book/Hutchinson, 1955), 19, 73–87.

51. Elizabeth Allston Pringle to Frederic Bancroft, July 12, 1908, Bancroft Collection, Columbia University Library, New York; Elizabeth Allston Pringle to Arnoldus Vanderhorst, October 29, 1921, APH-SCHS; *Mary Chesnut's Civil War*, ed. C. Vann Woodward (New Haven, Conn.: Yale University Press, 1981), xv–liii; Anne Montague Blythe, "Elizabeth Allston Pringle's 'The Woman Rice Planter': The *New York Sun* Letters, 1903–1912" (PhD diss., University of South Carolina, 1987), vi, xxxviii–xxxix, xlii. There are unsigned reviews of *A Woman Rice Planter* in the *New York Times*, November 30, 1913; *The Dial*, December 1, 1913; *The Nation*, January 8, 1914, 532; the *New York Sun*, October 18, 1913; and the *Chautauquan*, November 15, 1913, 221.

52. D. J. Jenkins (president of the Jenkins Orphanage, Charleston) to Elizabeth Allston Pringle, n.d., APH-SCHS; Jesse Spivey to Jane Allston Hill, February 20, [n.d.], APH-SCHS; Elizabeth W. Allston Pringle, *Rab and Dab*, ed. Anne Montague Blythe (Northport, Ala.: Seajay Press, 1984); Blythe, introduction, Pringle, *Rab and Dab*, xvii–ix.

53. On African American culture, see *Drums and Shadows: Survival Studies among the Georgia Coastal Negroes*, ed. Charles Joyner (Athens, Ga.: University of Georgia Press, 1987); Patricia Jones-Jackson, *When Roots Die: Endangered Traditions in the Sea Islands* (Athens, Ga.: University of Georgia Press, 1987); Margaret Washington Creel, *"A Peculiar People": Slave Religion and Community-Culture among the Gullahs* (New York: New York University Press, 1988); Guy and Candie Carawan, *Ain't You Got a Right to the Tree of Life* (Athens, Ga.: University of Georgia Press, 1989), and the following by Charles Joyner: *Down by the Riverside: Folk Song in South Carolina* (Urbana: University of Illinois Press, 1971), 62–94; "The Creolization of Slave Folklife: All Saints Parish, South Carolina, as a Test Case," *Historical Reflections/Reflexions Historiques* 6, no. 1 (1979), 435–53; "'ALL the Best Stories': Narrative and Identity on the Slave Plantation," in *Papers: The Eighth Congress for the International Society for Folk Narrative Research*, ed. Reimund Kvideland and Torunn Selberg, 4 vols. (Bergen, Norway: The Society, 1984), 1:299–307; "'If You Ain't Got Education': Slave Language and Slave Thought in Antebellum Charleston," in *Intellectual Life in Antebellum Charleston*, ed. Michael O'Brien and David Moltke-Hansen (Knoxville: University of Tennessee Press, 1986), 255–78; "History as Ritual: Rites of Power and Resistance on the Slave Plantation," *Australasian Journal of American Studies* 5, no. 1 (1986), 1–9; "The Trickster and the Fool: Folktales and Identity among Southern Plantation Slaves," *Plantation Society in the Americas* 2, no. 2 (1986),149–56; "Gullah,"

in *Dictionary of Afro-American Slavery*, ed. Randall M. Miller and John David Smith (Westport, Conn.: Greenwood Press, 1988), 305–6; *Remember Me: Slave Life in Coastal Georgia*, Georgia History and Culture Series, ed. Mary Drake McFeely and Charles Joyner (Atlanta: Georgia Humanities Council, 1989); "Creolization," in *Encyclopedia of Southern Culture*, ed. Charles Reagan Wilson and William R. Ferris (Chapel Hill: University of North Carolina Press, 1989), 147–49; "Prica o dvije discipline: folkloristika i historija" (A Tale of Two Disciplines: Folklore and History), in *Folklor i povijesni proces* (Folklore and Historical Process), ed. Dunja Rihtman-Auguštin and Maja Povrzanović (Zagreb, Yugoslavia: Institute of Folklore Research, 1989), 9–22; "'A Single Southern Culture': Cultural Interaction in the Old South," in *Black and White Cultural Interaction in the Antebellum South*, ed. Ted Ownby (Jackson: University of Mississippi Press, 1993), 3–22; and "'Believer I Know': The Emergence of African-American Christianity," in *African-American Christianity*, ed. Paul Johnson (Berkeley: University of California Press, 1994), 18–48.

54. Elizabeth Allston Pringle to Charles Scribner Jr., August 19, 1920, APH-SCHS; Charles Scribner Jr. to Owen Wister, June 6, 1922, Wister Collection, LC; Pringle, *Chronicles*, v.

55. For discussions of Susan Petigru King, see Steven M. Stowe, "City, Country, and the Feminine Voice," in *Intellectual Life in Antebellum Charleston*, 305–14; and J. R. Scafidel, "Susan Petigru King: An Early South Carolina Realist," in *South Carolina Women Writers*, ed. James B. Meriwether (Spartanburg, S.C.: University of South Carolina Press for the Southern Studies Program, 1979), 101–15. Cf. Virginia Ingraham Burr, *The Secret Eye: The Journal of Ella Gertrude Clanton Thomas, 1848–1889* (Chapel Hill: University of North Carolina Press, 1990); Nancy Cott, *The Grounding of Modern Feminism* (New Haven, Conn.: Yale University Press, 1987); Mimi Reisel Gladstein, *The Indestructible Woman in Faulkner, Hemingway, and Steinbeck* (Ann Arbor, Mich.: UMI Research Press, 1986); Minrose C. Gwin, *The Feminine and Faulkner: Reading (Beyond) Sexual Difference* (Knoxville: University of Tennessee Press, 1990). Like Charlotte Perkins Gilman, Elizabeth Allston Pringle developed in her work, however implicitly, the fundamental idea of the absolute necessity for women to do "meaningful work" outside the home and the double bind experienced by women who do. See Sheryl L. Meyering, ed., *Charlotte Perkins Gilman: The Woman and Her Work* (Ann Arbor, Mich.: UMI Research Press, 1988), and Polly Wynn Allen, *Building Domestic Liberty: Charlotte Gilman's Architectural Feminism* (Amherst: University of Massachusetts Press, 1988).

56. Jones, *Tomorrow Is Another Day*, 44.

57. See Michael Kreyling, *Figures of the Hero in Southern Narrative* (Baton Rouge: Louisiana State University Press, 1987), 7, and David Leverenz, *Manhood and the American Renaissance* (Ithaca, N.Y.: Cornell University Press, 1989).

58. Cf. Mary Ryan, *Womanhood in America: From Colonial Times to the Present*, 3rd ed. (New York: F. Watts, 1983), 252, and Sarah Beebe Fryer, *Fitzgerald's New Women: Harbingers of Change* (Ann Arbor, Mich.: UMI Research Press, 1988).

Mother Mary Baptista Aloysius (née Ellen Lynch)

A Confederate Nun and Her Southern Identity

NANCY STOCKTON

Mother Mary Baptista Aloysius (1825?–87), born Ellen Lynch in Cheraw, South Carolina, served as mother superior of the Ursuline Convent and Academy in Columbia for almost thirty years (from about 1858 to 1887). She was buried in the churchyard of St. Peter's Catholic Church in Columbia in an enclosure housing the graves of the Ursuline teachers who served in the city's first Catholic schools. The small tombstones, surrounded by a low iron fence, reflect the prescription for humility that the nuns followed. In contrast to the grander monuments devoted to the priests, the simple stones have an impersonal quality that suggests the lack of individuality (called "singularity") allowed these nuns. Baptista's stone, however, is topped with a larger cross and, though by no means ostentatious, it draws the eye. It signifies the higher status she enjoyed as a popular mother superior.

In the 1990s, a priest in South Carolina took on the task of organizing a book from a collection of letters Mother Baptista wrote over the course of her life to her brother, Patrick Lynch, but he died before he could complete the task. Significantly he entitled his work in progress "The Letters of the Sister of Bishop Patrick Lynch." To him this singular woman was of importance solely because of her brother, who, during the Civil War era, was famous as an esteemed intellectual and popular third bishop of the Diocese of Charleston. Yet Mother Baptista's letters, now housed in the archives of the Diocese of Charleston, South Carolina, are important for the rare glimpse they provide into the world of this southern Catholic nun—a woman whose existence was constrained by the traditions of her church and her region but who found a type of freedom in the religious life.

Baptista possessed a clear understanding of the limitations of her gender, which she accepted as ordained by God, but living within boundaries was evidently not difficult for her. Although she had no natural children of her own, her roles as teacher and mother superior provided her with many opportunities to fulfill any maternal desires she might have had and to wield significant influence within her sphere. Like many a southern lady, she was outwardly submissive to men but inwardly confident, and she had a definite impact on the world around her. She was a proud woman who considered herself neither common nor ineffectual. Indeed, she likened her position as mother superior to that of her brother Patrick, the renowned bishop. In a letter to him written in 1877, she declared: "Oh! I'm so tired of being SUPER(ior). Don't you get VERY tired of being bishop?"[1] Mother Baptista, in spite of being a Roman Catholic religious, and in spite of her rejection of the much glorified married state, became a popular, confident leader charged with considerable responsibility.

Yet, throughout Baptista's life, Catholics were a distinct minority in the South and despised by many for their religion, which the Protestant majority regarded as suspect at best and traitorous at worst—believing that American Catholics' supreme loyalty was always to the pope in Rome, not to the president in Washington. One of the reasons that Irish Catholic immigrants who came to the United States after the 1840s potato famine were met with such a harsh reception was the widespread idea that Catholicism was incompatible with the democratic, republican nature of American society. Historian Ray Allen Billington described this pervasive anti-Catholic sentiment: "The average Protestant American of the 1850s had been trained from birth to hate Catholicism; his juvenile literature and school books had breathed a spirit of intolerance. . . . ; his religious and even his secular newspapers had warned him of the dangers of Popery; and he had read novels, poems, gift books, histories, travel accounts, and theological arguments which confirmed these beliefs."[2] Historian John Tracy Ellis has insisted that "the Catholic Church was the most disliked and suspect of all the American churches of the mid-nineteenth century."[3]

In the North and the South, nuns' celibate and often cloistered way of life was the cause of much speculation. In the years between 1830 and 1860, the country was flooded with anticonvent literature and demands that nunneries be investigated. As Baptista was growing up, a proliferation of notorious "convent books," pulp books advertised as revealing the secrets of the deviant life in convents and filled with lurid tales of shocking sexual abuse and murder, inspired violent, usually anti-Irish, reactions. The most notorious of these, *The Awful Disclosures of Maria Monk*, was first published in 1836. Monk's sensational tales of "nuns left to starve in the cells or have their flesh burned off their

IMAGE OF THE RUINS OF THE URSULINE CONVENT
(LEFT) AND RICHARDSON STREET, COLUMBIA, S.C.,
LOOKING SOUTHWARD TOWARD THE STATE HOUSE

After the fire of February 17, 1865, this was all that was left of the massive, seventy-two-room Ursuline convent, which stood at the southeastern corner of Richardson and Blanding streets. The image was created by illustrator Theodore R. Davis and appeared in the July 21, 1866, issue of *Harper's Weekly*. From the newsletter of the Historic Columbia Foundation, *Historically Speaking* 43, no. 3 (Winter 2005). Courtesy of the Historic Columbia Foundation, Columbia, S.C.

bones with red-hot irons" and tales of sexually exploited and disappearing nuns and infants who were baptized and then strangled would have incensed devout Catholic families such as the Lynches.[4] There were several attacks on Catholic institutions in the North. In 1834, after the prominent Presbyterian minister Lyman Beecher, father of Harriet Beecher Stowe, gave three anti-Catholic sermons in Boston, lower-class Protestant rioters burned down the Ursuline convent in nearby Charlestown. The Boston elite, including Beecher, condemned this act but outrage at the idea of young girls being subjected to secret Irish Catholic brainwashing or sexual violation led to the mob violence.[5] Antebellum America also witnessed a nativist political movement beginning in the 1840s that coalesced into the Know-Nothing movement of the 1850s. Know-Nothings claimed that the large numbers of Irish Catholic immigrants who entered the United States after the potato famine were the greatest threat yet to the survival of the American republic.

Anti-Catholic sentiment was readily apparent throughout the heavily Protestant South, including South Carolina. Although early South Carolina (Charleston in particular) has a historical reputation for having been tolerant of religious differences, the nature of this religious toleration is often misunderstood. There were economic incentives to being an open colony regarding religion, but members of minority faiths did face a degree of discrimination. The very word "toleration" implies an unequal power relationship. Many reviled the "papists." These included members of the Anglican majority who had come from England, where fear and hatred of Catholicism was entrenched in law and custom, as well as the early Huguenot settlers, French Protestants driven from France by Catholic intolerance. Many southerners viewed Catholicism as anti-intellectual and bigoted as well as un-American. For example, in 1845, South Carolina statesman James Henry Hammond complained bitterly about his colleague Edmund Bellinger's conversion to Catholicism, saying, "Bellinger joined the Catholic Church last winter and is full of it now. It is melancholy to see an intellect like his so prostrated by bigotry. . . . His mind is perfectly closed to reason and common sense. . . . Nothing is too silly or too wicked for belief."[6] Hammond spoke for many when he visited Rome and announced that it was the center of a faith "primitive and deadening."[7]

Though parts of Alabama, southern Louisiana, and Maryland had large numbers of Roman Catholics, in the nineteenth century even these areas were nonetheless part of a Protestant-dominated society. Most residents of South Carolina, with its large Protestant majority, considered it to be a Protestant state and "South Carolina values" to be synonymous with English Protestant values, despite the state's history of religious tolerance and sizable numbers of Jews and Quakers as well as Catholics. Roman Catholics had to adopt a defensive posture. To many antebellum Protestants, according to scholar Jenny Franchot, Catholicism "played the fiction to Protestantism's truth, the failure to its progress, the weaker femininity to its superior masculinity."[8] It is ironic that in this hierarchical southern culture (in which a way of life prevailed that at the highest level mimicked the habits of the Old World nobility of England), the anglophilic Episcopal Church, favored by the majority of the politically and socially dominant planters, was not considered to be inimical to the egalitarian values of America. Though many young aristocrats in the state played at medieval jousting and engaged in other displays popular during the age of chivalry, the leaders of early South Carolina drew a distinction between what was "English," what was "American," and what was "southern." More importantly, they wanted to make clear what the South was not, and it was not a Roman Catholic land. In nineteenth-century South Carolina, being Catholic—with few exceptions—brought with it lower social status and doubts about one's loyalties. There are many accounts of such negativism toward Catholicism in the Old South. Some southerners took great pride in the overwhelmingly Protestant nature of their society, seeing it as one of the superior aspects of southern society in comparison to the more heterogeneous North.

Baptista, however, felt very much at home in her native South Carolina and had no difficulty reconciling her unpopular "foreign" faith with her identity as a daughter of the South. On the contrary, she believed that Catholicism was a religion well suited to the region. After all, a religious denomination constructed around an indisputable and supposedly beneficent hierarchy was hardly irreconcilable with the patriarchal South. And though she and her family were of Irish descent, she apparently felt no more kinship with the lower-class, urban-dwelling Irish Catholics of the North than she did with other ethnic groups. She was condescending in reference to the newly arrived from her own land of origin and occasionally laughed at their brogues, for example, spelling the word "biography" as "biORgraphy!" in reference to an Irish woman in one of her letters to Patrick.[9]

Ellen Lynch was born into a well established, prosperous, slave-holding family that had emigrated from Ireland in 1819. The Lynches were well-assimilated southerners who happened to be of Irish descent and Roman Catholic. Her life story reminds us that South Carolina was not a religiously homogenous society, but it also demonstrates that even devotees of a despised faith could be accepted in southern society under the right circumstances. One condition of such acceptance was adherence to certain southern traditions and values that were sacrosanct.

The Lynch family had established itself in Cheraw, a booming town in the South Carolina Upcountry; Cheraw appeared on English maps as early as 1740 and was incorporated in 1820. Most of the early settlers were English, Scots, French, or Irish. Mother Baptista's father, Conlaw Peter Lynch, was born in Magheraveely in County Fermanagh. He was a builder by trade and was recruited to settle in Cheraw to assist in the development of the community. The fact that Peter had been invited to move his family to Cheraw no doubt made their transition from Ireland easier. He designed and built the impressive Town Market Hall, St. Peter's Catholic Church, and many private homes that are now local landmarks. Ellen, born after her parents arrived in Cheraw, was named after her mother, Eleanor MacMahon, whose family was well established in County Monaghan.[10]

The prosperous family firmly planted themselves and their unapologetic Catholicism in South Carolina society. Three of the five daughters in the Lynch family became nuns, and the oldest son, Patrick, a bishop. In addition, Baptista's brother John, a respected physician in Columbia who became the surgeon general of South Carolina and a professor of medicine at the university in Columbia, was so broadly esteemed that the entire city closed down for his funeral service. Ellen Lynch's daily life in Cheraw seems to have been affected only tangentially by anti-Catholic prejudice. Her family's position as "the leading Catholic family of Chesterfield District" and the prosperity this implied allowed the Lynches the freedom to practice their faith without fear.[11]

The family benefited from its association with first bishop of the Diocese of Charleston, a Dubliner, John England, and from his efforts to reconcile Catholics and Protestants in the state. A member of many secular organizations, including the exclusive Charleston Literary and Philosophical Society, England encouraged the normalization of American Catholicism throughout the country, not only in South Carolina. Patrick Lynch had been educated in Rome and was the protégé of Bishop England. Back in 1832, in a pamphlet designed to influence South Carolina Protestants, the bishop had blamed anti-Catholic prejudice on the British, who, he claimed, exaggerated Catholic misdeeds. He used the pages of the newspaper he founded, *The United States Catholic Miscellany*, to apologize whenever there might be a Catholic slight to southern life and values. He emphasized the compatibility of Catholicism and the slaveholding plantocracy of South Carolina. He said both were patriarchal systems with power concentrated at the top and both depended on the submission of the majority to the rule of the minority. Also, at a time in which southerners expressed fear of the urban, immigrant, Yankee flavor of American Catholicism, Bishop England promised a southern brand of Catholicism just as racialist as any Protestant denomination.

For successful Catholic families such as the Lynches, South Carolina society was fairly accommodating. The experience of the Lynch family was consistent with the general rule that the social status of a Catholic family in the nineteenth-century South correlated to its financial position and the extent to which its members interacted and intermarried with elite Protestants.[12] One can see in Baptista's correspondence mention of the names Pinckney, Delage, Bellinger, and other prominent Catholic families with whom the Lynches were acquainted or to whom they were related. Most of these families had members who had married into Protestant families.

This small group of landed South Carolina Catholic families intersected at several points, one of which was at school. When Baptista, no doubt with the influence of her powerful brother, was appointed superioress at the popular Ursuline convent school in Columbia, the pupils included daughters of generals, judges, planters, governors, and senators—though there were some exceptions to this pattern: one account has Mother Baptista "amused at seeing the grand niece of Gen. (Robert E.) Lee side by side with Mary Hogan, the daughter of the cow-driver of Charleston."[13]

In her position as mother superior, Baptista became keenly aware of the advantages of associating with South Carolina's Protestant elite. "The Heywards & Middletons are her family," she wrote of one potential convert to Catholicism who had asked for her help. "Judge of my surprise & sadness when I heard thro the reports of her servant in Columbia that she is disreputable! If she is what her servant reports, I must let her know I cannot instruct her."[14] She counted this as a great loss. Baptista was an interesting example of a Catholic religious who never doubted her church's doctrine that it was the one and only true faith, the only avenue to heaven, yet was able to interact successfully with the Protestant elite and was even entrusted with the education of their daughters.

Baptista and her siblings, educated and accustomed to wealth and creature comforts, were at home among gently raised people familiar with a gracious lifestyle. She once had a letter from Patrick complaining about the "mean" stationery she used that offended him. He asked her to use paper that is "pink in color—pleasant and cheerful." She promised to use proper paper, saying, "ever since you told me what an unpleasant effect mean stationery had on you I keep the best I have for you."[15] Socially they were far from attending cotillions with the exclusive Lowcountry elite, but they were much further removed from the impoverished and disease-ridden Irish Catholics who were digging canals in Charleston and Columbia or living in the squalor of northern tenements.

The Lynches regarded slavery not only as an inevitable feature of southern life but as morally justified. The acceptance of slavery—the defining institution of southern life—was a prerequisite for anyone who wished to be judged truly southern. In accepting slavery, the Lynch family was hardly alone among American Catholics north or south. Pope Gregory XVI published the apostolic constitution *In supremo apostolatus* in 1839 condemning human enslavement and the international slave trade, but American Catholic prelates circumvented this by interpreting the decree as a ban on the transatlantic slave trade, not on existing domestic slavery.[16] In their view, owning slaves who were born into slavery was quite different from profiting by bringing new slaves into the country. Historian James McPherson has written that "the Catholic Irish in both Ireland and America during the nineteenth century possessed cultural values that were in many ways antithetical to modernization."[17] This conservatism manifested itself in the racism prevalent among them in the North and the South. In 1862 Archbishop John Hughes of New York insisted that although northern Catholics (overwhelmingly Democrats) were in full support of the U.S. Constitution and the government, they would "turn away in disgust" if they were called on to fight for the abolition of slavery.[18] Prosperous Catholics in the South were as likely to own slaves as any other members of the elite.

In fact, southern Catholics were convinced that their religion made them better slave masters. The rationalizations coming from pulpits throughout the South, Catholic as well as Protestant, asserted that the institution of slavery saved the slaves from the fate they would have endured in their native Africa and gave them the opportunity to be baptized as Christians. Roman Catholics went one step further and believed that Catholic slave owners were offering their converted slaves eternal life, the heaven denied to non-Catholics. It was the norm for religious orders in the South to own their own slaves. Members of the Lynch family, including Patrick, who owned many slaves, clearly considered themselves to be benevolent masters who were more caring than most slaveholders owing to the superiority of their religion. Patrick wrote about his concern—which he considered to be a decidedly Catholic one—that slave families not be separated.[19]

Baptista seemed to share the common belief that an American slave society could be the ultimate expression of Christian responsibility. She too stated that slaves were better cared for by Catholics than by Protestants and that their chances for salvation were better because they had the opportunity to convert. In her letters to Patrick, Baptista mentioned slaves or slavery only rarely, giving the impression that it was such a part of the fabric of southern life that she did not often find it worthy of note. Baptista did mention, however, that she pitied the slaves and hinted that she could understand the impulse for abolition, at least intellectually. Occasionally she mentioned a slave's ill health. And, as was the case with many southerners who expected loyalty from former slaves, her postemancipation letters revealed a more vehement racism as she associated the freedmen with the South's northern invaders and disdained them as much as she disdained their liberators. In reference to an 1876 court case involving a family friend, she called a witness against him "a big blubber-lipped negro," implying that this should invalidate his testimony.[20]

Baptista was also at home with nineteenth-century southern ideas about woman's nature and social role. She considered the religious life a positive good, as meaningful as being a wife and mother. The feminine virtues, such as "purity," "piety," "submissiveness," and, to a degree, "domesticity," which according to historians were accepted at the time as normal, natural, and even divinely inspired in women, were also represented in her calling as a nun.[21] Certainly the acceptance of male authority was beyond question. Furthermore, the Catholic Church offered her something that was not an option for most young women of Protestant backgrounds: the opportunity to pursue a career and satisfy personal ambition as a religious. Curiously, despite Protestant attacks on convent life as subversive of true womanhood, the single feature of the nineteenth-century Catholic Church that gained the most approval was the selfless labor of nuns. Their work with the poor and sick was recognized prior to the Civil War, but they received extravagant praise and gratitude for their heroic service nursing both sides during the war.

Baptista recognized how popular the nursing religious orders were. After an upsetting trip in which she had disguised herself as secular to avoid potential anti-Catholic harassment, she wrote to Patrick, "I cannot tell you the disagreeable time I had on the Mississippi River with gamblers, rogues, etc. on board. I was obliged to keep my room almost altogether."[22] She had learned a valuable lesson about the advantages a nun traveling alone could secure. Before her next trip she wrote, "I never intend to disguise myself as a secular again when traveling so I think I will assume the costume of the 'Sisters of Mercy of Charleston' which is so universally known and respected throughout the U. States."[23] Many Protestant women envied the selfless work of nuns and their opportunities for service. Wealthy South Carolina native Grace Brown Elmore was in her early twenties when she wrote during the Civil War that "I have often thought that if I were a Catholic, the Sisters of Charity would be my choice of all positions in life. I have longed to go to the poor and needy. I've wanted an interest of that kind in life, but there has been no opening."[24] The avenue offered to women by the religious life surely appealed to many who desired a life other than the idealized but isolated one of service to husband and children within one's own home.

Becoming a nun was certainly an acceptable and well-regarded choice for daughters of Catholic families such as the Lynches. The decision to enter the religious life would have been as natural for a young Catholic woman of the nineteenth century as the decision to marry and have children was for a young Protestant woman. Ellen, at least in her extant letters, does not appear to have struggled with her initial decision. She apparently considered her "love of God" as the defining feature of her life. Becoming an Ursuline enabled Baptista to do "the work for which I entered religion, viz, the overcoming of human nature."[25] In addition, choosing this vocation freed her from such earthly concerns as childbearing and a husband's control. Baptista was a strong-minded woman. And becoming a mother superior, or "lady superioress" as she was sometimes called, in a state where her family was well known and respected gave her the freedom to express her strong personality with few restraints.

A common misconception at the time was that Catholic women were forced into convents if they had no marriage prospects. Mother Baptista's life story suggests an alternate view. Many women, perhaps a majority, who pursued the religious life were not there against their wills: they were not reacting to an unfortunate lack of marital possibilities as many Protestants assumed. These women regarded a religious vocation as a positive good and sometimes compared it to a Protestant's choice to marry. When she was deciding on an order to join, Baptista remarked that it was "as good Bishop Reynolds says, like ladies in the world selecting a husband."[26] Some nineteenth-century photographs depicted young women dressed as brides as they took their religious vows.

Careful planning, a dowry, and acceptance by an often particular and discerning individual order were all part of the process of becoming a religious. It was a serious business in which both sides sought desirable matches, and convents rarely accepted anyone without financial means. After she was in the position of choosing who would be admitted to her convent, Mother Baptista revealed in her letters just how careful and calculating she was. In reference to one likely prospect, a young woman who would bring with her a tidy "dowry" including slaves, Baptista wrote: "I wonder . . . if we could count upon Louise for our novitiate. You see I am looking to number one. It seems to me I have heard something of her having a latent vocation for our order & as the Irishman said 'I'll take her and the *nagers* too!'"[27]

This was serious business to Baptista: being a practical mother superior, she "prayed for some well educated postulants with some fortune."[28] But she was always concerned about the sincerity of the prospects' devotion and their suitability for the religious life. Temperament, attitudes, and motives were also considered as she decided whom to admit. Baptista expressed doubts about the suitability of some girls from St. Augustine, Florida, who were "desirous of becoming Ursulines. . . . [I]t would however cost those hot-blooded Spanish dames something to conform to our Rules—but all things are possible with God's grace."[29] Baptista had a letter of application from a Miss Southhall of North Carolina but was disinclined to accept her because she preferred "pious, sensible & well-informed postulants. I must say that the tone of this letter is too much like Miss Lancaster's—too inflated to please me. I never like these vocations that arise from disgust of the world, or in other words, from wounded pride unacknowledged. I prefer those who can enjoy society, admire its beauties & love them, too, but love God more."[30] She seemed averse to the image of a convent as a haven for unhappy, bitter spinsters.

Just as nineteenth-century mothers were charged with the religious education of their children, women such as Mother Baptista took as their mission the religious improvement of others. This included schooling girls to recognize that their primary functions must be as wives and mothers. An enduring irony is that schoolgirls were taught that this was to be their lot in life by single women who were neither wives nor mothers and who were rarely controlled on a daily basis by men. The nuns in the schools were not encouraging female revolution of any kind, even though, ironically, their example might have had the effect of modeling independent behavior in many girls.

One scholar, Linda Lierheimer, has suggested that stricter gendering of religious roles in the Catholic Church in late eighteenth-century France encouraged the positioning of women as the principal transmitters of culture from their seats of power in the home. According to Lierheimer, "Ursulines were instrumental in bringing about this new status quo. In the classroom, their goal was to create good Christian mothers who would see to the proper religious upbringing of their children."[31] The same effect may be seen in American Catholicism of the nineteenth century. Some scholars see the teaching nuns as co-conspirators in a misogynistic church obsessed with gender boundaries. A typical exposition of the party line of Catholic education in nineteenth-century America can be found in an article written by a nun in 1874: "With a woman it is a question of feeling, with a man it is a question of reason." She goes on to assert that it is a poor education indeed that encourages women "to rival men in professions unsuited for their sex."[32]

From these perspectives Catholic educational philosophy posed no threat to the conservative Protestant dominance of South Carolina. Correcting unorthodox views and tendencies was the drumbeat of Catholic teaching, and knowing one's place was paramount, a perfect complement to the South's demand that one stay within social and gender boundaries. The whole of southern culture depended upon a strict adherence to the social hierarchy instituted by the patriarchal system. Defenders of traditional roles insisted that if one component of "southern civilization" should collapse, then the whole system might tumble. Most significantly, many believed that any challenge to the subordinate position of women might lead to a challenge of the subordinate position of blacks. Historian Anne Firor Scott stated that in the mid-nineteenth century, "southern women were almost a decade behind the more emancipated eastern and western women."[33] The concept of hierarchy was one with which the Catholic Church was familiar, and its support of this central philosophy made it compatible with southern values. Nuns in Catholic schools were not consciously encouraging female revolution.

A different scholarly perspective suggests that, in terms of role models, the impact of Ursuline teachers such as Baptista may have had an empowering effect that went beyond academic education and Catholic doctrine. Historian Emily Clark presents the nun as an "ideological outlaw" who rejected "the dependant state of marriage that was ideally prescribed for Protestant women, and by her overt example she made manifest what was possible for women not obligated to defer publicly to a husband." Clark's revisionist study of the early Ursulines of New Orleans suggests that nuns throughout antebellum America drew aside "the ideological veil of domesticity to reveal the capacity and ambition of American women."[34]

If in fact Baptista was an insurrectionist, it was clearly not intentional. Baptista, in enlisting Patrick's advice on "good Catholic school books such as you used for grown boys, particularly on the subject of chymestry, philosophy and history," displayed a decidedly traditional outlook. She wrote, "I know there is a good deal of humbug in putting such books into the hands of school girls but it is one of the humbugs of the age to which we must yield, but always bearing in mind that they are *only* our *bait* for enticing souls of children."[35] There is no suggestion in her letters that she was an advocate of new ideas about woman's nature or social role, even if her life could serve as an example of female empowerment. Mother Baptista was but one of the thousands of nuns who spoke often of the proper Christian sphere of women as being limited to lives as wives and mothers while not choosing that life themselves.

In one respect Baptista had a more "modern" perspective in her attitudes toward the lives of nuns. Before settling permanently in Columbia, she lived in a number of other convents and spent several months at the Ursuline Convent in New Orleans, where the influence of the Spanish and French Catholic heritage was still in evidence. This included "grating," an Old World custom that required a grated screen be placed between nuns and any visitors to a nunnery. The grates often had curtains that could be rolled down to effect further separation. This was a common feature of cloistered life, although many convents in the United States had by this time abandoned the practice. One letter written in January 1855 made it clear that Baptista disdained it:

> I don't believe in being caged like a wild beast from your family. . . . You must not be disedified at my American prejudice to grates my dear Brother. They may have been necessary long ago, when customs and education were different but I do not believe they are now, at least in the United States. Experience teaches me that they do not exclude the weaknesses of human nature for I have seen as great perfection & regularity without grates as with them.[36]

She left New Orleans shortly thereafter.

In most respects, however, Baptista appears to have been a thoroughly conservative person. In her correspondence with her brother Patrick she often adopted the complimentary and deferential manner then expected of southern ladies. A letter in which she stated: "I bow to your superior wisdom in this as in all things" was typical. In another letter she offered detailed instructions on how to run a successful church fair, including tips about "tasty milliners and mantua-makers" and then ended with blatant flattery: "However, you know much more than I do about such affairs."[37] In the 1870s, Baptista organized an attempt to gain compensation from the government for the 1865 burning of the Ursuline Convent in Columbia. She outlined a complex plan through which to demand an indemnification of 100,000 dollars and then—after clearly showing herself to be a savvy negotiator—added, "However, I am not a proper judge in the matter, & only speak like an ignorant woman, not knowing the ways of the world."[38]

Thus, though Baptista had strong political opinions, it was characteristic of her to expound intelligently to Patrick on a point and then end with a self-effacing disclaimer. For example, in 1863 she wrote that "the various generals, Bencks, Pope, etc. had been before the war, *violent knownothings* as was *Lincoln*—such being the case, I hope Providence will frustrate their designs & never permit even a nominal union. It may be, that with states as with people, quarrels but increase their friendships & union, but I could never understand that principle, therefore, I am totally opposed to a reunion & hear no one speak of such an idea here—. (What folly for a cloistered Nun to offer an opinion on politics!)"[39] Impressed with an article Patrick wrote for *Catholic World*, she displayed her grasp of history in a letter praising him: "What splendid testimony, & how puerile these Cavillers look beside it. Protestants have jumped over Medieval time thro' aversion to the Church & hence are ignorant of much they could learn from her libraries. Your argument is a splendid argument against them."[40]

Baptista and her family sided firmly and fully with the South during the Civil War and Reconstruction. She was as prosouthern in her ideology as any Protestant nineteenth-century South Carolinian. She lamented the horrifying upheaval of the Civil War but fervently supported the Confederacy and prayed continually for a southern victory. "I am truly sorry to see by today's paper of the troops landing at Beaufort. May God and our Blessed Mother protect us."[41] She entreated the Virgin Mary to protect the southern troops, especially General Pierre Gustave Toutant Beauregard, a Catholic from New Orleans who commanded Confederate troops in Charleston for much of the war. In 1863 she wrote to her brother that "we will pray particularly for Beauregard, the head and leader, from whom so much is expected & upon whom so much depends. If he is a good Catholic our Blessed Mother will protect him."[42]

Mother Baptista and her brother Patrick were unwavering in their support of the southern cause. She wrote poignantly of her wish that Mary would cover the young soldiers with her mantle when they were sleeping out in the cold. She had the girls at her convent school make a flag for the Emmett Guard of Columbia as a student project, which was presented to the soldiers by Patrick, by then Bishop Lynch, at their encampment on Sullivan's Island.[43] Patrick, a man who had used his talents to foster greater trust between the Protestant power elite of South Carolina and Catholic leaders, was so identified with the southern cause that he was sent to Europe by Judah Benjamin, the Confederate secretary of state, to win recognition by the Holy See.[44] He reported back from Paris to Benjamin that "I heard everywhere expressions of admiration for our valour, and of sympathy for our cause."[45]

Baptista is often mentioned heroically in the accounts of the infamous burning of Columbia in 1865. She became a legend in her own time for showing no fear of General William Tecumseh Sherman or his army, even as the nuns fled from their burning convent, their habits singed by the conflagration. The general's reputation as the lowest of the low among many South Carolinians was not helped by the story that he burned the convent despite giving his word to Baptista—who had courageously sought out his promise that it would be spared. There are many versions of this story, including one in which Baptista is described as having been acquainted with Sherman's Catholic wife and using that connection to protect the convent. (Sherman was himself a baptized but nonpracticing Catholic, although his family of origin was Episcopalian.) The Pinckney family, related to the Lynches, has an oral tradition recounted by Mary Pinckney Powell in her book about her family:

> Mother Baptista, having been a classmate of General Sherman's wife, did not hesitate to ask for guards for the Convent, and was assured by the General that the Convent would be protected. On the morning following the fire, while the nuns and students were huddled together in the graveyard, the General approached to explain the reason for the destruction of the Ursuline home. To make amends, he offered the Mother Superior the choice of any house remaining standing in the City for her sisters and young ladies. With her dignified and aristocratic bearing, with her grey blue eyes fixed on the face of General William Tecumseh Sherman, she replied to his offer: "General, are these houses yours to give?"[46]

Another version is that Baptista sent a personal note to Sherman requesting a guard for the convent, introducing herself as once having taught in the convent where his daughter Minnie was then attending school. Sherman penciled an order on the note that the convent was to be guarded.[47] This story is supported by an 1873 letter from Baptista to an unnamed person recounting that General Sherman's daughter had been a student in an Ursuline convent in Brown County, Ohio, when Baptista was there as a teacher. The burning of the convent led to an enduring bitterness toward Sherman, compounded by the burning of her beloved Cheraw by his men.

After the war Baptista continued her work, rebuilding from the ruins and nursing her lingering resentment of the Yankees. She continued to see the world through the lens of her Catholicism. She did, however, come to see the destruction of her convent as a blessing in disguise. On February 15, 1869, two days before the fourth anniversary of their being "burned out" of their convent and school by Sherman's forces, a day that had become "a day of thanksgiving" for the sisters and their students, Mother Baptista took a moment to write her older brother: "Everything is looking beautiful, fresh and calm this morning & the air is balmy and delightful. As I look out all nature seems dancing in the sunshine of our Lord's glory & goodness." The Ursulines celebrated every year with a day of recreation and paused to appreciate how much better things were than during the war. They had a new convent just outside Columbia. But Baptista, like many white South Carolinians of the era, never fully forgave the North or forgot their blue-coated invaders. Even on a beautiful day, as she wrote about the beauty of God's creation, she took a shot at the former adversaries:

The various kinds of birds enjoying the breeze that sways the tops of the trees are so very tame & fearless that they come in on the piazza as if to enjoy the pianos which seem to attract them. The little sparrows, wrens, & tomtits are quite domesticated while the mocking birds are busily building their nests in the jassimine vine near. The blue jays (I call them Yankees) are intruding themselves every where with their loud unmusical voices.[48]

Mother Baptista never abandoned her belief that to be southern made one superior to nonsoutherners, just as being Catholic made one superior to non-Catholics. For her there would always be a natural fit between her denomination and her southern homeland. She had no use for South Carolina's Reconstruction government and often used the term "Yankee" as a slur. In a letter to Patrick she noted that their mother likened northern scoundrels of Reconstruction to Protestant, pro-English "Orangemen" who used to "swear anything against the Catholics." She wrote, "What a government! . . . This is only one instance of the many, being enacted, of cruelty & injustice. They ought to read 'Valentine Mc-Clutchy'" (a popular 1845 novel by Irish author William Carleton critical of the abuses of the Orangemen). She concluded by noting that she "hope[d] soon we shall see a different sort of government."[49] In an 1876 letter Baptista informed Patrick that a family friend had been falsely accused of being one of the "Ellenton rioters" in Columbia. She attributed this turmoil to "this new element down here" who target property holders who were rich before the war and try to get money out of them "by hook or crook." She was a passionate admirer of former Confederate brigadier general John Smith Preston, a wealthy aristocrat of Irish Protestant descent who had been an ardent champion of secession and continued to defend it long after the war. In 1877 she wrote to Patrick: "Truly he is a *nobleman*. . . . We had quite a long talk about religion & he really edified me by his humility & deep sense of unworthiness on the sight of God. I believe he is a Catholic at heart."[50] In 1877 she also granted (in her mind) honorary Catholic status to Governor Wade Hampton, who presided over the return of "home rule" to the state that year: "How worthy of all praise is Gov. Hampton! What beautiful self government & Christian fortitude. He ought to be a Catholic & may, I pray."[51]

When Mother Baptista died in 1887 from typhoid fever, she was deeply mourned in the national Catholic press. We can learn much from her life. Though the wartime burning of the Columbia convent destroyed valuable records, Baptista's long correspondence with her brother together with other sources reveal much not only about this interesting woman but also about Catholics in the nineteenth-century South. In many ways Baptista closely resembled other South Carolinians of her race and class. She shared many of their ideas, including a belief in the rectitude of slavery and the right of secession. She stood out as an extremely devout Catholic in an overwhelmingly Protestant state and region, and her adherence to Catholicism was absolute. Though she had many friends among Protestants, in private she had a pronounced bias against them that was wholly consistent with, if not required by, her religion. She once wrote to Patrick concerning her seriously ill brother Conlaw who seemed to be dying of yellow fever that "he has always been a good Catholic. . . . It would be better for Almighty God to take him out of this life now when he is young and I hope in a state of Grace than that in after years he should live to marry a Protestant and perhaps lose his soul and those of his children." But she found Catholicism to be congenial with the prevailing values of her state and region. Indeed, she considered Catholicism to be ideal for a southerner with its emphasis on hierarchy and patriarchy. Ellen Lynch, Mother Baptista, lived within boundaries as strong as the iron fence that encloses her remains today. Yet this strong-willed woman managed to find a type of freedom in the religious life that suited her well. As Robert Frost once said, freedom is "feeling easy in your harness." The Ursuline Order offered her a framework within which she could successfully express her deep religious convictions and talent for leadership.

NOTES

1. Mother Mary Baptista (hereinafter cited as MB) to Patrick Lynch (hereinafter cited as PL), Columbia, S.C., first Sunday in Lent, 1877, Archives of the Diocese of Charleston, S.C. (hereinafter cited as ADC).

2. Ray Allen Billington, *The Protestant Crusade, 1800–1860: A Study of the Origins of American Nativism* (New York: Macmillan, 1938), 345.

3. John Tracy Ellis, *American Catholicism* (Chicago: University of Chicago Press, 1969), 83.

4. Maria Monk, *The Awful Disclosures of Maria Monk* (1836; rpt., London: Camden, 1939), 42, 87, 90.

5. Joseph Gerard Mannard, "'Maternity of the Spirit': Women Religious in the Archdiocese of Baltimore, 1790–1860" (PhD diss., University of Maryland, 1989), 260.

6. *Secret and Sacred: The Diaries of James Henry Hammond, a Southern Slaveholder*, ed. Carol Bleser (New York: Oxford University Press, 1988), 151.

7. Drew Gilpin Faust, *John Henry Hammond and the Old South: A Design for Mastery* (Baton Rouge: Louisiana State University, 1982), 193.

8. Jenny Franchot, *Roads to Rome: The Antebellum Protestant Encounter with Catholicism* (Berkeley: University of California Press, 1994), 14.

9. MB to PL, Columbia, February 15, 1868, ADC.

10. Lynch family genealogy, ADC.

11. David C. R. Heisser, "Bishop Lynch's People: Slaveholding by a South Carolina Prelate," *South Carolina Historical Magazine* 102, no. 3 (2001): 242.

12. Nancy Stockton, "'I Wonder Who Will Pray for Me When I'm Dead?' Elite Catholic Women in Nineteenth-Century South Carolina" (MA thesis, The Citadel, 2004).

13. Richard C. Madden, *Catholics in South Carolina: A Record* (Lanham, Md.: University Press of America, 1985), 94.

14. MB to PL, Columbia, October 25, 1861, ADC.

15. MB to PL, Columbia, March 8, 1868, ADC.

16. Heisser, "Bishop Lynch's People," 238.

17. James M. McPherson, *Ordeal by Fire: The Civil War and Reconstruction* (New York: Knopf, 1982), 21.

18. Ibid., 273.

19. Heisser, "Bishop Lynch's People," 244–45.

20. MB to PL, Columbia, December 1, 1876, ADC.

21. Barbara Welter, "The Cult of True Womanhood: 1820–1860," pt. 1, *American Quarterly* 18, no. 2 (1966): 151–74.

22. MB to PL, New Orleans? April 15, 1855, ADC.

23. MB to PL, Columbia, April 27, 1858, ADC.

24. Grace Brown Elmore, *A Heritage of Woe: The Civil War Diary of Grace Brown Elmore, 1861–1868*, ed. Marli F. Weiner (Athens, Ga.: University of Georgia Press, 1997), 20.

25. MB to PL, Columbia, n.d., ADC.

26. MB to PL, Cincinnati, Ohio, 1855, ADC.

27. MB to PL, Columbia, February 28, 1858, ADC.

28. MB to PL, Columbia, October 25, 1861, ADC.

29. MB to PL, Columbia, February 28, 1858, ADC.

30. MB to PL, Columbia, Ash Wednesday, 1864, ADC.

31. Linda Lierheimer, "Female Eloquence and Maternal Ministry: The Apostolate of Ursuline Nuns in Seventeenth-Century France" (PhD diss., Princeton University, 1994), 441–42.

32. Sister Mary Francis Clare Cusack, "Let Women Be Educated Carefully, with a Sense of Their Future Power and Influence, 1874," in *Gender Identities in American Catholicism*, ed. Paula Kane, James Kenneally, and Karen Kennelly (Maryknoll, N.Y.: Orbis Books, 2001), 58.

33. Anne Firor Scott, *The Southern Lady: From Pedestal to Politics, 1830–1930* (Chicago: University of Chicago Press, 1970), 152.

34. Emily Clark, *Masterless Mistresses: The New Orleans Ursulines and The Development of a New World Society, 1727–1834* (Chapel Hill: University of North Carolina Press for the Omohundro Institute of Early American History and Culture, Williamsburg, Va., 2007), 5, 6.

35. MB to PL Columbia, n.d., ADC.

36. MB to PL, New Orleans, January 2, 1855, ADC.

37. MB to PL, Columbia, July 21, 1863, ADC.

38. MB to (unidentified), Columbia, July 1873? ADC.

39. MB to PL, Columbia, January 28, 1863, ADC.

40. MB to PL, Columbia, May 7, 1872, ADC.

41. MB to PL, Columbia, December 10, 1861, ADC.

42. MB to PL, Columbia, February 19, 1863, ADC.

43. Madden, *Catholics in South Carolina*, 82.

44. David C. R. Heisser, "Bishop Lynch's Civil War Pamphlet on Slavery," *Catholic Historical Review*, 84, no. 4 (1998): 681.

45. PL to Judah P. Benjamin, Paris, June 20, 1864 (cited in Madden, *Catholics in South Carolina*).

46. Mary Pinckney Powell, *Back Over Home: The Heritage of Pinckneys of Pinckney Colony, Bluffton, South Carolina* (Columbia, S.C.: R. L. Bryan, 1996), 135.

47. Madden, *Catholics in South Carolina*, 95.

48. MB to PL, Columbia, February 15, 1869, ADC.

49. MB to PL, Columbia, December 1, 1876, ADC.

50. MB to PL, Columbia, February 21, 1877, ADC.

51. MB to PL, Columbia, February 22, 1877, ADC.

Mary Boykin Chesnut

Civil War Redux

ELISABETH SHOWALTER MUHLENFELD

More than a century has passed since the publication of *A Diary From Dixie*, a book by Mary Boykin Chesnut (1823–86) that was destined to become recognized as one of the most important works to emerge from the Civil War. It has taken all of that time for Chesnut to be accorded full rank as an important writer. We have only now come to grasp the scope of Chesnut's literary vision and, in so doing, to understand the woman herself. Though relegated to the sidelines, she carved out a role as hostess of wartime salons and as astute observer. Drawing on her wide acquaintanceship, political acumen, and broad reading, she recorded not only political and military developments but also the perspectives of soldier and civilian, slave and master, as she chronicled the Civil War from the home front. Viewing her original diary entries alongside the narrative journal she developed from them allows the reader to appreciate her skill as a writer and to see through her eyes the Confederacy in crisis.

The first edition of Chesnut's only book was so severely cut and edited that none of its readers could possibly have appreciated the magnitude of the author's achievement. Even its full title—*A Diary From Dixie, as Written by Mary Boykin Chesnut, wife of James Chesnut, Jr., United States Senator from South Carolina 1859–1861, and Afterward an Aide to Jefferson Davis and a Brigadier-General in the Confederate Army*—provides ironies, submerging the writer in a sea of praise for her husband, a well-born but minor player in the vast crisis that was to become our nation's defining struggle.[1] Mary Chesnut, who had never given her book any title, disliked the term "Dixie" and detested the song, which she said "never moved me a jot."[2] More troublesome, the blithe title—provided by the *Saturday Evening Post* that ran five long excerpts prior to book publication—proclaimed the work an untutored diary.

MARY BOYKIN CHESNUT AND HUSBAND JAMES CHESNUT JR.
Courtesy of Martha W. Daniels.

Although the first truncated edition omitted many of Chesnut's most vivid passages, *A Diary From Dixie* quickly became a valued source for historians, who were impressed with the cache of primary material it provided and charmed by its witty author. Novelist Ben Ames Williams read it and was so fascinated that he not only based a central character on Chesnut in his novel *House Divided* but subsequently undertook to edit a second edition of her work.[3] Williams's edition, published in 1949, was far more readable and attracted fresh attention to Chesnut. It contained half again as much manuscript material as the 1905 version but was heavily edited, smoothed and "improved." Although he apparently had in hand various manuscript versions, Williams did not mention a crucial point: that Chesnut's book was *not* a diary, *not* an original daily record, but an elaborate revision of the author's Civil War journal, written two decades after the war.

Nevertheless, sophisticated readers encountering the new edition responded to it as literature. Edmund Wilson in *Patriotic Gore* pronounced it a masterpiece and admitted himself puzzled by its literary quality: "The diarist's own instinct is uncanny. Starting out with situations or relationships of which she cannot know the outcome, she takes advantage of the actual turn of events to develop them and round them out as if she were molding a novel."[4] Critic Daniel Aaron in *The Unwritten War* saw Chesnut's *Diary* as "more genuinely literary" than any Civil War fiction, all of which lacked Chesnut's "evocative description[,] . . . trenchant comment, and down-to-earth realities." Aaron accorded Chesnut "the eye and ear of a novelist." "One feels in reading her remarkable diary," he wrote, "that she may have deliberately employed the form of a fictional memoir."[5]

Despite two editions of her work and seventy years of interest by historians, almost no scholarship had been done on Chesnut until 1975, when C. Vann Woodward undertook a new and complete edition of the Chesnut journals.[6] Knowing that the published editions were not, in fact, the diary Chesnut kept in the 1860s, Woodward initially intended to publish that original material. As he became immersed in the project, however, he was so impressed with Chesnut's masterful revision that he decided to publish it in a nearly complete, scholarly edition entitled *Mary Chesnut's Civil War*. Yet as an historian he found himself unable to ignore a number of important passages in the original diary (of which only those volumes covering February to early December 1861 and parts of January through July 1865 still exist). These, including a few recovered entries that Chesnut had erased, Woodward interspersed within the text of his edition, noting their provenance. By providing this plain evidence of multiple versions, Woodward clarified Chesnut's work. In the process, however, Mary Chesnut ironically became both more widely admired as a writer (Woodward's edition won the Pulitzer Prize in 1982) and tainted as a primary source. One reviewer famously called Chesnut's work a hoax, "one of the most audacious frauds in the history of American literature."[7] To insure that the original 1860s diaries were readily available to historians, Woodward and I coedited them in 1984, making it possible for the first time for scholars to place passages from Chesnut's diary side by side with comparable passages in her 1880s revision.[8]

With each new edition, we have come to see Mary Boykin Chesnut and her artistry as more complex. Scholars have debated whether Chesnut's book of the 1880s should be read as autobiography, memoir, diary, journal, chronicle, or fiction; frustrated that it does not fit tidily into a genre, they have argued about what it should be called. Woodward himself called it a palimpsest, as did Steven Stowe; Michael O'Brien, a particularly astute reader, names it a "narrative journal," conflating terms Chesnut herself used separately.[9] By any name, Chesnut's work proved to be an early and rich tool for exploring the social history of the Confederacy, women's roles, and the intersection of private lives and public crisis. So complex is Chesnut's narrative that readers have found within it evidence of diametrically opposing points of view. Her work has been condemned as an example of "Lost Cause literature," praised as an exemplary feminist text whose author battles her culture's myths of sexual ideology, and analyzed as an ur-modernist work, presaging Woolf's *To the Lighthouse*.[10] Chesnut herself has been dissected more thoroughly than has her book. Scholars have scrutinized the text for clues to the author's psyche, judged her credentials as a feminist, and probed deeply her views on race and slavery—in each case, finding deep complexities.

Chesnut's book has long since taken its rightful place as the most famous firsthand account of southern society during the Civil War. Further, its author is now coming to be understood not as one of dozens of women diarists and letter writers of the Civil War era and not even as the best woman diarist but as one of the best of our nineteenth-century writers, period. We know, however, relatively little about Chesnut's life beyond its basic outlines. To learn of the woman herself, and of the world in which she lived, we can most profitably turn to her writing.

Mary Boykin Miller Chesnut was born in Statesboro, South Carolina, in 1823, the eldest child of Mary Boykin, of an old and respected South Carolina family, and Stephen Decatur Miller, a self-made lawyer and former U. S. congressman. A strong proponent of Nullification, Miller was serving in the South Carolina legislature at the time of Mary's birth. He would be elected governor five years later, and to the U. S. Senate in 1830. Thus, throughout Mary's childhood, politics was in the very air she breathed. Mary was educated first at home, learning there to read and write and instructed by her maternal grandmother in the womanly arts and duties associated with running a large plantation. After attending school for two or three years in Camden, at twelve she was enrolled in a Charleston boarding school run by an indomitable Frenchwoman, Ann Marson Talvande, where she spoke only French or German during school hours.

Madame Talvande, who possessed what Mary later described as "the fiercest eye I have ever seen in a mortal head," was a strict taskmaster and kept a close watch on her young charges, but thirteen-year-old Mary managed to be seen walking on the Charleston Battery in the moonlight with James Chesnut Jr., newly graduated from Princeton. Governor Miller decided to remove his daughter from gossip and took her for several months to his cotton plantation in rural Mississippi, a state just emerging from frontier status. She returned briefly to Madame Talvande's school, but her formal education ended abruptly with the death of her father in 1838. Three weeks after her seventeenth birthday in 1840, she married and went to live with James at Mulberry, his family's plantation near Camden.

The new Mrs. Chesnut came to Mulberry expecting, in due course, to assume her prescribed role as wife, mother, and mistress of the household—a position for which she had been carefully educated. Fate had other plans. Her in-laws, James Chesnut Sr. and Mary Cox Chesnut, in their sixties at the time of her marriage, retained control of lands and household for twenty-five more years. Far more devastating, James and Mary remained childless, a lack Mary felt acutely. Thus, the first twenty years of her marriage were difficult, and her relationships with her in-laws and even her husband were often tense. Hers was a restless, gregarious personality, and she found life at Mulberry and in the provincial village of Camden stultifying. In later years, she would say of it: "A pleasant, empty, easy going life. If one's heart is at ease. But people are not like pigs; they cannot be put up and fattened. So here I pine and fret."[11]

James Chesnut Jr. spent the years before 1860 in public service, eventually presiding over the state legislature. In 1858 he was sent to the U. S. Senate. In Washington, his wife was finally in her element. Of necessity, hers was a social role, and yet she was a far more astute politician than her husband. She possessed intelligence, wit, a reputation as a "literary" lady, a facility for languages, a marked skill as a conversationalist, and charm. Women were occasionally uneasy in her presence, but men—some of the most powerful men of her time— were drawn to her.

As hostility between North and South grew in the fall of 1860, James Chesnut Jr. resigned his Senate seat and returned to South Carolina to help draft an ordinance of secession. His wife, who loved to pun, was succinct: "*I am not at all resigned.*"[12] Deeply reluctant to leave Washington, she nevertheless cast her lot with her state and became an ardent supporter of Jefferson Davis, whose wife, Varina, was a friend.

As war became a certainty, Mary Boykin Chesnut began to keep a journal. At first she wrote in an elegant red leather-bound diary with gilt edges and a brass lock, but as the privations of wartime cut off supplies she continued her journal in anything she could find, at last recording the bleak aftermath of civil war in the blank pages of an old recipe book. The journal was a private one, kept under lock and key. Portions of it that survive contain notes hurriedly jotted down, designed to remind her later of people, events, opinions, conversations, and impressions of the moment. Many of her entries are almost cryptic; all are utterly candid. After meeting South Carolina governor Francis Pickens, she wrote, "old Pick was there with a better wig—and his silly and affected wife."[13] After dining at someone else's house, she declared, "I can give a better dinner than that!"[14] Chesnut recorded whatever occurred to her as she was writing in her diary, taking no time to separate the trivial from the important. She seldom paused to reflect on the scene around her, something she often did in her re-vised journal of the 1880s. Rather, Chesnut wrote to amass material that could be winnowed later.

From the first, Chesnut understood that the events to which she was witness were of major historical significance, and she recognized that she was in an excellent position to "cover" the war. She was in Charleston when Major Robert Anderson moved into Fort Sumter, in Montgomery for the inauguration of Jef-ferson Davis, and in Charleston during the firing on Fort Sumter, where James served as aide to General Pierre G. T. Beauregard. In all these settings, Mary's hotel quarters served as salon in which the men engaged in forming the new government and their wives congregated. She spent most of the next several months in Richmond and recorded a city pulsing with excitement. She waited with Varina Davis for news of the battle at Manassas and visited the first sick and wounded of the war. Always, she wrote in her journal, sometimes express-ing there her fears for her country and her outrage over the antics of the men in positions of authority: "This war began a War of Secession," she wrote as early as March 1861. "It will end a War for the Succession of Places." By August, when her husband seemed unable to decide whether to go into the army or stand for reelection to the Confederate Senate, she exploded in her journal, "Jeff Davis ill & shut up—& none but noodles have the world in charge."[15]

As a woman Mary could neither join the army nor hold office, and her frus-trations frequently found their way into her journal. "Oh," she moaned in April 1861, "if I could put some of my reckless spirit into these discreet cautious lazy men." She hoped James would be appointed ambassador to France; failing that, she wanted him to be reelected senator, not least because she wanted to avoid having to go home to Mulberry. At one point, she wrote, "I wish Mr. Davis would send *me* to Paris—& so I should not *need* a South Carolina Legislature for anything else." Back in Camden, her husband's apparent indifference to the war raging in Virginia infuriated her: "*Now*, when if ever man was stirred to the highest for his country & for his own future," James seemed oblivious. "If I had been a man in this great revolution—I should have either been killed at once or made a name & done some good for my country. Lord Nelson's motto would be mine—Victory or Westminster Abbey."[16]

In December 1862 President Davis appointed James colonel and summoned him to Richmond as a personal aide. This appointment suited Mary Chesnut perfectly. She rented quarters close to the White House of the Confederacy; Chesnuts and Davises visited almost daily. In Richmond, as in Charleston, Montgomery, and Columbia, Chesnut's renown as a hostess assured that she had a constant round of visitors teeming with interesting conversation, much of which found its way into her journal. During her stay in Richmond, Mary and Sarah Buchanan ("Buck") Preston, the lovely daughters of Columbia friends, came for extended visits—these were but two of the many young people who were drawn to Chesnut throughout the war, in whom she delighted and who represented to her the children she had never had.

The summer and fall of 1863 were marked by family illnesses and deaths, which occasioned travel to Flat Rock, North Carolina, Camden and Columbia in South Carolina, and Alabama, where she visited her mother as well as her brother's and sister's families. Back in Richmond by November, Chesnut once again poured her energy into the social and political life of the city. Unable to serve the war in any other capacity, she saw her role as hostess of a wartime salon as a way to provide support to the soldiers she welcomed—officers as well as enlisted men, so long as they were of "good family." Her living room provided distraction from the losses, pain, and sheer exhaustion they suffered, a safe space for men serving in the Confederate government to cement friendships and engage one another socially and for the women of Richmond society to speak frankly. She watched romance bloom under her roof in the midst of war, as the beautiful Buck Preston was wooed by the wounded war hero General John Bell Hood—a doomed romance that seemed to track the unraveling of Confederate hopes for victory. James Chesnut chafed against what Mary later called "The Bright Side of Richmond," excoriating his wife for taking part in charade parties gotten up by the ladies of Richmond to lighten the despair of the Confederate capital after Gettysburg and Vicksburg.[17] The death of his mother in 1864 made James anxious to return to South Carolina, and so in May, President Davis promoted his friend to brigadier general and gave him command of the South Carolina Reserves.

The Chesnuts moved to Columbia, living first with the Prestons, and then in a nearby rented cottage, where in October 1864, Jefferson Davis stopped to visit on his way back to Richmond from a trip to the western front. In Columbia, Chesnut rose early to visit the sick and wounded in surrounding hospitals, welcomed her own nieces and Maggie Howell, Varina Davis's young sister, for long visits, read voluminously as always, and continued to hold open house, now often frequented by generals without troops. Sherman's siege of Atlanta and then his army on the march provided the grim omnipresent drumroll.

In late January 1865, as the South fought on to what she knew was inevitable defeat, Chesnut was forced into exile. Yielding to private despair at times, she publicly met adversity with good humor, noting wryly that she had thought to bring plenty of books to Lincolnton, North Carolina, where she fled while Sherman burned Columbia, but no one would accept her Confederate money for food. "I am bodily comfortable, if somewhat dingily lodged," she wrote, "and I daily part with my raiment for food. We find no one who will exchange eatables for Confederate money. So we are devouring our clothes."[18]

Two months later, she had moved again, to three vacant rooms in Chester, South Carolina. Again she kept open house as old friends were drawn to her — the Preston daughters and General John S. Preston, General Hood, Governor Milledge L. Bonham of South Carolina, Senator Clement Clay, General and Mrs. Louis Wigfall and others. "Night and day this landing and these steps are crowded with the elite of the Confederacy, going and coming. And when night comes . . . more beds are made on the floor of the landing place. . . . The whole house is a bivouac."[19] It took ten days for news of Lee's surrender on April 9, 1865, to reach the Chesnuts. Among her last visitors were Varina Davis and her children, fleeing unknown fates.

The Chesnuts returned to Camden. Mary continued to write in her journal occasionally through June, chronicling her disgust at the familiar petty grievances that marked village life and her anger at relatives uninterested in hearing any more about the war. Miserable from the emotional exhaustion of four years, she noted in her last entry only one remaining pleasure: "We have so much more [produce] than this establishment consumes, I am enabled to carry baskets of vegetables to my destitute friends."[20] But gradually, her depression lifted. James finally inherited Mulberry when his ninety-three-year-old father died in 1866, though beyond that his inheritance included not only huge debts he was never able to repay but also a host of relatives and former slaves dependent on him. The Chesnuts were by no means poverty stricken. When visitors came, Mary could and did don her antebellum Paris dresses and set her tables with fine china and crystal. But her scale of living had changed dramatically. She took over the responsibilities of running the cottage industries that supplied the plantations, assisted in overseeing farming affairs, and established a small butter and egg business that brought pin money into the household.

Perhaps to earn money, and certainly to amuse herself, she decided in the early 1870s to try her hand at fiction and worked on two novels more or less simultaneously.[21] One was a largely autobiographical novel she called *Two Years— or The Way We Lived Then* that deals with a schoolgirl at Madame Talvande's French School for Young Ladies in Charleston who is taken by her father to a raw cotton plantation in Mississippi. This novel, which provides perhaps the fullest and best extant description of a southern girls' boarding school of the period, includes plot elements drawn from the popular adventure tales of the Old Southwest. The other was a Civil War novel, entitled *The Captain and the Colonel*, Mary Boykin Chesnut's first effort to use, in palatable form, the materials of her wartime journals. By the mid-1870s, ten years had elapsed since the war, and she had had time to gain a very different perspective.

In an 1876 memoir for her nieces and nephews, she indicated that change in perspective very clearly, in a brief passage remembering abolitionist John Brown's famous 1859 raid:

> I remember . . . I saw in the Charleston papers, an account—of a speech from Senator Chesnut—and [one about] John Brown[s] raid. I was so stupid—I did not read [about] the raid at all—engrossed by my own small affair—and yet John [Brown]'s Raid—meant a huge war—revolution—ruin to us all and death to millions—and the speech—well it was a good speech—and there was the end of it.[22]

In short, the elapsed time between the war itself and 1876 had enabled Chesnut to step back from her own "small affairs" and see quite clearly the astounding scope of the national cataclysm through which she had lived. Not surprisingly, then, when Chesnut sought an epigraph for her novel of the war, she selected the following poem, perhaps her own:

> Spider! thou need'st not run in fear about
> To shun my curious eyes:
> I won't humanely crush thy bowels out,
> Lest thou should eat the flies;
> Nor will I toast thee with a damned delight
> Thy strange instructive fortitude to see;

> For there is one who might
> One day roast me.[23]

This little poem begins with the speaker watching a spider dashing around in instinctive terror (lest the giant human speaker in the poem crush it or roast it over a fire just to watch it burn). But the perspective changes dramatically; there is a far larger, more powerful force that might by analogy "roast" the speaker. The image is reminiscent of the famous passage by Jonathan Edwards in his sermon "Sinners in the Hands of an Angry God," in which he envisions the sinner dangling over the fires of hell like a spider suspended by a silken thread, awaiting the inevitable. This movement in perspective from the small affairs of the individual to imminent destruction by a crushing and inexplicable power is a dominant theme in the novel itself and would become essential to the revised journal of the 1880s.

The Captain and the Colonel is the story of the Effingham family of South Carolina: a mother and three daughters, Margaret, Susan, and Emily, all of whom live a life of beauty, ease, graciousness, and regularity. In its early chapters the novel follows a classic pattern of novels of manners: the three daughters are all of marriageable age. The plantation next door is owned by eligible bachelor and close family friend Charles Johannis, modeled on Mary Chesnut's nephew, John Chesnut, the "Cool Captain" of *Mary Chesnut's Civil War*. Visiting Johannis is a friend, Collingwood. Johannis has secretly loved Emily since she was a child. Both Margaret and Emily fall in love with Collingwood, Collingwood falls in love with Emily and confesses to Johannis. Susan tattles and creates complications. Margaret seethes with jealousy. Into all this comes the Civil War, which Chesnut talks about and alludes to rather awkwardly, primarily by drawing on a few settings and anecdotes from her own experiences.

In the novel, the central figure is the mother, a woman with some of the characteristics of the author herself. Even as a young woman, Joanna (née Hardhead) is described as "Queen Joanna" or "Regina." Her family acknowledges her right to rule, primarily because she is more intelligent and more decisive than they, and she is often depicted as a military tactician. At one point, for example, as she tries to quash a romance under her roof, military metaphors abound: "When the smoke of the battle field had blown away, Mrs. Effingham felt she had used her great guns in vain. Victory had not perched upon her banners. The foe was in motion all along the line. . . . 'To think a child of mine could be so insolent. . . . But I will conquer her yet.'"[24]

As the war drags on, Joanna's pride in her power and her control erodes. She runs a large war hospital in Richmond, but her tireless work and her efforts to rebuild, repair, and regroup at war's end become a mind-numbing way of life. Chesnut's protagonist comes to be painfully aware of her impotence. She goes from being a force of nature to the helpless victim of natural forces over which she has no control. At one point near the end of the novel, the story is told of a neighbor who has selfishly hidden away a hundred bales of cotton, insuring himself a personal fortune in the face of his neighbors' poverty. But as he brags of his foresight, the cotton is struck by lightning and goes up in flames. "For a hundred yards round, it was hot as hell!" cries the teller of the tale in wild excitement. "Not a lock of that cotton is left." Here the planter is like the spider in the novel's epigraph; some power far beyond his understanding is roasting him.[25]

Chesnut makes very clear in the novel the connections between the personal and the global. The revolt of Joanna's younger daughter, Emily, against her mother's absolute power is juxtaposed against "the grand revolt of the southern lands—and disaster after disaster." Toward the end of the novel, Susan tells of the death in childbirth of her best friend only hours after the woman had learned of her husband's death on a battlefield: "'I sat up all night trying to keep that poor little baby warm—with hot flannels—and as near as we could get to the stove. It was of no use. It died before day. And so they were all buried together——. These chairs are very hard and uncomfortable,' cried Susan. 'How I miss my rocking chair! And the room is so close.'" As she speaks, Susan walks to a window "where every pane was broken"; here is personal grief within the context of universal desolation.[26]

Although at the end of the novel, all three sisters find husbands and marry, only Emily, the youngest, has made a love match; the other two, like their mother before them, have simply secured support. Marriage and family, the traditional "happy endings" of Victorian novels, offer no solace. Even the newly freed slave women remain in bondage. "I stopped to look at a black girl," says Susan Effingham after Lee's surrender. "She was yelling at the top of her voice to some one behind me. It was delightful to see her ecstasy. . . . 'Look here—see me—I am free as a bird.' I foresaw a husband for whom she must bake and brew—wash and sew—she will only exchange masters."[27]

Chesnut's efforts at fiction are interesting for two reasons. First, they deal with themes that she later would develop effectively in her revised Civil War journal, including women's roles, the relationships of blacks and whites, and the impact of history—public and private—on the individual life. Second, these draft novels show the care and deliberation with which Chesnut, at that point in her mid-fifties, was teaching herself to write, to handle dialogue and description, to use imagery, to parallel characters and events, and to speak with a clearly defined narrative voice.

From very early in the war, Chesnut had had in mind that at some point, she would revise her journals for a general readership. Indeed, the entry with the earliest date in the 1860s diary reads very differently from all subsequent entries, and was almost certainly written months after February 18, 1861, the date it bears. Clearly a deliberate introductory essay, it begins, "I do not allow myself vain regrets or sad foreboding. This southern Confederacy must be supported now by calm determination—& cool brains. We have risked all, & we must play our best for the stake is life or death." In this entry, she introduces characters in a way no diarist writing simply for her own eyes would do ("Col. Colcock, formerly member of Congress & of U. S."), and provides a background statement about her politics and the political "mixed marriage" in which she has lived: "My father was a South Carolina Nullifier—Governor of the state at the time of the N[ullification] row & then U. S. Senator. So I was of necessity a rebel born. My husband's family being equally pledged to the Union party rather exasperated my zeal—as I heard taunts & sneers so constantly thrown out against the faith I had imbibed before I understood any thing at all about it. If I do yet."[28]

Chesnut made a brief attempt to revise her journals shortly after the war and an extended effort in the mid-1870s, expecting simply to smooth them out, transform notes into complete sentences, and delete the most personally revealing tidbits. As she worked, she apparently came to know that she did not want her book to be a record of daily domestic trifles. (Of the letters of Jane Welsh Carlyle, wife of Thomas Carlyle, she once wrote, "She had two motions—the one around her Sun—or brilliant husband—is delightful—the harder she hits him—the better fun—but when she turns on her own axis—and thrusts her homely details under our noses by the guise—she is a bore.") Rather, she wanted to focus on the tumultuous scene around her. Doing so, however, would require a thoroughgoing reconception rather than a mere polishing.

Accordingly, Chesnut bought a supply of notebooks in 1881 and began yet another revision of her Civil War journals in earnest—a task still incomplete at her death in 1886. The work was exhaustive, for in the twenty years since she had begun the journal she had had time to sort out the significant from the trivial and to find in trivialities emblems of the whole. Though she preserved the diary format and took care not to alter fact or admit anachronism into her book, the diary slowly became a carefully structured and dramatic literary work.

By analyzing comparable passages in each version, the transformation of diary into book becomes clear. The crisis over Fort Sumter provides a case in point.[29] In her diary, Chesnut records her distress on April 12, 1861: "Mr. Chesnut sent off again to Anderson. The live long night I toss about—at half past four we hear the booming of the cannon. I start up—dress & rush to my sisters in misery. We go on the house top & see the shells bursting. They say our men are wasting ammunition."[30]

More than twenty years later, in her revised journal Chesnut carefully develops this incident as a deliberate narrative, beginning with a clear description of the situation: "I do not pretend to go to sleep. How can I? If Anderson does not accept terms—at four—the orders are—he shall be fired upon." Like any good writer, Chesnut works to build tension, sustaining a sense of immediacy:

> I count four—St. Michael chimes. I begin to hope. At half-past four, the heavy booming of a cannon.
>
> I sprang out of bed. And on my knees—prostrate—I prayed as I never prayed before.
>
> There was a sound of stir all over the house—pattering of feet in the corridor—all seemed hurrying one way. I put on my double gown and a shawl and went, too. It was to the housetop.
>
> The shells were bursting. In the dark I heard a man say "waste of ammunition."[31]

Here, even the little comment about wasting ammunition, now placed in the mouth of an anonymous man, serves as an ironic contrast to the high patriotism and drama of the moment.

In her 1861 diary, Chesnut ends her account, "Good news. Nobody hurt on our side." By the time she revised her work in the 1880s, she wrote, "Do you know, after all that noise and our tears and prayers, nobody has been hurt. Sound and fury, signifying nothing. A delusion and a snare." Here her allusion to Macbeth suggests the theatrical quality of Fort Sumter; her comment foreshadows the real war to come, suggesting by "a delusion and a snare" that the high expectations with which the bombardment of Fort Sumter imbued the South were themselves a trap. And Chesnut includes one more passage of importance here, one that would initiate a theme barely mentioned in the original diary in 1861 but woven throughout the great work of the 1880s—the inscrutability of the slave population: "Not by one word or look can we detect any change in the demeanor of these negro servants. Laurence [James's manservant] sits at our door, as sleepy and as respectful and as profoundly indifferent. So are they all. They carry it too far. You could not tell that they hear even the awful row that is going on in the bay, though it is dinning in their ears night and day. And people talk before them as if they were chairs and tables. And they make no sign. Are they stolidly stupid or wiser than we are, silent and strong, biding their time?"

Chesnut's 1861 diary entry just following the bombardment of Fort Sumter captures perfectly the excitement of the moment, but her description is almost cryptic: "Monday 15th—16th—17th—18th—& 19th—20th, 21st—22nd—23rd. During this time—the excitement, &c, was so great I had never a moment to write. I drove every evening on the battery. Manning, Wigfall, John Preston, &c, men without limit best us at night. Mrs. Cheves came & her sweet little girls. Mrs. Frank Hampton as perfectly charming as ever. Barnwell Heyward—Mary Kirkland—every body, every thing happened. Mr. C, Manning & Miles carried Russell to the Forts—& Wigfall, drunk, insulted him. Poor Mrs. W. James Simons sat under the yellow flag for safety. They call him hospital Jimmy." This diary entry conveys euphoria ("every body, every thing happened"), but little else: a list of people she saw, a dig at Louis Wigfall, and some nasty gossip that James Simons had proved himself to be a coward. In her revised journal, however, Chesnut uses this moment to develop a wonderfully ironic picture of society, high to low, moving from the social to the serious:

> Home again. In those last days of my stay in Charleston I did not find time to write a line.
>
> And so we took Fort Sumter. Nous autres. We—Mrs. Frank Hampton &c, in the passageway of the Mills House between the reception room and the drawing room. There we held a sofa against all comers. And indeed, all the agreeable people South seemed to have flocked to Charleston at the first gun. That was after we found out that bombarding did not kill anybody. Before that we wept and prayed—and took our tea in groups, in our rooms, away from the haunts of men.
>
> Captain Ingraham and his kind took it (Fort Sumter) from the battery with field glasses and figures made with three sticks in the sand to show what ought to be done.
>
> Wigfall, Chesnut, Miles, Manning &c took it, rowing about in the harbor in small boats, from fort to fort, under the enemies' guns, bombs bursting in air, &c&c.
>
> And then the boys and men who worked those guns so faithfully at the forts. They took it, too—their way.

In revising her account of this first major episode of the Civil War, Chesnut moves quite deliberately both to broaden her lens and to control it, categorizing in a litany that resembles waves of artillery the myriad people who have come to Charleston—the ladies who blossom from frightened isolates into social directors, the middle-aged burgers accustomed to providing oversight, the negotiators, the strategists, and the young recruits who quietly follow orders. War here is an extended party—a vanity fair.

To craft her picture of the Confederacy, we see Chesnut in example after example transforming first-person statement into dialogue, rearranging incidents and thoughts within a given entry or contiguous entries to heighten their dramatic import, and seizing the symbolic moment to construct rich pictures of her world. In June 1861, at Sandy Hill, the Chesnut's summer plantation, Chesnut's original diary records a brief incident: "I woke in the night, heard such a commotion, such loud talking of a crowd—I rushed out, thinking what could they have heard from Virginia, but found only Mrs. Chesnut had smelled a *Smell*—& roused the whole *yard.*" The incident ends with the simple note: "One of Col. Chesnut's negroes was taken yesterday with a pistol."[32] In the 1880s, Chesnut uses this incident to create a fully realized dramatic vignette of plantation life with all its ironies, teeming with able-bodied slaves racing around to do the bidding of one elderly, deaf, white woman—all providing an ironic juxtaposition to the war raging in the background. In the process, she sketches a delicious portrait of her mother-in-law. The whole is alive with movement and sensory power: sight, sound, and smell.

Last night I was awakened by loud talking and candles flashing—everywhere tramping of feet—growls dying away in the distance, loud calls from point to point in the yard.

Up I started—my heart in my mouth. Some dreadful thing had happened—a battle—a death—a horrible accident. Miss Sally Chesnut was screaming . . . from the top of the stairway—hoarsely, like a boatswain in a storm. . . .

I dressed and came upon the scene of action.

"What is it? Any news?"

"No, no—only, mama smells a smell. She thinks something is burning somewhere."

The whole yard was alive—literally swarming. There are sixty or seventy people kept here to wait upon this household—two-thirds of them too old or too young to be of any use. But families remain intact. Mr. C has a magnificent voice. I am sure it can be heard for miles. Literally he was roaring from the piazza—giving orders to the busy crowd who were hunting the smell of fire.

Mrs. C is deaf, so she did not know what a commotion she was creating. She is very sensitive on the subject of bad odors. Candles have to be taken out of the room to be snuffed. Lamps are extinguished only in the porticoes—or further afield. She finds violets oppressive. Can only tolerate a single kind of rose. Tea roses she will not have in her room.

She was totally innocent of the storm she had raised and in a mild sweet voice was suggesting places to be searched.

I was weak enough to laugh hysterically. The bombardment of Fort Sumter was nothing to this.[33]

Like its source, this version also ends, "Yesterday some of the negro men on the plantation were found with pistols"—in reality a far more serious threat than the smoldering rags that had caused the smell. But now Chesnut again sounds the theme of black inscrutability: "I have never seen aught about any negro to show that they knew we had a war on hand in which they have any interest." Neither do they betray any sense of the absurdity that their lives depend on carrying out the fiats of a frail elderly woman who cannot abide the smell of a snuffed candle or a violet.

In this rich scene, the world of Mulberry's "yard" is permeated by threats. The war just beyond the horizon is linked to the domestic by its comparison to the bombardment of Fort Sumter. Smoldering fire threatens to destroy hearth and home, not to mention the lives of innocent sleepers. The Negroes turn out to be armed—the long-dreaded insurrection subject only to the unknowable emotions of the slaves dashing around to the orders of white master and bellowing old maid. And yet, with humor and irony just shy of hysteria, the scene is broadly comic.

It is also a scene of *chaos*, a governing theme of the book as a whole, the riot of emotions and events and people that *are* a disrupted society. Readers of Chesnut often note the difficulty of working through long passages of unattributed dialogue, snatches of conversation, puns, nicknames, unidentified allusions. Particularly when Chesnut is capturing the sense of general conversation and gossip, she makes no effort to link words to speaker but lets the chatter wash over the reader as if he were thrust into the drawing room knowing no one and left to make sense of the matter by himself. The reader feels as if the "diarist" has recorded *everything*. To achieve this chaos, though, Mrs. Chesnut exercised a rigorous selectivity on her material, often discarding half of the original diary material, shaping and amplifying the rest.

The fact that chaos whirls incessantly throughout the book does not belie the overarching structure of *Mary Chesnut's Civil War*. War, of course, provides the scaffolding: the book begins with the prelude to conflict, moves through four long years of civil war, and ends with war's aftermath. Chesnut herself provides the key metaphor: family. Civil war can be understood as family torn asunder in a painful divorce. "We separated because of incompatibility of temper. We are divorced, North from South, because we hated each other so," she writes.[34]

To bring her themes to life, Chesnut uses her own family, particularly the men closest to her. Chesnut's father-in-law, James Chesnut Sr., monarch of all he surveys, serves as archetype of the antebellum world. In 1861, James Chesnut Sr. is a vigorous, courtly man; by 1865, we see him uncomprehending, "blind, deaf—apparently as strong as ever, certainly as resolute of will. . . . Partly patriarch, partly grand seigneur, this old man is of a species that we will see no more. The last of the lordly planters who ruled this southern world. He is a splendid wreck. His manners are unequaled still, and underneath this smooth exterior—the grip of a tyrant whose will has never been crossed."[35] Chesnut's portraits of her father-in-law throughout the entire revised journal punctuate her most evocative passages about plantation life.

Just as old Colonel Chesnut personifies the antebellum world, husband James Chesnut Jr., statesman, first senator to resign his seat, looking handsome as he dashes about Charleston in a red sash, represents the Confederacy—marked in Chesnut's mind by high ideals marred by anachronistic beliefs and indecisions. It is Chesnut's nephew John Chesnut ("Johnny," the model for her hero in *The Captain and the Colonel*), who becomes the "Cool Captain" in her revised journal, the cheerful young man, "the very perfection of a lazy gentleman who cares not to move unless it be for a fight, a dance, or a fox hunt," who, following Appomattox, can put the past aside and stride forward. In the original diary, Johnny appears only occasionally, although Mary and James are deeply fond of him and proud of his service. In the book of the 1880s, however, he assumes increasing importance at war's end. It is Johnny who wants to get on with life: "And Johnny! His country in mourning, with as much to mourn for as country ever had! . . . That cold, calm, unmoved air of his is only good form. Under all he is as volatile, as inconsequent, as easily made happy, as any lighthearted son of the South. To my amazement he wants me to give a picnic at Mulberry. Just now I would as soon dance on my father's grave." Mary Chesnut isn't ready to give a picnic, but clearly her nephew bespeaks the future.[36] There is no hint in Chesnut's revised journal, written in the early 1880s, that Johnny had in fact died in 1868. Chesnut as writer has trumped Chesnut as historian.

Perhaps the most complex issue Mary Boykin Chesnut had to deal with as she transformed diary into book was slavery. Chesnut's portrayal of slaves and slavery deserves far more attention than can be accommodated here, for her treatment of the defining element of her society is multifaceted, and her own thoughts and emotions regarding slavery are complex. She shared the racism of her era and could be especially demeaning when defending the ladies of the slaveholding South (who "live in negro villages" and "strive to ameliorate the condition of these Africans in every particular" by "utter self-abnegation") against the attacks of the likes of Harriet Beecher Stowe ("What self denial do they practice? It is the cheapest philanthropy trade in the world—easy. Easy as setting John Brown to come down here and cut our throats in Christ's name"). Stowe's abolitionism both fascinated her and roused her ire. "Think of these holy New Englanders, forced to have a negro village walk through their houses whenever they saw fit—dirty, slatternly, idle, ill-smelling by nature (when otherwise, it is the exception)."[37] And yet her portraits of her own servants are fully realized, evenhanded, and often affectionate. Occasionally she skewers a maid or butler for a foolish act or remark, but she saves her most trenchant digs for her white relatives and acquaintances. When she is in a critical and ironic mode, no one escapes, black or white.

Ample evidence exists that Chesnut developed abolitionist sentiments as a teenager and remained unalterably opposed to slavery all her life.[38] In her original Civil War diary, she finds the sight of a slave auction sickening. Although she believes in 1861 that "the Bible authorizes marriage & slavery—poor women! Poor slaves!"—she famously muses, "I wonder if it be a sin to think slavery a curse to any land. Sumner said not one word of this hated institution which is not true. Men & women are punished when their masters & mistresses are brutes & not when they do wrong. . . . God forgive *us*, but ours is a *monstrous* system & wrong & iniquity."[39] As C. Vann Woodward notes, "No Southerner and few Americans went further than that." [40]

Some critics have sought to show that Chesnut softened her opposition to slavery in the twenty years between diary and book and that, in solidarity with her class during Reconstruction, her racist sentiments intensified. The criticism is unwarranted. She did not include the above passage in her book principally because it occurs in the original diary in the middle of a period of extreme tension with her husband (something that also gets deliberately left out of the book of the 1880s). Her strong expression of anger about slavery is clearly tied to the miscegenation that the system perpetuates: "We live surrounded by prostitutes. . . . This only I see: like the patriarch of old our men live all in one house with their wives & their concubines, & the Mulattoes one sees in every family exactly resemble the white children—& every lady tells you who is the father of all the Mulatto children in every body's household, but those in her own, she seems to think drop from the clouds or pretends so to think."[41] Importantly, these famous passages written in March 1861 show Chesnut fully aware that slavery is at the heart of the conflict unfolding before her, and although in the original diary slaves and the subject of slavery seldom appear, throughout her book of the 1880s, she insures that it is never far from the reader's mind.

Critics who have concentrated principally on the passages quoted above and a few others have failed to realize how completely the fact of slavery and slave culture permeate the book. The murder by slaves of Chesnut's relative Betsy Witherspoon dominates the months of September and October 1861. Chesnut handles the episode brilliantly, unveiling facts as if she is writing a mystery story, fully aware of the importance of character in the understanding of motive. She shows the consternation caused by the murder; the fear of slave insurrection, usually just below the surface, now laid bare; the interdependence of slave and master; the wishful thinking of the whites that their slaves can be counted on to care for them as "family." As war marches on, Chesnut tells of savage Adam McWillie, who punished slaves by putting them in hogsheads with nails driven in all around and rolled them downhill, and of her own unnamed "lovely relative[,] . . . [b]eautifully dressed, graceful, languid[,] . . . [s]oftly in dulcet accents regretting the necessity she labored under" to send a Negro child out to be switched, and the woman who politely called her servants "aunt" and stood on a stool to box their ears.[42] Chesnut writes about a toy, the proud possession of Robert E. Lee's nephew Fitzhugh Lee: a mechanical slave boy that, when wound up, danced "Ethiopian minstrel fashion" while "Fitz Lee [sung] corn-shucking tunes."[43] And she provides a remarkably detailed picture of the work done by the house slaves at Mulberry, trained by her venerable mother-in-law to be on call in the middle of the night to warm a second nightgown with irons kept always at the ready should their mistress become cold.

Particularly when she is in Camden, Chesnut the observer provides many glimpses of slave culture, always from a distance. She looks down from her third story window at Mulberry to see the half a dozen coachmen laughing, talking, "hookling" gloves, and "small footmen . . . playing marbles under the trees."[44] She goes one afternoon to the "negro church on the plantation" at Mulberry, and listens to the minister preach "hell fire—so hot I felt singed" and Mulberry's elegant driver Jim Nelson pray with such fervor that "I wept bitterly."[45] But for the most part, she shows the reader the eerie inscrutability of the slaves from earliest days of the war until its end. As news comes of Lee's surrender, Chesnut agonizes over how her world could have come to ruin. "And these negroes" she observes, "—unchanged. The shining black mask they wear does not show a ripple of change—sphinxes."[46] Taken on the whole, Mary Chesnut's diary of the Civil War perhaps presents a fuller and more nuanced picture of white and black living side by side through the Civil War years than any other book of the era.

Unfinished at her death and unpublished in any form for almost twenty years thereafter, the diary is an enormous work. In the form of a diary, it uses the steady accrual of quotidian moments to weave a broad picture of a society—of white and black, of highborn and low, of country and city life, of the motives and emotions that lay behind political, military, and domestic events, and of the views expressed in drawing rooms, across dining tables, in churches, railroad cars, and hospitals throughout the South from the beginning of a glorious war to the end of a way of life. Concluding as it does in 1865, what her book cannot reveal is how its author carefully and patiently wrote and rewrote, created and revised and recreated the world that powers beyond her had destroyed. We are only just beginning to appreciate that artistry.

NOTES

An early version of this essay was presented at the seventy-first annual meeting of the University South Caroliniana Society, University of South Carolina, Columbia, April 21, 2007, and was published in the program for the seventy-second annual meeting, April 28, 2008. It draws heavily on my previous work on Mary Chesnut, in particular *Mary Boykin Chesnut: A Biography* (Baton Rouge: Louisiana State University Press, 1981).

1. *A Diary From Dixie*, ed. Isabella D. Martin and Myrta Lockett Avary (New York: Appleton, 1905). Five long excerpts from the book appeared in the *Saturday Evening Post* on January 28, February 4, February 11, February 18, and February 15, 1905.

2. *Mary Chesnut's Civil War*, ed. C. Vann Woodward, ed. (New Haven, Conn.: Yale University Press, 1981), 722 (hereinafter cited as MCCW).

3. Ben Ames Williams, *House Divided* (Boston: Houghton Mifflin, 1947); *A Diary from Dixie*, ed. Ben Ames Williams (Boston: Houghton Mifflin, 1949).

4. Edmund Wilson, *Patriotic Gore: Studies in the Literature of the American Civil War* (New York: Oxford University Press, 1962), 279–80.

5. Daniel Aaron, *The Unwritten War: American Writers and the Civil War* (New York: Knopf, 1973), 251, 259.

6. Bell Irvin Wiley, *Confederate Women* (Westport, Conn.: Greenwood, 1975), had included a chapter on Chesnut; see also Margaretta P. Childs, "Chesnut, Mary Boykin Miller," in *Notable American Women, 1607–1950: A Biographical Dictionary*, ed. Edward T. Jones, 3 vols. (Cambridge, Mass: Harvard University Press, 1971), 1:327–30.

7. Kenneth S. Lynn, "The Masterpiece That Became a Hoax," in *The Air-Line to Seattle: Studies in Literary and Historical Writing about America* (Chicago: University of Chicago Press, 1983), 51.

8. *The Private Mary Chesnut: The Unpublished Civil War Diaries*, ed. C. Vann Woodward and Elisabeth Showalter Muhlenfeld (New York: Oxford University Press, 1984) (hereinafter cited as PMC).

9. C. Vann Woodward, "Mary Chesnut in Search of Her Genre," in *The Future of the Past* (New York: Oxford University Press, 1989), 250–62; Steven M. Stowe, "City, Country, and the Feminine Voice," in *Intellectual Life in Antebellum Charleston*, ed. Michael O'Brien and David Moltke-Hansen (Knoxville: University of Tennessee Press, 1986), 314; Michael O'Brien, "The Flight Down the Middle Walk: Mary Chesnut and the Forms of Observance," in *Haunted Bodies: Gender and Southern Texts*,

ed. Anne Goodwyn Jones and Susan V. Donaldson (Charlottesville: University Press of Virginia, 1997), 112.

10. See, for example, Kendra Lynne McDonald, "The Creation of History and Myth in Mary Boykin Miller Chesnut's Civil War Narrative" (PhD diss., Ohio State University, 1996); Melissa Mentzer, "Rewriting Herself: Mary Chesnut's Narrative Strategies," *Connecticut Review*, 14, no. 1 (1992): 49–55; and O'Brien, "The Flight Down the Middle Walk," 112.

11. MCCW, 251 (November 30, 1861).

12. PMC, 10 (November 10, 1860).

13. Ibid., 54 (April 4, 1861).

14. Ibid., 14 (February 27, 1861).

15. Ibid., 49 (March 28, 1861), 151 (September 1, 1861).

16. Ibid., 63 (April 27, 1861), 122 (August 12, 1861), 179–80 (October 17, 1861).

17. Chesnut wrote three drafts of a series of episodes that took place in early January 1864 involving charades parties, apparently polishing a complex segment of her book for separate publication. The last draft bore the title "The Bright Side of Richmond. Winter of 1864—Scraps from a Diary." This was likely the last time she worked on the Civil War material.

18. MCCW, 733 (February 26, 1865).

19. Ibid., 789 (April 19, 1865).

20. PMC, 263 (June 26, 1865).

21. A third novel, titled variously "Manassas" and "Susie Effingham," has been lost except for a ten-page manuscript fragment numbered 411–19, including two pages numbered 415. This third attempt at fiction seems to have combined elements from both *The Captain and the Colonel* and *Two Years—or The Way We Lived Then*.

22. Manuscript memoir about her sister Catherine Williams, entitled "We Called Her Kitty," transcribed in Elisabeth Showalter Muhlenfeld, "Mary Boykin Chesnut: The Writer and Her Work" (PhD diss., University of South Carolina, 1978).

23. *Two Novels by Mary Chesnut*, ed. Elisabeth Showalter Muhlenfeld (Charlottesville: University Press of Virginia, 2002), 1.

24. *The Captain and the Colonel* in *Two Novels*, 48.

25. Ibid., 88.

26. Ibid., 99.

27. *Two Novels*, 95.

28. PMC, 3–4.

29. The following compares April 12, 1861, and April 23, 1861, in PMC, 59, 61, and MCCW, 46–47, 51.

30. PMC, 59.

31. MCCW, 46.

32. PMC, 84 (June 21–23, 1861).

33. MCCW, 77–78. Entry is dated June 10, 1861, but contains copies of letters written after that date. Chesnut likely failed to note the beginning of a new entry dated June 21 or 23 as she was revising.

34. MCCW, 25 (March 1861).

35. Ibid., 815 (May 18, 1865).

36. Ibid., 811 (May 10, 1865).

37. Ibid., 245 (November 27, 1861).

38. See Muhlenfeld, *Mary Boykin Chesnut*, 59, 32, 109–10; MCCW, xlviii–li.

39. PMC, 21 (March 3–4, 1861), 42 (March 18, 1861).

40. MCCW, xlix.

41. PMC, 42 (March 18, 1861).

42. MCCW, 606–7 (May 1864), 435 (1862–63).

43. Ibid., 590 (March 19, 1864).

44. Ibid., 251 (November 30, 1861).

45. Ibid., 214 (October 13, 1861.

46. Ibid., 794 (April 23, 1865).

Frances Neves and Her Family

Upcountry Women in the Civil War

SARA MARIE EYE

Voices of elite white women resonate throughout the historical record of Civil War South Carolina. The diary of South Carolinian Mary Chesnut exemplifies the plantation mistress memoir, and many other women of her class left letters or memoirs recording their wartime experiences. Yet, as countless scholars have observed, the planter class represented only a fraction of the total southern white population. Other southern whites of the antebellum period, usually referred to as "common whites" or "plain folk," constituted a varied group made up of slaveholders who owned small numbers of slaves, "yeomen," who worked their own land and relied on their own labor, and landless whites. These common whites outnumbered the planters. Yet their lives—particularly those of the women—are decidedly less well known, because these less affluent rural white women left few writings to preserve their experiences for posterity.

Indeed, the relative paucity of sources relating to common whites of the South continues to confound Civil War scholars. The clamor of the planter class for secession and war and their calls to arms would have amounted to little more than hollow posturing without the acquiescence of common whites. Most nonelites supported the secession effort once the war began, some reluctantly, acting from a sense of honor and loyalty to their states. Nestled mostly in the mountainous regions of the Confederate states, Union sympathizers rejected the secessionist zeal that swept through the region. There were pockets of Union sympathy even in South Carolina, despite its reputation as the primary instigator of secession. Civil War historians have long sought information about the experiences and ideas of common whites in an effort to understand why most plain folk aligned themselves with the planter class but others remained

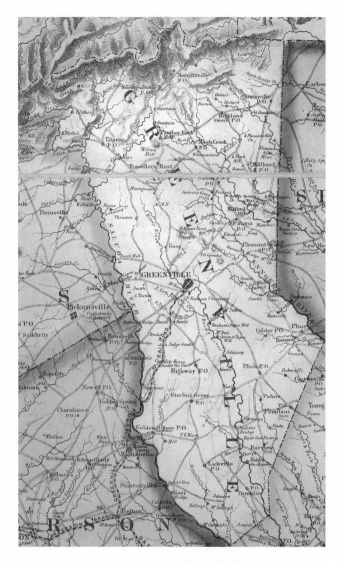

MAP OF MUSH CREEK

Courtesy of South Caroliniana Library,

University of South Carolina, Columbia.

loyal to the Union. But with few records to guide them, answers to these questions have remained elusive.

Given this context, the correspondence generated by Frances Neves and the women of Mush Creek is as significant as it is exceptional. A daughter of a South Carolina yeoman, Frances Neves was sixteen when the state voted to secede from the Union in 1860. She and her family lived in a small, closely knit rural community that lay along Mush Creek, a stream in the upper region of Greenville County. When three Neves sons left to fight for the South, Frances and other female Mush Creek relatives began a correspondence with them that lasted throughout the war. The brothers, stationed primarily on James Island in the defense of Charleston, shared the letters with fellow soldiers in their unit, safeguarded them, and brought them home to Mush Creek at the war's end.

With the analysis of these documents, the obscurity of hill country whites in South Carolina begins to fade away and a rural community of nineteenth-century common white women materializes. Their letters convey the disposition, temper, humor, and frame of mind of this part of the South Carolina home front and add to our knowledge of how the lives of common white rural women differed from those of the planter class. The correspondence attests to how the distinctive conditions of their prewar lives significantly influenced their home front experiences and differentiated them from white women elsewhere in the state and why, in a region of divided loyalties, allegiance to and preservation of their own small community transcended all other claims. In contrast to the common white women studied by historian Laura Edwards, who suffered great deprivation and danger during the war, the women of Mush Creek never experienced food shortages. Their geographic isolation protected their community from becoming a battlefront.[1] Their family and community life provided them greater resiliency in the face of wartime hardships compared to many other South Carolina women, who suffered more from the absence and loss of men, who experienced greater material deprivation, and who witnessed the general collapse of the community's infrastructure. In response, despite concern for the welfare of men and frustration with the war, the women of Mush Creek did not revolt against the Confederacy to the degree that yeoman women in other communities did. However, the reverberations of the Civil War nonetheless reached the far corners of Mush Creek. The letters written by these women reveal how they clung fast to their community and prewar way of life throughout the Civil War.

In the decades leading up to the Civil War, residents of the Mush Creek community had little choice but to develop strong family and communal ties and to rely on one another. J. Hardin Marion, an early twentieth-century South

Carolina State Supreme Court justice, described nineteenth-century residents of upper Greenville County as "remote and isolated by the inaccessibility of their mountain homes." "For a century or more they lived in a world apart," he said, "practically untouched and uninfluenced by the currents and tides of social and economic progress which flowed and rose and ebbed in the great world beyond their mountain barriers."[2] Though scholars might question Hardin's depiction of the region as "untouched and uninfluenced" by urban markets in the Midlands and the Lowcountry, certainly geography limited the inhabitants' exposure to other communities. Approximately thirty-five miles from the western North Carolina boundary, Mush Creek wound along the foothills of the Appalachian Mountains that lay along the North and South Carolina border. Like neighboring communities of Glassy Mountain, Traveler's Rest, the Dark Corner, and Hogback Mountain, geography determined the settlement's name: Mush Creek was a tributary of the North Saluda River.[3]

In the upper part of Greenville County, thickly wooded land had been sold cheaply to white settlers, who cleared large tracts to build settlements and produce crops. By 1850, a scattering of roughly hewn roads wound through the mountains serving as passageways from Greenville to Asheville, North Carolina, the next major town to the northwest. Wagons loaded with goods intended for markets in urban centers such as Columbia and Charleston traveled precariously through the Greenville Upcountry. Drovers from Tennessee, North Carolina, and Kentucky used these roads to drive cattle, mules, turkeys, and hogs through the mountains. Small streams, heavy vegetation, and wet weather often made roads impassable, particularly in winter and spring. In such circumstances travelers laid planks and poles across cavernous mud holes to continue their passage northwest or southeast.[4]

Often referred to as "the settlement" by its inhabitants, the Mush Creek community included a scattering of families that lived along this western offshoot of the North Saluda River. For most of the nineteenth century, Mush Creek lacked a local government in any form. The post office operated out of individual homes, and the position of postmaster shifted occasionally from one neighbor to another. The 1860 federal census records do not recognize Mush Creek as a separate entity; rather, they incorporate the community into the Enoree District, a collection of small communities that included Sandy Flat, Lima, Tyger, and others. Mush Creek residents' strong kinship ties extended into these neighboring communities. Largely self-sufficient, families traveled only infrequently to Greenville to sell surplus crops and to attain goods not manufactured in the community.[5]

Like many in the settlement, Frances Neves's family made its living from agriculture. Indeed, farming dominated the Enoree District, and most farmers cultivated mainly subsistence crops. Farmers raised corn and wheat and sold surpluses in Greenville markets. Yeomen also harvested tobacco, but their crops never reaped much of a profit. Cotton was also cultivated by 1850 but never at the rate found in the South Carolina Midlands and Lowcountry.[6]

Large slaveholders were rare in Greenville County. Small slaveholders peppered the country, but it was not unusual for cultivation and harvesting to be done by the families of small farmers. Tenant farming and the hiring of free black labor by white farmers provided viable labor sources for farmers with larger tracts of land and for mill owners. In the Enoree District, the 1860 population was overwhelmingly white.[7] Gristmills and foundries supported agricultural production.[8]

Albert Alsey Neves, Frances's father and the head of the household, appreciated the value of owning land. Acquired mostly in the 1840s and 1850s, Alsey Neves's farm consisted of 126 workable acres by 1860. The farm produced mainly corn and livestock.[9] In acreage and crop production, the Neves farm mirrored those of their Mush Creek neighbors.[10] During the 1860 harvest season, the Neves farm produced seven hundred bushels of corn and the livestock tallied at nine cattle, three horses, twenty-eight hogs, and twenty-six sheep that produced thirty pounds of wool.[11] Alsey Neves owned no slaves; he rented to tenant farmers any acreage he and his sons could not work themselves. Like other yeomen, Neves worried over his ability to produce enough crops to provide for his children. When the war broke out, Neves hired black laborers to help with the workload while his sons served in the Confederate army.[12]

By 1860, the large Neves family included ten children, with three sons of conscription age. Several of the men in the community, including Alsey Neves and his sons, believed that no one should be forced to stay in any union simply because a distant government told them to do so. Others wanted no part of war whatsoever and retreated to what locals called "the Dark Corner," an even more remote, mountainous region where it was easy to evade Confederate conscription efforts. Age forty-four in 1860 and plagued with frequent bouts of rheumatism, Alsey Neves stayed on the farm in Mush Creek, but his sons understood that the time had come to serve and volunteered for the Confederacy.[13]

All the eligible sons—William, John, and George Washington—volunteered to fight with Company A of the Palmetto Brigade.[14] In August 1861, when William, the eldest son, left for war at the age of twenty-five, he was still a bachelor. At social gatherings, he played the fiddle, told stories, and developed a reputation as a flirt. Of the Mush Creek women, he wrote, "The mountain girls handsome and fair; With sparkling eyes and silken hare; Have charming looks bewitching smiles; And kick a drunkard twenty miles."[15] John Neves, age twenty-two, also lived at home when South Carolina seceded, and went off to war alongside his elder brother. Only seventeen in 1860, the youngest brother to fight in the war, George Washington, or "Wash," did not volunteer immediately. Though married with children, he left by January 1862 to join his brothers in the Palmetto Brigade. Prone to illness, Wash returned to Greenville County periodically throughout the course of the conflict in order to recover.[16]

As the men went off to war, the women began writing their letters. This was not necessarily an easy task. Ann Neves, the mother in the family, was not illiterate but found writing difficult. In addition, she was busy. Five years older than her husband, Ann represented a firm maternal figure for her children and performed the lion's share of household duties.[17] By 1860, the eldest Neves daughter, Martha, had married Andrew Waldrop and lived with him a few houses away from the Neves farm.[18] Their second daughter, sixteen-year-old Frances, was then the eldest girl remaining on the farm. The other three, Mary, Emily and Harriett Ann, ages fourteen, thirteen, and twelve, respectively, helped Frances and their mother in the home and aided in the care of eleven-year-old Thornton and eight-year-old Benjamin.[19] Frances held a particular rapport with her eldest brother William and corresponded with him more frequently than the other women. Frances wrote most of the Neves family letters, and so it is often her perspective that we get on the family's way of life and on that of the common folk in this region of the South Carolina Upcountry.

In the Mush Creek Community, geography and weather played significant roles in determining how the Neves women lived. They were self-reliant, able to improvise, and accustomed to working hard for basic daily provisions. They relied on a communal network that reduced their needs for resources external to the settlement. They understood the precarious nature of forces greater than those within their control and experienced a level of uncertainty in the most basic elements of their lives, such as schooling and religion.

Evangelical religion was a cherished part of the Neves women's belief system and a crucial part of their upbringing, but because of their surroundings, worship practices were irregular at best. Alsey and Ann Neves reared their children as Baptists, but with no Baptist church yet built in Mush Creek, they often attended religious services in nearby communities of Lima or Tyger. At times, the weather proved too daunting for the venture, particularly in winter. During an unusual March snow, Frances admitted to her brother William, "We have some very cold weather hear for the time of year. There was preaching [at] Tyger today but I did not go[.] [I]t was so cold I did not want to go."[20] Owing to the scarcity of churches and the difficulties of travel, meetings were sometimes held in secular locations, such as schools or post offices. Sometimes the Neves family traveled for naught; on one occasion, Frances wrote, "Mary and Emily and Thornton went to meeting today to New Liberty but they sed there want no preaching."[21]

When services were offered, the children seized the opportunity to socialize as well as practice their faith. Mary Cox, a Mush Creek neighbor and Neves cousin, reported to William Neves in 1863 that "cosin we hav had a good meeting at Lima and I wish that you could hav spent that week with us[.] I think perhaps you could hav enjoyed your self fine for there was severl nice Ladies that tended the meeting and you could of past time much better than in camps or at least I think so."[22] The daughters also commented that their father occasionally attended church meetings to discuss business matters, which suggests the need to make the most of all social gatherings. Although their attendance at religious services was somewhat irregular in practice, there is no suggestion of a lack of piety among the Neves women. Rather, their irregular attendance at formal worship service demonstrates the difficult physical environment in which the family lived.

Similarly, educational opportunities for women depended on circumstances beyond the family's control. Schooling hinged on the availability of teachers and facilities and on the number of students who could attend and pay tuition. Although the Neves daughters worked on their farm, they attended school when conditions favored it. Weather sometimes curtailed schooling, as in February 1862—"Miss Goodletts schol begins tomorrow," wrote Frances. "I think she will have a bad time as it is very cold and cloudy now."[23] When students could not attend, teachers' salaries disappeared. On the eve of the war, Frances Neves noted that a teacher left because of low school attendance: "Alsey Dill has not bin home since he first went of[f]," Frances wrote. "We heard that he did not have verry many scolars."[24] Frances again worried over the continuation of classes when a new instructor, Mr. Stuart, charged 4 to 5 cents per child, depending on age.[25]

Despite these obstacles, by the beginning of the war, Frances Neves had attended school for ten years, although the length of the attendance per year remains unknown. Frances, and most of the Neves children, received an education of dubious quality. This is clear in their grammatical errors as well as their use of phonetic spelling associated with the regional dialect. Nonetheless, they exhibited a desire to attend school whenever possible and pride in the education they received. Emily Neves made this clear in declaring to her brothers that "it is with the grates[t] pleasure that I avale my self to drop you a few lines witch will inform you that we are all well. I go to school ever day to miss Goodlet[.]

she dose not have many s[c]olars." Emily then listed sixteen students as her classmates.[26] For Frances Neves and her sisters, literacy conveyed to them an exceptional and possibly even elite status within their own community, a status they cherished.

The Neves family's yeomen status dictated that Frances and the other Neves women contribute significantly to domestic production. Most women's work centered on generating food and clothing for the family's immediate needs. The care of some livestock also fell periodically to the women, although it is not clear how much this responsibility increased during the war when the men were away. For instance, Ann Neves helped raise the sheep on the farm. In the winter of 1862, she proudly reported to her sons that she had nine new lambs.[27] Mush Creek women spun and wove fabric, sewed pants, shirts, dresses and socks, and if time permitted, earned additional income through specialized tasks including carding and dying fabric. Frances Neves described an incident in 1863 where Mary Nicol dyed fabric at no charge: "Mrs. Nicol found the indigo & died the wool for your uniform she would not have any pay for it[.] [I]t is a very nice pale blue."[28] Other women produced pieces of clothing for sale. Eliza Pool, a Neves cousin that lived in Bellvue, South Carolina, a nearby community located southwest of Mush Creek, wrote to her cousins in 1863 that "I have been staying with Mrs Nancy Rosamond learning the milenery's trade[.] I have got so I can make a right nice hat or at least I think so but it is a very difficult traid to learn."[29] In addition to carrying out their daily domestic chores, the Neves women and their neighbors also created their own network through which they sold goods and services, using their skills to bring additional income into the home.

The women of the family understood they also had new tasks to complete directly related to the war. Ann Neves considered it her responsibility to prepare her sons for the journey. She and the Neves daughters went to work to provide the young men with their uniforms. Throughout the conflict, Ann kept vigil over the boys' material needs. Although only one of the extant Neves letters was written by Ann, she often relayed messages through her husband or her daughters, and usually focused on material necessities. In 1862 she directed her sons to keep her informed of their clothing needs, "William i am verry glad you can pat[c]h your pants and darn your socks[.] John i want to no if you can pat[c]h your pants and darn your socks[.] John i will send you a pare of pants and two shirts by Mr[.] hotsclaw[.] William i have cloth like John to make you pants and shirts and your[s] too Washington[.] . . . [I] want to no how your socks holes out so i can be a prepareing more."[30] Like other mothers in the North and South, Ann Neves was determined to provide for her sons with whatever was available to her.

Material shortages complicated such tasks as providing uniforms in South Carolina and across the Confederacy. Historian Mary Elizabeth Massey described how, in response to clothing and textile shortages, women learned "knitting, carding, spinning and weaving," but they knew much less about manufacturing cloth. Like the Neves family, women of lower classes and who lived in rural regions had retained the "art" of making clothes. However, the tools for preparing clothing, including wool cards, dyes, and corset stays, were hard to come by, and their scarcity hindered many common women's efforts to produce their clothing, so that by the fall of 1863 "the clothing situation was critical."[31] Despite Mush Creek's relative self-sufficiency, Frances frequently documented her struggles to obtain needles and thread. In March 1863, she traveled several miles south of Mush Creek to a textile mill to try and secure some thread: "I & Martha [Bailey] went to the factary yesterd[ay] but we never got nary bunch of threat[.] [W]e went to Greens. & Weavers[.] [T]hey wont sell no threat for money. I beg[g]ed Green for just one bunch but it did not do any good he sed that it would be five weeks before he could let out any thre[a]t."[32] Ann complained about a shortage of dye for uniforms: "The shirts are so lite i cant get nothing to die with but barke and that onte die."[33]

Though trying, clothing shortages were not as problematic as limited sources of food. Because of the war, land and labor formally dedicated to food production were lost to the war effort. Fruits, vegetables, sugar, and coffee also disappeared off of many tables in southern homes.[34] Like other women on the home front, the Neves women improvised "ersatz" or substitutes for goods in short supply. They boiled rye as a coffee substitute, but other items proved to be more challenging to replace. The city of Greenville offered a source for paper when it became scarce toward the end of the war. Massey noted that among those foods in short supply, meat was "nonexistent" in many areas, but this "would never have been so serious had it not been for a shortage of salt" for curing it. The absence of salt proved the most problematic for the Neves family. William Neves eventually secured salt from his camp and sent it to his relatives in Mush Creek in the final years of the war.[35]

Still, the Neves family letters reveal that, despite these deprivations and in contrast to many other nonslaveholding white women, the Mush Creek women never suffered severe food shortages. Crop harvests provided relatively steady sources of food throughout the war, except during periods of harsh weather. Rather than implore the men of their family to return home because of shortages in sustenance, the Neves women sent parcels of food to their encamped relatives. Sisters and cousins proudly detailed the food items they were sending to the Neves brothers, including seasonal fruits such as peaches and watermelons.

In the winter of 1862, Martha Bailey described the food she would prepare upon the brothers' return: "William when you come up I will kill the old Goblar and bake some rye and have a big time."[36] The ability of the Neves women to maintain a healthy supply of food stemmed both from the tradition of subsistence farming and from their isolation from enemy activity in their mountain homes. Unlike many southern women elsewhere, they were not plagued with plundering armies feeding themselves off the food stores of civilians in their paths.[37]

Although the Neves family maintained a fairly steady food supply during the war, the absence of men had a significant impact on their lives. As the conflict progressed, Confederate legislators passed several conscription acts to meet the personnel needs of the Confederate military. Eventually, Mush Creek found itself populated mostly by older men, younger boys, and women. That Alsey Neves never served in the military and that he was able to hire blacks to help replace the labor of his sons undoubtedly eased the burden of the Neves women.

In neighboring Spartanburg County, fellow yeoman Emily Harris struggled to adapt to the absence of her husband, David Golightly Harris. Although somewhat more privileged and more educated than the Neves women, Harris tended to the daily management of the family farm. In the fall of 1863 she confessed, "I shall never get used to being left as the head of affairs at home." She felt the burden of supervising the farm, ten slaves, and seven children and viewed herself as "constituted so as to crave a guide and protector. I am not an independent woman nor ever shall be."[38]

Unlike Harris, Frances Neves and other Mush Creek women experienced only a slight shift in gender roles, primarily in the social realm, which they readily embraced. Mush Creek women took it on themselves to keep social norms intact, particularly regarding the supervision of proper masculine behavior of boys in their pre- and early teens. The Neves women happily reported to the brothers and sons on James Island that the women had corrected improper behavior among young men, including laziness and excessive flirtation. They often suggested that, had the men been there, the boys would not have behaved improperly in the first place. Ann Neves informed her sons that she had righted the situation but that they had missed a scene: "william you and John out to of bin here this morning to see all these big boys elford dill ben boswell and John bailey and thornton i recken tha thot tha was grown."[39] Frances Neves, only in her mid-teens, reported that she considered striking one of the boys to keep them in line: "[W]e went to a party last night to Mr Childers you aught to have bin up ther to of seen the little boys a flow around they think them selves agreat deal biger than ever you did when you was at a party or any thing else I wanted to slap them over."[40] Indeed, the women seemed to have few qualms about assuming more masculine, authoritative attitudes. In a November 1861 letter to her cousins William, John, and Washington Neves, Mary Cox happily reported that, at a social gathering, several women played a game in which the women pretended to fight as soldiers: "The Company of lades is in fine sparits[.] . . . I think you will have to com and Drill them or thay cant kill a yankee[.] Mis[s] Hilda Hightower is capten and Sally goodwin is first lieutenant."[41]

The Neves family's ability to read and write became an invaluable skill during the war. As news of the war traveled to the remote South Carolina Upcountry, individuals gathered at public places including the post office in Traveler's Rest to have news read to them out of Greenville County newspapers and from correspondence of their more literate neighbors.[42] Civil War companies often consisted of men and boys from the same communities; Mush Creek and surrounding areas comprised Company A of the Palmetto Light Artillery Brigade. The Neves brothers relayed information from Mush Creek women to other community members in their company. In 1861, Mary Cox pleaded to her cousins, "I want you to tell William Hood his foks is well[.] Tell all your mess howdy for me and speachely my sweetheart."[43] Two years later, Mush Creek resident Mary Nicol presented a letter written by William Neves to Frances and Nicol asked her to read the letter aloud to her. Frances delightedly informed William, "Mrs. Nicol come round by hear[.] . . . [I]t pleased her powerful for you to mention her boys name in a letter[.] I told her that you nearly always sed something about them."[44] Through the Neves family's letters, messages disseminated throughout the settlement.

Letters from Frances Neves and her female cousins reveal a growing concern for the safety of the Mush Creek men as the war news worsened. Unlike other nonslaveholding white women, however, they did not repudiate secession or the Confederacy, nor did they advocate desertion on the part of Confederate soldiers.[45] Surprisingly, Frances Neves was still calling for Confederates to beat the Yankees through 1863. This may have been due in part to her father's influence. He remained loyal to the Confederacy throughout the course of the war and grew frustrated as neighboring men's loyalty wavered, an irresolution exacerbated by Confederate conscription legislation that forced men to serve against their will. The Neves brothers demonstrated their allegiance by fighting for the South and remained steadfast in their support for the cause.[46]

Despite a relatively high level of support for the Confederacy, however, the women's letters make clear their primary goal was the safe return of soldiers rather than Confederate victory at all costs. Frances Neves applauded Confederate victories and wished for the success of the Confederate cause. But when the Neves men left for war at its outset, Frances expressed reservations about the family's sacrifice, feelings that grew over time. She resented conscription; in an 1862 letter, she complained, "I hear that the Governor has called for some more men out of South Carolina[.] I think if it be true it will take the last man about her for they aint many now."[47] When her brother George joined the Confederate army in January 1862, Frances confessed to William, "I thought it was bad enough you went off but you know it is a great deal wors for him to go."[48] Two weeks later Frances confided to her brother, "Jane Tinsley sed she was agoing to have a big party when all of the boys gets back but I fear they will never all get back a live again[.] William I dreamed last night that they had made pease and you all was a coming home[.] I hope my dream will come to pass soon."[49] Ultimately she hoped that Confederate efforts would succeed and allow Mush Creek relatives to return home.

Frances's cousin Mary Cox also expressed doubts about the war effort, even before the passage of conscription laws. On Christmas Day 1861, Cox attempted to contact her cousin William Neves before he left Greenville County. She hoped she could convince him to reconsider his decision to join the Confederate army, saying: "Wm if you are not gone to war, dont go first let them rip, we are ruined any how."[50] Cox's comment suggests she was pessimistic about the chances of success for secession and not sure the cause was worth her cousin jeopardizing his life. In March 1862, Cox again lamented the departure of local men for the battlefront, though this time she seemed more hopeful, writing, "It is a sad time indeed to think that our best freinds and dear relation is about to part from us but I trust it wont be long tell peace will be restored to our happy land one time more and you all may able to return to your homs and best freinds and dear relations again."[51] A year later, Mary confessed to her cousins, "[W]e hav a melancolly time now but I hope it wont be so long[.] I think if peace was made now and you all could come home I could enjoy myself better than I ever did in my life."[52] Cox longed for the return of her friends but expressed less worry about whether or not the Confederacy was victorious.

Despite her concern for her brothers, Frances Neves seemed more hopeful regarding a Confederate victory than her cousin Mary. Keeping abreast of developments in the war, in February 1863 Frances confided to William, then stationed near Charleston, that "I hear that they are expecting an actact on Charleston daily now. I hope if the Yankees does actact Charleston they will get defeated again."[53] In July, after the battle of Gettysburg and the surrender of Vicksburg, Frances wrote again to her brother. "It looks like the yankees is every wher now I am so sory to hear of them getting Vicksburg but I sopose the families were nearly starveing there[.] I am very anxious to hear from Charleston now & will be as long as they expect an attact there."[54] On James Island, South Carolina, the Neves brothers and other Mush Creek soldiers waited and prepared for Union attempts to take Charleston. Local militias comprised largely of young men in their mid- to late teens or of men in their forties remained on the home front to defend Upstate towns and communities.[55] These forces tended to be small and inexperienced. When pockets of Union troops skirmished with Confederates near Asheville, North Carolina, the news traveled to Mush Creek and neighboring communities, alarming their residents. In November 1863, Eliza Pool confessed to her cousin William, "I heard yesterday they were moving the women and children from Asheville and if they did not send on some help the yankes they would be through here in a short time." She doubted the organization and strength of the local forces and pleaded with her cousin. "I think you all had better quit James Island and com up this way to fight yanks[.] I dont know whether to fight them or to run but I reckon I had better make me a little union flag and wave it at them if they [come at] me, now dont you think I am the most cowardly cousin you have[?]"[56] Though Pool made light of protecting herself with a homemade Union flag, her letter raises questions as to whether or not women on the home front remained loyal, especially when they faced confrontation with opposing troops.

On the subject of deserters the women of the settlement also had mixed feelings. In an 1863 letter to her brothers, Frances Neves observed that two acquaintances had returned from the war, one as a deserter. "Ben Thornell is at home on furlough.," she wrote. "I heard that Ern Lemons had runaway from the army & was at home."[57] She continued to other topics in her letter, however, and made no negative statements about the deserter. In an 1865 letter, she longed for military authorities to pursue deserters that stole supplies from a neighbor. She professed to her brothers that "[The Torys] went & robed Tandy Goodletts wife the other night[.] I am in hopes they will do something with the Torys before they come back."[58] Frances objected to the deserter's act of stealing from a member of her community but made no comment on the issue of disloyalty or desertion itself. On several instances when men in the family returned home to recover from sickness, her father urged them to return quickly lest they be mistaken for deserters. Neves ordered his sons to inform their captain of their brother's imminent return to the Palmetto Brigade: "Wash is get[t]ing on tolerable well considering his attact was vary severe[.] [I]t was fever[.] [H]e has no fever now[.] [H]e sets up some little yesterday & today tel the captain not to report him abssent he will come as quick as posable or as he is able to come he will not wait to get able for duty."[59] Neves strongly encouraged his son to return to the battlefield, even if he was not yet "able for duty." However, the Neves women did not rush their brother's return; in their view his illness brought a coveted, albeit brief, sojourn from danger and for them, from loneliness and worry.

Frances's cousin Martha Bailey also did not condemn deserters or shirkers. She narrated an incident involving shirkers writing to her Neves cousins: "There was muster up in the old field a sunday[.] all they companys was called together and I herd John say that them dark carner fellers turned out and he said after they cried like a child and they said that they was not able to go." Bailey not only avoided passing judgment on the men who would not serve but also felt compelled to defend one that she knew had been ill. "I know," she wrote, "that Jim Hood is not able to go by his look."[60]

Mush Creek resident Martha Robison, who lost her fiancé to the war, expressed much more hostility toward deserters than Frances or Martha Bailey. Robison wrote to William Neves, informing him of the death: "Ther will be a draft here in greenville next week will I am glad tha ar a going to draft thes men back here because the have as much right to go a[s] any of you boys you know tha ar nothing but cowards will you must be a brave fellow and stand up to youre part will I have had very bad luck my sweet hart come home ded but i have got another one but i never shall see no body tha i love half as good as i did him that is ded."[61] Her hostility seems, however, to have stemmed from her personal sacrifice rather than a political ideology. Robison turned her grief into resentment for deserters and a determination that other men take the same risks as the one she had loved and lost.

Mush Creek women grew increasingly anxious as war casualties mounted and clearly wanted the long, miserable affair to end. As the Confederacy fell into decline, the increasing death toll reverberated loudly in the small hamlet of Mush Creek. In Greenville County, wooden coffins arrived on trains, and crowds gathered to listen as the identities of the dead were read aloud.[62] Frances Neves described to her brother the return of two Mush Creek soldiers: "Elie Goodlet came home last friday and was burried at cross rode c[h]urch on sunday and Ben Frank Barton came on saturday and was burried yesterday at tiger[.] [T]hey was a great many people there[.] [H]e was burried in military form." She continued, "David Bailey is geting better but is not able to go back yet he aims to go back a monday."[63] In this tightly networked community, losses echoed beyond the immediate family's household, as a "great many people" attended Ben Barton's funeral. When a soldier died, the news quickly spread among neighbors. It is remarkable that even at this point none of the women openly begged male family members to desert and come home. They neither condemned the Confederacy nor embraced the Union.[64] Rather, following the example of Alsey Neves, they remained steadfast in their desire for peace and their loyalty to the Confederacy.

The Neves women were remarkably fortunate: their loved ones returned home safely from the Civil War. In April 1865, William, John, and George Neves were discharged from the Confederate army in North Carolina and eventually made their way back to Greenville County.[65] They grieved, however, for the loss of friends from their community. Although the exact number of dead and wounded from Greenville remains unknown, in 1901, 158 families filed for pensions on behalf of Greenville County soldiers who died during the war.[66] Like other women in the nation, both in the North and the South, Mush Creek women attempted to move on after four years of bloody conflict.

The women of the Neves family were fortunate in other respects as well. Their father never had to leave home and could afford to pay black laborers when manpower was short, and at the close of the war, their brothers and sons returned home able to resume their work. In these respects, the Neves women were exceptional, even within their own community. But other women of Mush Creek shared with them some advantages relative to women elsewhere in coping with the war itself and moving on after the war.

Due in part to isolation and to sheer luck, they were generally distant from the war's fighting. Union forces entered Greenville County only once, in May 1865, in response to rumors that Jefferson Davis had fled from Richmond to the Deep South via the South Carolina Upcountry. Their community escaped Union invasion as well as severe confiscation of material goods by the Confederate army, unlike many other southern mountain communities. In comparison, wives and daughters of business owners and middle-class merchants in a besieged Charleston and a burned Columbia lost much of their livelihood if not their homes. Women on the small farms that lay in the path of Sherman's March through South Carolina lost much of their personal property to the Union army. Slaveholding families who had invested their wealth in land and slaves suffered great economic loss with the collapse of slavery at the end of the war.

In coping with the war and its aftermath, the women of Mush Creek and their community could be said to be more fortunate than wealthier slaveholding women. Before the Civil War, many elite women relied heavily on slave labor for the most basic daily household duties. When the war began, and white men left for the battlefield, many elite white women assumed the role as head of the plantation, a role that included the supervision of slave societies and slave labor. With emancipation, elite women assumed many of the domestic tasks previously carried out by house slaves, tasks with which many of these privileged white women were unfamiliar and for which they were quite unprepared.

Additionally, emancipation signaled the collapse of their social structure, which rested on the institution of slavery and provided the framework of elite white women's lives.

The Neves family's tradition of subsistence farming as well as their distance from large planters proved invaluable to them both before and during the war. They were already accustomed to hard work in their home before the war; little changed after the war. Relative isolation from large planters and from urban centers facilitated their tolerance of material deprivation and their ability to survive after the collapse of southern planter society. Rather than witness the disintegration of their community, they saw the bonds within their settlement strengthen. The Neves letters also suggest a possible new social authority for the women, although it is not clear if this pattern continued after the war.

No doubt the women of Mush Creek and other white women in South Carolina had some wartime experiences in common. All were shut out of the process of making the decisions that led to the bloody conflict yet shared the repercussions of these decisions. But in this tumultuous period in American history factors, including race, class, gender—and region—shaped the varying and multifaceted lives of women and dramatically affected the ways that women on different parts of the home front experienced the war. The letters of Frances Neves and the Mush Creek women expand our knowledge of an understudied group of southern women and further our understanding of the impact of the Civil War in South Carolina.

NOTES

1. Laura Edwards, *Scarlett Doesn't Live Here Anymore: Southern Women in the Civil War Era* (Urbana: University of Illinois Press, 2000), 69, 85.

2. Cited in Mann Batson, *A History of the Upper Part of Greenville County, South Carolina* (Taylor, S.C.: Faith Printing Co., 1993), 93. J. Hardin Marion served as justice of the South Carolina State Supreme Court from 1922 to 1926.

3. Batson, *History*, 10–12 and 18.

4. Mann Batson, *Early Travel and Accommodations Along the Roads of the Upper Part of Greenville County, South Carolina, and Surrounding Areas* (Taylors, S.C.: Faith Printing Co., 1995), 10–11 and 57–64.

5. Conversation between author and Anne McCuin, Greenville County Historical Society, January 16, 2007; *1860 Federal Census, South Carolina, Greenville County*, South Carolina Department of Archives and History, Columbia, South Carolina (hereinafter cited as SCDAH).

6. A. V. Huff, *Greenville: The History of the City and County in the South Carolina Piedmont* (Columbia: University of South Carolina Press, 1995), 112–13.

7. *1860 Federal Census, South Carolina, Greenville County*, SCDAH.

8. There were 379 whites and 2 blacks (Batson, *History*, 324–28).

9. Register of deeds, grantee index to conveyances, 1787–1913, 241, Greenville County government inline (www.greenvillecounty.org/history); *1860 South Carolina Agricultural Index, Greenville County*, SCDAH.

10. Thomas A. Wall, "Upcountry during the Civil War, 1861–1865," research paper, Furman University, photocopy at South Caroliniana Library, University of South Carolina, Columbia, South Carolina (hereinafter cited as SCL), 2–3.

11. *1860 South Carolina Agricultural Index, Greenville County*, SCDAH.

12. *1850 South Carolina Slave Schedule* and *1860 South Carolina Slave Schedule*, SCDAH; Wall, "Upcountry," 9.

13. Alsey Neves to W. P. Z. F. Neves (hereinafter cited as WPZFN), October 11 and October 18, 1863, Neves Family Papers (hereinafter cited as NFP), SCL.

14. Fannie Neves, May 1, 1919, and George Washington Neves, November 27, 1919, Confederate Pension Records, South Carolina, Greenville County, SCDAH.

15. William Neves, n.d., NFP, SCL.

16. *1860 Federal Census, South Carolina, Greenville County*, SCDAH, and Wall, "Upcountry," 4.

17. Ann Neves (hereinafter cited as AN) to WPZFN, February 9, 1862, NFP, SCL.

18. *1860 Federal Census, South Carolina, Greenville County*, SCDAH.

19. *1850 Federal Census, South Carolina, Greenville County* and *1860 Federal Census, South Carolina, Greenville County*, SCDAH.

20. Frances Neves (hereinafter cited as FN) to WPZFN, 29 March 1862, NFP, SCL.

21. FN to WPZFN, March 23, n.d., NFP, SCL.

22. Mary A. Cox (hereinafter cited as MAC) to WPZFN, October 3, 1863, NFP, SCL.

23. FN to WPZFN, February 9, 1862, NFP, SCL.

24. FN to WPZFN, April 9, 1861, NFP, SCL; *1860 Federal Census, South Carolina, Greenville County*, SCDAH.

25. FN to WPZFN, March 18, 1863, NFP, SCL.

26. Emily C. Neves to WPZFN, April 27, n.d., NFP, SCL.

27. FN to WPZFN, February 14, 1862, NFP, SCL.

28. FN to WPZFN, July 21, 1863, NFP, SCL.

29. Eliza Pool to WPZFN, July 19, 1863, NFP, SCL.

30. AN to WPZFN, February 9, 1862, NFP, SCL.

31. Mary Elizabeth Massey, *Ersatz in the Confederacy: Shortages and Substitutes on the Southern Homefront* (Columbia: University of South Carolina Press, 1952), 86–98.

32. FN to WPZFN, March 19, 1863, NFP, SCL.

33. Ibid.

34. Massey, *Ersatz in the Confederacy*, 55–63.

35. Wall, "Upcountry," 2; Huff, *Greenville*, 115.

36. Martha Bailey to WPZFN, February 9, 1862, NFP, SCL.

37. Huff, *Greenville*, 143–44.

38. *Piedmont Farmer: The Journals of David Golightly Harris, 1855–1870*, ed. Philip N. Racine (Knoxville: University of Tennessee Press, 1990) 3, 14, and 309.

39. AN to WPZFN, February 9, 1862, NFP, SCL.

40. FN to WPZFN, January 2, 1862, NFP, SCL.

41. MAC to WPZFN, November 9, 1861, NFP, SCL.

42. Batson, *Early Travel*, 111.

43. MAC to WPZFN, November 9, 1861, NFP, SCL.

44. FN to WPZFN, July 21, 1863, NFP, SCL.

45. Edwards, *Scarlett Doesn't Live Here Anymore*, 88–90.

46. Alsey Neves to WPZFN, October 11, 1863, NFP, SCL.

47. FN to WPZFN, February 28, 1862, NFP, SCL.

48. FN to WPZFN, January 10, 1862, NFP, SCL.

49. FN to WPZFN, January 28, 1862, NFP, SCL.

50. MAC to WPZFN, December 25, 1861, NFP, SCL.

51. Martha Cox to WPZFN, March 20, 1862, NFP, SCL.

52. MAC to WPZFN, August 13, 1863, NFP, SCL.

53. FN to WPZFN, February 8, 1863, NFP, SCL.

54. FN to WPZFN, July 13, 1863, NFP, SCL.

55. Huff, *Greenville*, 135–37.

56. Eliza Pool to WPZFN, November 2, 1863, NFP, SCL.

57. FN to WPZFN, August 19, 1863, NFP, SCL.

58. FN to WPZFN, January 8, 1865, NFP, SCL.

59. A. A. Neves to WPZFN, August 2, 1863, NFP, SCL.

60. Martha Bailey to WPZFN, January 26, 1862, NFP, SCL.

61. Martha Robison to WPZFN, March 21, 1862, NFP, SCL.

62. Huff, *Greenville*, 138.

63. FN to WPZFN, November 14, n.d., NFP, SCL.

64. Edwards, *Scarlett Doesn't Live Here Anymore*, argues that yeoman women openly challenged the Confederacy and demanded the release of the men in their families from military service, 88–90.

65. Fannie Neves, May 1, 1919, and George Washington Neves, November 27, 1919, Confederate Pension Records, South Carolina, Greenville County, SCDAH.

66. Brent H. Holcomb, *South Carolina's Confederate Pensioners in 1901* (Columbia, S.C.: South Carolina Magazine of Ancestral Research, 2001).

Lucy Holcombe Pickens

Belle, Political Novelist, and Southern Lady

ORVILLE VERNON AND GEORGANNE BURTON

In one of her many obituaries, Lucy Petway Holcombe Pickens (1832–99) was described as "one of the most famous women of the South, and one whose name will live in history."[1] Such hyperbole had followed her throughout her life. Holcombe was the quintessential southern belle. Beautiful, accomplished, charming, flirtatious, wealthy, and deferential toward men, Lucy excelled on all counts.[2] Yet this typical belle was atypical in some ways. For instance, she published a political novel when she was only nineteen, prompted by her keen interest in politics and her love for a dashing young man involved in an 1851 scheme to seize Cuba. Her marriage to Francis W. Pickens of South Carolina placed her in the limelight but also in a number of demanding situations in which she thrived. When Pickens was appointed as the U.S. minister to Russia, she accompanied him to the court of the Czar and proved to be a great asset; the letters she sent home from there again demonstrated her talent for writing as well as her perceptive insights into another culture. Her behavior as the wife of the governor of South Carolina during the secession crisis, her actions during the Civil War and Reconstruction, her involvement in the creation of Confederate memorials, also indicated exceptional ability and drive.[3] An extravagant hostess, this uncrowned "Queen of the Confederacy" was confidante to many southern political leaders. More renowned for her beauty than for her intelligence, she had both in abundance. And despite her apparent acquiescence to male authority, she declared privately, "Submissiveness is not my role."[4]

Born in La Grange, Tennessee on June 11, 1832, Lucy was the second child of five. She and her older sister Anna Eliza remained close throughout their lives. Lucy's mother, Eugenia Hunt Holcombe, taught her daughters as well as her two sons, John Theodore and Philemon Eugene, to read, write, understand

LUCY HOLCOMBE PICKENS

Courtesy of Gus Graydon and Orville Vernon Burton.

mathematics, and appreciate music. Lucy became fluent in French and was a good singer and adequate on the piano, though she preferred singing to playing the piano because she loved facing an audience.[5] Her father, Beverly Lafayette Holcombe, taught his children to ride. His love of horses carried over into a love of horse racing, which cost the family dearly; his gambling losses took their entire cotton profits. Gambling was not his only problem; a loan cosigned for a friend cost them their beautiful home, "Westover," on the outskirts of LaGrange. Although Lucy's maternal grandfather gave them another home in LaGrange, less isolated than the plantation, as an adult Lucy greatly feared debt. The girls attended La Grange Female Seminary, and Lucy's mother continued to supervise their education and religious training.

Eugenia Holcombe placed a high value on education for her daughters. According to a diary entry on January 18, 1840, she wished for them to be "carefully educated" and "thoroughly informed," adding "A good education will make them independent." Partly because Eugenia Holcombe wanted Lucy to experience life away from home where she was so indulged and also because she wanted the girls to learn English grammar and literature, French, and German, she arranged for them to attend the Moravian Institute, a strict religious school in Bethlehem, Pennsylvania. In February 1846, Lucy was thirteen and did not want to leave her family. Nonetheless, she and her sister Anna went by wagon to Memphis, by steamboat to Wheeling, Virginia (now West Virginia), by train to Philadelphia, and by stagecoach to Bethlehem, traveling for about three and a half weeks to reach the school.[6]

Eugenia also furthered Lucy's education in other ways. To stimulate an interest in political affairs she took her and Anna to Nashville to watch the proceedings of the Tennessee state legislature. Eugenia recorded in her diary in January 1850, "The legislature is now sitting. I am here with my daughters and our friends. All join me in thinking and expressing their admiration and love for two of the loveliest of their sex."[7] From an early age Lucy learned that, whereas women could not wield power in the same manner as the men she observed on the floor of the legislature, there were other methods. And that an intelligent woman who also had highly developed social instincts and skills could accomplish much, even in a highly patriarchal society. In some of her later writings in which she discussed education for women, Lucy denied that men disliked learned women. She wrote that, "A woman with liberal information, one who comprehends, fully and correctly, the principles and propriety, not only of the intellectual but social world, may exert on society a great and good influence. Woman has great power, if she would realize and accept it."[8]

While the girls were at school, Beverly Holcombe bought land near Marshall on the Texas frontier in order to establish a new plantation, "Wyalucing," and grow cotton and wheat. Texas, having declared and won its independence in 1836, was admitted to the United States in December 1845. When the girls finished at Moravian early in 1850, they left Tennessee with their mother to join their father and brothers at their new home. Lucy would develop a deep love for Texas.

When Lucy was nineteen, her informal education took a dramatic turn. In 1851 she was strongly affected by the quest of some of her acquaintances, including her first love, Lieutenant William Crittenden of Kentucky, to take Cuba from the Spanish. It is unclear how she first met the dashing Kentuckian, the nephew of U.S. Attorney General John J. Crittenden, but this much is known. On one of many family trips to visit friends, the Holcombes went to see the current Governor John Quitman of Mississippi and his wife, Eliza at Monmouth Plantation, their stately home near Natchez. There Lucy met the group of conspirators gathered to plan their expedition including the leader, a handsome and flamboyant Cuban named Narciso Lopéz who had barely escaped during a previous such attempt, and Laurent Sigur, editor of the *New Orleans Delta News*. These men were called "filibusters," a term then used for men who invaded another country in violation of federal neutrality laws. Filibustering had particular appeal in the South and Southwest including Texas; many were frustrated by the failure of the U.S. government's attempt to purchase Cuba and its unwillingness to support Lopéz's efforts to take it by force. Governor Quitman, a hero of the Mexican-American War who had advocated annexation of all of Mexico, had been tempted to accept the command of this venture; he believed that such imperialistic efforts were part of America's "Manifest Destiny" and that acquisition of Cuba, a slave society that would then become a state, would enhance the South's political power.[9] The men were charmed by the lovely Lucy Holcombe, and she was charmed by their rhetoric of freedom and independence.

The next planning meeting for the Cuban venture took place on July 31, 1851, at Sigur's plantation home, near New Orleans, and Lucy was again present. On the morning of August 3, 1851, Lopéz's vessel, the *Pampero*, sailed from New Orleans. This was an illegal and supposedly secret expedition as the US government had prosecuted supporters of Lopéz's first expedition (dropping charges after southern juries would not convict them), but the departure was permitted by sympathetic New Orleans port officials. Among the enthusiastic throng of supporters saluting and waving good-bye to the expedition was Lucy Holcombe.[10]

Despite being in disrepair, the ship sailed early. Crittenden, who worked in the Louisiana Custom House and was privy to inside information, had notified

Lopéz that the federal government was planning to impound their vessel. Lopéz decided he could not wait for all his recruits. Crittenden was supposed to have commanded a Kentucky regiment, six hundred well-trained and disciplined soldiers from Kentucky and Indiana, but they had not yet arrived. Lopéz thought Crittenden and his men could come later, but Crittenden would not be left behind. So before the ship left New Orleans he enlisted 114 young men from the city streets and signed them on as the First Regiment of Artillery.[11]

The invasion was a disaster. The Spanish had learned of their plans and had already suppressed a premature uprising of Cuban planters that was to assist Lopéz. While Lopéz and the main force moved inland, Crittenden and about fifty of his men who had remained to guard supplies were surrounded. They tried to escape in four small boats but were captured. These fifty were summarily tried and executed by firing squad on August 16. Many of the other men, including Lopéz, were captured in the following weeks. On September 1 Lopéz was executed in front of a large crowd in Havana by garrote, or slow strangulation with an iron collar.[12]

From prison in Cuba, Crittenden wrote two last-minute letters. The first, to his uncle, the Attorney General, asked him to "do me the justice to believe that my motives were good."[13] The other letter was to an unknown Dr. Lucien Henley. It may be far fetched to hypothesize that it was to Lucy Holcombe, who had the same initials. Yet, the need for secrecy was uppermost. If Crittenden wanted to write to Lucy, he would need to take precautions to protect her from possible indictment. The letter was short and to the point ("I will die like a man") and signed "Yours, Strong in Heart, W. L. Crittenden."[14]

Holcombe family history tells of Lucy Holcombe's great love for Lieutenant William Crittenden who is sometimes described as her fiancé. Her reaction to his execution, however, was not what might have been expected. Lucy was profoundly grieved but not faint of heart. She poured her grief into an attempt to defend the failed mission and aid its surviving members. In 1851 it was difficult for a woman to speak out on national and international affairs let alone condemn the actions of the men in charge of U.S. foreign policy. Though Lucy passionately wanted to sway public opinion on this issue, she knew that her image as a southern belle precluded overt political activity. Writing was therefore the most effective means available to her. Though only nineteen, Lucy had already been writing poetry and scattered prose. Now, she wrote a novel *The Free Flag of Cuba; or, The Martyrdom of Lopéz: A Tale of the Liberating Expedition of 1851*, published under the pseudonym of H. M. Hardimann.[15]

Holcombe's avowed purpose in writing was to vindicate the Cuban expedition and Narciso Lopéz, to persuade the world that the venture had been undertaken in the name of a noble cause, and to promote the idea that the men who were executed in Cuba were martyred heroes. She used her novel to condemn American policy toward Cuba and to try to affect a change from official neutrality regarding Spanish dominion of the island to one of active engagement in pursuit of freedom for Cuba. At the very least, she wanted the U.S. government to come to the aid of the men taken in the invasion who, at the time she wrote the novel, were still in captivity.

The novel is a romance. Like Sir Walter Scott whose work was wildly popular in the antebellum South, Holcombe makes references to knights and chivalry; the male protagonists leave home to perform heroic deeds and earn honor and fame. She accurately depicts the geography, soldiers, and history of the expedition and her writing is fluent and articulate, though the novel contains overblown descriptions common in the mid-1800s.[16] In describing Crittenden's death, Holcombe wrote about how he had defiantly refused to be blindfolded or to bow down: "Thank heaven, the noble form of Crittenden, the gallant Kentuckian, bowed not even in death, and his glorious lips gave to history the immortal words: 'An American kneels but to his God.'"[17] In it William Crittenden is described as flirting with the heroine, "Mabel" at the Sigur party. Holcombe described Crittenden as the ideal man in appearance, charm, and honor. His large eyes were "fearless," and he exuded a "half tender, half defiant charm." He held a rose and said he had been instructed to present it "to the most beautiful woman in the city. I can go further. I offer it to the most beautiful woman in the world." He gave it to Mabel.[18]

Although her ostensible reason for writing her novel was to advocate freedom for oppressed people, Lucy's novel is also a defense of slavery. Indeed her novel was one of many proslavery novels written in response to the popular Uncle Tom's Cabin.[19] When she spoke of the defense of freedom, she was speaking of freedom for white Cubans whom she perceived as slaves to Spanish tyranny—not the 436,000 people on the island who were actually enslaved. In fact, many white southerners feared that the Spanish government would yield to pressure from England and free the Cuban slaves.[20] In the novel Holcombe's protagonist, Narciso Lopéz, promoted Cuban liberation partly on the grounds that Spain meant to cast on Cuba "the undying stain of African equality."[21] Like other southerners at this time, Holcombe did not see the irony of her position, that the tyranny of the Spanish over Cubans was much less oppressive than that of whites over enslaved Africans.

Holcombe's novel reflected ideas about human nature, race, and gender widely held at the time. In her novel good looks were as important as they are in Harlequin romances of today. Eyes revealed character. Foreheads were important because of the racial implications in the then-popular study of phrenology. One of her women protagonists was noted for "extreme whiteness" except for "the rare beauty" of blue temple veins. Feminine temperament was calm, spiritual, gentle, timid, and clinging.

Similar to many other women writers of the time, Holcombe introduced the idea of woman suffrage only to reject it. Opposition to woman suffrage was strong in the South, where the right to vote was thought to be commensurate with manhood and white supremacy. And yet, Holcombe's expectations for women and gender roles were more complex than one would expect from a young southern girl in 1851. Although her heroines stated unequivocally that they favored customary roles for men and women, Holcombe allowed some flexibility in her female characters.[22]

The two women protagonists were best friends from school at the Moravian Institute in Pennsylvania, the school Lucy and her sister had attended. The character Mabel Royal, as Lucy later confided to a dear friend in South Carolina, was modeled after Lucy herself.[23] Thus it is not surprising that although her female characters reflect a standard gendered formula, Holcombe still presented charming, beautiful women interested in political debate. In her development of Mabel, she seemed to be exploring a wider range of acceptable feminine behavior, thus endorsing an ideal for women that she herself could accept.[24] One of the points Holcombe addressed was whether an interest in politics meant that a woman was not feminine. Both women characters were well read and interested in politics. One worried, "Are you not afraid of being called strong-minded?" But Holcombe defended political reading.[25] She believed women should take an interest in politics and encourage men to take the right political stand. Holcombe gave her female characters individuality that male authors of the time did not.[26] Although they have the traditional power of a southern belle, namely, romantic appeal, Holcombe also gives them intellect. In her own way, by allowing her female protagonists to voice strong opinions without losing — indeed while adding to their charm — Holcombe was stretching the limits of women's political boundaries.

Holcombe played it both ways. On the one hand she was coy about her manuscript in a letter to Governor Quitman to whom she had dedicated the novel. In reference to a critique of her book, she said that the author gave too much credit "to a romance which has only the power of a woman's pen." According to Holcombe, women were "morally superior" but only as equal intellectually as men allow.[27] On the other hand, her novel clearly shows women as the intellectual equals of men. Knitting together her high regard for female intellect, feminine influence, republican ideology, and political romanticism, Holcombe affirmed that a woman has the same right to an opinion as a man does without upsetting the natural order of male supremacy.

Holcombe tied the attempted liberation of Cuba to the American Revolution and compared the sacrifices of her female characters to that of the wives and daughters of American patriots. (Her grandfather, Philemon Holcombe Jr., was with Lafayette at the Yorktown surrender of the British and gave his son, Lucy's father, the middle name "Lafayette.")[28] Invoking a complex of assumptions about women's roles in the new nation that historians have dubbed "republican motherhood," she asked, "What would our revolutionary mothers say to the American women who seek to stay an arm uplifted in such a cause?"[29] Her message for her women readers was: be willing to sacrifice your loved ones for a just and honorable cause. Ten years later, Lucy would defend the Confederacy with similar arguments. The López expedition was an abject failure but, in her view, a noble one: and Holcombe's novel, in an uncanny and fascinating way, presaged the rhetoric of the Lost Cause.

At twenty-two, having lost her beloved and worked through her grief by writing her novel, Lucy turned her attention to her future and her prospects for marriage. In the summer of 1857 Eugenia took her daughter to White Sulphur Springs, Virginia. Wealthy people might vacation at the Springs to bathe in the healthful waters, but more often than not, they went there to meet suitable marriage partners. Lucy needed a mate if she were to move from southern belle to plantation mistress. Obviously she had many advantages on the marriage market and many suitors. Benjamin Perry, state senator in South Carolina and good friend of the man who became Lucy's husband, declared that "she was preeminent for her beauty, intelligence and accomplishments. She was, most deservedly, the belle of the South."[30]

At White Sulphur Springs, Lucy Holcombe sought a certain type of man. Speaking through the fictional character Mabel, Lucy described her "ideal lover." He would be "tall and good-looking, with a cold, quiet manner, and large commanding eyes—a perfect prince of knowledge, at whose feet I was to sit with timid wonder and love; who was to guide me with his mightier will, and with an affection only shown to myself, he was to charm me by this tenderness, and awe me by his superiority."[31]

Instead she found Francis W. Pickens. A southern aristocrat by birth, Pickens was a congressman, a grandson of General Andrew Pickens of Revolutionary War fame, and son of Andrew Pickens, governor of South Carolina in 1817. Pickens was born on a plantation on the Toogoodoo River, St. Paul's Parish, Colleton District, S.C., April 7, 1805. He graduated from the University of South Carolina, studied law, and entered the law firm of Eldred Simkins and George

McDuffie (both of whom served as congressmen). In 1834, John C. Calhoun said he was "the most promising man in the state."[32] Described as "hospitable, generous, kind by nature," he also was proud and overbearing.[33] Lucy probably liked all those things about him. She surely appreciated that in the early 1840s, even before he met her, he was an advocate for Texas statehood.[34] In June 1856 Pickens had been chosen as an elector from South Carolina and cast his vote for his good friend James Buchanan, who won election as president.

Still, Pickens hardly fit Lucy's ideal description. As depicted a decade later by northern journalist Sidney Andrews, Pickens was "a battered old wreck—short and squarely built, with a large and squarish head, a broad and flat face, a small and insignificant nose, round and piggish eyes, and broad high forehead."[35] More important, perhaps, he was wealthy. In the U.S. Census of 1860, Pickens was listed as having 45,000 dollars worth of real estate and 244,206 dollars worth of personal estate in Edgefield, South Carolina; he also owned plantations in Alabama and Mississippi and more than three hundred slaves. The South Carolina plantation of Edgewood included 2,250 acres of land in cultivation, and a beautiful old home with lovely gardens.[36]

Francis Pickens was lovesick for Lucy Holcombe. His courtship letters to Lucy (her replies have never been found) show romantic imaginings, flowery language, exorbitant flattery, and also an annoying neediness. A letter written November 1857 contains his typical phraseology: "No earthly power shall ever shake my deep devotion to you. I love you without calculation. I love you because my heart beats instinctively in holy sympathy with your spirit and it is beyond my power to control it and beyond the power of any one to divert it."[37] Lucy stalled. Courting was one arena in which the woman had some power, power that ended once she married.[38] In addition, her family was hesitant to accept him as her husband. Pickens had been widowed twice and had five living daughters; four daughters from his first marriage were close to Lucy's age, and several were not pleased by their father's infatuation with the beautiful young woman. Pickens was older than Lucy's mother, and he lived too far from Texas. On the other hand, he was honest and faithful to obligations.[39] Lucy needed someone with wealth so she would not have to suffer the disappointments her mother endured as a result of her father's indebtedness. She also wanted someone who had influence, who traveled in prestigious company, to whom she could be a political asset, and upon whom she could wield some influence—in short, a person worthy of her. At this time Pickens, a good friend of President James Buchanan, was confident he would win election to the U.S. Senate from South Carolina. Yet Pickens had enemies, he lacked charisma, and in the end he was not chosen for the Senate seat. Defeated in politics and apparently also defeated in love, Pickens accepted an offer from Buchanan to be the minister to Russia. He wrote to Lucy on January 27, 1858, to let her know and to say that he realized she was cutting off the relationship: "I suppose as you seem to desire it, this terminates our correspondence."[40]

But Lucy did not desire it. Quite possibly the allure of accompanying Pickens as his bride to the Russian court may have influenced her decision. In addition, however lovely, Lucy was approaching twenty-six years of age—an advanced age for a southern belle. At any rate she finally accepted the proposal of the fifty-one year old Pickens, and he traveled to Texas for the wedding. Some have speculated that Lucy's reasons for the marriage included "her grief for Crittenden."[41] One of her Texas friends credited her with saying that, having exhausted her romantic feelings in that tragic first relationship, if she married it would be for position.[42] Lucy and Francis married at the Holcombe home on April 26, 1858. That night Eugenia recorded in her diary, "My precious darling Lucy as long my companion is married and nearly broken my poor heart."[43] In any event, after shopping in New York, the newly married couple left the country one month later and again Eugenia wrote of her sadness: "She is gone to Russia and I am inconsolable."[44]

The Pickens traveled first to England where Francis met Queen Victoria. Lucy wrote, "I must tell you that Col. P. was presented to the Queen, not myself, as it was not a 'drawing room' but only a levee for gentlemen."[45] From England they went to France where they met Napoleon III. Letters from Lucy about her travels were full of vibrant detail and insight. She observed that British nobility "do not go out in very much finer style than ourselves, only a greater display of servants"; that France under Napoleon was "unhappily governed"; and that "there is nothing real in European society but its hollowness."[46] Excerpts from some of her letters were reprinted in the *Memphis Eagle and Enquirer*.[47]

Lucy was delighted with the opportunities for shopping in these new and exotic places. In France she bought gifts for family and friends back home; in Russia she purchased furs and tea sets. Not to be outdone by Lucy, Francis had busts of marble sculpted of himself and of Lucy. But his spending sometimes overwhelmed and worried her, as she so feared debt. She wrote Anna on receiving a particular gift that "Col. P. bought me the other day a lace pocket handkerchief at $40.00 and I almost cried with vexation. I thought of Mother so often saying, 'if I had a million, I would never be so foolish as to give $50 for a handkerchief.' He of course thought I was delighted."[48] When Francis calculated his wealth two years later in 1860, he found that they had been overspending and were in debt over 17,000 dollars.[49]

The Pickens arrived in St. Petersburg July 6, 1858. Lucy met the Czar and

Czarina, Alexander II and Maria Alexandrovna, at a glittering dinner party and ball held at the palace less than two weeks later.[50] She was mesmerized by the splendor of the palace and wrote about "looking with all the wonder and delight of a child on this magnificence, which is so new to my republican eyes."[51] Her beauty caught the not-so-republican eye of the Czar who showered her with jewelry and other gifts; this led to gossip, but she established a friendship with the Czarina and kept herself out of compromising situations. She wrote Anna, "In a society like this, where the existence of virtue is *not believed* in by men, mine has not been a position free from incidents but I have conducted myself with such prudence that my husband tells me, he loves me more for my dignity and goodness, than for my beauty and intellect."[52] Despite the magnificence of the palace and her friendship with the Czarina, Lucy Pickens found Russian society vacuous "beyond belief." "If you advance an idea, you are looked at with a kind of well-bred disgust. You are valued for what your wear, and by the rank you have in court."[53]

Their daughter and only child, Eugenia Frances (nicknamed Douschka, Russian for "little darling," by her godmother, the Czarina), was born in the Russian royal palace on March 14, 1859.[54] When she was pregnant Lucy had written her sister that she would be disappointed if she did not bear a son: "It is so natural for you and Mother to say, 'don't set your heart on a son,' but it is already set, and I could not help feeling sorry, tho' I will thank God for which-ever he sends if it is only healthy and well formed in body and mind. I try to feel this but no human being could imagine my sore disappointment in a girl."[55] Yet no hint of that prejudice would mar Lucy's relationship with Douschka to whom she was devoted.

In the late fall of 1859, Francis Pickens became deathly ill and took a long time to recuperate. He was ready to return to America. Moreover, after John Brown's raid at Harpers Ferry on October 16, 1859, he wanted to be on the political scene in the United States. Lucy was also homesick and eager to be with her mother, who was ill. She begged Francis to let her go immediately, but he would not grant permission. To placate Lucy he promised that they would buy a place in Texas and that he would help her father pay off his debts.[56] He never did buy land in Texas, and Eugenia recorded in her diary that "poor Lucy deceived her-self with promises of being with us that will never be fulfilled."[57] Lucy wrote to Anna, "My dear sister the best of men are selfish and incapable of sacrifice even for the person they love best on earth. . . . He (like all other men) loves his own comfort and happiness better than mine."[58]

On April 17, 1860, Pickens resigned his post as minister to Russia and awaited a replacement, which would not arrive until September. Meanwhile, on April 23, the Democratic National Convention convened in Charleston, South Carolina to select its candidate for president. The absent Francis Pickens, was considered as a potential nominee. According to the *New York Journal of Commerce*, Pickens was "conservative" [meaning not a "fire eating secessionist"] and "as such was kept down in his own state. He is a high-minded, honorable, patriotic and able man."[59] The convention split on the platform of a national slave code, and the delegates went home.

At this time Francis was not in favor of secession. Lucy was probably also opposed at this point. Her beloved state of Texas had annexed itself to the United States rather than remain an independent republic. When writing her novel just a few years earlier, Lucy was clearly not interested in stirring bad feelings between North and South. Indeed, like a number of other southern writers who believed it was "woman's duty to ensure sectional harmony," she depicted close friendship between her southern and northern protagonists.[60] Lucy Pickens had gone to school in the North, had friends in the North, and knew that even anti-slavery northerners were not the raving radicals often depicted in the southern press. She used the Mississippi River—"that generous river, knowing neither north nor south, but alike kissing the frozen banks of the snow-hill states, and the sunny shore of the flower-dowered south"—as a metaphor to connect the two sections and used the friendship between her two heroines to suggest that they should stay on friendly terms.[61]

Passion and ambition changed both Lucy and Francis Pickens, however, and they were both caught up in secessionist fervor. Upon arriving at his home in Edgefield, South Carolina, in November 1860, Pickens gave a speech pandering to the assembled crowd. He urged secession as a "clear and indisputable right of a sovereign people." As a favor to his old friend President James Buchanan, Pickens urged that secession not take effect until Lincoln's "hostile incoming government" took office in March 1861.[62] He soon dropped even that request. In Columbia, South Carolina, addressing the General Assembly, he declared it would be preferable to "cover the state with ruin, conflagration and blood rather than submit."[63]

In December 1860, the General Assembly selected Francis Pickens to be the next governor of the state, which it almost certainly would not have done had he continued to advocate moderation. Three days after his inauguration, he was in Charleston where he announced that the Declaration of Secession had passed in the Secession Convention. South Carolina leaders seceded with the clear expectation that other southern states would follow and that the Confederacy would be formed. In the meantime, however, the former state became an independent nation, the Republic of South Carolina.[64] Governor Francis W.

Pickens was now Chief Executive and Commander in Chief of the new republic and Lucy Holcombe Pickens was the First Lady. Shortly thereafter Lucy wrote to her father from Charleston, South Carolina, "I am where duty and honor demand me, and whatever dangers surround me, I will be with God's help true to my name and blood."[65]

Zealots in Charleston wanted Governor Pickens to order an immediate attack on the three federal forts in Charleston, South Carolina: Fort Moultrie, Castle Pinckney, and the uninhabited, half-built Fort Sumter, but Pickens believed that the better policy was to wait. On December 26, 1860, however, Major Robert Anderson of the First U.S. Artillery spiked the guns at Fort Moultrie and, under cover of darkness, left with a small detachment of troops for Fort Sumter in the mouth of the harbor. Local secessionists, who had demanded the surrender of all national property, were outraged. Many pressured the governor to order the capture of Ft. Sumter. He ordered the placing of cannons around the harbor, the occupation of Castle Pinckney and the empty Fort Moultrie, and the seizure of federal arsenals, but he still did not want to initiate an outright attack on Sumter.

On January 5, 1861, President Buchanan tried to send reinforcements to Fort Sumter, an effort that might have gone undetected except for advance notice to South Carolinians. Significantly, Francis Pickens was forewarned of the plan by Louis Wigfall, U.S. senator from Texas, originally from Edgefield, South Carolina, and a friend of Lucy Pickens. When the *Star of the West* approached, Pickens was ready. South Carolina troops fired on the U.S. vessel, which turned around. Many South Carolinians applauded Pickens, but there were other southerners, including Jefferson Davis, who urged caution. He told Pickens that the federals at Fort Sumter were nothing but an irritant, "a point of pride."[66] Pickens concurred; the state lacked military supplies and a navy. Tensions were high, but the situation seemed under control, so Lucy made a trip to Texas to see her ailing mother.

In early February, representatives from South Carolina, Georgia, Alabama, Mississippi, Florida, and Louisiana, convened in Alabama for the Montgomery Conference where they drafted a provisional constitution for the Confederacy. Jefferson Davis was inaugurated as its president on February 18, 1861. On her way back to South Carolina, Lucy traveled to Alabama and met with Davis on March 16, 1861. There is no known record of the meeting, but, even if it were purely a social visit, her meeting the new president of the Confederacy would have been helpful to her husband.[67] On April 3, 1861, the ratification of a constitution for the Confederacy ended the separate existence of the Republic of South Carolina.[68] South Carolina was officially part of the Confederacy and Francis and Lucy were no longer Chief Executive and First Lady of a republic deemed by some "too small to be a nation and too large to be lunatic asylum!"[69]

Pickens had hoped that the Confederacy would assume the problem of Fort Sumter rather than depend on South Carolina and that proved to be the case. Without bearing responsibility for initiating action, Governor Pickens urged Confederate leaders to move immediately, to take Fort Sumter before Lincoln took office. He reasoned, "Mr. Buchanan cannot resist, because he has not the power. Mr. Lincoln may not attack, because the cause of the quarrel will have been, or may be considered by him as past."[70] On March 6, 1861, two days after Abraham Lincoln's inauguration, General Pierre Gustave Toutant Beauregard arrived in Charleston to oversee the military situation. Francis wrote Lucy that the general had five hundred men ready to storm the fort.[71]

On April 6 Lincoln asked Robert S. Chew, a government clerk, to travel to South Carolina and inform Governor Pickens that the federal government was sending provisions to Ft. Sumter. Pickens delivered the letter to Beauregard.[72] On April 12, Beauregard ordered the South Carolina militia, now constituted as Confederate troops, to fire on Fort Sumter. The outbreak of hostilities at Fort Sumter precipitated Lincoln's call on April 15 for seventy-five thousand volunteers for a ninety-day tour of military duty. With Lincoln's call to arms, the Confederate expectation that Lincoln meant to coerce the South was confirmed. Like countless others who had hoped civil war would be averted, Lucy fully supported the South once "the war came."[73]

During the first two years of the Civil War, Lucy's role as wife to the governor of South Carolina involved entertaining and morale building, but she also served as his secretary until one was finally hired. In addition, Lucy was clearly an unofficial but influential advisor, adept at political maneuvering. She was a great asset to her husband who, as governor, earned a reputation for being arrogant and overbearing. She loved to entertain and even enemies of her husband enjoyed her company. Famed South Carolina diarist Mary Chesnut wrote that Governor Pickens "will outwit them all yet, with the aid of the lovely Lucy, who is a host in herself."[74] In another entry, Chesnut described the flirtatious interaction between Lucy and one of Francis's enemies, William Porcher Miles, who had served, like Francis, as a U.S. congressman from South Carolina.[75]

On the whole, Francis Pickens was not popular. Some Civil War scholars have written that, though Pickens was a very capable man, his ability to govern was thwarted by his political opponents. His history as a moderate and a late-comer to secession, and his efforts to temper more hot-headed South Carolinians including urging restraint on those who had wanted to seize the federal forts right away, made some of them doubt the strength of his commitment to their cause.

The South Carolina leaders that had constituted themselves as the secession convention and then refused to dissolve themselves, had given the governor a surprising degree of authority given South Carolina's tradition of resistance to executive power. But after Pickens had been in office but a year, they reversed course and instituted a Second Executive Council, with executive and legislative power, one that often thwarted Francis, virtually stripping him of power.[76] Mary Chesnut, whose husband was a member of the new council and on the other side of this dispute, wrote, "There is to be a council of safety—a bundle of sticks and crutches for old Pickens." She also wrote about Lucy's reaction to the council: "Mrs. Pickens was bitter against the convention for giving Governor Pickens these guardians—of this guard of honor, or this council, call it you will. It means that Governor Pickens has been felt to need aid and council."[77]

Mary Chesnut did not like Lucy Pickens, and the feelings were surely mutual. Their husbands were rivals for power in the state and in the Confederacy. In January 1862 Mary called on Lucy: "We flattered each other as far as that sort of thing can be done. She is young, lovely, clever—and old Pick's third wife. She cannot fail to hate us. Mr. C put as a sort of watch and ward over her husband."[78] Feelings between the two women continued to deteriorate. Later that month Mary wrote, "The governor's lady was there—she received in state. She did not rise from her chair as we spoke to her—we are only of the governor's council. Young Moses—Franklin Jr.—is secretary to Governor Pickens. He hung over the lovely Lucy, standing or bending over her from the back of her chair. It suggested the devil whispering in Eve's ear in the primeval days."[79]

Lucy apparently wrote anonymous letters criticizing her husband's enemies. Regarding a letter to the editor that was critical of James Chesnut, Mary Chesnut gave this account: "The editor was asked for the writer's name. He gave Little Moses, the governor's secretary. When Little Moses was spoken to, in a great trepidation he told that Mrs. Pickens wrote it and got him to publish it. So it dropped, for Little Moses is such an arrant liar no one believes him. Besides, if that sort of thing amuses Mrs. Pickens[,] [l]et her amuse herself."[80] Chesnut found it amusing when a friend called Lucy "The governess" because "it is the easier to say than the Governor's wife." But she also offered some positive comments about Lucy Pickens, complimenting her looks and her skills as a hostess.[81]

Like other women during the Civil War, Lucy worried about men folk in battle. Mary Chesnut recorded in her diary on June 11, 1862, that according to her husband, Lucy was particularly anxious because "her brother and her brother-in-law are either killed or taken prisoners."[82] And like many other women in the South, Lucy Pickens did her best to aid the Confederacy, including making sacrifices. The exigencies of war required and enabled elite and yeoman women to make more substantial contributions to family and community than ever before. They transformed their everyday church groups, sewing circles, and benevolent societies into organizations to support the war effort. Women became teachers and nurses. Like other women, Lucy helped raise funds for the Confederacy, but with her unusual resources and dramatic flare she upped the ante.

One of the events she held at Edgewood was a fundraising venture for which she displayed her outfits from the Russian court.[83] In addition, according to family legend, Lucy financed a legion with some of the jewels given to her by Czar Alexander II. Lucy designed the legion flag, which included the star of Texas reminiscent of the "free flag of Cuba." She presented it to the Holcombe Legion, named after her, commanded by Colonel P. F. Stevens, superintendent of the Citadel Military School in Charleston.[84] The legion suffered many dead and wounded in June and July 1863 around Vicksburg.

Thanks to her friend, Christopher Memminger, Confederate Secretary of the Treasury, Lucy's likeness was placed on Confederate treasury notes, the 1 dollar bills of 1863 and the 100 dollar bills of 1864.[85] She was one of the few women whose image has ever appeared on a national currency. For this and other reasons, she was sometimes called in the press the "uncrowned queen of the Confederacy, or "Lady Lucy."[86] Lucy Pickens was a clear beneficiary of the Old Order, enjoying the tributes that came her way owing to her beauty, social skills, and prominence.

Francis's two-year term ended, and on December 18, 1862, he and Lucy returned to Edgewood. They still had enslaved servants, houseguests came often, and they hosted dinner parties. But it would not be the same; power and political intrigue were in Columbia. Several years later Lucy wrote, "I do so dislike practical duties but am ashamed & grimace at the truth of the confession."[87]

In 1863 Lucy met a new resident of Edgefield, Clara Victoria Dargan, a poet and a writer fluent in French who recorded some very interesting impressions of Lucy at this stage of her life. Dargan, originally from Winnsboro, South Carolina, came to Edgefield to work as editor of the literary department of the *Edgefield Advertiser*.[88] Despite a negative first impression they became good friends. When they met in early 1863, Dargan wrote in her diary, "Mrs. P. and her confrere Miss Floride Cunningham called on me. Mrs. P. wore her full suit of Russian sable furs and a superb velvet cloak. She is rather affected I think and very vain of having been Mrs. Governor—people still call her the Empress."[89] It was probably a pleasure for Lucy to have such a cultured friend. In what was probably a reference to Crittenden, Lucy told Clara that she had once loved deeply.[90]

In November 1864 Lucy's father died, and she went to Texas. Francis remained in Edgefield where he worried about her safe travel through war zones. People needed a pass to get across the Mississippi River into Texas, but she apparently had no difficulty. Lucy Pickens was still with her mother early in 1865 when William Tecumseh Sherman turned to the Carolinas and marched through Columbia, which fell to Federal troops on February 17 and went up in flames that night. Confederate troops evacuated Charleston the next day. By April 1865 the war was officially over.

As an early step in Reconstruction, President Andrew Johnson appointed a provisional governor for South Carolina, Benjamin Perry, who had remained a loyal Unionist. Perry was a good friend of Francis and Lucy, and they hoped this would work to Francis's benefit and that he would receive amnesty when he signed the loyalty oath of allegiance to the Union. In September 1865, Francis was chosen as a delegate to a convention which drew up a new state constitution for South Carolina, a constitution that, put together by wealthy white conservative delegates, abolished slavery but restricted voting and office holding to white males. "This is a white man's government," explained Governor Perry, "and intended for white men only."[91] Francis Pickens offered the motion that the state repeal the "ordinance passed in convention, 20th December, 1860, withdrawing this state from the Union."[92] Journalist Sidney Andrews reported that Pickens "eats his humble pie with some ostentation."[93] The U.S. Congress, however, rejected South Carolina's new state constitution; Reconstruction would not be that simple.

The Pickenses experienced nowhere near the suffering endured by many in those years. Nevertheless, Lucy Pickens wrote her friend Clara about "a gloom dark & bitter indeed to all who love our desolate & helpless land." Again likening the position of a relatively privileged group to that of slaves, she wrote "[T]he dreary clanking of our chains comes shuddering on every breeze."[94] After Emancipation, many house servants on the Pickenses' Edgewood plantation, including Lucinda, Lucy's maid, who had accompanied her to Russia, remained in the household, now earning a small stipend plus room and board. Francis Pickens made the usual arrangement with his free agricultural workers: labor contracts providing housing, clothing, food, a small sum, and a portion of the crop. However, the "faithful" valet Tom, who had also accompanied Pickens to Russia, chose to move north. Pickens's great wealth had evaporated. He lost plantations in Mississippi and Alabama. Yet he still owned his South Carolina land, and Lucy still owned jewels. Pickens felt his losses keenly. After the war, he wrote to Lucy somewhat insensitively that their financial hardship was partly due to not having a son: "I have no sons to work & to help me or I might be independent." He cared a great deal about Lucy's family, but in that same letter he wrote, "I shall be most happy for your dear sister to live so near in Augusta if it suits her, and I only wish I could offer her any substantial aid, but I am far too poor for that." About Lucy's mother, however, he wrote, "Our precious dear mother say to her I will always give her a home, as long as I can be able to plough a corn patch."[95] In June 1866 Francis said he was planting only half of what he had planted in 1850.[96]

Pickens bemoaned the fact that the government turned down his request for amnesty because he had too much money. He wrote to Lucy, "I know I am not worth it, except in your jewelry, if it be I am equal owner of that. I know I own my wife and that she is worth over one million in hard money, but then the gove[rnment] will not value her that high."[97] For a while they lived by selling pieces of her jewelry and gifts she received from Alexander II. Lucy wrote her friend Clara about their economic situation in 1867: "The whole of our State is almost in a state of destitution. We are able to live comfortably still, having the supplies of the Plantation but are greatly reduced & entirely without means. Unless there is a successful crop this year, God only knows what will become of us as a people."[98] Moreover, debt problems grew as more people became dependent on Francis. Historian C. Vann Woodward and others fault Lucy for the debt problems Francis faced, claiming "her extravagance helped drive her husband far into debt."[99] To be sure, Lucy lived life extravagantly, but so did Francis.

Lucy and Francis received heartbreaking news on June 5, 1867 of the death of Jeannie Pickens Whately, Pickens's nineteen-year-old daughter from an earlier marriage. A year and a half later, on January 25, 1869, Francis died. Lucy Pickens was a widow at age thirty-six. Her mother came to be with her over the next year.

Lengthy visits from family and friends were common. Now that Francis was gone, Lucy's brother Theodore moved to Edgewood to help her, along with a wounded Confederate veteran, a Major Kirkland, who came for dinner and stayed. Lucy also had long visits from Anna's daughters from Texas.[100] When Eugenia returned to Marshall in 1870, she, with Anna's help, took in boarders and sold off parcels of land. From time to time, Lucy and Douschka also helped Eugenia and Anna in Texas. Eugenia died February 17, 1873. Anna could not meet the mortgage obligations on the Texas home place, and so it was auctioned off in May 1874. African Americans in the community purchased it and turned it into Bishop College.[101]

In the mid-1870s, violent clashes between whites and blacks occurred throughout the South, but the scale of battle was nowhere as great as in South Carolina, and in South Carolina, nowhere as great as in Edgefield. The local militia was commanded by a former slave, Captain Edward Tennant. A dashing of-

ficer who bore himself with dignity, Ned Tennant was both a symbolic and sub-
stantive threat to southern white hegemony. Whites asked Republican governor
Daniel H. Chamberlain's permission to disband Edgefield's black militias, and
Chamberlain, who endorsed African American voting rights but also wanted
to cultivate moderate whites, gave assent. Led by Lucy's stepson-in-law, former Confederate General Matthew Calbraith Butler, one thousand white men
searched for Tennant's militia throughout the county. Tennant and his troops,
of course, were unwilling to relinquish their weapons to Butler's group. Instead
they marched twenty-five miles through a country swarming with whites and,
arriving in full force at Edgefield Courthouse, they surrendered their weapons to African American state senator and regimental commander Lawrence
Cain. Potential violence was averted, but the political outcome for freedmen
was disastrous.[102]

Butler and Brigadier General Martin Witherspoon Gary organized armed
bands of horsemen, attired in symbolically defiant "Red Shirts." They intimidated and attacked potential black voters and killed Republican officials and
community leaders. Lucy's reaction to the violence is not known, but her daughter played a dramatic role in restoring white supremacy. In the election of 1876,
seventeen-year-old Douschka rode at the front of a group of more than seven
hundred armed and mounted Democrats in red shirts, who seized control of
the Edgefield County Courthouse, outnumbering the few federal troops and
preventing African Americans from voting. According to Benjamin Tillman,
later a South Carolina governor and senator, "Gary's doctrine of voting early
and often changed the republican majority of 2,300 in Edgefield to a democratic
majority of 3,900."[103] Some whites honored Douschka for this bravado, calling
her "The Joan of Arc of Carolina."[104]

The life of Lucy Pickens was by no means over, and she continued striving
to exert influence, now through work on memorials. In 1866 she accepted an
appointment as a Vice Regent of Mount Vernon's Ladies' Association for the
state of South Carolina. Women in this association raised money nationwide
to purchase and restore George Washington's home place. In 1876, she attended
their annual meeting, enjoyed it thoroughly, and made good friends with other
women on the council.[105] Over the next twenty-two years, Lucy attended the
annual meetings. In her role as representative from South Carolina, she was in
charge of refurbishing and decorating a small dining room at Mount Vernon.
Always a lover of the outdoors, she was put in charge of the Garden and Green-
house Committee.[106] In appreciation, the Daughters of the American Revolution named their Washington, D.C., chapter the Lucy Holcombe Chapter.[107]

In 1891 she was chosen president of the local Ladies Memorial Association and assigned the task of fund-raising for a Confederate monument in Edge-field's town square. The newspaper reported that Mrs. Pickens, as president of the Edgefield Confederate Monument Association, announced that the associa-tion had collected 647 dollars, and she urged her audience to express interest in the matter, "not in money," but "in efforts to further the cause among their people." Some of the Confederate survivors asked her to pass the hat, and "this she did with sad but consummate grace." She thanked all present "in the name and memory of the immortal Confederate dead of Edgefield."[108] Her efforts to memorialize the Confederacy, just as her efforts to memorialize the Lopéz ex-pedition, show how Lucy Pickens sought to perpetuate in a wide audience her image of the South. (The monument was erected shortly after her death.)

Lucy wrote to her sister on August 3, 1881, that she was going on a busi-ness trip to England. Her economic situation was such that "I have lost all my property but E [the Edgewood plantation] and that not secure."[109] When she returned from England, she seemed to have secured her finances, and she began planning for Douschka's marriage to Dr. George Dugas of Augusta, Georgia.[110] Douschka spent a great deal of time with Lucy at Edgewood, taking over much of the management of the plantation.

At the end of July 1887, Lucy traveled to Marshall, Texas, for the funeral of her sister, Anna Eliza Greer. An even more profound tragedy overcame Lucy six years later, in August 1893, when Douschka died suddenly, apparently from a fever. She was thirty-four; Lucy was sixty-one. She thereafter helped care for her grandchildren.

Lucy Holcombe Pickens lived to see the beginning of the Spanish American War of 1898 and North and South come together to end Spanish dominion of Cuba. In exhorting her readers in 1851 to support the Cuban expedition, Hol-combe had portrayed the Spaniards as brutes. In the years after she published *Free Flag of Cuba* such images would grow more harsh and more commonplace in U.S. media and public opinion. When Holcombe described in her novel the coffin of Lopéz, she wrote that "the flag of the American republic, and the free flag of Cuba, were shrouded and crossed above the chieftain's head."[111] This scene foreshadowed a drawing she may have seen in her later years, a tableau adver-tising the Spanish-American-Cuban War. It featured Union and Confederate veterans shaking hands in front of a little blonde, curly-haired girl with a crown reading "Cuba," her wrists adorned with chains broken asunder. Behind the scene is the Cuban flag in the middle of two draped American flags representing a reconciled North and South freeing "Little Cuba." At the time Americans en-gaged in many rituals of reconciliation — even as the North chose to overlook the restoration of white supremacy and the disfranchisement of African Americans in the South. Holcombe's work definitely foreshadowed this late nineteenth century phenomenon when North and South chose war with Spain and white reconciliation in the United States over racial justice.[112]

Lucinda, the former slave, married in 1880, and continued to visit Lucy from time to time. In August 1899, during one of these visits, both women caught a fever. Lucy died on August 8, Lucinda on August 11. In a eulogy for Lucy Holcombe Pickens at a meeting at Mount Vernon, one of her friends, Mrs. Sweat from Massachusetts, stated, "The imaginary kingdom, the Confederacy, which to many was only an ill-considered political experiment, was to her a glorious reality, a faith, a religion, and she gave it a loyalty that only strengthened as it became hopeless."[113]

Examining the life of Lucy Petway Holcombe Pickens opens a window into her times and the perspectives of wealthy white southern women. She was hardly typical. Few women, even from the wealthy and most prominent families, enjoyed such opportunities and adventures or took such full advantage of those that came their way. Although traveling broadened her world, none of her letters and writings reflected any dissonance with her proslavery values or any revolt against the constraints tradition imposed on women. Like many other elite southern women, she kept "a tenacious hold of traditionalism."[114]

She seemed to be content with the indirect influence permitted to her sex and particularly adept at its use. Throughout her long life she pressed gingerly against the restrictions placed on her sex while defending white paternalism as the natural and correct way to live.

NOTES

1. Belle Walsh, "Mrs. F. W. Pickens Dead," *Charleston News and Courier*, August 9, 1899, 15.

2. Carol Bleser and Frederick Heath, "The Clays of Alabama: The Impact of the Civil War on a Southern Marriage," in *In Joy and In Sorrow: Women, Family, and Marriage in the Victorian South*, ed. Carol Bleser (New York: Oxford University Press, 1991),135; Anne Firor Scott, *The Southern Lady: From Pedestal to Politics 1830–1930* (Chicago: University of Chicago Press, 1970).

3. Emily L. Bull, "Lucy Pickens: First Lady of the South Carolina Confederacy," *The Proceedings of the South Carolina Historical Association, 1981* (1982): 5–18; Marli F. Weiner, "Lucy Pickens," in vol. 17 of *American National Biography*, ed. John A. Garraty and Mark C. Carnes (New York: Oxford University Press, 1999), 473–74; Francis B. Simkins, "Lucy Petway Holcombe Pickens," *Notable American Women, 1605–1950: A Biographical Dictionary*, ed. Edward T. James, 3 vols. (Cambridge, Mass.: Harvard University Press, 1971), 3:64–65. Elizabeth Boatwright Coker, *India Allen* (New York: E. P. Dutton, 1953).

4. Lucy Pickens' papers are spread among a number of collections located in the Library of Congress, the South Carolina Department of Archives and History, the Southern Historical Collection at the University of North Carolina, Chapel Hill (hereinafter cited as SHC), the Perkins Library at

Duke University, Durham, North Carolina, and the South Caroliniana Library at the University of South Carolina (hereinafter cited as FWP-SCL). The quotation on submissiveness is from her miscellaneous writings in the Perkins Library. She would often write notes like this on scraps of paper to use later in her writings. See also, Elizabeth Wittenmyer Lewis, *Queen of the Confederacy: The Innocent Deceits of Lucy Holcombe Pickens* (Denton, Texas: University of North Texas Press, 2002),141. Lewis used the quote as a title to Chapter 18 of the book.

5. Lewis, *Queen of the Confederacy*, 10.

6. Eugenia Holcombe diary, January 18, 1840, 5, Pickens Papers, FWP-SCL.

7. Eugenia Holcombe diary, January 1850, FWP-SCL.

8. Jack T. Greer, *Leaves from a Family Album* (Waco, Tex.: Texian Press, 1975), 16, quoted in Lewis, *Queen of the Confederacy*, 25.

9. Lopéz was originally from Venezuela; Robert E. May, *John A. Quitman: Old South Crusader* (Baton Rouge: Louisiana State University Press, 1985), 238). Later the term *filibuster* was used to refer to a tactic for delaying action in the U.S. Senate. See also C. Vann Woodward, Robert Middlekauff, James M. McPherson, James T. Patterson, David M. Kennedy, Daniel Walker Howe, *The Oxford History of the United States*, Oxford University Press, 103-107.

10. Antonio Rafael de la Cova, "Ambrosio José Gonzales: A Cuban Confederate Colonel" (PhD thesis, West Virginia University, 1994), 210; Woodward et al, *Oxford History*, 106.

11. De la Cova, "Ambrosio Jose Gonzales," 200.

12. Some of the survivors managed to get back to the United States. Those imprisoned were released in 1852, after the United States paid damages to Spain. A foremost authority on the Lopéz expedition is Tom Chaffin, *Fatal Glory: Narciso López and the First Clandestine U.S. War Against Cuba* (Charlottesville: University Press of Virginia, 1996), 216–18; Woodward et al, *Oxford History*, 106.

13. Chaffin, *Fatal Glory*, 215.

14. Lewis, *Queen of the Confederacy*, 45.

15. In the mid-nineteenth century, women made up a large part of the readership in the United States. Holcombe fits precisely into the paradigm described by Mary Kelley in which women writers at this time secretly wanted to be creators of culture while at the same time preferring to tell themselves and others that they were simply private domestic women. Mary Kelley, *Private Woman, Public Stage: Literary Domesticity in Nineteenth-Century America* (New York: Oxford University Press, 1984), 184. See also Paula Baker, "The Domestication of Politics: Women and American Political society, 1780–1920," *American Historical Review* 89, no. 3 (1984): 643.

16. Henrietta M. Hardimann, *The Free Flag of Cuba; or, The Martyrdom of Lopéz: A Tale of the Liberating Expedition of 1851* (New York: De Witt and Davenport, 1855). See also *The Free Flag of Cuba*, ed. Orville Vernon Burton and Georganne B. Burton (Baton Rouge: Louisiana State University Press, 2002).

17. Burton and Burton, eds., *The Free Flag of Cuba*, 142–43.

18. Ibid., 123.

19. Harriet Beecher Stowe, *Uncle Tom's Cabin* (1851–52; rpt., New York: Bantam, 1981).

20. Philip S. Foner, *A History of Cuba and Its Relationship with the United States, 1845–1895* (New York: International Publishers, 1963), chap. 6.

21. Burton and Burton, eds., *The Free Flag of Cuba*, 173.

22. In her study of southern women writers, Elizabeth Moss argued that their writings show "an alternative standard for feminine behavior," that upper-class women in these novels could "participate in contemporary political discourse while remaining within the bounds of accepted feminine

behavior." Elizabeth Moss, *Domestic Novelists in the Old South: Defenders of Southern Culture* (Baton Rouge: Louisiana State University Press, 1992), 18.

23. Clara Victoria Dargan Maclean diary, April 6, 1863, Clara Victoria Dargan Maclean Papers, Manuscripts Department, the William R. Perkins Library, Duke University, Durham, North Carolina (hereinafter cited as WRPL).

24. On prevailing ideas about women's nature and social role at the time, see Barbara Welter, "The Cult of True Womanhood, 1820–1860," pt. 1, *American Quarterly* 18, no. 2 (1966): 151–74.

25. For women as avid readers of the political press in the antebellum period, see Ronald J. Zboray and Mary S. Zboray, "Political News and Female Readership in Antebellum Boston and Its Region," *Journalism History* 22, no. 1 (1996): 2–14, and Ronald J. Zboray and Mary S. Zboray, "Whig Women, Politics, and Culture in the Campaign of 1840," *Journal of the Early Republic* 17, no. 2 (1997): 277–315.

26. Nina Baym has argued that woman's fiction is de facto feminist because such work "advocate[s] an individualism that had not traditionally been a woman's option." Nina Baym, *Woman's Fiction: A Guide to Novels by and about Women in America, 1820–1870* (Ithaca: Cornell University Press, 1973), xx).

27. Henrietta H. Hardimann to John A. Quitman, January 1855, John A. Quitman Papers, Mississippi Department of Archives and History, Jackson.

28. J. Walker Holcombe, "Lucy Holcombe Legacy Lives in Washington, D. C.," *Harrison County Historical Herald*, 7, undated clipping, Lucy Holcombe Collection, Harrison County Historical Society, Old Courthouse, Marshall, Texas (hereinafter cited as LH-HCHS).

29. See Linda K. Kerber, *Women of the Republic: Intellect and Ideology in Revolutionary America* (Chapel Hill: University of North Carolina Press for the Institute of Early American History and Culture, Williamsburg, Va., 1980).

30. Benjamin Franklin Perry, *Reminiscences of Public Men* (Philadelphia: J. D. Avril, 1883), quoted in John B. Edmunds, *Francis W. Pickens and the Politics of Destruction* (Chapel Hill: University of North Carolina Press, 1986), 137.

31. Burton and Burton, eds., *The Free Flag of Cuba*, 116.

32. Some say Francis was born in 1805 and some say 1807. See John B. Edmunds, *Francis W. Pickens and the Politics of Destruction* (Chapel Hill: University of North Carolina Press, 1986), 20, 183 fn. 3.

33. Ibid., 10.

34. Ibid., 73.

35. Sidney Andrews, *The South Since the War, As Shown by Fourteen Weeks of Travel and Observation in Georgia and the Carolinas* (1866; rpt., Boston: Houghton Mifflin, 1971), 50.

36. U.S. Census records, cited in Orville Vernon Burton, *In My Father's House Are Many Mansions: Family and Community in Edgefield, South Carolina* (Chapel Hill: University of North Carolina Press, 1985), 48; Edmunds, *Francis W. Pickens*, 139; newspaper clippings, FWP-SCL.

37. Francis W. Pickens (hereinafter cited as FWP) to Lucy Holcombe, November 28, 1857, FWP-SCL.

38. Steven Stowe, *Intimacy and Power in the Old South: Ritual in the Lives of the Planters* (Baltimore, Md.: Johns Hopkins University Press, 1987).

39. Edmunds, *Francis W. Pickens*, 128.

40. FWP to Lucy Holcombe, January 27, 1858, Pickens Papers, WRPL.

41. Bull, "Lucy Pickens," 8.

42. James Henry Rice Jr. *Glories of the Carolina Coast* (Columbia, S.C.: R. L. Bryan Company, 1936), 118. Personal files of Mrs. Chas. A. Beehn, Marshall, Texas, LH-HCHS.

43. Eugenia Holcombe diary, April 26, 1858, 28. FWP-SCL.

44. Eugenia Holcombe diary, April 26, 1858, 28, FWP-SCL.

45. Greer, *Leaves from a Family Album*, 66.

46. Ibid., 64, 66, 85.

47. Ibid., 63.

48. Lucy Pickens (hereinafter cited as LP) to Anna Greer, December 20, 1859, FWP-SCL.

49. Edmunds, *Francis W. Pickens*, 141.

50. Ibid.

51. Greer, *Leaves from a Family Album*, 71.

52. Ibid., 89.

53. Ibid., 85.

54. This is eight months after her initial, brief meeting with the Czar, so it is highly improbable that Douschka was the Czar's daughter, as was bandied about in local gossip.

55. LP to Anna Greer, January 9, 1859, FWP-SCL.

56. Edmunds, *Francis W. Pickens*, 142.

57. Eugenia Holcombe diary, June, 1861, 29, FWP-SCL.

58. LP to Anna Greer, 1859, Pickens-Dugas Papers, Southern Historical Collection, Manuscripts Department, Wilson Library, University of North Carolina, Chapel Hill (hereinafter cited as SHC).

59. *New York Journal of Commerce*, April 28, 1860, quoted in Edmunds, *Francis W. Pickens*, 145.

60. Moss, *Domestic Novelists in the Old South*, 27.

61. Burton and Burton, eds., *The Free Flag of Cuba*, 81.

62. *Edgefield Advertiser*, November 28, 1860.

63. Edmunds, *Francis W. Pickens*, 152.

64. Charles Edward Cauthen, J. Tracy Power, *South Carolina Goes to War, 1860-1865* (Columbia: University of South Carolina Press, 2005), 79, 80.

65. LP to Beverly Lafayette Holcombe, January 1, 1861, Pickens-Dugas Papers, SHC.

66. Edmunds, *Francis W. Pickens*, 159.

67. Jefferson Davis to FWP, March 18, 1861, FWP-SCL.

68. Cauthen and Power, *South Carolina Goes to War*, 90, 91.

69. James L. Petigru, quoted in Lacy K. Ford Jr., *Origins of Southern Radicalism: The South Carolina Upcountry, 1800–1860* (New York: Oxford University Press, 1988), 371. Ford cites Sally Edwards, *The Man Who Said No* (New York: Coward-McCann, 1970), 65.

70. Edmunds, *Francis W. Pickens*, 162.

71. Ibid., 162–63.

72. *The Collected Works of Abraham Lincoln*, ed. Roy P. Basler, 9 vols. (New Brunswick, N.J.: Rutgers University Press, 1953–55), 4:323–24.

73. Abraham Lincoln used this phrase in his second inaugural address (*Collected Works*, 8:332–33).

74. *Mary Chesnut's Civil War*, ed. C. Vann Woodward (New Haven, Conn.: Yale University Press, 1981), 287 (hereinafter cited as MCCW).

75. Ibid., April 3, 1861, 40.

76. Wallace Hettle, *The Peculiar Democracy: Southern Democrats in Peace and Civil War* (Athens: University of Georgia Press, 2001), 102-123.

77. MCCW, January 7, 1862, 274–75.

78. Ibid., January 7, 1862, 275.

79. Ibid., January 1862, 285; Franklin J. Moses Jr. began his career as Governor Pickens's private secretary, was terminated by the Second Executive Council, served in an artillery unit, and after the war became a Republican and in 1872, the governor of South Carolina. He was despised as a "scala-wag" by many white South Carolinians. Moses's father was from a Jewish background but "Young Moses," as Chesnut called him, was raised as a Protestant. Robert N. Rosen, *The Jewish Confederates* (Columbia: University of South Carolina Press, 2000), 393.

80. MCCW, February 25, 1862, 297.

81. Ibid., June 25, 1862, 395.

82. Ibid., June 11, 1862, 375.

83. Lewis, *Queen of the Confederacy*, 163. Lewis cites the Clara Victoria Dargan Maclean diary, Clara Victoria Dargan Maclean Papers, WRPL.

84. Information from reminiscences in the personal files of Mrs. Chas. A. Beehn, Marshall, Texas, LH-HCHS.

85. H. D. Allen, "The Paper Money of the Confederate States with Historical Data," *The Numismatist* 31, no.7 (1918): 287–311. A Web site (http://www.csacurrency.com/csacur/index.htm [accessed June 4, 2007]) devoted to Confederate money shows pictures of the bills that have Lucy Pickens on them (fourth issue, 1862, and fifth issue, December 2, 1862).

86. *The Tennessee Encyclopedia of History and Culture.* http://tennesseeencyclopedia.net/ (accessed October 27, 2008).

87. LP to Clara Dargan, June 2, 1866, Pickens-Dugas Papers, SHC.

88. http://famousamericans.net/claravictoriadargan.

89. Clara Victoria Dargan Maclean diary, Clara Victoria Dargan Maclean Papers, WRPL.

90. Ibid.

91. "Speech of B. F. Perry," in *Journal of the People of South Carolina, Held in Columbia, South Carolina, September 1865* (Columbia, S.C.: Julian A. Selby, 1865), 14.

92. Edmunds, *Francis W. Pickens*, 176.

93. Andrews, *The South Since the War*, 50.

94. LP to Clara Dargan, June 2, 1866. Pickens-Dugas Papers, SHC.

95. FWP to LP, September 4, 1865, Pickens Papers, WRPL.

96. Edmunds, *Francis W. Pickens*, 178.

97. FWP to LP, September 4, 1865, Pickens Papers, WRPL.

98. LP to Clara Dargan, Pickens papers, SHC.

99. MCCW, 40 fn. 6.

100. Lewis, *Queen of the Confederacy*, 178.

101. Bishop College occupied the home until 1950, when it was demolished.

102. Orville Vernon Burton, "Race and Reconstruction: Edgefield County, South Carolina" *Journal of Social History* 12, no. 1 (1978): 31–56.

103. Benjamin R. Tillman, "The Struggle of 1876: How South Carolina Was Delivered from Carpet-Bag and Negro Rule," speech delivered at the Red Shirt reunion, Anderson, S.C., 1909.

104. John Hope Franklin, *Reconstruction: After the Civil War* (Chicago: University of Chicago Press, 1961), 209.

105. Lewis, *Queen of the Confederacy*, 187.

106. Ibid., 190.

107. J. Walker Holcombe, "Lucy Holcombe Legacy Lives in Washington, D.C." *Harrison County Historical Herald*, 7, undated clipping, LH-HCHS. One overstated newspaper account in the Holcombe Collection, written years later, reported that Lucy remained influential in politics ("The Pickens Family," *The (Columbia, S.C.) State*, January 31, 1910, 6 ff.

108. Tricia Price Glenn and Tonya A. Browder Taylor, *Remembering Edgefield, 1891* (Johnston, S.C.: Old Edgefield Publishing Co., 2003), 167.

109. Lewis, *Queen of the Confederacy*, 188.

110. Ibid., 189.

111. Burton and Burton, eds., *The Free Flag of Cuba*, 191.

112. This tableau by Captain Fritz Guerin is featured on the jacket cover of Nina Silber, *The Romance of Reunion: Northerners and the South, 1865–1900* (Chapel Hill: The University of North Carolina Press, 1993). See also Gerald Eugene Poyo, "Cuban Émigré Communities in the United States and the Independence of Their Homeland, 1852–1895" (PhD diss., University of Florida, 1983); Louis A. Pérez Jr., *The War of 1898: The United States and Cuba in History and Historiography* (Chapel Hill: University of North Carolina Press, 1998).

113. Lewis, *Queen of the Confederacy*, 197.

114. Drew Gilpin Faust, *Mothers of Invention: Women of the Slaveholding South in the American Civil War* (New York: Vintage Books, 1996), xiii, points out that this was the case for many elite southern women.

Contributors

ORVILLE VERNON BURTON is the Burroughs Distinguished Professor of Southern History and Culture at Coastal Carolina University. He was previously a professor of history and sociology at the University of Illinois and director of the Illinois Center for Computing in Humanities, Arts, and Social Science. A Furman University graduate, he received his PhD in American history from Princeton University in 1976. He has published more than a hundred articles and is the author or editor of ten books, including *In My Father's House Are Many Mansions: Family and Community in Edgefield, South Carolina* and *The Age of Lincoln*.

GEORGANNE BURTON is an independent scholar, researcher, and freelance editor. She received her BA and MA from the University of Illinois. Among her publications is *The Free Flag of Cuba: The Lost Novel of Lucy Pickens*, edited with Orville Vernon Burton.

SARA MARIE EYE received her doctorate in history from the University of South Carolina in 2008. Her dissertation is entitled "Left to Our Fate: South Carolina White Women during the Civil War and Reconstruction." She received her undergraduate degree from Western Carolina University and her master's degree from Virginia Tech. Eye's areas of specialization include women in the nineteenth-century South, the Civil War, nineteenth-century Appalachia, and digital history and new media. She is currently teaching in the History Department at the University of South Carolina.

CHARLES JOYNER recently retired as Burroughs Distinguished Professor of Southern History and Culture at Coastal Carolina University. He also taught at the University of California, Berkeley, the University of Mississippi, and the University of Alabama and was an associate of the Du Bois Center at Harvard University and a visiting professor at the University of Sydney in Australia. An alumnus of Presbyterian College, he holds doctorates in history from the University of South Carolina and in folklore and folklife from the University of Pennsylvania. Joyner is the author of *Down by the Riverside: A South Carolina Slave Community, Shared Traditions: Southern History and Folk Culture, Folk Song in South Carolina*, and *Remember Me: Slave Life in Coastal South Carolina*. He is coeditor of *Before Freedom Came: African-American Life and Labor in the Antebellum South*.

ALEXIA JONES HELSLEY is an instructor in history at the University of South Carolina Aiken and a historical consultant. She is retired from the South Carolina Department of Archives and History. Helsley received her MA in history from the University of South Carolina and her BA from Furman University. Her fields of interest include South Carolina history, the revolutionary and antebellum South, and Roman Britain. Helsley's publications include *South Carolinians in the War for American Independence, Beaufort, South Carolina: A History; A Guide to Historic Beaufort, South Carolina;* and *A Guide to Historic Henderson County, North Carolina.* Helsley also was a contributor to the *South Carolina Encyclopedia* and the *Encyclopedia of Antislavery and Abolition.* In 2006 she received the Governor's Award for her work in promoting archives in South Carolina.

JOAN MARIE JOHNSON teaches women's and southern history at Northeastern Illinois University in Chicago and is the cofounder and codirector of the Newberry Library Seminar on Women and Gender at the Newberry Library, Chicago. She received her PhD in history from the University of California, Los Angeles, in 1997. Johnson is the author of *Southern Women at the Seven Sister Colleges: Feminist Values and Social Activism, 1875–1915* and *Southern Ladies, New Women: Race, Region, and Clubwomen in South Carolina, 1898–1930* and the editor of *Southern Women at Vassar: The Poppenheim Family Letters, 1882–1916.*

VALINDA W. LITTLEFIELD is an assistant professor at the University of South Carolina. She received her BA from North Carolina Central University and her PhD in history from the University of Illinois, Urbana-Champaign. Littlefield is a scholar of the history of women, African Americans, and education, with an emphasis on southern African American women and African American history from 1877 to the present. Her publications include several articles on African American educators and her book on southern African American women schoolteachers during the Jim Crow era is forthcoming from the University of Illinois Press.

ELISABETH SHOWALTER MUHLENFELD is the president of Sweet Briar College. Before coming to Sweet Briar in 1996, she was dean of undergraduate studies and a professor of English at Florida State University. Showalter received her BA from Goucher College, her MA from the University of Texas at Arlington, and her PhD from the University of South Carolina. She is the author of four books, including *Mary Boykin Chesnut: A Biography,* as well as coeditor (with historian C. Vann Woodward) of Chesnut's original diaries, *The Private Mary Chesnut: The Unpublished Civil War Diaries.* Muhlenfeld has also edited *William Faulkner's* Absalom, Absalom! *A Critical Casebook* and *Two Novels by Mary Chesnut.* She currently serves as chair of the Women's College Coalition.

AMRITA CHAKRABARTI MYERS is an assistant professor of history at Indiana University in Bloomington, Indiana. Originally from Canada, she received her BA and MA degrees at the University of Alberta-Edmonton. Myers earned her PhD in African American history and women's history from Rutgers University in 2004. An historian of the black female experience in the United States, she is interested in the intersection of race, gender, freedom, and citizenship in the Old South. Her book on free black women in antebellum Charleston is forthcoming from the University of North Carolina Press.

LAURA ROSE SANDY is a lecturer in American history at Oxford Brookes University in the United Kingdom. She received her BA, MA, and PhD in history from the University of Manchester. Sandy's research has been supported by a Mellon Research Fellowship, an Economic and Social Research Council Postdoctorate Fellowship, a John D. Rockefeller Library Fellowship from the Colonial Williamsburg Foundation, as well as research fellowships from the International Center for Jefferson Studies, Charlottesville, Virginia, the Virginia Historical Society, and the Institute for Southern Studies, University of South Carolina. Her fields of study are slavery, labor, race, class, gender, colonialism, and southern studies. Sandy's research focuses on plantation overseers who lived and in colonial Virginia, South Carolina, and Georgia. Sandy's book, *Between Planter and Slave: The Social and Economic Role of Plantation Overseers in Colonial Virginia and South Carolina,* is being published by the University of South Carolina Press.

CONSTANCE B. SCHULZ is professor emerita at the University of South Carolina from which she recently retired as professor and codirector of the public history program. She received her PhD from the University of Cincinnati in 1973. Schulz has been a Fulbright Distinguished Lecture/Research Scholar at the University of York in England and a Fulbright Distinguished Lecturer in Southern History at the University of Genoa in Italy. She has published extensively on public history and on historical documentary photography. She has been supported by a National Endowment for the Humanities grant for 2008–10 to create a digital documentary edition of the papers of Eliza Lucas Pinckney and Harriott Pinckney Horry. She is the editor of *Michigan Remembered, 1936–1943: Photographs from the Farm Security Administration and the Office of War Information*; *A South Carolina Album, 1936–1948: Photographs from the Farm Security Administration, Office of War Information, and Standard Oil of New Jersey Documentary Projects*; and (with Elizabeth Hayes Turner) *Clio's Southern Sisters: Interviews with Leaders of the Southern Association for Women Historians.*

CHRISTINA SNYDER is an assistant professor of history and American studies at Indiana University, Bloomington. She graduated from the University of Georgia with a BA in anthropology and received her PhD in history from the University of North Carolina, Chapel Hill, in 2007. Snyder spend two years as a Barra Postdoctoral Fellow at the University of Pennsylvania's McNeil Center for Early American Studies. Her current book project, *Captives of the Dark and Bloody Ground: Native Americans and Bondage in the Early South,* is forthcoming from Harvard University Press.

RANDY J. SPARKS is a professor of history at Tulane University specializing in the history of the U.S. South, American religion, and the Atlantic World. He received his PhD from Rice University in 1989. His publications include *The Two Princes of Calabar: An Eighteenth-Century Atlantic Odyssey, Religion in Mississippi*, and *On Jordan's Stormy Banks: Evangelicalism in Mississippi, 1773–1876*. He is coeditor (with Bertrand Van Ruymbeke) of *Memory and Identity: Minority Survival among the Huguenots in France and the Atlantic Diaspora* and (with Jack P. Greene and Rosemary Brana-Shute) of *Money, Trade, and Power: The Evolution of Colonial South Carolina's Plantation Society*.

MARJORIE JULIAN SPRUILL is professor of history at the University of South Carolina. She was previously associate provost at Vanderbilt University and a professor at the University of Southern Mississippi. She received her BA from the University of North Carolina, Chapel Hill, a master's degree from Duke University, and a master's and PhD from the University of Virginia. In 2006–7 she was a fellow at the Radcliffe Institute for Advanced Study, Harvard University. An authority on the American women's rights movement and the American South, Spruill is the author or editor of numerous books, including *New Women of the New South: The Leaders of the Woman Suffrage Movement in the Southern States; One Woman, One Vote: Rediscovering the Woman Suffrage Movement; VOTES FOR WOMEN! The Woman Suffrage Movement in Tennessee, the South, and the Nation; Hagar*, a 1913 prosuffrage novel by Mary Johnston; and *Jailed for Freedom*, a 1920 memoir about suffrage militancy by Doris Stevens. She is coeditor (with William A. Link) of *The South in the History of the Nation: A Reader, One Woman, One Vote: Rediscovering the Woman Suffrage Movement*, vols. 1 and 2, and (with Elizabeth Payne and Martha Swain) of a two-volume anthology, *Mississippi Women: Their Histories, Their Lives*.

NANCY STOCKTON is a doctoral candidate in American history at Tulane University. She teaches at Loyola University in New Orleans. Stockton received a BS in sociology from the College of Charleston in 1977 and her master's degree in American history from The Citadel in 2004. Her dissertation is titled "All along the Watchtower: Fears, Spheres, Religion, and the Feminine Contours of White Supremacy in New Orleans, 1877–1900." Stockton's major fields of interest include the late nineteenth-century South, especially elite women's intellectual history, and religion, racism, and imperialism in the Gilded Age.

BERTRAND VAN RUYMBEKE is professor of American history at the Université de Paris VIII at Saint-Denis. He is the author of *From New Babylon to Eden: The Huguenots and Their Migration to Colonial South Carolina* and coeditor (with Randy J. Sparks) of *Memory and Identity: The Huguenots in France and the Atlantic Diaspora*; (with Jean-Louis Breteau and Françoise Knopper) of *Protestantisme et autorité/Protestantism and Authority*; (with L. H. Roper) of *Constructing Early Modern Empires: Proprietary Ventures in the Atlantic World, 1500–1750*; (with Bernard Cottret, Lauric Henneton, and Jacques Poitier) of *Naissance de l'Amérique du Nord: Les acts fondateurs, 1607–1776*; and (with Mickaël Augeron and Didier Poton) of *Pour Dieu: La cause et les affaires* and *Racine et mémoires*, vols. 1 and 2 of *Les Huguenots et l'Atlantique: Histoire, mémoire et patrimoine.*

EMILY WEST is a senior lecturer in American History at the University of Reading in the United Kingdom. She received her PhD from the University of Liverpool. Her research interests are in the history of U.S. slavery and the antebellum South, with particular emphasis on the lives of slave women and the relationships between enslaved spouses. She is currently researching the experiences of free people of color who sought enslavement in the American South and slaves who were wet nurses in the antebellum era. She is the author of *Chains of Love: Slave Couples in Antebellum South Carolina* and many articles on family, marriage, and slavery in the American South.

CHARLES WILBANKS is an associate professor of speech communication in the Department of English Language and Literature at the University of South Carolina. His areas of specialty include eighteenth- and nineteenth-century American public address and civil-religious rhetoric. He received an MA from the University of Houston and a PhD from the University of Nebraska. His most recent books are *The American Revolution and Righteous Community: Selected Sermons of Bishop Robert Smith* and *Walking by Faith: The Diary of Angelina Grimké, 1828–1835.*

Index